ADDITIONAL PRAISE FOR *THE IRAN THREAT*

"Alireza Jafarzadeh's book is a must-read. Jafarzadeh is one of the foremost authorities on modern Iran, and his book is a unique collection of information you can't find anywhere else. From the inner-workings of Mahmoud Ahmadinejad's regime to the Iranian nuclear threat, he gives a unique and insightful perspective to the current situation in Iran."

—*Rita Cosby, Host of* MSNBC Investigates

"As Iran relentlessly drives toward nuclear-armed status, world leaders shift gears and quicken their search for diplomatic exit ramps in a race against time to avoid war. As diplomacy fails, problematic military strike scenarios against Iranian nuclear sites abound. In his excellent book, *The Iran Threat*, Alireza Jafarzadeh creatively offers another option: Empower the Iranian people to seize control over their own country from the illegitimate clerical leadership. *The Iran Threat* will be on the "Must read" list of policy makers from Washington to Moscow as well as from Baghdad to Beijing."

—*Professor Raymond Tanter, Georgetown University and President, Iran Policy Committee*

"No one outside Iran has a better idea of what the regime in Tehran is up to than Alireza Jafarzadeh, whose *The Iran Threat* offers an important assessment of today's circumstances. He also presents vital ideas for dealing with a rogue government as it attempts to acquire nuclear weaponry."

—*Daniel Pipes, Director, Middle East Forum*

"Alireza Jafarzadeh knows Iran and the terrorist nature of Islamic fascism. He charts the Iranian regime's political development and efforts to become a nuclear power. He analyzes U.S. policy and failures to date to contain the Iranian threat. Anyone concerned about world peace and security should read this book."

—*Donna M. Hughes, Professor and Carlson Endowed Chair, University of Rhode Island*

THE IRAN THREAT

President Ahmadinejad and
the Coming Nuclear Crisis

ALIREZA JAFARZADEH

THE IRAN THREAT
Copyright © Alireza Jafarzadeh, 2007.

First published in 2007 by
PALGRAVE MACMILLAN™
175 Fifth Avenue, New York, N.Y. 10010.

PALGRAVE MACMILLAN is the global academic imprint of the Palgrave
Macmillan division of St. Martin's Press, LLC. Macmillan® is a registered
trademark in the United States, United Kingdom and other countries. Palgrave is
a registered trademark in the European Union and other countries.

ISBN–13: 978–1–4039–7664–2
ISBN–10: 1–4039–7664–3

Library of Congress Cataloging-in-Publication Data

Jafarzadeh, Alireza.
    The Iran threat : President Ahmadinejad and the coming nuclear crisis / Alireza
Jafarzadeh.
        p.   cm.
    Includes bibliographical references and index.
    ISBN 1–4039–7664–3 (alk. Paper)
    1. Iran—Military policy.   2. Nuclear weapons—Iran.   3. Iran—Foreign
relations—1997–   4. Security, International.   5. Ahmadinejad, Mahmoud.   I.
Title.
UA853.I7J34   2001
355.02'170955—dc22

                                                                                2006050346

A catalogue record of the book is available from the British Library.

Design by Letra Libre, Inc.

First edition: February 2007

10   9   8   7   6   5   4   3   2   1

Printed in the United States of America.

CONTENTS

To those brave and patriotic members of the Iranian resistance network inside Iran who have risked their lives in order to serve not only the Iranian people but also humanity by exposing the most secret aspects of the Iranian regime's nuclear weapons program.

Without them, I would not have been able to write this book, and the world would not have known about a nightmare awaiting them.

Their reward is a liberated and free Iran.

PROLOGUE

Just as this book was about to go to press, the United States' 2006 midterm elections shifted the balance of power in Washington, D.C. The primary factor in the Republicans' loss of majorities in both the House and the Senate, analysts agreed, was the Iraq War. With the insurgency becoming more powerful, terrorism on the rise and the acts more bloody, the casualties of coalition troops and Iraqi civilians mounting, and the cost of the war exceeding $1.8 billion per week, American citizens expressed their frustration in the voting booth. Changes were subsequently made in the cabinet level of the United States administration, and a handful of study groups were formed to seek solutions.

The problem in Iraq is neither a civil nor a sectarian war. The main threat to Iraq is neither al Qaeda nor the Sunni insurgents—they both are cause for major problems, but neither can take the whole future of Iraq as hostage. Rather, Iraq is now a battleground for the clash of two alternatives: the Islamic extremist option, which gets its orders from Tehran and seeks to establish an Islamic republic in Iraq, and a democratic alternative seeking a pluralistic democracy in the country. The former seeks sectarian violence and fans the flames of civil war, while the latter seeks to ease tension, provide security and stability and establish democratic institutions.

A crucial factor in the escalating chaos in Iraq was, and continues to be, the Iranian regime's devastatingly effective infiltration of Iraq's political, military, social, and religious infrastructure. Immediately after the coalition invasion of March 2003, Iran's leaders exploited the situation and launched a no-holds-barred mission to control Iraq's elections, militias, and power structure at every level. The leaders in Tehran had been waiting for such an opportunity since the end of the Iran-Iraq War in the late 1980s, and the upheaval of Operation Iraqi Freedom was a gift beyond their wildest dreams. The door to Iraq flung open, they leapt at the chance to fulfill their long-held goal of installing an Islamic Republic in Iraq that mirrored their own.

Under the present circumstances there appears to be no hope for an improvement of the situation in Iraq; many are genuinely concerned that the crisis could spread beyond Iraq's borders. Some suggest bringing in the Iranian regime as part of the solution to the Iraqi problem.

But the Iranian regime is the main problem, not a part of the solution in Iraq. Over the past three years, hundreds of books and thousands of articles and essays have been written about Iraq; various committees and study groups have been formed to tackle the Iraqi problem and offer a solution. But few have pinpointed the root cause of the problem in Iraq, let alone offered a solution for the blazing crisis in the region.

This book is timely as it details Iran's destructive role and its grand agenda for Iraq; its ambitious nuclear weapons program; President Mahmoud Ahmadinejad's background, worldview, and regional and global agenda; as well as discussing viable policy options to deal with the Iranian threat in Iraq and within Iran, its global terror network and nuclear weapons program.

I was strongly encouraged by many of my colleagues and friends within the Washington beltway, in the media, and my dear Iranian countrymen and associates to write this book, as I have been involved with these issues for nearly three decades—in the most unique way, at times. For all their wise suggestions, sincere criticism, valuable information, useful ideas, and unselfish contribution, I am most grateful.

My sole enemy, the ruling regime in Tehran, is certainly very unhappy, to say the least, about the publication of this book, as it further exposes its anti-Iranian and anti-human policies in Iran, uncovers its ominous designs for the world, and offers solutions and hope for both the Iranian people and the world community in terms of ending the Iran threat. It is this hope that has made writing this book very worthwhile.

November 29, 2006
Washington, D.C.

MY IRAN

. . . for the heart of the shallow ones is an army camp.

—Hafiz, from *Ghazal 31*

When I gained political asylum in the United States in the mid-1980s, I viewed the plight of Iran under the control of Ayatollah Ruhollah Khomeini and the mullahs as a crisis for my countrymen and women back home. But twenty years later, I and the rest of the world realize that Iran is everyone's problem. The all-too-real possibility of a nuclear-armed Iran has put the globe on high alert since the regime's secret nuclear program was uncovered in 2002, and events in 2006 reveal that the regime is speeding up its race to the bomb. Confronting this nuclear showdown demands a deep and thorough understanding of Tehran's motivations and goals, particularly as they apply to its nuclear weapons program. This book analyzes three new characteristics of the Iranian regime that I consider central to the Iranian nuclear threat: the takeover by the military of the nuclear program, the transfer of nuclear facilities to underground tunnel complexes, and the acceleration of the nuclear weapons program since Mahmoud Ahmadinejad became president in July 2005.

Leaders throughout the world are divided over whether the consequences of a nuclear-armed Iran are too horrifying to allow. In an interview with CBS Television, President George W. Bush told Iranian rulers, "Your designs to have a nuclear weapon or your desire to have the capability of making a nuclear weapon are unacceptable."[1] Similarly, French President Jacques Chirac said that Tehran "must understand that for the international community, the prospect of an Iran with nuclear military capability is unacceptable."[2] On the other hand, Russian President Vladimir Putin said that he is convinced that "Iran does not intend to produce nuclear arms. . . . In this context, we will continue cooperation with Iran in all areas, including the nuclear energy field."[3] There are others who believe that the international community should learn to live with a nuclear-armed Iran.

Why focus on Iran's nuclear threat when other countries with a history of unfriendly relations with the United States, such as North Korea and Pakistan, have also developed the bomb? Iran's case is unique in the worst possible way. The driving force of the regime is a long-held ambition to spread its repressive brand of Islamic extremist rule throughout the Middle East and beyond. Anyone who thinks that this expansionist zeal has faded with time and that Iranian leaders have been on a slow, inevitable course toward moderation has only to listen to one speech by Ahmadinejad. The regime may have toyed with the outer trappings of a reformist attitude in the 1990s, but the current government has given up that charade, and Ahmadinejad is the most authentic voice of the regime since Khomeini himself lambasted the United States as the "Great Satan."

The export of "Islamic" rule is written into the Iranian regime's constitution, and the religious zealots and military commanders who rule Iran have never been more serious about achieving it. Most world leaders have not taken Iran's religious imperatives seriously, but we can no longer afford to ignore this ideology. When Ahmadinejad rants about religious government as the only answer to the world's problems, he is dead serious. He speaks for every mullah in power, including, of course, the Supreme Leader Ali Khamenei, who has the first and last word on every decision in Iran. Khamenei does *not* speak for the vast majority of Iranians, the at least 95 percent of the population who are not fundamentalist Muslims and who do not support the repressive, inhumane, and economically destructive policies of the mullahs.

Also inherent in Tehran's version of Islamic rule is a lack of an ethical standard that would forestall the actual use of nuclear weapons. Tehran's leaders have no moral ambiguities about using nuclear weapons to annihilate "global arrogance" and clear a path for radical Islamic rule. Combine the regime's radical drive to export Islamic rule with a nuclear first-strike capability, and you have the most rogue nuclear state imaginable. Independent, non-state-aligned terrorist groups are no match to a state sponsor of terror that has the geopolitical clout of being the world's fourth-largest supplier of oil. If the Iranian regime is not prevented from building a nuclear weapon, its clout will turn into wanton nuclear aggression.

This book reveals the full story of Iran's secret nuclear weapons program, evidence of which I first revealed in 2002. A press conference that I held in August of that year ignited worldwide alarm about a nuclear-armed Iran and helped uncover 18 years of secret Iranian atomic activity. These revelations were based on evidence uncovered by the Iranian regime's number-one enemy, the main Iranian opposition group, the People's Mojahedin Organization of Iran (PMOI), also known as the Mujahedin-e Khalq (MEK).[4] The MEK is a member organization of the parliament in exile, the National Council of Resistance of Iran (NCRI). The intelligence gathered by MEK members in Iran has proved correct many times over and has been the main factor in compelling the International Atomic Energy Agency (IAEA) to inspect Iran's nuclear sites. President George W. Bush emphasized in March 2005 that these revelations had come from a unique source: "Iran has concealed a nuclear program," he stated. "That became discovered—not because of their compliance with the IAEA or NPT—but because a dissident group pointed it out to the world."[5]

I worked for many years as the Washington, D.C., media director and chief congressional liaison for the National Council of Resistance of Iran, U.S. Representative Office (NCRI-U.S.), which has gained strong support from Congress over the years. In 1992, for example, 219 members of the U.S. House of Representatives—a majority—signed a statement that read, "We are convinced that support for the National Council of Resistance will contribute to the achievement of peace and stability for all the countries of the region." The same type of recognition and support was expressed in 2001 by majorities in the parliaments of Italy, Belgium, and Luxembourg and in Britain's House of Commons. The 1992 U.S. Congress document enraged the Iranian regime, of course, which had already begun complaining to the United States in public speeches and Friday prayer sermons about the freedoms of "Iranian terrorists" who were feeding the U.S. Congress with misinformation. A bipartisan group of 32 senators in 2001 as well as 150 members of the United States House of Representatives in 2002 described the MEK as a "legitimate resistance movement."[6]

The 2002 revelations that blew the lid off Iran's secret nuclear program showed that the regime had developed two top-secret nuclear sites, one in Natanz, where a huge uranium-enrichment plant was being built under the guise of a desert eradication project, and the other in Arak, where a heavy-water project was hidden behind a front company, Mesbah Energy.[7] Both of these projects, run by the Atomic Energy Organization of Iran (AEOI), had gone undetected by both the IAEA and western intelligence services. The Iranian nuclear program suddenly became the world's biggest security threat, and the regime had a lot of explaining to do. Many more revelations about Iran's covert nuclear program followed, all based on facts uncovered by the opposition.

I have devoted my career to revealing the truth about the Iranian regime and to supporting the establishment of democracy, human rights, and political pluralism in my homeland. For me, the tragedy of Iran is both globally relevant and utterly personal.

Growing up in Iran in the 1960s and 1970s, I never imagined that my country would one day become a theocratic dictatorship and one of the most brutal regimes in world history. Nor did I foresee my career as a whistle-blower on Iran's secret nuclear weapons program. But the Iranian revolution of 1979, which for a few brief months filled Iranians with hope, quickly degenerated into the battleground of a supreme leader who envisioned Iran as a launching pad for spreading Islamic fundamentalism throughout the region.

My first exposure to political unrest in Iran occurred when I was 16 years old. That year, one of my relatives, an older cousin, was arrested by SAVAK (*sazemane amniat va ettela'at keshvar*), the shah's notorious secret police. My cousin's parents explained to our family that he had opposed Shah Mohammad Reza Pahlavi and thus SAVAK picked him up and took him to Evin prison. I recall asking a lot of questions about what my cousin had said, why he was opposed to the shah, and what he tried to accomplish. Even though I was too young to understand the entire story, this was my first exposure to the political realities of Iran, and it affected me deeply. Years later, my curiosity flared again when I tried to understand the motives of the supreme leader, Ayatollah Ruhollah Khomeini, as he usurped the leadership of the anti-shah movement, replaced the secular government with a clerical regime, and began killing his dissenters.

Other than the story of my cousin, politics were not discussed much in our home. I grew up in Mashhad, the second largest city in Iran, located in the northeast, close to the border of the former Soviet Union and Afghanistan. Millions of pilgrims stream through Mashhad every year to visit the shrine of the Imam Reza, the eighth imam, one of the holiest sites of Shia Islam. My father was a merchant with a retail and wholesale business in office supplies, stationery, and candy. He was the sole distributor of many items for the entire Khorassan Province, so he did a good business. A hard worker who had started his business from scratch, my father provided us with a house in a nice neighborhood that mingled with the University of Mashhad, and he also provided college educations for me and my four brothers and sisters. Regarding politics, my father was apolitical except at large family gatherings, where he would gossip with relatives about the incompetent government and the shah's excesses.

My father set high standards for each of us, such as when I was in the fifth grade and he insisted that I attend English classes sponsored by the American consulate at the local Iran-America Society. I was completely lost at first because the class was conducted entirely in English, but I stayed with it through every level and eventually received my diploma. The American consulates sponsored many similar organizations at the time. There were also many American companies, educational and social institutions, tourism industry organizations, non-governmental entities, and thousands of military personnel and defense contractors working on a variety of projects in Iran.

Looking back on my family's religious life and talking about Islam with many Iranians over the years, I believe that we were typical of the majority of Muslims in our country. We prayed five times a day and observed the fast of Ramadan, but I would not describe us as a religious family. We went to the mosque only for special occasions such as a family funeral or a major religious holiday like the Martyrdom of Imam Ali (the first Shiite imam and the Prophet Muhammad's son-in-law). My father also followed the Islamic teaching of giving 20 percent of his income every year to the poor, but he gave it directly to people he knew and trusted rather than to a local cleric, as was the traditional custom. This annual tithe was a small example of my father's generosity; we all remember how often he went out of his way to help people. When a major earthquake hit the southern part of our province near Kakhk in August 1968, for example, he packed the car with blankets and food and drove me and one of his friends to the devastated area to get these supplies to survivors. I was then 12 years old, and witnessing this stricken region, in which 30,000 people were killed, as well as witnessing my father's quick willingness to do whatever he could to help, left an impression on me that I will never forget.

Our family traveled extensively throughout Iran; the outer appearances of Islam that were instituted by the ayatollah after the revolution do not reflect the actual religious practices of people that I observed in Mashhad, Tehran, and many cities and even villages throughout the country. Ninety-eight percent of Iran's population is Muslim, and the vast majority is Shiite, but the people are not fanatic. We have no history of extremism, and the clerics played no serious role in society before the Khomeini regime came to power in 1979. There were no Friday prayers in those years, and people obtained the services of a mullah for their wedding or paid a lower-level clergyman to read the Koran over someone's grave after a funeral. For many Iranians, that was the extent of the clerics' role.

I recall one particular custom practiced by my mother that illustrates the largely superficial role of the clergy in everyday life. Once a month for many years, my mother hosted a very traditional yet informal "religious" ceremony of mourning at home called *Rowzeh*, in which women got together to socialize under the guise of a small ceremony. As a child I attended all of these events, as well as those held in our relatives' homes. In the midst of the talking and snacking, the little girls would spot the mullah through the window and run around yelling, "*Agha* is coming! *Agha* is coming!" This was the nickname for the cleric whose job it was to go house to house on appointment and conduct religious ceremonies. The women stopped talking, threw on their full-length black chadors, set out a chair for the mullah, and sat on the floor. (As a boy attending these gatherings with my mother, this sudden transformation always astonished me.) After the mullah gave his short reading—accompanied by the women's loud, obligatory crying—he made some final comments, collected his fee, and walked out. As soon as he left, everyone threw off their chadors and started laughing and talking about the mullah. "Did you see his *turban?*" At each of these gatherings in women's homes, it was common to poke fun at the mullahs.

The larger reality of the world outside—the shah's corrupt and repressive regime—was no laughing matter, however. This became clear to me when I entered Aryamehr (now named Sharif) University of Technology in Tehran—perhaps the most prestigious technical university in Iran—as a freshman in 1974. The shah had instituted significant police forces on university campuses throughout Iran to quell student protests against his government. Although I was focused on my engineering program and had little knowledge about any opposition groups, it was impossible to ignore the anti-shah movement. My initiation into this fact of life took place when I stopped for a moment to watch an on-campus student demonstration one morning. Suddenly the antiriot police or guard, who had their own office on the campus, ran toward the crowd, and the students scattered while still chanting. As I naively stood by, one guard began running toward me, and I realized he meant business. I ran into the nearby library—no guard members would enter the buildings unless they had a special permit—and frantically asked the librarian why they were chasing me if I hadn't done anything. She laughed and said, "That's the way it is here. Once you're here, you're part of it."

Gradually there were strikes; some days I would go to class only to find students standing at the door and whispering, "We're not going to class today." I gradually got involved, reading anti-shah pamphlets originally out of curiosity, and later out of interest. Anti-shah slogans on the walls, in the libraries, in the halls and other places repeatedly caught my attention and soon became a topic of discussion with my friends who were also getting into politics. When I started writing anti-regime slogans on the walls myself, I knew a fire had been lit inside me. In protest of the shah's repressive policies, on many occasions some classes refused to take exams and simply handed in blank sheets of paper. As a result, no students got grades that academic year; all our credits were nullified. My father urged me to apply to schools in the United States, and I decided to start out at Ohio University in Athens, which one of my cousins was already attending.

Studying abroad was not unusual for Iranians at this time; in the 1970s, approximately 100,000 Iranian students attended colleges or universities outside Iran.[8] In 1975, like every other student on his or her way to a foreign school, I had to sit in a mandatory group session, being briefed about the regulations for our trip and about how we should handle our grades, transfer credits, and remain compatible with the Iranian education system. The officer (perhaps a SAVAK employee) told us, among other issues, that outside Iran there were a number of dangerous people—student groups, anti-Iran troublemakers, terrorists, "Islamic Marxists." We must stay away from people like that, he said, because SAVAK is watching them and SAVAK is watching us.

The contrast between the campus in Tehran and the campuses at the colleges I attended in the United States was overwhelming. Here was an open society with open discussions: students who wanted to discuss Iran actually put up signs in the student union to meet at a specific time and place! It was exciting to see, but one year in college in Iran still kept some fear of SAVAK in me. There was a palpable fear factor in the foreign universities at the time, especially for those who wanted to go back to Iran, and everybody wanted to go back. Students were afraid that SAVAK had its own spies at our schools, and it took at least a year for me to stop looking over my shoulder while participating in anti-shah meetings and discussions. I transferred to the University of Michigan at Ann Arbor the following year. By that time my fears had faded as I became an active participant in group meetings, discussions, on-campus speeches, and anti-shah demonstrations. When I returned to Iran in the summer of 1977 for family visits, I could easily sense that things had begun to unravel—people were criticizing the regime in a more open way, my high school friends were now talking politics, and my college friends had become so involved in anti-shah activities that some of them had been jailed by SAVAK. This only heightened my involvement in anti-shah activities when I returned to the United States to complete my studies. When I completed my bachelor's degree, I entered a master's program in civil engineering at the University of Texas at Austin in January 1979.

Throughout 1978, the anti-shah movement in Iran heated up to a new level and made headlines in the United States. The more I learned about the violent crackdowns by SAVAK and about the shah's weakening position, the more interested I became in talking to students about finding a better solution for Iran. The following February, Ayatollah Ruhollah Khomeini assumed power after the people overthrew the shah, and I had to go back to see what was happening. During that visit in the summer of 1979, which turned out to be the last time I stepped foot in Tehran, I witnessed Khomeini's brand of justice and realized that things were headed in the wrong direction.

People like me had no idea of Khomeini's real intentions. The general public threw their unconditional support to Khomeini with all their hearts and minds. This is a leader who is religious, we thought, a man of God who will bring us spirituality, prosperity, and freedom, and will end all the misery. With the exception of some of the opposition groups, such as the Mujahedin-e Khalq, who were keenly aware of Khomeini's real intentions (by virtue of dealing with his disciples in the shah's prisons for many years), millions gave him carte blanche. But when a friend invited me to court to watch the trial of one of the people accused by Khomeini of killings, I got a cold dose of reality. Seated at the front was the judge, Sheikh Ali Tehrani, a cleric who is married to Supreme Leader Ali Khamenei's sister. There was no lawyer for the accused who stood before him, and no jury. In less than half an hour, the judge accused the man of killing certain people at a certain time and place, and an anonymous man stood up in the gallery and made more accusations. The accused did not have a chance to say anything on his own behalf before the judge sent him away and called for the next prisoner. I knew nothing about the legal system, but I thought, could it really be like this? No papers were exchanged. No official protocol was in place. No right to appeal. Who were these people?

The next morning I went to a remote cemetery near Mashhad called Khajeh Abasalt to visit relatives' graves with my family. I walked over to a crowd and learned that they were burying a man who had appeared in court the previous day. When they lifted the white cloth from his face I could not believe my eyes—it was the man convicted in court the previous day. He had been shot that morning. That was the way things were operating in Iran six months after the revolution.

A few months after I returned to Texas, student followers of Khomeini stormed the U.S. embassy in Iran and launched the hostage crisis. Khomeini's entire cabinet resigned in the wake of this radical move in November 1979, and he consolidated power by promoting clerics into all positions of power. Khomeini imposed an oppressive code of "Islamic" law and managed to get a nationwide approval vote for the regime's newly drafted constitution, despite its rejection by the Mujahedin-e Khalq. In Texas, I finished my master's degree and began work on a Ph.D. in 1981, but the mass executions in Iran that began that summer distracted me from my work. Dissidents had been handed a death sentence by Khomeini, and 50 to 100 executions were being carried out each day. Several thousand executions were tallied in the following 12 months, my friends and relatives among them. I used every opportunity to talk about this wave of killings, from speaking to church groups to giving interviews to local TV news programs and to the *Austin American Statesman*. I reached a crisis of my own and decided to leave school and devote myself full-time to getting the word out about the Iranian regime. I needed to be a voice for my people when they needed me most.

My first serious step was to move to New York to work with student groups and human rights activists who were sympathetic to the Mujahedin-e Khalq and who were trying to get the issue to the United Nations General Assembly. The issue had already received the attention of the United Nations Human Rights Commission, and in December 1985 everyone's work finally paid off. My colleagues and I managed to hold a press conference at the main headquarters of the United Nations for women political prisoners who had escaped Iranian jails with torture scars on their bodies. The press conference and the chilling stories of the torture victims, who also met with many United Nations missions, stunned many member-state delegations and the media. That month, a resolution was passed for the first time at the General Assembly condemning the Iranian regime for its flagrant violation of human rights.[9] In 1985, I took another big step and moved to Washington, D.C., to focus my efforts on the U.S. Congress. There I informed members of Congress about Iran's abuses of women's rights and freedom of speech and about its support of terrorism. In the meantime, I started dealing with the media and soon became a media spokesperson for the People's Mujahedin of Iran press office (PMI Press).

Over the next ten years I came to know many more people involved in the organized opposition, particularly those in the National Council of Resistance of Iran, the political coalition that has set up an Iranian parliament in exile in Paris. During this period, I began representing this coalition as its media spokesperson and eventually became its chief congressional liaison. This gave me nearly full access to the information coming from the coalition's vast network of resistance workers in Iran.

From 1985 to 2003 I managed, along with my colleagues, to gather significant support on the Hill for condemning the violations of human rights in Iran and for supporting the establishment of democracy there. We also began releasing crucial information about the Iranian regime's role in terrorist attacks around the world. In 1995, based on evidence gathered by the Mujahedin-e Khalq sources in Iran, I exposed Tehran's role in the deadly bombing of the Jewish community center in Argentina, where nearly 90 people were killed. In 1997 I revealed the details of how Iran masterminded the Khobar Towers bombing in Saudi Arabia, where 19 American servicemen were killed, and in 1998 I revealed that Iran had test-fired a Shahab–3 missile with a range of 880 miles, allowing it to target most of the capitals in the Middle East. All of these announcements provided leaders with crucial facts about Iran's role in global terrorist events and its expanding weapons program, but the two nuclear revelations of 2002 actually changed the course of history.

Speaking out about the regime at press conferences, in lectures, in articles, and as a foreign affairs analyst on the Fox News Channel and other mainstream media has had its price. My father in Mashhad was repeatedly harassed by the Ministry of Intelligence and Security (MOIS) after I began activist work in New York and Washington, and he was eventually arrested and jailed for several months. The regime accused him of providing funding and assistance to Iran's main opposition movement. In exchange for his release, they ordered him to go on national TV and denounce me. When he refused, they kept pressuring him and told him to sign a letter asking Supreme Leader Khamenei to forgive me. He still refused, and they said that because he was not willing to denounce his son, he must be in agreement with his son. The pressure continued even after he was released, and for years he was barred from leaving the country. With three of his children living outside Iran this was a devastating hardship. In the last years of my father's life, when he spent most of his time in the capital, Tehran, the grilling continued. My father finally managed to tell me his story of those years of pressure by the Iranian regime before he died in 2004.

I have lost several mentors, close associates, and friends to the regime—people who devoted their lives to the resistance movement. One was Professor Kazem Rajavi, the brother of the Iranian resistance leader Massoud Rajavi and the first ambassador to the United Nations after the revolution; he resigned from the United Nations when Khomeini began purging and suppressing his opponents. Anticipating his fate in the hands of the Iranian regime's terrorists, Rajavi once told the *New York Times* that "we're writing the history of human rights with our blood."[10] A Swiss magistrate, Jacques Antenen, concluded at the end of his investigation that a group of 13 regime assassins, carrying passports marked "on mission," were the perpetrators of Rajavi's murder.[11] According to a warrant issued by Antenen, the alleged murderers flew back to Iran on the afternoon of the killing. The warrant also noted that an international warrant had previously been issued for the arrest of the 13 alleged members of the hit squad, including Tehran's ambassador to Germany, Mohammad Mehdi Akhondzadeh Basti.[12] Some 162 members of Congress called Dr. Kazem Rajavi "a great advocate of human rights, who had dedicated his life to the establishment of democracy in his homeland." Mrs. Zahra Rajabi, a senior figure in the NCRI, was killed by a hit squad in 1996 during a trip to Turkey, where she was helping refugees who had fled Iran. Akbar Ghorbani, who had moved to Turkey, was kidnapped and tortured to death and buried in the outskirts of Istanbul in January 1992. When they were questioned about other crimes, the assassins confessed to Turkish police and told the police where the body was buried. Another colleague of mine, Hossein Abedini, was shot on his way to Istanbul airport in March 1990 and miraculously survived. And Mohammad-Hossein Naghdi, the former Iranian charge d'affaires in Italy who had defected and was the NCRI representative in Italy, was assassinated in March 1993 in Rome.[13]

Inside Iran, the regime's most infamous attack on the opposition took place in the summer of 1988, when tens of thousands of political prisoners were executed on direct orders of Khomeini. The *Sunday Telegraph* reported in 2001, "More than 30,000 political prisoners were executed in the 1988 massacre—a far greater number than previously suspected."[14] In 2003, Amnesty International declared September 1 the "International Day in Remembrance of the Massacre of Political Prisoners" in an effort to bring this crime to greater public awareness. That massacre reminds all of us that there is always a price for freedom, and that if you want to help your people embrace freedom, you have to be ready to pay that price.

Since the closing of the NCRI-U.S. office in 2003 (I explain the circumstances surrounding this event in chapter 12), I have continued to reveal facts about Iran's nuclear weapons program and terrorist activities. Despite a struggle to overcome the imbedded set of ideas about Iran and its opposition groups that permeates U.S. policy, I am extremely gratified about the progress made in the last few years. It has been a difficult but worthwhile challenge to get the facts to the people who need to hear them. That more than a hundred members of the U.S. House of Representatives and dozens of senators support the resistance as the way both to establish freedom and democracy in Iran and to end Iranian terror is a matter of public record. In a statement issued on November 21, 2002, for example, 150 bipartisan members of Congress wrote:

> We now have a historic opportunity to base our policy towards Iran on reality rather than on futile hopes of "moderation" within a brutal theocracy. Let us recognize the efforts of those who struggle against the repressive, terrorist and destabilizing Iranian regime.[15]

In August 2001, in a bi-partisan statement, 32 senators endorsed a "policy statement on Iran." The statement said that U.S. policy should reach out to those working to establish a democratic and pluralistic system in the country. In this context, the statement concluded, "Support for the democratic goals of the National Council of Resistance of Iran and its president-elect, Mrs. Maryam Rajavi, whose objectives are supported by the majority of Iranians, can contribute to peace, human rights, and regional stability."

I have worked with many people like these members of Congress who understand the issue and realize the urgency of halting Iran's nuclear weapons threat and its destabilizing role in Iraq. But at the same time, the old policy is so deeply rooted, so intertwined at every level of government that it bogs down the prospect of a new policy toward Iran. This is the inertia that I have faced for more than two decades, but the Iranian terrorist and nuclear threat is so central and urgent now that I understand that the real work is just beginning.

My contribution to that work in the form of this book opens with a profile of Ahmadinejad, covering his childhood in an upper-middle-class Tehran household to his military career and government posts. Part I explores how Ahmadinejad ascended to the presidency of the regime, his mission, and how he has been executing this mission as president. Part II describes the ideology of Khomeini, an ideology that remains the bedrock upon which the regime's policies and decisions are made, and that is so clearly reflected in Ahmadinejad's radical attitude and rhetoric. Part III covers Iran's role as the world's most active state sponsor of terror, from its direct terrorist operations (ops) to exterminate critics of the regime to its devastating mission in Iraq. Part IV provides details about every aspect of Iran's nuclear program, from the organization of cover-up strategies and nuclear smuggling to the deceptive cat-and-mouse games the regime plays with the IAEA. This part also describes Iran's push to hide its nuclear program underground, and Ahmadinejad's role in speeding up the mullahs' race for the bomb. Finally, Part V provides a discussion of the global consequences of a nuclear-armed Tehran and ideas for a practical and effective United States policy toward Iran that could end the Iranian threat.

PART I
A STUDY IN TERROR

CHAPTER 1

CHILD OF THE "REVOLUTION"

I am a child of the revolution . . . and if there is a danger for this revolution and
our nation then I am ready for it.

—Mahmoud Ahmadinejad, May 2005

Mahmoud Ahmadinejad's activities in the first decade of the revolution took him
to several fronts of battle. The military post that sources say he assumed while
still an undergraduate student in Tehran, something not mentioned in his official
biography and revealed for the first time in the following chapter, most likely
groomed him to become a religious zealot not only in ideology but in action. As a
young militant Islamic fundamentalist and Khomeini insider, Ahmadinejad was
the quintessential child of Khomeini's hijacked revolution, operating wherever
the regime needed him to go and carrying out six distinct types of operations
from 1979 to 1989. Sources say his military career and radical Islamic calling
began at the university, which he entered as a serious and highly religious student
in 1975. His personal story begins in a small corner of the desert.

Soon after his fourth child was born, Ahmad Saborjhian decided to move his
family from Aradan, a village at the edge of the salt desert of north-central Iran.
After running two businesses, a grocery store and later a barbershop, Mr. Saborjhian wanted to find better opportunities than the sheep- and cattle-farming villages of Semnan Province could provide. But before moving to the capital city, he
decided to increase his chances of success by changing his family name. Saborjhian, derived from the Farsi word *sabor* (thread painter), denotes one of the most
humble jobs in the province's traditional carpet industry. To leave that regional
trace behind and make a fresh start, Ahmad expanded upon his first name, which
means "virtuous" and is another name used for the Prophet, Muhammad. He

added *nejad* (race) to form Ahmadinejad, "virtuous race" or "Muhammad's race." Name changing was common among many people who moved from the villages to the cities, and Ahmad's choice reflected his intensely religious outlook.[1]

Ahmad had already named his new son with another variant of the Prophet's name. Mahmoud, born on October 28, 1956, was six months old when the family moved to the Narmak district in northeastern Tehran.[2] From his youngest years, Mahmoud lived up to his heavily Islamic names, immersing himself in the Koran from a very early age and trying to get into religion classes as early as age 10. "They threw him out because he was too young," said one of his cousins, "but he would insist, saying, no, no, I know how to read the Quran."[3] The Ahmadinejad family eventually had seven children, each growing up in a devout household where their mother, whom friends and relatives called Seiyed Khanom, "Madam Descendent of the Prophet," maintained a strict code. When she hosted religious gatherings at the house, for example, she hung a curtain to separate the men and the women, and she did not sit next to a man unless he was a close relative.[4] Like other very traditional Muslim women, Mrs. Ahmadinejad wore the full-length black chador that covered everything but her eyes.

Ahmad Ahmadinejad did well for himself in Tehran, finding a new trade in the ironworks industry. He owned the house in the upper-middle-class Narmak district, in a neighborhood called Nezam-Abad, and he sent Mahmoud to an expensive private high school, called Daneshmand, in another part of the district. An acquaintance of mine who attended this high school with Ahmadinejad recalled that there were several public schools much closer to the Ahmadinejads' home, but the family had the means to send Mahmoud to one of the most prestigious schools in Narmak. The tuition at Daneshmand cost nearly 35 times as much as the tuition at any of the local schools.

Even though the family had means, Ahmadinejad's parents preferred to keep the furnishings of their home plain to the point of austerity. "The family was not poor, but they were living very simple lives," said one of Ahmadinejad's second cousins. Ahmadinejad retained these tastes for himself, prompting the cousin to say in 2005, "His life is not luxurious at all. There are no sofas in his house in Tehran, only cushions and rugs."[5]

The family's humble style coincided with its conservative religious practices. Ahmadinejad's classmate observed that the Nezam-Abad neighborhood was home to many highly religious families and known throughout the city for the dramatic heights of its Shiite mourning ceremonies. On the religious mourning days, which memorialized the death and martyrdom of Imam Hossein (the third Shiite imam) with rituals that sometimes included self-flagellation and self-cutting, the largest gatherings and processions were conducted in south Tehran, the Bazaar area, and Nezam-Abad. "The youth, who on other days did not look or act like devout Muslims, would participate in the mourning and self-desecrating fundamentalist acts," he recalled. Not surprisingly, the environment was ripe for recruiting young men into radical Islamic groups. "The strong, traditional religious social structure of Nezam-Abad, along with the existence of several influential mosques and *Hosseinyiehs* (religious sermon houses), had rendered this area one of the special social bases of Hizbollah," he recalled.

Ahmadinejad's education included classes in English at private language institutes, which boosted his grades in English in high school. "Such extracurricular English classes were very expensive," said his classmate, "and only the upper-middle-class or wealthy families could afford them. Definitely, no 'son of a blacksmith' could afford attending such a program."

The "blacksmith" label became attached to Ahmadinejad's father during the 2005 Iranian presidential campaign, presumably based on someone's English translation of *ahangar*, which is more correctly translated as "ironworker." The difference is significant because Ahmadinejad's father earned a healthy income working in the metals trade, enough to buy a house that he later sold for the equivalent of 70,000 U.S. dollars, a virtual fortune in Iran. But amazingly, the "son of a blacksmith" title clings to Ahmadinejad to this day. To many, "blacksmith" conjures up the image of a leather-aproned worker in a one-man shop, and this concept fit well with the poverty-conscious "man of the people" persona that the regime crafted about Ahmadinejad.

Ahmadinejad was among the top students at Daneshmand, usually ranking second or third in his class. The school offered three tracks of study: natural sciences, literary studies, and mathematical sciences, and Ahmadinejad took the mathematics track. According to a longtime friend of Ahmadinejad interviewed by *Newsweek*, he played a lot of soccer and "he didn't chase girls."[6] Sports were his main social outlet—he also hiked in the nearby Alborz Mountains—but in school he did not go out of his way to be friendly. On the contrary, he "always acted as if he was above others," recalled my source. "He looked down at other students and derided and ridiculed them." Ahmadinejad told people that he did not have to study hard, but "the truth was very much the opposite"; he worked to portray himself as something he was not. When the students got together to compare answers after exams, for example, he "pretended that he couldn't care less about his grades." If he found out that he had given an incorrect answer, he would make a point of waving it off as though it did not matter. He also set himself apart with his wardrobe, never wearing the current styles that all the other teenagers preferred. "Ahmadinejad always put on a jacket or an overcoat," recalled his classmate. "He never had long hair. He actually looked much like he looks today, except he didn't have a beard in high school."

My acquaintance also stated that Ahmadinejad held a grade point average of "just above 17 out of a total of 20" when he graduated from Daneshmand in 1975, which was better than most. He also did well in the national university entrance exams that year, ranking 130th overall.[7] This earned him entry into the civil engineering program at the University of Science and Technology, located in his home district of Narmak.

By the mid-1970s, student unrest over the shah's repressive regime had flowed into the universities. Iranians were terrified by the arrests and executions carried out by the shah's secret service, SAVAK, and would no longer tolerate the shah's lavish lifestyle and economic policies that drove more people into poverty. The student activists evolved into three basic camps: the Marxists; the secular Muslims and intellectuals who envisioned a secular democratic state—that is, the Mujahedin-e Khalq (MEK); and the radical Islamic fundamentalists, many of whom were apolitical and were mostly involved in reading religious books and writings. The fundamentalists later supported Khomeini when he came into the picture in 1978 and 1979. The Marxists and the MEK were the dominant groups until Khomeini's network grabbed control of the mosques and took over the religious movement in the months preceding the fall of the shah. The Mujahedin-e Khalq's organizational capabilities were nearly annihilated by the work of SAVAK, and later by a bloody coup within the MEK, all of which left the Khomeini followers with little challenge when they usurped the leadership of the anti-shah movement in 1978.

In his first year at the university, Ahmadinejad fell in with the religious political movement and found his calling. Not only was he the personification of the ultraconservative, highly religious mentality that Khomeini would soon enlist for taking over the revolution; Ahmadinejad immediately rejected the intellectuals and their secular political ideals. The effects of this new calling were evident after his freshman year. "Ahmadinejad was from a fanatically religious family," said his classmate, "and it was obvious that during his first year at college he had socialized with politico-religious people and had become even more religious." His religious zeal soon put him at the center of Khomeini's student movement.

When the major student demonstrations against the shah began in the late 1970s, Khomeini was sitting in exile in Najaf, Iraq, closely following the riots and strikes. Khomeini realized that a leadership vacuum had been created: many of the leaders of the student organizations and opposition groups, including the Mujahedin-e Khalq, were killed by the shah or were in the shah's jails. But the mullahs, who had kept their network of clergy totally intact, were not targeted by the shah's network. Many were collaborating with the shah, so once Khomeini saw the opportunity, he consolidated his power with the clerics and usurped the leadership of the revolution from the opposition groups. Everything was timing. It was a unique historic opportunity; Khomeini happened to step in at the right place at the right time.

Ahmadinejad and his fellow Islamic radicals were fueled by Khomeini's vision of a government in which zealous, uniquely qualified Islamic leaders control the "simple-hearted" lower classes. This sense of superiority is rampant in Khomeini's set of published speeches called *Velayat-e Faqih* (Guardianship/Rule of the Jurist), released in the decade preceding the revolution but little noticed at the time. In a section about recruiting the people to his revolutionary ideas, he gives instructions on inflaming the masses to a militant defense of Islam.

Khomeini stressed the role of religion in arousing these masses into a powerful force, explaining that "all segments of society are ready to struggle for the sake of freedom, independence, and the happiness of the nation, and their struggle needs religion. Give the people Islam, then, for Islam is the school of jihad, the religion of struggle . . . so that they may overthrow the tyrannical regime imperialism has imposed on us and set up an Islamic government."[8] In the future, Ahmadinejad's push to bring the regime back to its "pure" revolutionary roots and reject western "bullying" would echo these ideas. Khomeini's total fusion of religious radicalism and politics as a means to define Iranian independence would show up in Ahmadinejad's countless speeches about Iran's "right" to nuclear technology, his call to wipe Israel off the map, and his condemnation of the imperialist United States.

Another crucial aspect of Khomeini's ideology that was burned into the minds of his student followers was his all-or-nothing approach to Islamic rule. Khomeini claimed that anyone who rejected his ideas rejected the Islamic faith as a whole: "Any person who claims that the formation of an Islamic government is not necessary implicitly denies the necessity for the implementation of Islamic law, the universality and comprehensiveness of that law, and the eternal validity of the faith itself," he said.[9] This was typical of the message that Iranians would hear after the revolution: If you do not accept Khomeini's version of Islam and Islamic rule—which were no more than a collection of dogmatic, rigid, feudalistic, medieval ideas contrary to the true teachings of Islam—then you are not a Muslim. As with all tyrannical dictators, there was no gray area with Khomeini.

Initially, Khomeini flatly denied any interest in getting involved in postrevolutionary Iranian politics. While in Paris, he had said in response to a question about his future that he would go to Qom and teach theology. Once in power, however, he installed himself as supreme leader. The person in this politico-religious position, according to Khomeini's writings in exile, would act as the safeguard who ensured that neither Islam nor the people would fall into decay: "Were God not to appoint an Imam [high-ranking Islamic scholar—he was clearly talking about himself] over men to maintain law and order, to serve the people faithfully as a vigilant trustee, religion would fall victim to obsolescence and decay." Without such a leader, "men would fall prey to corruption; the institutions, laws, customs, and ordinances of Islam would be transformed . . . resulting in the corruption of all humanity."[10]

By his senior year at the University of Science and Technology, Ahmadinejad had risen to the top of the militant Islamic student movement. By then, Khomeini had positioned himself as the indisputable driving force of the movement, and many students had adopted his firebrand ideology. After the fall of the shah, Ahmadinejad founded the Islamic Students Association at his university, and in July 1979 he was selected to be the representative of the university who would attend regular meetings with Khomeini. After a series of these student gatherings with the ayatollah, Ahmadinejad cofounded the Office for Consolidating Unity between Universities and Theological Seminaries (OCU).[11]

This OCU, underwritten by the regime, was the brainchild of Ayatollah Mohammad Hossein Beheshti, Khomeini's closest confidante. Beheshti needed to establish a student fighting force to combat the rapidly expanding membership of the Mujahedin-e Khalq, which was one of Khomeini's gravest concerns. In the early days after the revolution, the radical Islamic fundamentalists had already established themselves as the strongest student movement, followed by the Marxists and the MEK. The MEK's organizational structure had been severely shattered under the shah, and the surviving leadership and key members of the organization were released from the shah's jails only three weeks before the revolution, when the people stormed the prisons and released the political prisoners. However, the MEK, which emerged with a still sizable social support but little organizational ability, soon staged its come-from-behind move in the universities as the pro-Khomeini students were riding high. Khomeini immediately began using his network to put down the non-Islamic groups, and the Marxists lost much of their ground. Other groups were divided and disarrayed.[12] But despite this situation the MEK was rapidly on the rise because of the enormous popularity of the speeches of its leader, Massoud Rajavi.[13] His message of democracy, human rights, intellectual diversity and freedom, and other progressive ideas chipped away at Khomeini's base among young Muslims. There were six major universities in Tehran that set the pace for the entire student movement in Iran both under the shah and in post-Khomeini Iran. These universities were Tehran

University, Aryamehr (later changed to Sharif) University of Technology, Polytechnic (Amirkabir Industrial) University, Science and Technology University, Melli (Beheshti) University, and Tarbiat Moaalem University. The major universities in other parts of the country were in Shiraz (south), Tabriz (northwest), Mashhad (northeast), and Isfahan (central). Within months, the Mujahedin-e Khalq became the dominant force in all the universities throughout the country. As a result, Beheshti met the challenge head-on by forming the OCU and enlisting its leaders, including Ahmadinejad, to put down the MEK primarily.

Members of the OCU central council met regularly with Khomeini, but they also held their own planning sessions. It was during one of their own meetings that two of the members brought up the idea of storming the United States embassy in Tehran. According to former OCU members who reported on this event in 2005, Ahmadinejad was present at the meeting.[14]

The controversy over whether or not Ahmadinejad took part in the embassy takeover, which escalated into the 444-day American hostage crisis, erupted immediately after his election in the summer of 2005 when a photograph surfaced that apparently showed him holding the arm of one of the blindfolded hostages in the embassy compound. The intelligence community investigated the photograph and decided that it was not Ahmadinejad, but that decision did not address the question of whether or not he was involved in the ordeal. He was the cofounder of Khomeini's most important student organization and therefore was in the supreme leader's inner circle. It is unrealistic to think that he would step away from an operation of this magnitude, organized by his own group. My information suggests his high-level involvement.

Once those students began climbing the embassy walls, it was clear that the plot had at least the tacit approval of Khomeini—if indeed the plot was not ordered by him—or they would have been dragged away within minutes. Most important, Khomeini exploited the hostage crisis as a way to eliminate the secular, western-educated, suit-and-tie-wearing interim government. Within hours of the students' takeover of the embassy, which was not put down by Khomeini, Prime Minister Mehdi Bazargan and his entire cabinet resigned in protest. This is exactly what Khomeini was waiting for.

Khomeini had used Bazargan and his Freedom Movement of Iran network, as well as the remnants of the National Front who shared the cabinet posts with Bazargan, to win western backing for his rise to power. With that already achieved, it was now time for the mullahs to take over and consolidate power. The Bazargan administration, first praised by Khomeini as the *Dowlate Imam Zaman* (the government of the Imam of the Age [Mahdi]), was now totally out of the picture. All other "liberals" within the regime were gradually purged in the months that followed. Khomeini then turned over the government to the *Showray-e Enghelab* (Revolution Council) dominated by clerics and headed by his confidante, Ayatollah Mohammad Hossein Beheshti. This created a new administration made up of Khomeini's followers, both clerics and nonclerics, and he began to focus on the embassy issue as his rallying point for inflaming anti-American sentiment. He defined this event as the second revolution, more important than the first because it was Iran against the United States. The embassy became the "Den of Spies" that represented everything evil and corrupt about the United States and the West. Khomeini drew a line that gave him a justification for punishing and executing the students, professors, intellectuals, and any others who opposed his regime. After the embassy takeover, there were only two types of people in Iran, according to Khomeini: those who supported the hostage taking and all the anti-American fervor that went with it, and those who did not and were by extension lackeys of America.

The embassy takeover, which had already resulted in the elimination of the "liberals" from the government, gave Khomeini more ammunition for eliminating political freedoms, establishing an "Islamic" government, and confronting the expanding Mujahedin-e Khalq. Khomeini realized that if the group continued to grow, it would spread well beyond the younger generation, so he committed heavy resources to his 1980 crackdown on the MEK and non-Islamic student groups. This purge was so important to the regime's survival that Khomeini called it the "cultural revolution," targeting the universities and educational institutions.[15]

Ahmadinejad's role in this phase of the revolution was critical to Khomeini, who needed the radical Islamic youth and other highly committed followers to develop a specific military unit that would become the lifeblood of the regime.

In March 1980, the Iranian regime gave all political student groups who had set up offices in various universities throughout Iran three days to evacuate. Ahmadinejad's cohorts were instrumental in physically attacking the student groups who were clearly defying the regime's orders to turn over the universities to the ayatollahs. In June 1980, Khomeini ordered the universities closed for three years and formed the Council of Cultural Revolution to overhaul the entire educational system, purge all the students and faculty, and make the universities "Islamic," turning them into the bedrock of the Islamic fundamentalists. Government-run agencies and revolutionary institutions such as the Islamic Revolutionary Guards Corps (IRGC) could have a quota as high as 40 percent of students for the new educational systems in the universities. The students were to be the children of the most devout religious zealots and the regime's key officials.

CHAPTER 2

SON OF THE REGIME: AHMADINEJAD'S RISE UP IRAN'S MILITARY AND POLITICAL RANKS

The foundation of the world's arrogance will collapse very soon and the flag of Islam will be raised.

—Mahmoud Ahmadinejad, January 2005[1]

They named it *Vahed-e Ettelat-e Sepah*, the Islamic Revolutionary Guards Corps Intelligence Unit. Khomeini's regime rushed to form this new intelligence organization in 1979, as the shah's SAVAK had disintegrated overnight when the shah's government fell. Khomeini needed his own committed intelligence force to help round up and silence opponents of the regime, and the agents of the IRGC Intelligence Unit were trained to disrupt events and demonstrations, intimidate dissidents, and interrogate prisoners.[2] This unit became the most prestigious section of the IRGC, an elite unit of agents with virtually no constraints over their methods. In short, the Intelligence Unit was Khomeini's answer to SAVAK.[3]

According to my sources, Ahmadinejad, who was among the first to join the Islamic Revolutionary Guards Corp while a student at the University of Science and Technology, may have joined the Intelligence Unit early on. This post is not listed in his biography on his Web site, nor does it appear in articles or other research on Ahmadinejad's history that I am aware of. I received this information from my sources in Iran in June 2006, and if it were true it could solve the mystery of a wide and mysterious gap in Ahmadinejad's questionable biography. Throughout my research in Farsi and other sources, I have not found any writings or speeches in which Ahmadinejad explains the inconsistencies in his official biography.

During the U.S. embassy takeover and hostage crisis that lasted from November 1979 to January 1981, Ahmadinejad, these same sources say, worked as the chief interrogator in the IRGC, questioning the American hostages, according to my sources inside Iran. His leadership role among the group of young, devoted, and radical Islamic students who made up the first group of the unit would show how early the regime recognized and used his skills.

Six former hostages told the American media they recognized Ahmadinejad as one of their captors when they saw him on television coverage and in photos during the 2005 Iranian presidential elections. William A. Gallegos, who lives in suburban Denver, told the Fox News Channel, "I remember him being one of the leaders at the beginning of the takeover. He was also present during my interrogations. He did not take part, but was present in the background and he always seemed to be in charge of the guards who watched over us." Kevin Hermening of Mosinee, Wisconsin, who had been a Marine guard at the embassy, recalled the man he believes was Ahmadinejad asking him for the combination to a safe. "His English would have been fairly strong. I couldn't say that about all the guards," Hermening said. "I remember that he was certainly direct, threatening, very unfriendly." Other hostages—Chuck Scott, William J. Daugherty, and Don A. Sharer—agreed that Ahmadinejad was one of the hostage-takers.[4]

In his profile of Ahmadinejad written for the American Foreign Policy Council, Ilan Berman cites information published in *Al-Jazeera* when he states that Ahmadinejad was at the center of the event: "As a member of the radical 'Office for Strengthening Unity' during the Islamic Revolution, Ahmadinejad played a major role in planning and executing the 1980 takeover of the U.S. embassy in Tehran."[5] The official CIA report of August 2005 about Ahmadinejad's alleged participation in the hostage taking was not solidly conclusive. An administration official said the agency determined that they lacked the evidence to "conclude definitively" on Mr. Ahmadinejad's role. "It was similar to the Scottish court's not proven judgment," the source said.[6] However, some former hostages demanded that the CIA turn over this classified report that cast doubt on the involvement of Ahmadinejad in the 444-day hostage crisis in Iran. A retired Air Force colonel, David Roeder, recalled how in one interrogation session Mr. Ahmadinejad sat in a room and watched as his questioner gave the location and time that his son in Alexandria, Virginia, caught his bus for special-education classes and then threatened that his wife would receive fingers and toes of his son if he did not cooperate. "He did not say anything at the time, but it was clear Ahmadinejad was in control," Colonel Roeder said. "I am upset with the CIA that they leaked a classified document calling me a liar," he said. "If someone is going to tell me I'm wrong and I know I'm not, I would bet my life on it, I should at least have access to the data that led them to that conclusion."[7] Two other former hostages told CNN they remain certain Ahmadinejad was involved in plotting the takeover of the U.S. Embassy in Tehran in 1979.[8]

On orders of the supreme leader, members of the Office for Consolidating Unity (OCU)—of which Ahmadinejad was also a member—stormed Iranian universities, rounded up "dissident" professors and students, and beat them, all in the name of Khomeini's cultural revolution.[9] Many of their targets were arrested, imprisoned, tortured, and executed. *Newsweek* reported on May 5, 1980 that "As many as 50 students were killed when fundamentalists stormed university campuses in Teheran and the provinces. The bloodshed seemed to signal a violent new phase in Iran's Islamic revolution."[10] In an added measure to wipe out the student movement during this period, Khomeini shut down all the universities in Iran for three years.[11]

After Ahmadinejad's first stint at the battlefront at the start of the Iran-Iraq War in November 1980, he returned to Tehran to resume working in the IRGC, this time in the prisons that were filling up with political prisoners. The Intelligence Unit formed a strong alliance with Iran's prison system in this period, and Ahmadinejad was among the many agents who earned notorious reputations at such institutions as Evin prison in north Tehran, sources say. According to the Egyptian *Al-Ahram Weekly*, Ahmadinejad "developed a reputation as notorious interrogator and was believed to have worked . . . at Evin prison where thousands of political prisoners were tortured and executed in the 1980s."[12]

I have met and spoken with many political prisoners who survived this period, including one who recalled many interrogations by, he says, Ahmadinejad, known in Section 4 of Evin prison as "Golpa." (The interrogators at Evin and other Iranian prisons hid their identities by using pseudonyms and also by wearing sacklike coverings over their heads, similar to those worn by the Ku Klux Klan—the coverings were often removed once the prisoner was blindfolded. On some occasions, however, the interrogators removed their masks, which allowed the prisoners to identify them.) "In Section 4, Ahmadinejad was in charge of intense interrogation of the political prisoners arrested before June 1981," said the former prisoner who spent 6 years in Evin, Gohardasht, and Ghezelhessar prisons, "so that he could link them to the resistance network inside the prison and send them off for execution."[13] This tactic, of accusing long-held political prisoners of colluding with the resistance and then executing them, enabled the regime to kill more dissidents, even those arrested in early post-revolution months. In February 1982, this prisoner was transferred to Evin for additional interrogation and for supposedly wrapping up his case. "After a few days I was taken to Section 4. It was during that time that I was personally tortured and interrogated by both 'Fakoor,' the head of Section 4, and 'Golpa,' or Mahmoud Ahmadinejad."[14] He says he was able to identify Ahmadinejad because he saw his face many times at the prison. "Every time my blindfold would fall after being lashed with the cable, I would see Ahmadinejad's face along with other torturers. Each time they would tie the blindfold even tighter and continue the lashing," he said.

During the six years he says he was incarcerated and tortured, my interviewee learned a few details about Ahmadinejad that, along with information from other prisoners, corroborates information from my other sources in Iran that he was working with the Intelligence Unit of the IRGC. From early- to mid-1982, the prisoner recalled, Ahmadinejad was assigned to lead a project to map out and discover the organizational chart of the Mujahedin-e Khalq (MEK):

> He would compare the interrogation process of each section and try to extract information on the Mujahedin network among prisoners from high school students, universities, labor, and other sections. He conducted multiple torture sessions to extract this information, which is why many of those who broke down under torture and started to cooperate with the regime were directly linked with either "Golpa" or "Mirzaiee," the two pseudonyms that Ahmadinejad used as an interrogator.

This prisoner was transferred to solitary confinement in Evin's notorious 209 ward in the spring of 1982, where he says he had more chances to see Ahmadinejad's face and confirm his identity in his mind. "Ahmadinejad and Assadollah Lajevardi, the infamous Evin Prison warden, dubbed the 'Butcher of Evin,' used to come to my cell two to three times a week without masks or face coverings, to interrogate my two Mujahedin-e Khalq cellmates, Ibrahim Farajipour and Mostafa Nik-kar," he said. Both were later murdered. In this section of the prison, according to the prisoner who was only 19 years old at the time of his arrest in December 1980, Ahmadinejad was known as "Mirzaiee," as some of the interrogators would use different names in different units, and he worked very closely with Hamid Torkeh, the head of Section 6 in the 209 ward. A woman who had been a political prisoner in Shiraz for three years, from October 1982 to April 1985, explained to me that the prison interrogators repeatedly changed their pseudonyms in order to keep the prisoners from discussing who was torturing and interrogating who. "This would make it difficult for prisoners to coordinate their interrogation sessions and trick the interrogators," she said.[15] Five former political prisoners who had spent considerable time in Evin prison (from 3 to 5 years) confirmed that they had heard about an interrogator and torturer with the pseudonym of "Mirzaiee."[16] I interviewed another prisoner in August 2006, a 45-year-old man who had spent five years in Eshratabad, Ghezel Hessar, and Evin prisons from 1981 to 1986. Asked about who had jurisdiction in various parts of the prison, he said that during this period a certain section of Evin Prison was run by the Intelligence Unit of the IRGC, as opposed to other sections that were run by the Revolutionary Prosecutors Office. "The only section of Evin prison that was run by the Intelligence Unit of the IRGC was the 209 ward," he said.[17] Three other former prisoners confirmed that 209 ward was run by the IRGC. This is the section in which my other prisoner interviewee witnessed Ahmadinejad interrogating prisoners, further confirming that he may very well have been a member in the Intelligence Unit of the IRGC.

Another former prisoner, who spent five years in Evin and Ghezel Hessar prisons between 1981 and 1986, recalls that when in Ghezel Hessar around September 1983, Ahmadinejad accompanied Assadollah Lajevardi to this prison to select a number of prisoners to be taken to another prison in Karaj, known as Kanoon, for work. "He was very mean and not very talkative," said the prisoner, who had been a 22-year-old factory worker at the time of his arrest.[18] He said that Ahmadinejad used to come to Ghezel Hessar from time to time. "My cellmate told me that Ahmadinejad, who was upset with his non-cooperation, told him angrily that if he didn't cooperate he would 'personally make sure to fire your *coup de grace*,'" he said.

The frenzy of the U.S. hostage taking and the wave of political arrests of 1980 and 1981 led to more interrogations and torture. All of Khomeini's carefully selected and trained young militants were busy with the cultural revolution: One group demonstrated in front of the U.S. embassy by day, chanting "Death to America" in front of all the cameras, and at night moved on to organize attacks against Mujahedin-e Khalq offices.[19] The Mujahedin-e Khalq was still operating openly at that time, based in headquarters in Tehran and in many other cities throughout the country. They had managed to build a membership of more than 500,000 and were still growing.[20] Islamic radicals called this headquarters the "Den of Spies Number Two." Some stormed classrooms and meeting places to pull out suspected dissidents, while some worked inside the embassy, securing and interrogating the hostages. Some, like Ahmadinejad, were suspected of working double duty at the embassy and at Evin prison.[21]

The regime's intelligence operations gradually shifted away from the IRGC Intelligence Unit to the Ministry of Intelligence and Security (MOIS) after this ministry was founded in 1984.[22] The Intelligence Unit, however, lived to later partly merge with other units to form the notorious deadly terror machine known as the Qods (Jerusalem) Force of the IRGC. The Directorate of Intelligence of the IRGC continued to operate separately. Targeting and eliminating critics of the regime and supporting terrorist operations outside Iran are two fundamental activities of the Iranian regime, and both depend heavily upon the MOIS. As a result, it is ranked by experts as one of the Middle East's most extensive and active intelligence agencies.[23] The MOIS stands apart from every other ministry in Iran in that it reports directly to the supreme leader, has no oversight by the parliament or cabinet, and operates out of a secret budget.[24] What began as a group of young intelligence agents plucked from Iran's universities just after the revolution has evolved into a huge and highly secretive instrument of political repression.[25]

Ahmadinejad was made a senior commander of an elite section of the IRGC, which later became the Qods Force, as described in a Global Security.org profile: "Ahmadinejad was a senior officer in the Special Brigade of the Revolutionary Guards, stationed at Ramazan Garrison near Kermanshah in western Iran. This was the headquarters of the Revolutionary Guards' 'Extra-territorial Operations'— mounting attacks beyond Iran's borders." The report added that his work in this elite unit involved the "suppression of dissidents in Iran and abroad. He personally participated in covert operations around the Iraqi city of Kirkuk."[26] Describing Ahmadinejad's role in this unit, the *Sunday Times* of London wrote, "US intelligence sources . . . believe he became a key figure in the formation of the IRGC's Qods Force, which has been linked to assassinations in the Middle East and Europe."[27] Kenneth Katzman, a Specialist in Middle Eastern Affairs for the Congressional Research Service, and the author of *The Warriors of Islam: Iran's Revolutionary Guard*, told a Congressional Committee Hearing on Iran in July 2006 that Ahmadinejad "was a commander in the Guard during the 1980–88 Iran-Iraq war," adding that "his presidency is likely to only enhance the Guard's influence."[28] The Qods Force was created specifically to run special operations—terrorist attacks—outside Iran and to train Islamic terrorist groups.[29] This organization "is highly trained and well-funded," according to a *Washington Post* report in 2003, and "has provided instruction to more than three dozen Shiite and Sunni 'foreign Islamic militant groups in paramilitary, guerrilla and terrorism' tactics, according to a recent U.S. intelligence analysis." The article also stated that U.S. intelligence determined that the Qods Force had long-standing ties with al-Qaeda, agents in "most countries with substantial Muslim populations," and a training regime that included "assassinations, kidnapping, torture and explosives."[30]

According to the official Web site of the Iranian regime's president, Ahmadinejad "voluntarily joined" the IRGC in 1986, and many profiles that circulated after the presidential election of 2005 repeat this as a fact.[31] In truth,

Ahmadinejad had been part of the IRGC since 1979, primarily working on intelligence and security issues. If there was anything special about the year 1986 it may be that he spent more time at Ramezan garrison (the headquarters of the Qods Force) that year.[32] Many pro-Ahmadinejad web sites set up during his presidential campaign stated that Ahmadinejad took part in the Kirkuk operation in 1986, which was a Qods Force special operations mission deep inside Iraq during the Iran-Iraq War.[33] Such *Boroun Marzi* (extraterritorial) operations were commonly conducted by the IRGC, carried out by special, well-trained, well-qualified members in very risky situations deep inside enemy territory.[34]

The mid-1980s is a period in which Ahmadinejad's official biography is vague, overlapping and confusing at best. The biography claims that in 1986 he returned to the University of Science and Technology to begin work on a master's degree in civil engineering, yet it also states that during the Iran-Iraq War, he "was actively present as a member of the volunteer forces [Bassij] in different parts and divisions of the battlefronts, particularly in the war engineering division, until the end of the war."[35] If he was racing around the western fronts of the war from 1980 to 1988, it begs the question, how did he have time to go to graduate school in Tehran? The "volunteer" description could be seen as a weak attempt to hide his actual role in the terrorist special forces units (later to become the Qods Force).

In addition, the biography states that Ahmadinejad served for four years as the deputy governor and governor of the cities of Maku and Khoy in northwestern Iran, and two years as an "advisor," to the governor general of Kurdistan Province in the 80s, although it does not give specific dates for those positions.[36]

At the same time, sources say that during the eight-year Iran-Iraq War he engaged in special operations in Europe and the Middle East, targeting enemies of the regime. There are several Qods Force terrorist operations in which Ahmadinejad allegedly participated in the late 1980s and early 1990s, but the one that has come to the attention of European prosecutors took place in Vienna shortly after the Iran-Iraq War, in 1989. In July 2005, the Austrian member of Parliament Peter Pilz announced that he had received "very convincing" evidence that Ahmadinejad was part of the assassination plot that killed the Kurdish leader Abdolrahman Ghassemlou, the leader of the Iran-banned Kurdish Democratic Party. On July 13, 1989, Ghassemlou and two other members of his group were shot in the head and killed in a Vienna apartment, and Pilz asserted that his evidence identifies Ahmadinejad as the agent who delivered the weapons to the assassins a few days before the attack.[37]

The regime denied the accusations and dismissed them as a smear campaign against the newly elected president, but in doing so one Ahmadinejad defender brought up an important point. Ali Rabiee, an intelligence advisor to the former

President Khatami, was quick to give Ahmadinejad an alibi. At the time of the crime, he stated, "Mr. Ahmadinejad was only involved at the civil construction work in the governing offices of Maku and the province."[38] According to the regime's official biography, Ahmadinejad's four-year governorship job in north-western Iran coincided with his continuous military service at several battle-fronts in the Iran-Iraq War and his pursuit of a master of science degree in civil engineering at the University of Science and Technology. In my analysis, Ahmadinejad's political appointment as deputy governor and governor in Maku and Khoy, as well as his advisory role in Kurdistan were essentially front jobs on paper only, fabricated to hide his actual activities as part of the IRGC special forces (Qods Force) in the 1980s, especially in the Western Azerbaijan, Kurdistan, and Kermanshah provinces.

Iranian movie producer and filmmaker Mehdi Joorak, who was jailed by the regime and later released, was asked by the authorities to make a film as a way to make up for his prior opposition to the Iranian regime.[39] Joorak told me that he was approached by a personal friend of Mahmoud Ahmadinejad, at Ahmadinejad's request, to prepare an educational and training movie to be used by members of terror teams. Ahmadinejad, according to Joorak, worked directly with him on the project and told him that he had planned and carried out the assassination of an Iranian pilot who had defected from the country. Major Mohammad Hassan Mansouri, who had flown his fighter jet out of the country in 1982, was assassinated in Istanbul, Turkey in July 1987.[40] Ahmadinejad described the operation and his leading role in it to Joorak in detail. Ahmadinejad said, according to Joorak, that he was present at the site of the assassination, and returned to Iran by car once he was confident that Mansouri was dead. Joorak cooperated with Ahmadinejad by writing the movie script and the film was later produced and used in training sessions for the Iranian regime's terrorists. Two of my other sources, who have proven accurate in the past, corroborated Joorak's claim about the direct involvement of Ahmadinejad in the terrorist assassination of Major Mansouri.

If what sources say is true, Ahmadinejad's posts in the 1980s allowed him to serve the regime on six fronts: interrogating U.S. hostages, leading the closure of universities, questioning and torturing political prisoners, engaging in battles on Iran's western border in the Iran-Iraq War, conducting special operations inside Iraq with the special forces (later IRGC Qods Force), and killing the regime's enemies in Europe and the Middle East with the same special ops unit.

After the war, Ahmadinejad gradually shifted into a postwar phase, centered on politics and academics. In 1989, the University of Science and Technology made him a member of the faculty of the board of civil engineering. He then received another political appointment from a fellow IRGC officer, Ali Larijani, who had become Iran's minister of culture and higher education. Larijani named Ahmadinejad his cultural affairs advisor in 1993, a job that involved enforcing the Islamic ideals of the mullahs in various aspects of society. Moving up the political ladder, Ahmadinejad was appointed governor general of Ardebil Province in northwestern Iran in 1993, a post he held until 1997, when the new administration of President Khatami removed him.

In another deceiving aspect of his official biography, Ahmadinejad is portrayed as spending considerable time at the University of Science and Technology in the five years that he ran Ardebil Province, and as receiving his Ph.D. in transportation engineering and planning in 1997. Ardebil is about 400 miles away from Tehran, so it seems unlikely that he somehow managed to run the province and "write many scientific papers and [be] engaged in scientific research in various fields" during his teaching years. He also supervised the research of "students at M.S. and Ph.D. levels on different subjects of civil engineering, road and transportation as well as construction management" at the university.[41] The government job could not have made significant demands on his time if he was able to fulfill all these academic responsibilities.

Those who worked at the university with Ahmadinejad in the 1990s recall that he presented himself with radical, militant Islamic zeal that many others of his generation had shed. He looked the part, with the black-and-white checked Palestinian kaffiyeh covering his shoulders. Heshmatollah Tabarzadi, who had been a member of the OCU with Ahmadinejad in their early college days, said, "Ahmadinejad was less involved in political and cultural events of the university and more in military and operations." For Ahmadinejad and others like him, Khomeini's command to cleanse the universities of dissident thought was as urgent as ever because the ideals of the "revolution" were not only timeless, but meant to be exported to the rest of the world. In order for that to happen, Iran had to become a pure, devoted, and steadfast Islamic fundamentalist state. "Even in the 1990s he was one of the main players who disrupted the gatherings of intellectuals and opposition in the university," said Tabarzadi.[42]

The "military and operations" focus that Tabarzadi mentioned included Ahmadinejad's founding of an Ansar-e Hezbollah (Followers of the Party of God) section in Tehran during his teaching years, an activity included in his official biography.[43] This group, known for their signature black dress, acted as the mullahs' shock troopers, attacking student gatherings and demonstrations, storming student dormitories, and beating up students and other opponents of the regime with chains, clubs, truncheons, and knives.[44]

Ahmadinejad's closest adviser is Mojtaba Hashemi Samareh, also a former IRGC commander who spent many years at the Intelligence Ministry. One of my sources, who entered the University of Science and Technology the same year that Ahmadinejad did, told me that Ahmadinejad, along with his long-time friend, Mojtaba Hashemi Samareh, were the most hard-line, radical students at the university. He recalled that they led all the other Islamic fundamentalists at the time and "were always together before and after the revolution."[45] Mojtaba Hashemi later became Ahmadinejad's deputy as mayor in Tehran and was appointed as the special presidential advisor in August 2005.[46] In contrast to his rough approach to other associates, the president treats Mojtaba Hashemi with reverential respect, timorously standing behind him at prayers.[47] According to the news site Rooz Online, when Samareh headed the Foreign Ministry's Placement Office in the early 1990s he demoralized the diplomatic staff with his efforts to check the loyalty of those applying to serve in Iranian missions abroad. He composed a training program for a model Islamic diplomat that stipulated that an unfit diplomat was one who wore perfectly creased pants and polished, lace-up shoes and who grinned at strangers, a "Western" habit that demonstrated weakness to foreign visitors.[48]

Contrary to some media reports, Ahmadinejad is fully devoted to Supreme Leader Ali Khamenei. In a 2000 interview with Rooz, he emphasized his close contact with Khamenei during his student days as one of the founders of the Office for Consolidating Unity. He explained that he had been one of only four students who went to see Khomeini in the early days after the revolution, and that the supreme leader appointed Ali Khamenei to be the point of contact with Ahmadinejad and his associates. Ahmadinejad said he has been loyal to Khamenei ever since.[49]

As the dramatic events of 2003 in neighboring Iraq unfolded, the leaders in Tehran realized that they had an unprecedented opportunity to boost their plans for the region. After the Iran-Iraq War, the mullahs never lost sight of their goal to control Iraq, and after the coalition forces toppled Saddam Hussein's government in March 2003, a new door opened for them. Tehran knew that the United States was preoccupied with Iraq and had no immediate plans to force the Iranian nuclear issue with any deterrent actions. The mullahs became even more assured that the United States was not a threat when the United States made a deal with them at the start of Operation Iraqi Freedom. The United States received assurances that Iran would not fight against it in Iraq in exchange for Iran's demand that the Iranian opposition—the Mujahedin-e Khalq bases stationed along the Iran-Iraq border in the Iraqi territory—be targeted and bombed.[50] The bombing was followed by the United States complying with Iran's demands to disarm the MEK in hopes of pacifying Iran in Iraq and containing Iranian designs for that country. "In a meeting in January between U.S. and Iranian officials, and through messages subsequently delivered through British diplomats, the United States suggested it would target People's Mujahedin as a way of gaining Iran's cooperation to seal its border and provide assistance to search-and-rescue missions for downed U.S. pilots during the war," the *Washington Post* reported.[51] At the same time, Iran pushed its Iraqi agenda by sending thousands of its proxy group members into Iraq.[52] These fighters included the IRGC's Badr Brigade unit and the Supreme Council for the Islamic Revolution in Iraq (SCIRI), both formed by Iran in the early 1980s. The United States did not confront these groups, further convincing Tehran that it now had a historic opportunity to realize its long-held design in the region: namely, the establishment of an Islamic republic in Iraq, as part of a broader global Islamic rule. Upon his return from Iran to Iraq only a month after the fall of Baghdad, Ayatollah Mohammed Baqer al-Hakim, the head of the Iran-based Supreme Council for the Islamic Revolution in Iraq (SCIRI), said that he wanted "to put Islam and Sharia law at the top of the political agenda of the new Iraq," Agence France Press reported.[53]

In the chaos that followed the invasion of Iraq, the Iranian regime threw enormous resources into its mission to disrupt the political process in Iraq, from setting up new Shiite political parties to forming charities as covers for terrorist networks to smuggling improvised explosive devices (IEDs) across the border to be used against coalition forces.[54] The world only gradually discovered the extent of Iran's meticulously planned and heavily funded activities in Iraq. The basis for Tehran's investment in Iraq is its goal to install an Islamic government there. The invasion of Iraq was a gift to the mullahs, and other events further emboldened them to accelerate their plans for exporting the revolution. They sped up the covert nuclear program, only part of which had been exposed in 2002, by placing it primarily under the control of the IRGC and secretly advancing many research and development projects and moving facilities into underground tunnel complexes. In 2003 the regime began working on its list of hard-line candidates for the upcoming parliamentary elections in order to clear out the "liberal" factions that might slow down its plans. And it also paved the way for its candidate of choice to win the next presidential election, installing him in a new political post from which he could launch his campaign in 2005.

The Islamic Iran Developers Coalition, the party of ultraconservative hard-liners who run the Tehran city council, appointed Ahmadinejad the new mayor of Tehran in April 2003. His fifth political appointment since the end of the Iran-Iraq War, this position gave Ahmadinejad a much wider palette on which to project his radical fundamentalist ideology on society. He used the podium of city hall to extol the virtues of Islamic rule and preach about Iran's duty to export this type of government to the rest of the world. Ahmadinejad's ideology had only become more conservative and deep-rooted with time, and it was in perfect lockstep with the inner circle of clerics who rallied around Khamenei. The supreme leader and his top lieutenants in Tehran knew that the regime could survive only by repressing the population and suffocating the opposition. Putting Ahmadinejad on track for the upcoming presidency was a deliberate part of this strategy for survival.

Many of Ahmadinejad's mayoral speeches were throwbacks to the rhetoric of his glory days as a militant student leader. In one statement he declared that the executive branch of the government had lost its focus on the values of the Islamic revolution and that Iran had a "monumental historic duty" to fulfill the Prophet's mission and blaze the trail for a global Islamic movement.[55] He often spoke of the "culture of martyrs," a central theme of the small group of war veterans and hard-line fundamentalists who believed that dying in defense of Khomeini's ideology was the highest form of Islamic devotion. "Any society that has the spirit of martyrdom will remain undefeatable," he said, "and if we want to resolve today's social problems, we must return to the culture of martyrs."[56] He called for a better city government so that Iran as a nation would advance and fulfill its sacred duty: "Today our nation has a historical prophetic mission, and that is to put up an advanced society which would become an example for the world, in particular the municipal workers who have the main responsibility due to their sincere and devoted forces."[57] At a speech for a group of athletes in the IRGC Bassij forces, Ahmadinejad described the victory of the Islamic revolution and the Iran-Iraq War as "two great miracles" that had been accomplished by Iran's youth, and stated that the "third and greater miracle" will be the establishment of the "global Islamic government." This future depended on the young people of Iran who, with their "dynamic ideas based on the Islamic doctrine," would rebuild a better Islamic Iran.[58] After Iran's judo champion announced that he refused to enter a match with a "Zionist" judo opponent at the 2004 Olympics, Ahmadinejad, at an event in Tehran's Cultural Center, publicly praised him for his "courageous stand," adding, "Our youth have always made our country proud in many areas."[59]

The mayor put his ultraconservative ideas into action in Tehran with policies such as ordering men and women to use separate elevators in some public places. One hard-line member of the parliament defended this policy, saying, "It is not that we don't trust our youth, rather by taking this necessary action we have their dignity and safety in mind."[60] In November 2003, Ahmadinejad ordered the construction of four "women-only" parks in Tehran.[61] Ahmadinejad ordered the removal of billboards showing ads of British soccer star and heartthrob David Beckham.[62] He also built up the religious infrastructure of the city by revamping cultural halls into religious facilities and passing new policies to eliminate the financial separation of church and state. In September 2004, for example, the city council unanimously approved Ahmadinejad's resolution to exempt mosques and religious organizations from paying city fees and dues, a move that he felt was long overdue. "Support for the country's mosques and other religious centers is a duty and responsibility of the government," he said. "Unfortunately, there has not been much attention paid to this issue over the past 25 years."[63]

These fanatical, repressive policies earned Ahmadinejad the nickname "the Iranian Taliban" among the residents of Tehran.[64] With his harsh attitude, rumpled beige jacket, and medieval approach to public policy, he struck an odd profile in the city. But his rhetoric became even more outlandish and mystical when he began to campaign for the presidency, preparing the masses of the "revolutionary nation of Iran" to embark upon "monumental tasks of the world."[65]

CHAPTER 3

AURA OF OPPRESSION:
THE AHMADINEJAD PRESIDENCY

God willing, with the force of God behind it, we shall soon experience a world without the United States and Zionism.

Mahmoud Ahmadinejad, October 26, 2005[1]

Today our nation's great duty and prophetic mission is to prepare for the formation of the universal rule which can be accomplished by development of this land [Iran].

—Mahmoud Ahmadinejad, January 23, 2005[2]

The state media in Iran reveled in the outcome of the 2005 presidential elections, exclaiming that a man of the people had won because the people had spoken. The people voted for the humble mayor of Tehran because he spoke up for the poor and railed against corruption, because he had a clean past and people were fed up with the old guard. Ahmadinejad won on his own credentials by a popular landslide, they said. In reality, there was no such man-of-the-people platform, no popular surge of support, and certainly no majority vote.

Iran's election system, which is preposterously called "democratic," stipulates that a list of all potential candidates for national elections be screened by the Guardian Council, a panel through which Supreme Leader Khamenei exerts his authority over the executive and legislative branches. The Guardian Council consists of 12 members, six clerics appointed by the supreme leader and six members introduced by the parliament and approved by the supreme leader. This body also has the jurisdiction to veto legislation to make sure that all rulings are compatible with Sharia law. Effectively, the Guardian Council is the voice of the supreme leader. Candidates who want to submit their names to the screening list must register with the Interior Ministry. The five-day window for registration in the 2005 elections was May 10 through May 14, after which the Guardian Council took five days to review the registrants' competence.

There is no set number of candidates who will be allowed to run; the Guardian Council simply returns a list of those whom it has verified. The official list of candidates was announced by the Interior Ministry on May 25, and the candidates were given a campaign period of May 27 to June 15, with the election to follow on June 17. A special commission consisting of the chief prosecutor, the interior minister, the chief of radio and television, and one representative of the Guardian Council oversees the campaign process. Therefore, with the Guardian Council's presence intact, this commission can nullify anything that doesn't fall in line with Khamenei's wishes. All radio and television campaign programs of the candidates must be prerecorded, the commission schedules all the airings, and there are no debates.

The most conservative of the three main parties involved in the 2005 presidential election was the Osoulgarayan (Fundamentalists), a coalition of ultra-conservative Islamic fundamentalists loyal to the supreme leader. The front-runner of this group was Brigadier General Ali Larijani, Ahmadinejad's longtime fellow IRGC associate. The other top candidates from this faction were Brigadier General Mohammad-Baqer Qalibaf, former state security chief; Major General Mohsen Rezai, former commander and founder of the IRGC and also the secretary of the Expediency Council; and Tehran mayor Mahmoud Ahmadinejad.

At the opposite end of the political spectrum was the Eslahgaran, also known as the Reformist Front, which had been President Khatami's front. Mustafa Moein, Khatami's minister of science and higher education, and Mehdi Karrubi, a cleric and former speaker of the parliament, were the candidates from this faction. Situated between the two camps was Ali Akbar Hashemi Rafsanjani, associated with a party known as Hezbe Kargozaran-e Sazandegi (Servants of Construction Party). Iran's president from 1989 to 1997, Rafsanjani wanted to make a comeback after being defamed by corruption, scandal, the stigma of his extensive wealth, and his miserable showing in the February 2000 parliamentary elections. Khatami's vice-president and the head of the country's National Sports Organization, Mohsen Mehralizadeh, also entered the race.

Women were not allowed to run in the election because the Guardian Council had banned all the women on the potential candidate's list, citing the constitution of the Islamic republic, which states that the president of the country should be a male. Ahmadinejad reinforced this code of discrimination against women during his campaign when he stated, "Women will have no place in my cabinet."[3]

Ahmadinejad registered on the last day and expressed a cavalier attitude toward the process. Many assumed that he was going to drop out altogether when he seemed to hedge questions during registration week. As the deadline drew near, he told a reporter, "So? There are two and a half days left . . . there is still time."[4] He also began campaigning late in the official 20-day campaign season and was frequently questioned about whether he was actually in the race. "No need to hurry," he told a reporter five days into the campaign season.[5] He appeared very confident as the days ticked by, which puzzled the media in that there was no indication that he had anything to be confident about. He expressed an air of being above the campaign process, as though he had more important things to do and these things would sort themselves out. "I had a reason to be the last person to enter the presidential race," he said four days before the campaign cutoff, "and I will not be able to travel to all the cities given the time period." In the same statement, he sounded as though he would have plenty of time to listen to the concerns of all the provinces soon enough. "If elected, I plan to hold various meetings with different ministers so that we can resolve people's issues in different towns." He then claimed that the election would ultimately go his way, telling a crowd in Kashan, "The condition for the election will change in a way so that an Islamic governance will be established in the country."[6] In all respects, Ahmadinejad acted like a candidate who already knew the outcome of the election.

Ahmadinejad's campaign followed the same themes that he had stressed in mayoral speeches, highlighting the glories of martyrdom, the need to return to the pure Islamic values of the revolution, and the superiority of Iran's Islamic government over all other types of government. He unabashedly stressed the role of all Iranians in the regime's core mission to prepare the way for Islamic rule throughout the world. "The Iranian nation has a great duty," he said just before the candidate registration period, "and we must form a strong and advanced Islamic country which is a precursor for the formation of the global Islamic government."[7] He also vowed to solve social crises, such as by redistributing the nation's wealth to the poor, and he condemned government corruption.

He could have said anything, however, because it is very doubtful that it was his platform that got him into office. Ahmadinejad's hard-core IRGC background had caught the eye of Supreme Leader Khamenei, who decided that Ahmadinejad would be the most suitable choice to lock up complete ultraconservative control of the government. Through the Guardian Council's censure of pro-Khatami candidates in the 2004 parliamentary elections, Khamenei had cut out reformist elements of the legislative branch. By orchestrating Ahmadinejad's win, Khamenei's process was complete and made the presidency a zealous and aggressive mouthpiece for his radical Islamic agenda.

Ahmadinejad's campaign behavior seemingly reflected a carefully devised strategy behind the scenes—he did not stand out as a high-profile figure, so no one suspected that the supreme leader endorsed him. The foreign observers who were following the Iranian campaign closely predicted Larijani as the front-runner and assumed that he was Khamenei's favorite. In the sensational outcome, the media shouted that Ahmadinejad was an upset who had come out of nowhere, which was exactly how the supreme leader would have wanted it to look. Khamenei needed Ahmadinejad to come to power as a genuine, legitimate, come-from-behind guy who won the hearts and minds of the poor. This way they could combat accusations that Ahmadinejad won because of IRGC members stuffing the ballot boxes. It was a flagrantly fraudulent election, from the regime's inflated claims about voter turnout to the impossible claims of the final tally.

Before the June 17 election day, even the regime's own newspapers conceded that the people had little incentive to participate and predicted a low turnout. But on election day, the regime announced that 63 percent of the eligible voters turned out, obviously an inflated figure according to most accounts, and that Rafsanjani won the most votes. The Interior Ministry, which is officially in charge of counting the ballots and announcing the winner, made an early report that showed Rafsanjani with 21.9 percent of the vote, Karrubi with 19.9 percent, and Ahmadinejad with 18.6 percent. The ministry followed this up with a final count of Rafsanjani at 21.3, Karrubi at 19.7, and Ahmadinejad at 18.5. Because Rafsanjani did not receive a majority of 51 percent, the ministry would need to call a runoff election between him and Karrubi. But to everyone's surprise, the Guardian Council then announced that Ahmadinejad was actually in second place with 19.4 percent and that Karrubi was out of the running with only 17.5 percent. The Guardian Council also announced a total vote tally that was nearly 3 million votes higher than the Interior Ministry's count, all of which led to accusations of fraud and vote rigging. Never before had Iran experienced such an out-of-the-blue upset in a presidential election, and the outcry over the Guardian Council's hidden agenda was sensational and unprecedented.

Karrubi angrily charged that the Guardian Council had arranged an illegal voting scheme in order to install its candidate, saying that, if possible, "The Guardian Council would have appointed Ahmadinejad without any election." He claimed to have a tape that revealed Revolutionary Guard commanders ordering military personnel, including Bassij militia, to vote more than once. How was it possible, Karrubi wondered, that in the course of election day the Guardian

Council announced on television that one of the candidates suddenly had one million more votes?

Karrubi had also spoken out about the ultraconservative takeover of the 2004 parliamentary elections, but at that time he still held out faith in the system. "Many basic rights were violated in the last elections," he said in May 2005, "yet I will not turn my back on a system I spent my life for simply because certain reformers were disqualified." As a result of the parliamentary election fiasco, some called for international observers to be present at the presidential elections, but Karrubi tried to calm that debate, saying, "We are mature enough to hold a free and democratic election."[8] But Khamenei appeared to have proven him wrong, and after the June 17 election Karrubi wrote a protest letter to the supreme leader and resigned his posts as a member of the Expediency Council and as an advisor to Khamenei.

Mustafa Moein, the candidate who came in fifth, announced through a spokesperson that he had uncovered a voter fraud operation. He claimed that 140 billion rials ($15.5 million) had been spent in a vote-rigging project involving 300,000 members of Islamist militias.[9]

Ahmadinejad did not engage in the controversy but shrugged off the critics, saying, "Those who the people do not choose in an election always have the tendency to complain."[10]

In the week before the runoff election, no one expected Ahmadinejad to beat Rafsanjani, based on the simple logic of where the voters' affiliations would go. The only voters who would stand behind the ultraconservative candidate were the nearly 20 percent who voted for the conservative candidates (Qalibaf had gotten 14 percent, and Larijani had gotten 6 percent), which would give Ahmadinejad a total of 39.4 percent based on the first-round results. Ahmadinejad would certainly not get Karrubi's votes (17 percent), Moein's votes (14 percent), or Mehralizadeh's votes (4.5 percent). Based on the regime's own first-round results, Ahmadinejad's numbers just did not add up to a win. But after the election of June 24 the regime announced that Ahmadinejad won by a landslide with 62 percent of the vote over Rafsanjani's 36 percent, and that voter turnout was an incredible 60 percent.

Outrage erupted again over the results and the evidence of a vast IRGC network that had stuffed the ballot boxes of the thousands of voting stations throughout the country. Rafsanjani complained that "All the available resources of the regime were used in an organized and illegal way to intervene in the election."[11] One Interior Ministry voting inspector observed the vote rigging first-hand at the Rassoul-Akram mosque in south Tehran, where he saw officials stamping blank voting papers before the polls opened. The ballots were supposed to be stamped after a voter's identity had been verified, and when the inspector reported this abnormality to the poll monitors, he was told to "mind his own business." He claimed that the election was a conspiracy of the Guardian Council and the IRGC, since officials at the polling stations were all members of the Bassij and the IRGC.[12]

Nothing could change the fact that Khamenei had succeeded in placing his chosen hard-liner in the presidency. Ahmadinejad could now execute the supreme leader's mission of installing an Islamic republic in Iraq, facilitated by an Iranian nuclear weapons arsenal.

Ahmadinejad slipped into the presidential lifestyle with the same contrived humble style that he had developed as mayor of Tehran. Rather than move into the presidential palace, the shah's former residence and the home and office of the regime's presidents, he announced that he had chosen to keep living in his austere home with his wife and three children, and that he would travel to the palace for work. In reality, there is no indication that this is the case. He also retained the cheap cotton sports coat that had become his trademark as mayor and that appeared as a novelty item called the "Ahmadinejad jacket" in shops across the country after he became president.[13] In fact, he is hand in hand with a small clique of superrich mullahs who own or control the vast majority of the wealth and resources of the country.

Ahmadinejad, since taking office, has significantly escalated his number of spiritual speeches about Iran's duty to prepare for the "return of the Mahdi." Shiites believe in the twelfth imam, the Mahdi, who went into hiding and who will return to spread justice. They view the Mahdi as someone who symbolizes a society full of love, peace, and coexistence. But Ahmadinejad's bizarre perspective on this subject has made him the target of ridicule among the public and theologians alike. The fact that he needs to manipulate this religious concept for political purposes reveals both his lack of charisma and legitimacy, as well as the weakness of Supreme Leader Khamenei, who lacks the religious authority to boost Ahmadinejad. Ahmadinejad is now grasping at straws to survive.

Many theologians in Qom were speechless, for example, over his story about sensing an "aura" surrounding him during his address at the United Nations in 2005. He claimed that the assembly became enraptured with his words:

> I was placed inside this aura. I felt it myself. I felt the atmosphere suddenly change and for those 27 or 28 minutes the leaders of the world did not blink. When I say they did not bat an eyelid I am not exaggerating because I was looking at them and they were rapt. It seemed as if a hand was holding them there and had opened their eyes to receive a message from the Islamic republic.[14]

Convoluted and hypocritical spirituality has been a signature of Ahmadinejad's presidency. In a letter to Ahmadinejad, published on the Farsi-language website *Entekhab* in October 2005, a parliamentary member revealed that Ahmadinejad's cabinet had signed a written pledge with the Mahdi, which a member of the cabinet brought to the Jamkaran mosque in Qom and dropped in a well to be received by the Mahdi. A report published in the same website stated that close associates of Ahmadinejad believe that the reason he emphasizes the imminent emergence of the Mahdi is to justify Iran's nuclear ambitions. This is Ahmadinejad's manipulation of the concept that the Mahdi will return in a time of great turmoil; the rallying cry of "nuclear rights" is Ahmadinejad's justification for creating an atmosphere of global turmoil to signify that the Mahdi will come soon, the website reported.

Many senior Shiite clergies believe that those who claim to have seen the Mahdi before he actually emerges or take advantage of him are liars whose acts in the name of Islam are detestable. "Ahmadinejad certainly qualifies as one," a senior Shiite Ayatollah told me in November 2006. Ahmadinejad demagogically misuses the sacred concept of the Mahdi to arm his regime with nuclear weapons and to control the Iraqi Shiite holy sites in Najaf and Karbala.

At the other spectrum of Ahmadinejad's public speaking style is his confrontational approach, which reached a fever pitch in October 2005 with his call for Israel to be wiped off the map. "Our dear Imam [Khomeini] ordered that the occupying regime in Al-Qods [Jerusalem] be wiped off the face of the earth. This was a very wise statement," he said at an anti-Zionist conference. He also condemned and threatened any nation that acknowledged Israel's existence, saying, "Anyone who would recognize this state [Israel] has put his signature under the defeat of the Islamic world."[15] That was the first of two anti-Israel remarks that will undoubtedly go down in history as the most bizarre rhetoric of the twenty-first century. The second was his claim about the Holocaust, which he said "is a myth that has been used for 60 years by Zionists to blackmail other countries and justify their crimes in the occupied territories."[16] Ahmadinejad was relentless in his verbal attacks on Israel and left no doubt that the regime was intent on destroying the country with a military—presumably nuclear—strike. "Like it or not, the Zionist regime is heading toward annihilation," he said in April 2006. "The Zionist regime is a rotten, dried tree that will be eliminated by one storm . . . [because] its existence has harmed the dignity of Islamic nations."[17]

The president's burning defense of Iran's nuclear program, filled with defensive posturing and rhetoric about Iran's rights to nuclear technology, has only deepened the world's suspicions about Iran's secret nuclear weapons program. Ahmadinejad tried to divert the people from the glaring evidence of nearly two decades of illegal nuclear activity by putting the crisis in a nationalistic context.

Without mentioning the regime's public record of lying to the International Atomic Energy Agency (IAEA), Ahmadinejad defined the problem as just one more example of western aggression. "The enemies of the Islamic Republic [of Iran] are furious because the Iranian nation has dared to grow its self-confidence out of their domination sphere," he said in February 2006. "The foes cannot do a damn thing. We do not need you at all. It is you who need the Iranian people. . . . You can issue as many resolutions as you like and dream on. But you cannot prevent the Iranian nation's progress."[18]

In July 2006, when Europe offered Iran a new package of economic and nuclear incentives in hopes of persuading Tehran to halt its nuclear enrichment program, Iran refused to acknowledge the deadline for an answer. Rather than agreeing to respond in five days, as the EU requested, the regime said it would not have an answer until late August, and Ahmadinejad personally responded by scolding the West for putting pressure on the regime. He threatened that if the western nations continued in their demands, "they are the ones who will suffer."[19] On July 31, 2006, the U.N. Security Council resolved the deadline question by passing a mandatory resolution that instructed Iran to suspend its uranium enrichment and nuclear fuel reprocessing activities by August 31. Passed by a vote of 14 to 1, the resolution stated that if the regime did not comply, Iran would face "appropriate measures," under Article 41 of Chapter 7 of the UN Charter, which could possibly include sanctions. This resolution marked the first legal action taken by the U.N. against Iran over its nuclear program. Iran's immediate response was a tacit rejection of the resolution. Javad Zarif, Iran's ambassador to the U.N., dismissed it as lacking any legal foundation, stating, "Iran's peaceful nuclear program poses no threat to international peace and security and therefore dealing with this issue in the Security Council is unwarranted and void of any legal basis or practical utility."[20] Instead of suspending enrichment, Iran fed a new batch of uranium hexafluoride to a small cascade of centrifuges in Natanz as the August 31 deadline expired, according to the IAEA. Ahmadinejad's pivotal role in the regime's pursuit of nuclear weapons is discussed at length in Chapter 10.

Ahmadinejad's presidency has also seen an enormous expansion of power and influence transferred to the Islamic Revolutionary Guards Corps. In June 2006, the *Wall Street Journal* reported that the Guards "hold sway over a range of enterprises in Iran, particularly those involving exports and imports," including a massive new deal involving Iran's energy sector. The Iranian contractor Ghorb, an affiliate of the IRGC, had just won a $2.3 billion contract to develop two upcoming phases of the South Pars gas field in Iran. South Pars, which Iran shares with Qatar, is the world's largest gas field, and Iranian authorities had originally awarded the contract to a group of foreign and domestic companies led by the

Norwegian company Aker Kvaerner ASA.[21] The reassignment of the contracts to an IRGC-led company shows a shift in Tehran's priorities that will enrich the IRGC and grant increasing control to the elite militia.

The IRGC also acted upon its boosted status in 2005 when it shut down Iran's new international airport just one day after the facility opened its doors. Iran dissolved its contracts with the Austrian-Turkish group that had been slated to run the airport and replaced them with companies affiliated with the IRGC.[22]

Ahmadinejad's presidency is marked by repressive policies that harken back to the early years of the revolution. His fundamentalist ideology shows itself on the streets, in the jails, on the radio—virtually throughout the fabric of society. In October 2005, the president's Supreme Cultural Revolutionary Council publicized its intention to ban all western music, including classical, from state radio and television networks. The conductor of Tehran's symphony orchestra, Ali Rahbari, announced that he was resigning in protest. But first he scheduled a series of performances of Beethoven's Ninth Symphony, a piece that had not been heard in Iran since the revolution, and the symphony played to a full house each night. In December, Ahmadinejad ordered that the ban be put in effect throughout all the state's media outlets.[23]

Banning Mozart and Beethoven is perhaps the mildest of the new trends of repression in Ahmadinejad's new order. International news agencies reported that the already horrendous human rights record of Iran became worse after Ahmadinejad took office. Amnesty International issued public statements in 2006 about "signs that Iran is witnessing the start of a further harshening of repression" and that "executions in Iran continue at an alarming rate." It reported that there had been 28 executions in the first eight weeks of 2006 alone, and expressed its outrage over child executions and over the treatment and execution of political prisoners.[24] The European Union also observed this trend and published a statement in May 2006 about the "general increase in executions in Iran," which included a spate of 10 executions at Evin prison in Tehran.[25]

Amnesty International also reported that it had unconfirmed reports that the Ahmadinejad administration used political prisoners on death row as leverage in the nuclear crisis with Europe, the United States, and the IAEA by telling the prisoners that they would be executed if the IAEA reported Iran to the United Nations Security Council. Amnesty listed several Mujahedin-e Khalq (MEK) members who, it felt, were at risk over this threat, and said it was investigating the issue in February 2006.[26]

The same report stated that Iranians convicted of "enmity with God, corruption on earth, and murder" were subject to death by crucifixion for three days, cross amputation, execution, or banishment. Iran is a signatory of treaties outlawing child executions, but Amnesty stated that the Iranian regime executed at least eight children in 2005 alone.[27]

Journalists, bloggers, the homeless, ethnic minorities, peaceful Sufi mystics, young people at parties with both genders in the same room, bus drivers who go on strike for better wages—anyone who does not comply with the regime's hard-line, fanatical Islamic policies is in danger of arrest, torture, and execution in Iran. The regime violently puts down demonstrations by ethnic minorities such as the Kurds, Azeris, and Arabs, to the point that the prisons in some provinces are packed to four times their capacity. So many were arrested in Khuzistan Province in the first year of Ahmadinejad's presidency, for example, that 3,000 prisoners were packed into Karoun prison, which is built to house only 800. Repression of unrecognized religions escalated as well, especially against members of the Baha'i faith. Ayatollah Jannati, secretary general of the Council of Guardians, summed up the regime's contempt for all non-Muslim religions in a public speech in November 2005, declaring that "human beings, apart from Muslims, are animals who roam the earth and engage in corruption."[28]

Women, who already had few rights and suffered tragic abuses in Iran, also became a target in Ahmadinejad's government. A typical example was the violent shakedown of a peaceful demonstration in Tehran's Daneshjoo Park on International Women's Day in March 2006. One thousand women gathered at the park to stage a sit-in and hold banners with slogans about women's rights, and they were met by busloads of police, Bassij militia, and antiriot units. When the women refused to leave, the forces began beating them—even the elderly women—with batons and kicking them.[29] That is what International Women's Day taught the world about the lives of women in Ahmadinejad's Iran.

Ahmadinejad also put pressure on authorities to demand a stricter Islamic dress code, which compelled the courts to announce some new penalties. In Isfahan, for example, the courts proclaimed that women who did not wear the Islamic *hijab* head covering would be punished by lashing. Reports also surfaced about security guards at public buildings who are ordered to turn away women who are not dressed modestly enough, and about police who patrol and regulate what is sold in clothing stores.[30] In July 2006, Tehran's Imam Khomeini mosque hosted the country's first Islamic dress fair, in which ankle-length manteaus, or overcoats, and all-covering black chadors supplanted the styles favored by European designers. The 10-day event was organized by Iran's police force along with the commerce ministry and the state broadcasting corporation, IRIB.[31]

Ahmadinejad's presidency is a symbol of the regime's rock-solid agenda: repression of the people to stifle opposition and ensure the unpopular regime's survival, establishment of Islamic rule in Iraq as a jumping point for its establishment in the rest of world, and acquisition of nuclear weapons to facilitate that global mission. No element of this agenda displays a respect for, or even an acknowledgement of, human rights, creative expression, freedom, or democracy. As Ahmadinejad put it, "We did not have a revolution in order to have a democracy."[32]

The signature of Ahmadinejad's administration is confrontation. Khatami falsely portrayed himself as a president who would promote a civil society, rule of law, and a dialogue of civilizations. In contrast, Ahmadinejad emphasizes the domestic need to establish an ideal Islamic society and the external goal of founding global Islamic rule. He quickly fell into a pattern of exploiting the indecisiveness of the West and of growing increasingly confrontational. The more the international community failed to respond, the harsher he became and the more concessions he gained. His manipulation of international crises, his contempt for the West, his inflammatory rhetoric, and his militant demeanor all combine as a fitting symbol of the Iranian regime.

PART II
IRAN'S GRAND PLAN

CHAPTER 4

GLOBAL AMBITIONS: THE IRANIAN REGIME'S RADICAL FUNDAMENTALIST IDEOLOGY

Divine governments ... set themselves the task of making man into what he should be. To juxtapose "democratic" and "Islamic" is an insult to Islam. Because . . . Islam is, in fact, superior to all forms of democracy.

—Ayatollah Ruhollah Khomeini, 1979[1]

Ayatollah Khomeini may be gone, but the oppressive and tyrannical system he invented and installed in Iran is still very much alive. The ease with which he lied about his plans for the country, deceiving both the West and his own people, remains a dark inheritance of the regime. The most alarming evidence of this is that Iran successfully hid its nuclear program for 18 years until my sources exposed it in 2002. The underlying contempt that Khomeini bore for human beings, considering them nothing more than brutes who would destroy each other without his all-wise and strict leadership, is sealed into the laws of the land. And the radical Islamic zeal he promulgated, including the glorification of martyrdom for the sake of the regime, lives on in the mullahs' national call for suicide bombers to sign up for missions in Iraq.

A brief glimpse at Khomeini's legacy helps form a bridge to the present, in which the regime's actions are sending shock waves throughout the world—actions including its vocal hatred for Israel, for the West, and for nonfundamentalist Arab leaders; its refusals to follow international nuclear protocols; its bullying of other nations over criticisms about its long-covert nuclear program; and its imbedding and using a terrorist network in post-Saddam Iraq.[2] To understand Khomeini is to understand the radical ideology inherited by President Mahmoud Ahmadinejad and the mullahs. It explains how the regime justifies a policy of terrorism and deceit in dealing with foreign countries and with the International Atomic Energy Agency. And it also explains how Iranians have been forced to contend with a split from their traditional beliefs in the name of an Islamic republic, Khomeini style, that they never imagined when they dreamed of a new Iran without the shah.

The type of government that Khomeini installed in Iran after the so-called Islamic revolution was a surprise even to some of his closest advisers. No one was naive enough to expect a democracy patterned exactly after those of western nations, but at the same time, no one predicted that Khomeini would create a brutal dictatorship, complete with a police force set up to purge dissidents—a police force that surpassed the style of the shah's SAVAK and Stalin's secret police. While in exile, Khomeini denounced the shah's rule, railing that "freedom of expression and of the press have been destroyed and his police have massacred thousands of Iranian people."[3] No one in their wildest dreams imagined that Khomeini himself was capable not only of inflicting those same horrors, but of inventing even more horrific tortures. Who could picture the elderly, seemingly pious Khomeini launching a bloody campaign of mass murder against his own people? But when Khomeini revealed his true colors, killing those who opposed him both within Iran and outside it, the Iranian people realized that they had simply replaced one brutal tyrant with another. Khomeini had promoted a government based on the rich wisdom of Islam, but no one imagined that this included the authority to kill everyone who spoke against him.

Because of a specific set of circumstances, Khomeini discovered that he had a very good chance of stealing the revolution from other anti-shah groups, and steal it is exactly what he did in a few short months prior to the shah's escape from Iran. The Iranian people had envisioned a free society that reversed the oppressive system of the shah, and these revolutionary ideals are very much alive today in the hearts and minds of Iranians in Iran and throughout the world. But instead of contemplating what Iranians envisioned for their country, Khomeini crafted a theocracy based on the absolute rule of one man. This type of rule, defined in the constitution of 1979, was based on concepts Khomeini developed during his years in exile in Iraq. In those days, Khomeini envisioned supreme leadership as a role equal to nothing less than that of Prophet Muhammad (PBUH), the founder of Islam. A "worthy" leader who establishes an Islamic government, Khomeini declared, "will possess the same authority as the Most Noble Messenger (upon whom be peace and blessings) in the administration of society, and it will be the duty of all people to obey him."[4]

In Khomeini's mind, this position of ultimate authority was no dream, but instead a very real alternative for ruling Iran that would become reality when he took control of the antimonarchy Iranian revolution in 1979. Leading up to his takeover of power, Khomeini had provided many signals like the statement above about his plans for a spiritual dictatorship. The ayatollah shocked many Iranian Shiites in 1977, for example, when he broke from a central point of the religion by referring to himself as Imam Khomeini. The term "imam" was reserved for the first Shiite leader, Imam Ali, who had been granted that role by his cousin, the Prophet Muhammad, and for Ali's 11 male descendants. None of Iran's grand ayatollahs endorsed Khomeini's self-imposed title of imam, which reveals just how far astray Khomeini had wandered from Iran's Islamic tradition. With his severe expression and radically fundamentalist view of Islam, Khomeini reshaped Iran into an entity of his own design, based on his subjective interpretation of Islam.

Western leaders anticipated a lessening of the regime's dogmatic and repressive power structure during the 1990s when a few so-called moderate politicians appeared to be taking the country in a new direction, but the ascension of Ahmadinejad in 2005 as the regime's new president quashed any hope for such a new direction. The entire idea of a moderate group had been grossly inflated in the first place, because the supreme leader has absolute authority over all three branches of Iran's government, and moderation has never been on the agenda at the top of the Iranian regime.

WRITINGS AND RANTINGS: KHOMEINI BEFORE THE REVOLUTION

From his exile in Iraq and France in the late 1970s, Khomeini orchestrated his takeover of the anti-shah revolutionary movement in Iran. He had not lived in Iran for more than a decade, but he was keenly aware of all the factors that would collectively give him this opportunity.

Khomeini already had, in the period leading up to his expulsion from Iran in November 1964, a reputation for standing up to the shah. During his more than three decades as a religious teacher in Qom, Khomeini was vocally opposed to the shah's efforts for land reform and for decreasing the clergy's authority. In 1941, for example, Khomeini published a book entitled *Kashf al Asrar* (The Secrets Revealed) that refuted the shah and his regime.

Khomeini's *Resaleh Towzih al-Masael* (A Clarification of Questions), spelled out his fundamentalist interpretation of Shia Islam as it applied to every conceivable question of daily life. All senior clerics publish a similar collection of views on Islam, and Khomeini's release of this publication in 1961 preceded his elevation to the status of an ayatollah, the highest rank in Iran's Shiite clergy. Dictums from this book shed light on Khomeini's approach to Islam—dictums such as "the child . . . [who] chose infidelity [to be non-Muslim/an infidel] . . . will be asked to repent (and to return to Islam), else he will be executed"[5] and "Infidels . . . do not have the right to promote their religions and publish their books in Islamic countries . . . and it is incumbent upon Moslems that themselves and their children avoid their books and meetings."[6]

Khomeini's outspoken criticisms of the shah in the 1960s included a speech in October 1964 in which he lashed out against the United States' influence on the shah's government. The Majlis (parliament) had just passed a law granting diplomatic immunity to Americans in Iran, and in this speech—which was the final straw, the one that forced Khomeini into exile—Khomeini declared: "Let the American President know that in the eyes of the Iranian people, he is the most repulsive member of the human race today because of the injustice he has imposed on our Muslim nation. Today the . . . Iranian nation has become his enemy."[7]

Khomeini also accused the members of the Majlis of high treason and called on Iranians to protest the legislation: "By God, whoever does not express his outrage commits a major sin!" he said in the speech.[8] These rallying words were widely distributed both on leaflets and on cassette tapes, and a few days later Khomeini was arrested and exiled to Turkey. One year later he was allowed to settle in the Iraqi Shiite shrine city of Najaf, where he lived for the next 13 years and continued to teach, write, and occasionally utter a mild criticism of the shah's policies.

By 1969, Khomeini's ideas about the importance of Islamic law had evolved into a radical set of ideas about establishing an Islamic state. Khomeini explained this concept in a series of lectures that were later published as a book called *Velayat-e Faqih*, (Guardianship/Rule of the Jurist). One theme of this treatise, which the historian Shaul Bakhash described as "a blueprint for the reorganization of society" and "a handbook for revolution," involves unifying all Muslim countries under a common Islamic rule.[9] Khomeini said that by banding together in this way, Muslim countries could abide by the Koran's dictum to "be strong and well-prepared" and to fend off foreign "aggressors":

> If the rulers of the Muslim countries . . . join together like the fingers of one hand . . . then a handful of wretched Jews (the agents of America, Britain, and other foreign powers) would never have been able to accomplish what they have. . . . The verse: 'Prepare against them whatever force you can muster' com-

mands you to be as strong and well-prepared as possible, so that your enemies will be unable to oppress you and transgress against you.[10]

Most important—and most relevant to any discussion of the current Iranian regime—is the fact that Khomeini had no qualms about the violence that might come with fulfilling his goals. "It is our duty to preserve Islam. . . . The preservation of Islam is even more important than prayer. . . . It is for the sake of fulfilling this duty that blood must sometimes be shed. . . . We must understand this matter well and convey it to others."[11]

In the mind of Khomeini, human life was subservient to the cause of the Islamic republic. This is the ideology that took control of the revolution, and this is the ideology that continues to permeate the power structure in Tehran today. This bloodthirsty ideology of the regime flows from Khomeini's descriptions of Islam in 1969 to Ahmadinejad's searing statements against Israel and the United States in 2005. Proof of this worldview is found in the Iranian graveyards that contain the victims of those who dared speak out against this oppressive and radical force throughout the span of the regime.

HALF-TRUTHS AND OUTRIGHT LIES: KHOMEINI FOOLS THE WEST

As the anti-shah protests heated up in late 1978, the shah called on Saddam Hussein to expel Khomeini from Iraq because he thought that Khomeini's presence in the holy city of Najaf was giving him too much significance in the eyes of some of the anti-shah groups in Iran. France issued visas for Khomeini, his wife, and his aides, and they settled in the Parisian suburb of Neauphle-le-Château in October 1978.

Students, journalists, and others flocked to France to meet with Khomeini, who during his four-month stay in France gave more than 120 radio and press interviews and published approximately 50 speeches and declarations.[12] His well-crafted public relations strategy allowed him to portray himself as a moderate yet highly capable force for ending the shah's tyrannical rule, a reformer whose mission was to obtain justice and rights for the poor. The little house in France was revolution headquarters, where Khomeini spent hours on the phone every day with Ayatollah Morteza Motahari and Ayatollah Mohammad Hossein Beheshti, who led the Khomeini network in Iran. Khomeini also recorded daily messages that were sent to Tehran and distributed throughout the country.

In France, Khomeini worked out his strategy for overtaking the revolution, a strategy that included making false claims to win western support and to assure everyone, including the Iranian middle class, that he was a moderate who did not promote changing the country's social or economic systems. He went out of his way to allay the fears of those who thought that he would institute a conservative, repressive Islamic government, stating that although he was leading the revolutionary movement, he would not take any part in running the country after the revolution. "I will guide the people and let them choose the sort of government they want by universal suffrage," he told the *New York Times* in November 1978. "I don't have any intention to head this government or be part of it."[13] Odd words for a man who, a few months later, created a role for himself as the first absolute politico-religious leader in Iran's history.

Khomeini spoke blatant lies to politicians back in Iran, as well as to the international press: During a November 1978 meeting with Karim Sanjabi, leader of the Iranian National Front, he stated that Iran would be "democratic and Islamic."[14] In many of his interviews, Khomeini stressed that all voices would be respected in the new government. One of his aides, for example, told the *Washington Post* in November 1978 that Khomeini envisioned that all political parties would be legal in Iran after the fall of the shah. He quoted Khomeini as saying, "In the history of Islam, those who denied God were free to express themselves." In the same interview, Khomeini himself told the reporter that everyone would be included in designing the nation's reforms, which were "possible only with the total participation of all the population."[15] Khomeini further shored up this facade by directing his top mullahs in Iran to stay behind the scenes in order to support his statements that after the revolution they would not hold any executive positions but only work to bring moral and spiritual guidance to the people.

Western women journalists were ordered to cover everything but their faces and hands before meeting Khomeini for an interview, and this was a small hint of what was to come.[16] After taking control of the revolution, Khomeini's strict Islamic code ordered that women wear a head-to-toe black chador, be segregated from men in every grade of school below university, and also be segregated at swimming pools, beaches, and many other public facilities.[17] These were simply the outer trappings, however, of what many consider to be the regime's virulent misogynist attitude, one that has permeated the regime since its inception. Ali Akbar Hashemi Rafsanjani's embrace of Khomeini's attitude about women's rights were made clear in an interview he held in 1986, when he was president of Iran. He stated that there should be separate laws for men and women because men and women are so intrinsically different, from their brain size (men's are larger) to "the differences in body, height, sturdiness, voice, growth, muscle quality, physical strength, perseverance in the face of disasters and resistance to disease," all of which "show that men are stronger and more capable in all these areas."[18] These were not the words of a radical cleric ranting on a soapbox in some remote Iranian village; this was a public interview with the president of the country. And it occurred in 1986, the same year that the U.S. Supreme Court ruled that sexual harassment at work was a crime because it was a form of sex discrimination. As the rest of the world moved forward, the regime continued its backward strides.

Khomeini had decades to form his ideas about the ideal Islamic rule, and as the shah's hold on Iran spiraled into chaos, Khomeini worked relentlessly to ensure his ability to institute that rule. By the time that the shah imposed martial law in 1978, Khomeini had become known in the international press as the wise old holy man who would undoubtedly play a major role in the inevitable transformation about to shake Iran. He had successfully consolidated his power in the clerical community, and no one could challenge his standing. His presence in the press and the wide distribution of his uncompromising, vehemently anti-West messages gave him more visibility than other clerics in Iran who also called for a new government. The two most popular of these high-ranking ayatollahs, Seyyed Mahmoud Taleqani and Kazem Shariatmadari, could neither match Khomeini's fiery revolutionary tone nor gain the same amount of global recognition.[19]

A FIRST-PERSON WITNESS TO KHOMEINI'S RISE TO POWER

Ayatollah Jalal Ganjei, who knew Khomeini as a teacher and mentor for many years before the revolution, observed the ayatollah's rise to power firsthand. His perspective provides a first-person view of how Khomeini took control of the revolution and built a clerical regime based on corruption and a thirst for power. Ganjei fled Iran in 1980 after discovering that his name was on the regime's hit list of 3,000. Khomeini issued a fatwa against Ganjei, and since he left Iran, 13 of Ganjei's relatives have been killed by the regime, including his son. Once out of Iran, Ganjei joined the opposition coalition, the National Council of Resistance of Iran (NCRI), headquartered in a suburb of Paris. He currently serves as the chairman of the council's Committee on the Freedom of Religion and Denominations.

Ganjei was among the young religious students and scholars who grew up envisioning a democratic future for Iran during the era of Iranian parliamentarianism and Prime Minister Mohammad Mossadeq. "There was a group of us who believed in democracy for Iran," Ganjei said, "and we felt this could be brought about in Islam—in fact, this is guaranteed in Islam. That's why my family encouraged me to pursue religious studies."[20] In the course of his training with Ayatollah

Khomeini, Ganjei came to realize that his teacher was not the man that he and his colleagues thought he was.

During his seminary training in Qom, Ganjei formed a critical outlook of the traditional religious hierarchy, which viewed freedom and democracy as a threat to religion. He also criticized the religious system as rife with both moral and financial corruption, and steeped in demagoguery, deceit, hypocrisy, and false piety. Voices like Ganjei's were not welcomed, and "for that reason the new thinkers in the religious area who wanted a new perception in Islam and religion were pushed on the fringes," Ganjei said. "They were very much isolated by the old guard."

Ganjei explained that Khomeini's first step to power occurred after the death of the top Shiite leader of the day, Grand Ayatollah Boroujerdi, in the spring of 1961. "All those vying to replace him were not good choices," Ganjei said. "We knew that all of them were corrupt, and the only person who looked relatively better at the time was Khomeini. He looked to be less corrupt and less backward." At this point Ganjei decided to study with Khomeini, and over the next eighteen months the ayatollah was his mentor. During that same period the nation was rocked with opposition to the shah's new reforms, collectively known as the "white revolution." Ganjei recalled that this program "was very much resented by religious and political forces because it was not a reform against dictatorship, but very much strengthened the shah's dictatorship. That led to a major uprising in Iran in June of 1963 that was very bloodily suppressed. This was a turning point in Iranian contemporary history."

Before the shah's violent crackdown on his opposition, Ganjei and his colleagues had rallied around Khomeini. Only later did they realize that some of the ayatollah's ideas contradicted their most precious Islamic ideals. "We were so much in need of a good leader, we younger generation of religious students, that we did not pay attention to the fact that two of Khomeini's major slogans were very reactionary," Ganjei said. "One was that he showed very strong support for the big landowners, and also that he was against the right of women to vote. We weren't observant of these two realities of Khomeini at the time."

When the shah suppressed the June 1963 uprising, Khomeini was arrested and all his students were threatened. Ganjei fled to Najaf in Iraq, where he continued his religious studies. Unlike Qom, which had been a major theological center for only 50 years and attended only by Iranian students, Najaf was a 1,000-year-old center of learning that attracted Shiite students from all over the Muslim world. For the first time, Ganjei met students from as far away as Somalia and Kenya and was exposed to many different Shiite cultures. Unfortunately, he and his friends discovered that this deeply rooted international hub of Shiism contained some of the same corruption they had seen in Qom. "What was tragic was that there was some discrimination about how much allowance some students would receive," Ganjei said. "For example, some students from Africa got less financial aid because they were viewed to be from a lower-class country, while the Iranians got more financial aid because they were viewed in higher esteem. So it was very disturbing to us—why this difference? It was very striking given the Islamic criteria, particularly Shiite criteria; it was against all of our understanding." This observation carried more meaning when Khomeini arrived on the scene.

After a year in Turkey, Khomeini continued his exile in Najaf, and he began teaching there in 1965. "I enthusiastically enrolled in his classes," said Ganjei, "but what was sad for us was that he adopted the very same methods that we resented in order to checkmate his opponents." As a relatively young newcomer, Khomeini faced a strong and deeply entrenched religious hierarchy in Najaf. Ganjei and his colleagues observed Khomeini's actions as he worked to overcome these challenges and assert his authority. "For example," said Ganjei, "he started distributing financial aid only to those who were his pupils and his disciples. Traditionally you should have given to any theological students who needed help, but he devoted all of his resources exclusively to people who attended his class." Khomeini and other clerics were supported by Muslims who had a long tradition of donating 20 percent of the surplus of their incomes to religious leaders. "These were donations from people with very good intentions," said Ganjei, "but instead of distributing this equally among the needy theological students, Khomeini pushed for his own agenda to have a higher stature among his religious students. He wanted to rush to a prime position in the hierarchy, so he used every possible ploy to raise his stature."

Acts like this sparked doubts in the minds of Ganjei and his colleagues, but the final straw came when the ayatollah introduced a doctrine that represented nothing less than a betrayal of their core Shiite beliefs. "The departure point was 1970," Ganjei said, "when Khomeini introduced the doctrine of *velayat-e faqih*, the absolute rule of the religious jurisprudent. This doctrine had stark impacts on all of us who were looking for a way to establish democracy with the values of Islam. One was a scientific impact; the religious findings and citations that he made in his reference books to defend this doctrine were very weak. Throughout these years we had realized that Khomeini's arguments had a lot of deficiencies, they were not convincing, but given the popularity and the dream that we had, we overlooked it. But when this doctrine was introduced it was a shock to all of us."

The rude awakening of this doctrine forced the students to take a closer look at what Khomeini had been saying throughout the years. "That's when we started thinking, why does he support the landowners and why does he defend some kind of slavery and misogyny? In the past, when we ran into these kind of questions, we figured that they were issues of the future and that we would find a way out in the future." But the concept of the *velayat-e faqih* was too severe and too contrary to their beliefs to ignore. "The most profound impact of this was our realization that this teacher is committing a betrayal. The entire doctrine could be summarized in one sentence: absolute rule of the government under the grand mullah. Khomeini knew these grand religious leaders, what utterly corrupt people they were. He had said this himself on several occasions. He used to say that these mullahs had nothing to do with Islam, and now he himself was acting like them. So that's when I said good-bye."

Khomeini did not invent the doctrine of *velayat-e faqih*, but he reintroduced the concept that had been shaped 200 years earlier by an Iranian mullah named Ahmad Naraghi. The doctrine consists of four pillars. (1) The set of Islamic laws, or Sharia, must be put into practice. "These laws, from how to do your daily prayers to how to stone a woman to death, must be implemented," Ganjei explained. "You see this repeated in the fundamentalist lexicon everywhere these days." (2) The grand ayatollahs and mullahs can understand these laws and pass ruling on them because they know the subject. (3) Power should be in the hands of the religious leaders who can discern and apply the laws. (4) Political Islam does not recognize any nationalist borders. "In Khomeini's famous will," said Ganjei, "he calls on all Muslims to have a unified Islamic government."

This doctrine did not create much antagonism when Naraghi first introduced it because in his time the Persian kings had a good relationship with the clergy. But Khomeini knew that in 1970 the doctrine would rouse hostility in Tehran. "When you were dealing with the shah or his father, this created an antagonistic situation," said Ganjei. "So when Khomeini introduced this idea, it meant that the shah's regime should go."

Ganjei and others opposed Khomeini's *velayat-e faqih* doctrine on every point, arguing that the entire concept falls apart at the very first pillar about Sharia. "The first concept, that these are religious rules, is absolutely irrelevant because this entire grouping of religious laws was put together 400 years after Muhammad's death. Most of it stands from the ideas of thinkers who represent their own way of thinking. Therefore, this is not original Islam." With the entire concept of Sharia in doubt, the other pillars have no basis to stand on, either. "Who says that the laws have to be implemented? Who says that the mullahs have to be the ultimate arbiters and the people who carry it out? The whole thing loses its validity," Ganjei said.

Ganjei's split with Khomeini put him at a crossroads. "I was married and had one child at the time, and I asked myself, what's the right thing to do? I was against the established religious hierarchy, but I decided to go back to Qom because there were new thinkers among the young people there with whom I could work. It didn't take very long to make many exchanges and meetings with various new religious thinkers and groups who thought more or less the same way as I did, and eventually I went to Tehran to be closer to them."

Modern thoughts about democracy and freedom based on Islam were not tolerated by the shah, and in 1972 Ganjei was arrested by SAVAK. "In the jail, several months after the interrogation and torturing was finished and I was taken to a common ward, I had my first encounter with members of the People's Mujahedin Organization of Iran," Ganjei said. "That's when I felt I had a lot of things in common in terms of our view and religious perception."

After 15 months in jail, Ganjei was exonerated by the military court and released. Although the religious establishment closed its doors to him, the general public was open to his ideas, and he gave sermons in mosques and at various meetings. "I had many, many sermons in Tehran, and for 20 days in Qom, which is the bastion of fundamentalist mullahs, I was known as the only spokesman for democratic and modern Islam, antifundamentalist Islam," Ganjei said. He found a receptive audience among the business and working classes that make up Iran's bazaar, as well as among the religious and academic intelligentsia. "I was told by some of those who teach in Qom that at the time some of the theological students decided to come and listen to my speeches, which they found more appealing than their traditional classes. When I was teaching in a more intellectual setting there was not an open seat, and many of these speeches were transcribed and distributed without my knowledge. That not only gave me a lot of stature, but it showed me how pervasive and deep was this potential new modern Islam among the Iranian people."

The clerical hierarchy tried to silence this movement. "All of this achievement was done in spite of ferocious and ruthless opposition by the religious establishment," Ganjei said. "They made charge after charge on me, saying, for example, that I was released because I cooperated with SAVAK. There was a very heavy smear campaign because of all the potential I saw." Eight months after his release, Ganjei was arrested again. "The shah's answer to this great potential was suppression," he explained, "and the torture was much more intensified this time around."

SAVAK prevented many political prisoners from being released at the end of their sentences, and Ganjei's second incarceration went 18 months beyond his two-year sentence. He was finally released and reunited with his family after a change in the political climate forced the shah's hand. "After Carter became president and there was this whole notion of human rights, the shah was under pressure and they could not keep me in jail much longer," Ganjei said. Although the official new policy called for a halt of executions, in reality the killings continued. "The shah eliminated the leaders of the democratic movement as much as he could," Ganjei said, explaining that SAVAK would execute them and then release a story that the prisoners were killed while trying to escape.

A shadow seemed to pass over Ganjei's face when he recalled Khomeini's campaign of lies in his last months of exile. "It's very sad for me because I knew at the time that this was not good for our nation. In this period when Khomeini left Iraq and came to Paris, he deliberately started telling outright lies and he kept lying and lying. That was very tragic. His interviews with the press are on the record and there is not a single reference to *velayat-e faqih* in any of them. He said that Islam is a defender of women's rights and that there is no difference between men and women, but he didn't believe this, it was an outright lie."

One of the most potent strategies that Khomeini used to convince Iranians that he intended to install a democratic government was the draft constitution he drew up while in exile. "They took the model from the Belgian and French constitutions and wrote in a modern style that was very appealing," said Ganjei. "Many copies were sent to Iran and they called it Khomeini's constitution, but this was absolutely a lie." Ganjei explained that the constitution's name for the new nation was the Republic of Iran, and there was no reference to Islam in the document. "The name of the parliament was the National Parliament of Iran," Ganjei said. "There was no mention of a Council of Guardians, a group of mullahs who would control everything, and no talk of *velayat-e faqih*."

Khomeini's appealing propositions reached a wide audience because he had the vast clerical network of Iran at his disposal. His ability to overtake the revolution was based on the power of the clergy to get his message across to millions of people in an effective way. Iranians no longer expected a nationalistic movement to rise up and replace the shah because the nationalist Mossadeq government had been destroyed in the 1953 coup d'etat engineered by the United States and Britain. After that coup, the only viable anti-shah movement in Iranian society was in the hands of the younger generation, the students who were looking for ways to depose him and institute a new government. In the late 1960s and early 1970s new intellectual movements started to form, including the Mujahedin-e Khalq (MEK), composed of more moderate secular Muslims, and Marxist movements such as the Fedayeen-e Khalq.

During this period, which Ayatollah Ganjei found so stimulating in Iran, the clerics were not an organized opposition force. Once the student movement escalated and expanded to the rest of the society in 1977 and early 1978, the mullahs and Khomeini himself were basically just trailing the events. People took to the streets in demonstrations, the shah suppressed them, and Khomeini would issue a statement denouncing what the shah had done. At the same time, the leading anti-shah organizations in Iran, such as the MEK, were badly damaged because their leaders were either imprisoned or executed. With this vacuum of leadership, Khomeini saw the opportunity to usurp the leadership of the revolution.

The clerical network Khomeini used was a well-funded and massive system that no other opposition group could match. The only other entity in Iran with a comparable reach throughout the country was the regime itself. The clerics had mosques that stretched from the capital of Iran through the other major cities, townships, and villages, all of which they could use to mobilize, communicate, and get their message across. But they did not need people to go into the mosques: the vast majority of Iranians who heard Khomeini's messages were not those who prayed in the mosques on a regular basis. The clerics took their message to the streets where the demonstrations had already begun, getting in front of the crowds to quote Khomeini's words in fiery speeches. No one tried to challenge them.

The regime had radio and television, but the mullahs had an extensive network of clerics that allowed them to dominate the situation and take control of the demonstrations. The messages came from Khomeini to the clergy who had religious authority, and this would give immediate authority to all the other clergy who spread the messages in various cities. Khomeini's fame and wide appeal automatically gave legitimacy to even the lowliest cleric in a small town because the cleric was on a direct pipeline to the grand ayatollah in Paris. In many cases, demonstrations that had been organized by a student organization or the MEK were overtaken by a mullah who stood up as a representative of Khomeini and proclaimed all the democratic plans the ayatollah had in store.

The clerics shouted Khomeini's words about the significance of freedom, about how Islam is compatible with freedom and with the open exchange of ideas, and about how the workers would be supported. Khomeini's message was a call to the common man. He offered the ultimate solution to a nation suffering under a corrupt, degenerate, western-influenced shah whose SAVAK paralyzed everyone with fear. Through the elaborate mouthpiece of Iran's clerics, Khomeini said that he was going to end all that; Iran would not be dependent on the United States but rely on itself and move forward. He even promised that he would make electricity free for the poor (which he never did). All of this was very appealing to the population, and no one had any idea that a repressive regime was on the verge of taking over. Millions of Iranians threw their trust and their faith in this man who looked spiritual, wise, and sincere. How in the world could we possibly think that he'd do anything bad?

Khomeini's prescription for Iran sounded like a rational, positive approach, and people took the ayatollah at his word. "He had made a commitment and said, 'This is my position,'" said Ganjei. "This was the commitment of an 80-year-old man with a white beard, a pious-looking man; he said, 'This is my word.'"

In December 1978 anti-shah groups organized peaceful demonstrations throughout Iran—in Tehran, the massive turnout numbered one million. A resolution was drawn up during this demonstration that called upon Khomeini to lead Iran. On January 16, 1979, the shah fled the country, and two weeks later, on February 1, Khomeini boarded a plane in Paris for Tehran. To the end, he continued to lie about bringing democracy and freedom to Iran; as he boarded the plane he thanked the French people "who have followed with interest the struggle for freedom of conscience and the way of democracy desired by all clear-minded Iranians."[21] Shortly afterward he landed at the Tehran airport to a hero's welcome.

POSTREVOLUTION WAKE-UP CALL: KHOMEINI'S REAL MOTIVES

In the early days after the revolution, Khomeini had both the political and the religious authority completely centered on himself, and he fully used the authority to his advantage. In those first weeks he played it very smart. The first administration that he appointed was nearly all western educated; there was not a cleric among them. With this cabinet Khomeini sent the message to the western countries that he had no intention of forming Islamic rule. While in exile, he had stated clearly that after the overthrow he would return to his role as a cleric in Qom, settling back in the theological school, but he never did.

Khomeini and the clerics dominated everything in the first phase of the revolution. In the beginning there was absolute freedom, political openness, release of political prisoners, freedom to express opinions and criticisms of the clerical leadership peacefully. But in a gradual and well-orchestrated campaign, Khomeini began to marginalize those whom he and his followers were calling the liberals, the western-educated technocrats. This campaign included stifling the cabinet by subordinating it to Khomeini's Revolutionary Council, a group of interim legislators whose identities were kept secret.[22] Then came the embassy takeover on November 4, 1979, just eight months after the revolution. The hostage taking was a carefully designed turning point that tilted the whole balance of power in favor of Khomeini and the clerics.

Khomeini's totalitarian style had also surfaced earlier, during the debate about what sort of government Iran would install. On March 30 and 31, 1979,

Iranians voted on a public referendum about the future of their country. Khomeini had narrowed the choice to one option: replace the monarchy with an Islamic republic, yes or no. Other parties had argued for a more open referendum offering Iranians the choice of an "Islamic" republic, or a "democratic" republic, or simply a "republic," but Khomeini refused. Four weeks before the vote he told a crowd that "democratic" was a western concept and inimical to Islam: "What the nation wants is an Islamic republic: not just a republic, not a democratic republic, not a democratic Islamic republic. Do not use this term, 'democratic.' That is the Western style."[23]

For all his talk on semantics, Khomeini's real reason for outlawing the word "democratic" was that it would give a political voice to groups that did not endorse Islam. "In the first government after the revolution," recalled Ganjei, "many wanted a democratic Islamic republic, because within the government there were some non-Islamic nationalists, but Khomeini said it must be called an Islamic Republic, not a word more or a word less, that's it."

Faced with no choice but monarchy or Islamic republic, Iranians voted to pass the referendum, and Khomeini declared April 1, 1979, as "The First Day of God's Government." Iranians then voted for an assembly of experts to write up a draft constitution, and clerics from Khomeini's Islamic Republic Party won a majority of the 73 seats, clearing the way for Khomeini's vision of Islamic rule to be written into law.

In May 1979, Khomeini created a new militia, the Islamic Revolutionary Guards Corps (IRGC), out of a collection of armed neighborhood *komiteh* (committees) who had protested against the shah before the revolution.[24] Numbering about 10,000, the IRGC's first task was restoring order in the cities; within two years, its role and its numbers increased dramatically. The IRGC became responsible for supporting Khomeini's monopoly on power, which meant hunting down and murdering opposition groups. By the end of 1981, the organization had grown to 50,000 and become Khomeini's domestic assassination machine.[25]

Khomeini set out to create an army of believers, trained as carefully in Islamic ideology as they were in arms and tactics. Article 144 of the constitution defined the type of recruits that would form the military, stating, "The Army of the Islamic Republic of Iran must be an Islamic Army, i.e., committed to Islamic ideology and the people, and must recruit into its service individuals who have faith in the objectives of the Islamic Revolution and are devoted to the cause of realizing its goals."[26]

The regime set about transforming the overall purpose of the military, which, according to Mostafa Chamran, Khomeini's minister of defense, had been "created to defend Zionism and Imperialism" under the previous "Satanic regime" (that is, the regime of the shah).[27] The Islamization of the regime's military was carried out by an organization called the Ideological-Political Directorate of the Armed Forces (IPD), which integrated radical Islamic propaganda into every level of military training. The officers who emerged from three years of this training and fundamentalist indoctrination were tailor-made for enforcing the regime's repressive doctrines and spreading its version of Islam to other nations.[28]

KHOMEINI'S ONE-MAN RULE AND LAUNCH OF IRAN'S EXPANSIONIST POLICY

The constitution of the new Islamic Republic of Iran, adopted in October 1979, transformed Khomeini's ideas about Islamic rule from political theory to legal fact. The all-or-nothing leadership style that he had outlined in his 1969 lecture series while in exile suddenly became the law of the land, granting control of the executive, legislative, and judicial branches of government to one absolute leader. There was no precedent in either Iranian or Shiite history for this role of supreme politico-religious ruler.[29]

In the broadest terms, Khomeini described the role of the *vali*, or leader, in this system as that of an adult taking responsibility for a minor. "With respect to duty and position, there is indeed no difference between the guardian of a nation and the guardian of a minor," he stated.[30] In 1979, ten years after he lectured about it, the idea was imbedded in the constitution to define the role of the absolute leader, or "Just Holy Person." The document states that this leadership role "is in accordance with the saying *'The direction of affairs is in the hands of those who are learned concerning God and are trustworthy in matters pertaining to what He permits and forbids,'*" and that this holy leadership "will prevent any deviation by the various organs of State from their essential Islamic duties."

The *vali*'s power, as stated in article 110 of the constitution, cancels out the legitimacy of presidential elections in Iran in that the candidates are subject to approval by the Guardian Council, a group appointed by the *vali*. Therefore, the candidates reflect not the choice of the people but the choice of the leader himself. The constitution also ushered in a new set of repressive policies and stripped away issues of freedom that many revolutionaries believed would be part of the new Iran. Women's rights would be ensured, according to article 21, but with an enormous qualifier: "in conformity with Islamic criteria." Anyone who dreamed of a free and open press quickly lost that notion in light of article 24, which stated that the press had "freedom of expression except when it is detrimental to the fundamental principles of Islam or the rights of the public." Who would define those principles? The *vali* and his top clerical leaders, of course. Political or intellectual opposition was outlawed in article 26, which declared that parties, organizations, and societies were allowed "provided they do not violate the . . . basis of the Islamic republic."

These provisions are tyrannical enough—and contrary to what Khomeini promised prior to the revolution—but the section of the constitution that is most relevant to world leaders and policy makers in the twenty-first century is the section that defines the regime's global mission and expansionist doctrine. Under the heading "The Form of Government in Islam," the constitution is crystal clear in explaining the regime's plan to export its form of Islamic rule throughout the world:

> With due attention to the Islamic content of the Iranian Revolution, the Constitution provides the necessary basis for ensuring the continuation of the Revolution at home and abroad. In particular, in the development of international relations, the Constitution will strive with other Islamic and popular movements to prepare the way for the formation of a single world community (in accordance with the Koranic verse *'This your community is a single community, and I am your Lord, so worship Me'* [21:92]), and to assure the continuation of the struggle for the liberation of all deprived and oppressed peoples in the world.[31]

Could a moderate legislator or even a president of Iran have any impact on this fundamental principle of the regime? The inability of so-called moderates to make significant changes in Iran in the 1990s proved that making such an impact is not only impossible, but a naive assumption based on the regime's clearly defined goals. Those who raise their eyebrows at Ahmadinejad's religious vocabulary need only look at the regime's constitution to see that he is not an anomaly but a sharply accurate personification of the regime's ideology and worldview.

As the author Mohammad Mohaddessin explains, this constitutional commitment to exporting the revolution is one of the two main pillars in the regime's policy. The military's role in achieving this first goal is outlined in a section of the constitution entitled "An Ideological Army," which states that these forces are responsible for "extending the sovereignty of God's law throughout the world."

The second pillar, also defined in the constitution, is repression of the opposition at home in order to maintain power.[32] One of the "Foundational Principles" of the government as stated in article 2 pronounces that "the Islamic Republic is a system based on belief in . . . the One God (as stated in the phrase *'There is no god except Allah'*), His exclusive sovereignty and right to legislate, and the necessity of submission to His commands." Khomeini, declaring himself God's appointed messenger, was responsible for ensuring that the people abided by that divine "legislation" and submitted to God's commands. This issue is further articulated in article 9, which states that "no individual, group, or authority, has the right to infringe in the slightest way upon the political, cultural, economic, and military independence or the territorial integrity of Iran under the pretext of exercising freedom."

Accordingly, anyone who disagrees with the absolute leader's laws or pronouncements commits blasphemy and violates the holy order, and neither God nor his earthly messenger would be merciful. In addition, the regime was justified in wiping out opposition groups and executing anyone who did not follow the letter of the law. Khomeini had long described his belief that opposing voices should be silenced. "Despite all the adornments with which He equipped it, God has never looked upon this world with mercy," he said in a 1972 lecture.[33] In April 1979, Khomeini explained that severe punishment, which at times may lead to death, is sometimes necessary because the culprit is like a cancer in society that must be cut out. "If the hands of four thieves are cut off in a public gathering [thievery] will end," he said. "If four people who are afflicted with prostitution are flogged, prostitution will die."[34]

EXECUTING THE "ENEMIES OF GOD": THE BLOODY WAKE OF REVOLUTION

The period of freedom of expression that immediately followed the revolution was brief. Khomeini would not compromise with political parties or opposition groups, and he quickly set up a network of organizations to threaten and terrorize all critics of the regime, whom he called *mohareb* (enemies of God).[35] The regime's tools for repression included the Islamic Revolutionary Guards Corps, Islamic Revolutionary Courts, Islamic Revolutionary Committees, the volunteer Guards Corps Mobilization (or *Bassij*), and operatives in government and business offices, schools, and universities.[36]

The new "guardianship" of the people cracked down on dissenters with a vengeance. The grizzly sentencing of four prisoners in July 1980 showed how the mullahs were ushering in a feverish era of terror: Two women who had been found guilty of prostitution and two men convicted of sexual offenses were buried in the ground up to their chests and stoned to death, with the sentencing judge throwing the first stone.[37] Thousands who voiced criticisms of the *velayat-e faqih* system were arrested as political prisoners and tortured, and by the summer of 1981 some 70 members of the main opposition group, the Mujahedin-e Khalq, were murdered, and several thousand more were imprisoned. That was merely a warm-up to the scourge of arrests and executions that began after the historic massacre of June 20, 1981, during a peaceful demonstration organized by the Mujahedin.[38] When 500,000 gathered in Tehran to show their disapproval of the mullahs' exchange of one dictatorship for another, the Islamic Revolutionary Guards Corps opened fire on the crowd under the direct order of Khomeini.[39]

The *Christian Science Monitor* reported that the regime "shot just about any leftist they could capture on the streets on June 20 [1981], including people who were simply carrying leftist leaflets. They then began looking into their prisons and hauling before the firing squad leftists who had been arrested earlier. . . . The ruling fundamentalists have been sending group after group of people before the firing squad."[40] The *New York Times* reported in April 1982 that the Mujahedin "were crushed with a wave of jailings, torture and executions that rivaled the worst days of Shah Mohammed Riza Pahlevi."[41] In postrevolutionary Iran, you either bowed and expressed allegiance or you were killed; there was no middle ground.

———————•◆•◆•———————

After Khomeini's death on June 3, 1989, the Assembly of Experts appointed a new *vali-e-faqih*, the midlevel cleric Ali Khamenei. Because the constitution demanded a high-ranking cleric for the position, the assembly immediately promoted Khamenei to ayatollah. The constitution was subsequently revised on July 28, 1989, to increase the power of the *velayat-e faqih;* without the overwhelmingly authoritative status that Khomeini had given the office, the assembly feared that the role of absolute leader would be weakened.[42] The assembly's changes to the constitution included dropping the requirement that the absolute leader be accepted by the majority of the people; instead, he was simply appointed by the Assembly of Experts. The original constitution stated that the role of the absolute leader could be replaced by a council of qualified members; this stipulation was also dropped so that supreme leadership would always be in the hands of one man. The prime minister position was eliminated, and the office of the president was made more dependent upon the *vali-e-faqih;* instead of being accountable only to the population, the president would now be accountable to the *vali* as well. The revised constitution also reduced the overall qualifications for the supreme leader, dropping the requirement that he be a *marja-e-taqlid* (the source of emulation). The new constitution also granted the supreme leader more power over the judicial branch by exchanging the five-member Supreme Judicial Council with one *vali*-appointed official.[43]

———————•◆•◆•———————

In an essay written for *Harpers* in July 1980, Fergus M. Bordewich of Columbia University described the new regime in Iran as "fascism without swastikas." He targeted the American press for being blissfully ignorant about Khomeini's agenda leading up to the revolution. Referring to a *Washington Post* reporter who had written that Khomeini planned to install an "open government," Bordewich said that the reporter "simply recorded what the ayatollah's spokesmen told him because he couldn't distinguish the ayatollah's philosophy from Aristotle's."[44] No one can afford to be this blind to the Iranian regime's goals in the first part of the twenty-first century. Tehran's most basic mission, written into the opening lines of the constitution, is to establish global Islamic rule. As Iran continues in 2006 to create chaos in Iraq—a crucial strategy in pursuing its global mission—one must give the regime credit for consistency. It has never wavered from the fundamental precepts of its founding constitution. By 2006, Iran's interest in controlling Iraq could no longer be ignored, thanks to hard evidence that it plays a major role in some of the deadliest attacks against coalition forces. President George W. Bush stated this fact in a speech on March 14, 2006: "Tehran has been responsible for at least some of the increasing lethality of anticoalition attacks by providing Shi'a militia with the capabilities to build improvised explosive devices in Iraq." He added that the IEDs that troops had seized "were clearly produced in Iran."[45]

Tehran's endless ambitions will not stop at forming new Islamic governments in Iraq and other Muslim states throughout the world. If the regime acquires nuclear weapons, it will be in a position to eradicate its enemies at the push of a button. The decision will be easy, based on a 25-year tradition of rule by a wholly manufactured, false version of Islam that justifies launching such an apocalypse.

PART III
THE SECRET INSURGENCY

CHAPTER 5

NEXUS OF TERROR

Intelligence indicates the persistence of contacts between Iranian security officials and senior al-Qaeda figures after Bin Ladin's return to Afghanistan. . . . There is strong evidence that Iran facilitated the transit of al-Qaeda members into and out of Afghanistan before 9/11, and that some of these were future 9/11 hijackers. . . . After 9/11, Iran and Hezbollah wished to conceal any past evidence of cooperation with Sunni terrorists associated with al-Qaeda. . . . We believe this topic requires further investigation by the U.S. government.

—*The 9/11 Commission Report*, 2004

Iran is ground zero for international terrorism.

The Iranian regime uses terrorism as a policy instrument to deal with both exterior and interior challenges to its survival. Outside Iran, its terrorist acts are used to blackmail and gain concessions from western countries; inside Iran, terrorism benefits the regime by boosting the morale and status of the Islamic Revolutionary Guards Corps (IRGC) every time it achieves a successful attack. This boost further enables the regime to confront the rising discontent of the population. Iran's Islamic Revolutionary Guards Corps considers itself part of a global network that is leading the way for the Islamic revolution to spread beyond Iran's borders, and without this international scope the IRGC would not enjoy a fraction of its prominence in Iran. But with its identification as being part of a much bigger entity in the Muslim world that is fighting America—the "Great Satan"—the IRGC has a high sense of purpose and elevated self-regard in Iran.

Each terrorism operation starts in Tehran, where the leaders choose their targets and develop the operations. Based on warrants previously issued for those involved in terrorist assassinations as well as other information, it can be inferred that the highest ranks of the regime are involved in each mission, including the supreme leader, the president, the chiefs of the Ministry of Foreign Affairs and the Ministry of Intelligence and Security (MOIS), and commanders of the IRGC and Qods Force. The Ministry of Foreign Affairs, for example, is key in each operation because it uses Iran's diplomatic system to move Iranian agents into the countries where the attacks will occur and to coordinate operations out of Iran's embassies and consulates. The head of the Ministry of Intelligence and Security coordinates its secret service agents to run the intelligence gathering for each operation. In the final phase, the attacks are carried out by either Qods Force officers or MOIS agents. If the terrorist operations are run through another terrorist group in a foreign country, the regime uses local agents or foreign nationals to carry out the attacks.

TERRORIST ACTS COMMITTED DIRECTLY BY THE REGIME

In 1979, Khomeini's regime made a direct strike against the United States with its support of the Iranian students' seizure of 52 Americans at the U.S. embassy in Tehran that ignited the 444-day hostage crisis.[1]

The other direct acts of terrorism committed by Iran are the attacks on people who oppose the regime throughout Europe and the Middle East. Several of the IRGC members and MOIS agents who worked the terrorist operations in Europe and the Middle East for the regime in the 1980s and early 1990s are now in the highest levels of power in Iran. According to an international arrest warrant issued by a Swiss judge in April 2006, Ali Fallahian, the mullah who currently serves as a security advisor to Supreme Leader Khamenei, allegedly masterminded the assassination of Kazem Rajavi, the National Council of Resistance of Iran's representative in Switzerland, on April 24, 1990.[2]

Fallahian was the minister of intelligence at the time of this terrorist operation, and in that capacity, Swiss investigating magistrate Jacques Antenen believes, he coordinated a team of 13 operatives, several of whom were MOIS agents, who gunned down Rajavi in broad daylight while he was driving home just outside Geneva.[3] Rajavi had been a vocal critic of the regime ever since resigning his post as Iran's representative to the United Nations in Geneva shortly after the 1979 revolution. He resigned in protest after Khomeini's government began arresting, torturing, and executing Iranians throughout the country. The clerics also made Rajavi's brother, the Iranian resistance leader Massoud Rajavi, the number-one target on their hit list.

Iran's policy of international terrorism had already made headlines in the spring of 1997 when a Berlin court preliminarily ruled that Iran's top leaders—

including Supreme Leader Khamenei—were part of a "special operations committee" that ordered the murder of four Iranian Kurds in exile in Germany. In 1992, two heavily armed men charged into the Mykonos restaurant in Berlin and shot Sadiq Sharafkandi, the leader of the Kurdish Democratic Party, and three of his colleagues. The investigation that ensued suggested that Iran's supreme leader, Khamenei; its president, Rafsanjani; and its foreign minister, Ali Akbar Velayati, were all directly involved in planning the mission. The judge who made the ruling, Frithjof Kubsch, specifically named the then Intelligence Minister, Ali Fallahian, as having directed the operation. The German authorities had issued a warrant for Fallahian's arrest in 1996.[4] The judge stated that Iran's political leadership ordered the killings in order to "silence an uncomfortable voice," and described the action as "an official liquidation measure ordered without a verdict." He also criticized the hypocritical nature of the regime, stating in his ruling, "The fact that this was ordered by the Government of a state that calls itself a 'state of God' changes nothing. This religious embellishment does not hide the fact that the concern of the ruling regime in Iran was to eliminate opposition beyond its borders." Peter Mollema, a spokesman for the European Union, stated that these revelations made it impossible for Europe to make any kind of progress in dealing with the regime "while Iran flouts international norms and indulges in acts of terrorism."[5] The Iranian authorities have continued to deny involvement in the killings, however.

The German court did not follow through on investigating Iran's top leaders for the crime; rather, in May 1997, Germany's federal prosecutor announced that there would be no follow-up. As reported in the *New York Times*, this decision to back off angered the United States because "it enabled European Union countries—Germany in particular—to maintain important trade ties with Iran and thus undermine American calls for Tehran's isolation because of its suspected support of international terrorism."[6]

Since Ahmadinejad became president, many Qods Force assassins and MOIS members, such as Fallahian, who made up the terrorist network are now high-ranking leaders in the regime. The MOIS has also intensified its intelligence-gathering operations in Europe during Ahmadinejad's term, and the international terrorist committee continues to target victims. During the uproar over an editorial cartoon about the Prophet Muhammad that was published in newspapers in late 2005 and early 2006, for example, the regime reportedly sent 12 agents to Denmark on orders to murder the cartoonist. According to the May 2006 report about this operation by G2 Bulletin, the agents traveled to Europe carrying Iranian and Pakistani passports.[7]

TERROR BY PROXY:
IRAN'S SUPPORT AND USE
OF GLOBAL TERRORIST ORGANIZATIONS

In addition to carrying out their own operations, the Iranian regime has long used foreign groups in the Middle East and elsewhere to carry out terrorist attacks outside Iran. This strategy holds multiple benefits for the Iranian regime. First, it gives the terrorist attacks a higher likelihood of success because they are executed by local operatives and therefore invite less suspicion. Second, it makes the terrorist attacks more difficult to trace back to Iran, an issue that became important to the regime when some of its agents in Europe were exposed in the 1980s. The Iranian Wahid Gordji, for example, an official at Iran's embassy in Paris, was brought in for questioning by French police in 1987 as the suspected ringleader of a group of terrorists who bombed Paris in 1985 and 1986. The pro-Iranian terrorists had killed 13 people and wounded 250 during that bombing spree. Gordji dodged arrest, however, when France and Iran made a deal for his release in exchange for a French diplomat held hostage in Tehran.[8]

A third benefit for the regime in using terrorist proxies involves Iran's recruitment efforts in each particular region where it uses these groups. By enlisting the help of foreign nationals and using them for attacks, the regime expands its network, gains new opportunities for spreading its version of Islamic fundamentalism, and recruits new followers. Many transnational Islamic terrorist groups receive their identity, funding, resources, political backing, and ideological incentive from Iran. The regime also works hard to promote this support by glorifying these groups in public statements, such as Ahmadinejad's glowing praise of Hezbollah in August 2005. "Success, victories and progress of this popular and faithful force in political, cultural, social and military domains of Lebanon are results of purity and reliance on God's will," he said during an official visit with the group's leader. Ahmadinejad stressed that the group's Islamic fundamentalist ideology—wholly inherited from the Iranian regime—should be "preserved and institutionalized as the main factor in the fight against enemies of Islam."[9]

IRAN-BACKED TERRORISM IN LEBANON

The regime's first terrorist act against the United States carried out by a foreign group came in 1983, when two bombings in Lebanon killed a total of 258 Americans. Intelligence surrounding the second of these attacks, the bombing of the U.S. Marine Corps barracks in Beirut in October 1983, provided clear-cut proof that Iran was responsible. This connection motivated the Department of State to add Iran to its list of state sponsors of terrorism on January 19, 1984, branding it as a regime that has "repeatedly provided support for acts of international terrorism."[10] Libya, Syria, and Cuba were already on the state-sponsor list that year, and North Korea and Sudan later increased the list to six. (Iraq was on the list from 1979 to 1982, restored to the list in 1990, and removed again in 2003; South Yemen was also on the list until 1990.[11]) Iran has been named the most dangerous and active state in this group every year since 1987.[12]

The first of the Lebanese attacks struck on April 18, 1983, when a suicide bomber ignited a truck filled with explosives inside the courtyard of the U.S. embassy in Beirut and killed 63 people, including 17 Americans. The blast was so intense that it leveled the eight-story building and sent a shudder through a U.S. Navy ship anchored five miles off the Beirut coast. A group calling itself the Islamic Jihad Organization—one of several pseudonyms for the Lebanese group Hezbollah (Party of God)—telephoned the Beirut office of Agence France-Presse to take responsibility for the bombing.[13]

Hezbollah, the Lebanese group designed as a resistance force against Israel, is not a Lebanese creation. Tehran created the organization in the early 1980s and is the sole role model for the group's goal to install Islamic rule in Lebanon. In 1983, Iranian cleric Fazlollah Mahallati created a secret religious governing body in Lebanon patterned after the highest levels of clerical leadership in Iran.[14] This leadership council was made up of Lebanese Shiite clerics who held the highest authority in the three Hezbollah headquarter regions of Lebanon: the Bekaa Valley, a governorate of the country that lies between Lebanon's two mountain ranges; the suburbs of southern Beirut; and southern Lebanon. The organization is known by several other names, including Organization of the Oppressed on Earth and Islamic Jihad for the Liberation of Palestine. The U.S. Department of State describes this "radical Shia group" as "closely allied with, and often directed by, Iran," and also states that Hezbollah is "known or is suspected to have been involved" in many terrorist attacks against the United States, including the Beirut bombings mentioned above.[15] The department also reports that the group receives "substantial amounts of financial, training, weapons, explosives, political, diplomatic and organization aid from Iran and Syria."

Hezbollah's most infamous leader, Imad Fayez Mugniyah, is considered the mastermind of the attack on the U.S. Marines barracks in Beirut in 1983. He was also indicted by a U.S. federal grand jury in 1987 for his involvement in the 1985 TWA flight 847 hijacking, but he was never caught. Mugniyah is considered to be as dangerous as Osama bin Laden, and before the al-Qaeda attacks on the United States on September 11, 2001, he was the most-wanted terrorist in the world. Reports surfaced in 2003 that the Iranian regime was providing a safe haven for Mugniyah and other members of Hezbollah, and as of 2006 Mugniyah remains on the FBI's Most Wanted Terrorists list.[16]

The 1983 U.S. embassy attack was the first of a rapid-fire series of Iran-coordinated attacks against Americans in Lebanon in the mid-1980s. Six months later, a truck bomb much like the one that struck the embassy blew up the U.S. Marine Corps headquarters in Beirut, killing 241 marines. At 6:20 A.M. on October 23, while most of the marines were still sleeping in the barracks, a truck filled with TNT rammed the sandbag barrier around the compound and ignited in the courtyard. The U.S. district judge who ruled in 2003 that Iran was responsible for the attack and therefore owed damage payments to the victims' families called the bombing "the most deadly state-sponsored terrorist attack made against United States citizens before September 11, 2001." The judge, Royce C. Lamberth, based his ruling on evidence gathered after the October 1983 attack that proved that Iran had approved and funded the Marine headquarters bombing. "Lamberth concluded that Hezbollah was formed under the auspices of the Iranian government, was completely reliant on Iran in 1983 and assisted Iranian Ministry of Intelligence and Security agents in carrying out the operation," CNN reported.[17]

The October 1983 terrorist bombing of the U.S. Marines barracks in Beirut led to a complete withdrawal of U.S. peacekeeping forces in Lebanon. Although there had been growing public and political opposition to keeping U.S. troops in Beirut, the bombing that killed 241 marines escalated that opposition and forced President Reagan to reverse his policy of not "yielding to terrorism."[18] In February 1984, Reagan called for a removal of the 1,600 marines who made up the U.S. peacekeeping force.[19] "We're trying to see to it that American citizens, and it doesn't matter whether they are Navy pilots in the Gulf of Sidra or medical students in Grenada, can no longer be attacked or their lives endangered with impunity," Reagan said.[20]

With this U.S. retreat, the Iran-backed terrorists won. As a *Newsweek* summary observed, the withdrawal of U.S. troops benefited Iran's cause in the entire region: "The Marines were forced out of Beirut not just by Syrian intransigence but also by Iranian-inspired terrorism. That can only increase the appeal of Islamic fundamentalism for many young Arabs—and sharpen the threat to the conservative Gulf regimes."[21]

Confirmation of Iran's role in this attack came out of the regime itself, in remarks by then minister of the Islamic Revolutionary Guards Corps Mohsen Rafiqdoust, who boasted in a speech before defense industry personnel: "In the victory of the revolution in Lebanon and many other places around the world, the United States has felt our power on its ugly body and knows that both the TNT and the ideology which in one blast sent to hell 400 officers, NCOs, and soldiers at the Marine Headquarters have been provided by Iran." His remarks were carried in Iran's state-run newspaper, *Ressalat*, in July 1987.[22]

The evidence used by Judge Lamberth was the same intelligence that convinced the Department of State to designate Iran as a state sponsor of terrorism in early 1984. By then, Americans had been struck by another terrorist hit, this time at the U.S. embassy in Kuwait. On December 12, 1983, a terrorist ignited a truckload of explosives in the embassy annex, killing three embassy workers. A few minutes later, six more people were killed when car bombs exploded at five different sites around Kuwait, each ignited by remote-control devices. The embassy bomber was a 25-year-old Iraqi who belonged to Hezbollah, which had already claimed responsibility for the bombings in Lebanon.[23] The Islamic fundamentalist terrorists who had masterminded the attack for months were arrested, and they confessed and became known as the "Kuwait 17" or "al Dawa 17," because some of them belonged to the Iran-backed al-Dawa political group in Iraq.

Tehran-backed bombings of American forces continued in Lebanon in the mid-1980s. On September 20, 1984, a car packed with 385 pounds of explosives and four Soviet-made rockets raced toward the U.S. embassy annex in Aukar, northeast of Beirut.[24] Guards fired on the suicide bomber, but he exploded the bomb and blew out part of the eight-story building, killing 24 people. The victims included two Americans from the U.S. Army and Navy. Just weeks after the bombing, the U.S. House of Representative's Select Committee on Intelligence said that reports had warned about such an attack and pointed to an Iran connection. These intelligence reports stated that there was a high potential for more bombings by the same Iran-backed groups that had bombed U.S. sites in Lebanon twice in 1983. "The panel reported that there were 'credible reports' in the months before the attack warning that terrorist groups, in particular Moslem fundamentalists with Iranian connections, were planning attacks against United States posts," reported the *New York Times* in October 1984.[25]

The Iranian regime had blood on its hands, and world leaders knew it. Looking back at this period, President Ronald Reagan's national security adviser, Robert McFarlane, said that by 1985 "the Iranian sponsorship of terrorism was [confirmed by] clear, solid evidence."[26]

Tehran also masterminded a long, terrifying hostage-taking crisis in Lebanon in the 1980s. Tehran built an extremely active coalition of terrorists who seized Americans and other westerners. The first American hostage, David Dodge, the president of the American University of Beirut, was kidnapped in

1982. The next American, Frank Regler, was kidnapped in February 1984, and in March, Tehran-sponsored terrorists kidnapped the CIA station chief in Beirut, William Buckley, who was killed by his captors two years later—U.S. officials believed that he died while being tortured in Iran.[27] Eighteen Americans were captured during the crisis, including the longest-held western hostage, the journalist Terry Anderson, who spent six years and nine months in captivity. By the time that the last American hostages were released in 1991, three had escaped and another three had been killed or died in captivity.[28]

In his memoir, *Den of Lions*, Anderson explains how Iran benefited from the hostage crisis in Lebanon. Hostage negotiator, Giandomenico Picco, according to Anderson, offered Iran a considerable amount in the field of public relations, which certainly involved, among other things, a UN finding that Iraq was primarily to blame for the Iran-Iraq war. That 1991 report by then UN Secretary General Javier Perez de Cuellar formally blamed Iraq for starting the war by attacking Iran—something Tehran had failed to obtain before.[29]

The hostage crisis in Lebanon was a striking example of how the Iranian regime could manufacture and subsequently exploit an international crisis by using terrorism.[30] Tehran wants to be known as the leading state sponsor of terrorism while having the least provable ties. It cleans its traces, but leaves enough of a trademark to show its ability to deal with all kinds of terrorist groups. Tehran wants to build this image in the minds of western countries, and during the Lebanese hostage crisis it worked the field both ways.[31]

Without a doubt, the Iranian regime was the main sponsor of the American hostage taking, while at the same time it offered assistance to the United States to negotiate the hostages' release.[32] Tehran created the crisis, and then offered help to resolve it. Iran insisted that its influence on the terrorists in Lebanon was solely ideological and spiritual and that it would use this influence to help obtain the hostages' release, but at the same time the regime was sending money to the terrorists in Lebanon for their use in confining, feeding, and guarding the hostages.[33] Just weeks after the last American hostages were released, the *Washington Post* broke the news that Iran not only financed the day-to-day upkeep of the hostages in Lebanon but paid the terrorists a bonus of $1 million to $2 million every time they released a hostage. The regime's purpose in giving these rewards, according to the U.S. official interviewed by the *Post*, was to "keep these people happy, quiet and on their side. They have long-term investments in Lebanon."[34]

The regime never lost sight of its long-term plan for Lebanon or for the rest of the Middle East—its plan to export the Iranian revolution. As the hostage crisis wore on, human lives were simply fodder for Tehran's goals, and President

Ronald Reagan was moved to describe these Iran-backed acts as "human trafficking" in 1987.[35]

Iran played a dirty game, releasing a hostage or two only to seize more later, which made negotiating with Iran a nightmare for U.S. officials. "If there is anything we have learned from the last two years it is that you cannot negotiate with the Iranians for hostages," one unnamed official told the *Christian Science Monitor* in 1987. "If we got two released, three more were taken." Another government source described the mix of Lebanese hostages and Iran as "disaster."[36]

Among the worst disasters was the covert arms-for-hostages deal manufactured by Tehran and some members of the Reagan administration. By 1985, Iran was in the middle of its war with Iraq and desperately needed arms—which it could not legally purchase from the United States—so the regime asked to buy weapons from the United States in exchange for releasing hostages. From the regime's perspective, the Lebanese hostage crisis was a win-win situation. It allowed the regime to attack the United States by seizing and torturing its citizens while simultaneously exploiting the crisis to buy much-needed weapons for the Iran-Iraq War. The Americans managed to get only three hostages released in exchange for a scandal that was the most damaging political crisis of Reagan's presidency.[37] Even worse, the deal did not stop the regime's hostage-taking spree—in 1987, Terry Waite was seized and accused of being a spy for the United States, and three American academics were taken hostage from Beirut University.[38]

One would think that years of such deceit and violence would drive home the lesson that the Iranian regime could not be trusted at any level and that its hatred of the United States was unwavering and nonnegotiable. Not so; in his January 1989 inaugural address, President George H. W. Bush gave a high priority to the American hostages held in Lebanon, whom he referred to as citizens "held against their will in foreign lands," and expressed his willingness to negotiate with Iran for their release. "Assistance can be shown here, and will be long remembered," he stated. "Good will begets good will."[39] Rather than create a hopeful atmosphere for negotiation, however, this offer of good will only invoked bad will in the form of a full-blown firebrand tirade out of Tehran. Seven days after Bush's address, Iran's president at the time, Ali Khamenei, blasted the president for daring to make demands on the regime. "The American president should know that we, not they, have conditions to set," he said at the weekly Friday prayer service at Tehran University. "These are our conditions: Stop being aggressive, stop your arrogant actions, discontinue the transgressions against the rights of the Iranian people and return what you owe us."[40] So much for approaching Tehran with hat in hand, looking for a rational discussion.

Iran had the United States by the throat during the western hostage crisis, and it relentlessly exploited the situation to win benefits. Iranian foreign minister Ali Akbar Velayati frequently voiced Iran's desire to help release the hostages if the United States was willing to show its good will explicitly on Iran's terms. He repeatedly called for the release of 735 Lebanese Shiites being held in Israeli jails, a move that he said would "create a good climate for the release of all hostages, including Western hostages."[41]

During the final negotiations for the release of the hostages, U.S. officials gradually woke up to the reality that Iran had complete control of the hostage situation. "We used to spend endless hours debating here the degree of Iranian control," a U.S. official told the *Washington Post* six weeks after the last American was released. "The evidence now is that [Iran's] control was 99.9 percent."[42] The regime's total control over the fate of the hostages became more evident during the final months of the negotiation process, when it exacted financial concessions from the United States. In November 1991, Iran received a $278 million payment from the United States for arms that the United States had impounded from the regime in 1979. Throughout the crisis, the regime had called for the return of arms and other assets that the United States had impounded during the first hostage crisis at the U.S. embassy in Tehran in 1979. The regime's claims for these items were being addressed at a U.S.-Iran claims tribunal at The Hague, but the United States sped up the process in 1989 when Iran made it clear that the funds would have an impact on the release of the hostages.[43] The United States agreed to pay Iran the multimillion-dollar payment on November 26, 1991; on December 4, the last American hostage was freed.[44]

Tehran's support of Lebanese terrorism in the 1980s also included support of airline hijackings. Three months after the September 1984 bombing in northeast Beirut, Iranian terrorist proxies killed two more Americans during the hijacking of Kuwait Airways flight 221. The hijackers diverted the flight to Tehran on December 3, 1984, and demanded the release of the Kuwait 17; two passengers who worked for the United States Agency for International Development were shot and killed when the demands were not met. Iran allowed the airliner to land and to remain at the airport as the terrorists killed the two passengers and continued to make their demands. Playing the crisis from both sides once again, the regime sent in a security force to storm the plane and arrest the hijackers, but rather than putting the terrorists on trial—as they promised the world they would do—they released them and allowed them to leave the country. Once again, Iran used the grisly tactics of terrorism by sponsoring these acts while seeking concessions from the West and trying to show a cooperative face. A U.S. Department of State official told the *New York Times* that the hijackers were the same Iran-backed terrorists responsible for the bombings in Lebanon: "We have intelligence that leaves no doubt that the hijackers are connected with the Iranian-sponsored terror network in Lebanon and elsewhere," he said.[45]

Six months later, on June 14, 1985, Iran-backed hijackers seized TWA flight 847 in another attempt to gain the release of the Kuwait 17. The terrorists forced the plane to land in Beirut and tortured and shot one of the military passengers, U.S. Navy diver Robert Stethem. Television viewers watched in horror as the hijackers dumped Stethem's body onto the tarmac, and for many this remains the most lasting image of the Iran-backed terrorism that wracked the 1980s. Although Iran denied any involvement in this hijacking, the regime could not hold back from blaming the United States and Israel for calling all the trouble upon themselves. In a trip to Syria during the crisis, Akbar Hashemi Rafsanjani, then speaker of Iran's parliament, announced that the hijacking was in retaliation for Israel's imprisonment of the 735 Lebanese Shiites. "The days the Zionists could abduct innocent Muslims with total impunity are gone," he said.[46] Khomeini had scathing remarks for the United States during the crisis as well, declaring that the United States was powerless in the face of the unity of the Lebanese people.[47]

After being held for 17 days, the 39 hijacked American hostages were released upon promises from Israel that the Shiite prisoners would be freed. Israel met this demand, releasing all the prisoners in stages over the next few months.[48] Terrorism remained an extremely profitable business for Tehran.

———————•◦•———————

The fighting that escalated in southern Lebanon and northern Israel in July 2006, following the kidnapping of two Israeli soldiers by Hezbollah, once again highlighted the fact that Tehran is the root cause of the crisis in the Middle East. Zalmay Khalilzad, the U.S. ambassador to Iraq, believed that the round of bombings and killings were orchestrated by Iran to deflect attention from the fact that the regime was "under more pressure to cooperate" with the West and halt its nuclear enrichment activities.[49] It is widely believed that Iran was the main instigator of the crisis and that it acted in an effort to divert attention from Iran's nuclear weapons program, spread the scope of Iran's conflict with the West into Lebanon, and overshadow its extensive destabilizing activities in Iraq.

On July 11, 2006, one day before the crisis ignited, Ahmadinejad warned the West that it must immediately end its support of Israel or all of the nations in the region would take action. "The storm of their wrath will not be confined to within the borders of the region," he said on Iranian state television, "and it will affect the governments that support [Israel].[50] The next day, Ahmadinejad followed up this threat with the declaration, "In the near future we will witness the rapid collapse of the Zionist regime."[51] That day, Hezbollah fighters made their raid into Israel, killing seven Israeli soldiers and kidnapping two others. Israel struck back with air attacks and the crisis quickly escalated.

Saeed Aboutaleb, a senior Iranian parliamentary member, was quoted in the *Aftab Yazd* newspaper saying that Lebanon is now the front line of the Islamic world. General Rahim Safavi, commander-in-chief of the Islamic Revolutionary Guards Corps, said that the futures of Syria, Lebanon, and Iraq are tied to one another. If they all join together, he added, they will "dominate the entire Middle East," thus revealing Iran's bigger regional agenda.

In a speech broadcast on state television, Khamenei demonstrated the dominant, Big Brother role that Iran plays in Lebanon. "The U.S. president says Hizballah must be disarmed. It's clear that (the U.S.) and Zionists want this, but it won't happen."[53] He added, "Lebanon was supposed to be turned into a center for Western culture but this country has instead turned into a center for Jihad and resistance and this is exactly the opposite of what the Western hegemonic powers wanted."[54]

TEHRAN'S ROLE IN THE KHOBAR TOWERS ATTACK

On June 26, 1996, terrorists blasted the Khobar Towers apartment complex in Dhahran, Saudi Arabia—home to approximately 2,000 American, French, British, and Saudi troops—with a truck bomb outfitted with 5,000 pounds of explosives. The massive explosion killed 19 servicemen, all from the United States, and wounded 372 more U.S. military personnel.

According to information that I received from sources inside the Iranian regime in early 1997, IRGC brigadier general Ahmad Sharifi masterminded the Khobar Towers attack. In a press conference that my colleagues and I held on April 16, 1997, we reported that the terrorists under Sharifi's supervision were flown from Tehran to Damascus in early 1996.[55] From there they were dispatched to the Bekaa Valley in Lebanon. Subsequently, they went to Saudi Arabia, where they carried out the truck bombing. The attack was a joint operation executed by the Iranian Ministry of Intelligence and Security and the IRGC's Qods Force. Sharifi remains a senior commander in the Qods Force stationed in Beit ol-Moqaddas Seminary in Qom.

In his 2005 autobiography, former FBI director Louis Freeh confirmed the Iranian tie to the Khobar Towers bombing. Freeh outlined the facts about Iran's role in the attack, facts that were uncovered during the FBI investigation (because American citizens were killed, the FBI had jurisdiction in the Saudi attacks):

> The new materials and information . . . showed almost beyond a doubt that the Khobar Tower attacks had been sanctioned, funded, and directed by senior officials of the government of Iran. The Ministry of Intelligence and Security and the Iranian Revolutionary Guard had both been in on the planning and execution. The bombers had been trained by Iranians in the Bekaa Valley of Lebanon, where the Iranian-backed Hezbollah is based. They had been issued passports by the Iranian embassy in Damascus, Syria, that allowed them to cross the border into Saudi Arabia.[56]

Freeh further explained that in 2000 the FBI was able to question one of the Saudi Shiites who was being held in connection with the Khobar attacks. This detainee, Mustafa al-Qassab, had met with the commander of Saudi Hezbollah's military wing, Ahmed al-Mughassil, in Iran in the late 1980s. "Al-Qassab laid out for us in detail the planning and logistics that had gone into the Khobar attack, traced the lineage irrefutably back to Tehran, and as far as I was concerned tied the whole package together for good," wrote Freeh.[57]

The *9/11 Commission Report* highlighted the fact that Iran supported Saudi Hezbollah and that "the evidence of Iranian involvement is strong" in the Khobar attacks.[58]

BLOODSHED IN SOUTH AMERICA: IRAN AND THE BUENOS AIRES BOMBING

The single deadliest terrorist act against Jews since World War II took place in Buenos Aires, Argentina, in 1994, when a suicide bomber targeted the headquarters of the city's Jewish community. Twenty-one-year-old Ibrahim Hussein Berro, a Lebanese citizen and a member of Iran-backed Hezbollah, drove his van through the gates of the Argentine-Israeli Mutual Association (AMIA) building and detonated his bomb. The blast leveled the seven-story building, killing 85 people and wounding more than 300.

In 1998 my sources, who were associated with the National Council of Resistance of Iran, revealed that the Iranian regime planned and orchestrated this now historic attack, working through its well-established intelligence and terrorist network operating out of the Iranian embassy in Buenos Aires. I presented the information to a bipartisan group of members of Congress, which included the chair and the ranking member of the subcommittee that had jurisdiction over this issue in the U.S. House of Representatives. When members of Congress shared the information with the U.S. Department of State, the Department of State later confirmed the material and much of the details in its response to the lawmakers.

The facts my sources revealed were shocking: Not only was Tehran behind the attack, but the plan appears to have had the final approval of Ayatollah Khamenei himself. The Iranian leadership refers to Argentina as the second Israel because it is home to approximately 250,000 Jews, and the decision to attack the headquarters of this community was made by Iran's Supreme National Security Council in a session chaired by Iranian president Akbar Hashemi Rafsanjani on August 14, 1993. During the two-hour session, which ran from 4:30 to 6:30 P.M., the Council delegated the operation to Qods Force commander Ahmad Vahidi. According to my sources, the commander's subsequent Qods Force Command Council meeting was attended by Morteza Rezai, commander of the IRGC counterintelligence unit; Tehrani, commander of the logistics division of the Qods Force; and a mullah named Ahmad Salek, Khamenei's representative in the Qods Force. Ahmad Reza Asghari, a Qods Force officer, was reportedly chosen by the council to carry out the attack plan in Argentina. Asghari went to Buenos Aires under the cover of a diplomatic appointment and settled into his "job" as the third secretary at the Iranian embassy. The Supreme National Security Council ordered Iran's Foreign Ministry and the Ministry of Islamic Guidance to provide Asghari with intelligence, facilities, and anything else he needed to carry out the attack.

My sources also revealed that a leader of the Iranian parliament, Ali Akbar Parvaresh, who was also a close confidant of Khamenei, was sent to Argentina the following December to meet with pro-Iranian Muslims and assess who among them would possibly cooperate in the operation. When Parvaresh returned to Iran, he provided a report about the status of these potential operatives directly to Khamenei. Two mullahs stationed in Buenos Aires, the cultural attaché Mohammad Abd-Khodai and his successor, Mohsen Rabbani, also reportedly met with anti-American Muslim groups in Argentina to recruit them for the bombing mission. They reported their findings about new agents to Iran's Ministry of Guidance.

The regime in Iran had decided in 1993 that Argentina was fertile ground for developing an intelligence and terrorist network because of its large population of Muslims, many of whom had migrated from Lebanon. The mission of the Iranian cultural attaché was to contact young Muslims in the hope of bringing them into the fundamentalist fold, thereby establishing an active, functioning network for operations in the country. This strategy was outlined in a Ministry of Islamic Guidance memo obtained by my sources, dating from 1993. The document outlines the alluring facts about Argentina as the regime saw them:

The estimated number of Arabs who have migrated to Argentina are around 400,000; about 250,000 of them are Muslims. Most of the Muslims who are in Argentina have come from countries like Lebanon, Syria, Jordan and other Arab countries. It should be stated that in the past few years, due to Islam's advancements in the world, in particular the victory of the Islamic Revolution in Iran, there has been a major change among them. . . .

The maturity of the Alavi [a branch of Shia Islam] youth coincided with the new Islamic movement in the world, in particular the Islamic Revolution. In their movement toward their origins, they express their indignation toward the Argentinean culture and there is no doubt in their kindness and affection towards the Islamic Revolution. . . . They are Alavi and claim to be Ja'ffari Shiite. They resent other countries and their only hope is the Islamic Republic. We should be more concerned with them and do more things for them. . . . their affection for Imam Khomeini is indescribable.

To take advantage of this opportunity, the regime sent more than 70 delegations from various terrorist or fundamentalist organizations to Argentina to cultivate a pro-Iranian Muslim network. One of the organizations that set up offices in Argentina was the Mostazafin (The Oppressed) Foundation, one of the largest financial conglomerates in Iran, which is run by the clerics. This foundation had a history of providing logistics for the Iranian regime's terrorist acts in several foreign countries. Another organization, the 15th Khordad Foundation, is the same financial group (also run by clerics) that raised the ransom on British author Salman Rushdie's head.

The information provided by NCRI sources about the Buenos Aires bombing included facts about travel to and from Iran by Qods Force members and highly placed Iranian officials. In 1993, for example, two members of the Qods Force with the last names Zareh and Karimzadeh traveled to Argentina and remained there for nearly three months. They made few contacts with other operatives and few visits to the embassy in an attempt to keep their presence virtually unknown. A senior delegation from the regime also made a trip to Argentina prior to the attack. In December 1993, five members of the Iranian parliament made the trip to meet with Iran-friendly Islamic groups, including an Alavi group that ran a radio station called Radio Ghebleh.

The final result of this elaborate two-year operation, which involved tremendous organization and covert activity, was the fatal blast on the Jewish community center. The high secrecy that characterized the entire mission made the ensuing investigation extremely difficult for Argentina's authorities, but they did make progress by using the information that I had shared with the U.S. Congress. First, the congressional delegation that received my information traveled to Argentina and met with the judge. The judge consequently traveled to Paris and met with other people associated with my sources, and the strong evidence and detail that he obtained aided him in determining Iran's role in the attack.

The authorities also gained insight from an Iranian defector named Abolqassem Mesbahi, who, like my sources in Iran, affirmed that the mission was personally directed by Khamenei and that Rafsanjani was also involved. Mesbahi also told the authorities that the regime paid $10 million to Argentina's president at the time, Carlos Saúl Menem, as hush money; Menem denies it.[59] A former Argentine police commissioner who had been jailed during the investigation also told the authorities that he and four of his brothers each received $500,000 as payment for outfitting a van with a bomb. The investigators surmised that payments of this size were too large for an individual terrorist group and could come only from a government-sponsored operation—adding to the mounting evidence about Iran's involvement.[60]

The judge leading the investigation of the attack committed against the Israeli-Argentine Mutual Association (AMIA) ordered the arrest, both nationally and internationally, of nine individuals, mostly Iranian citizens allegedly responsible for the bombing.[61] Iran successfully petitioned to Interpol that the warrants be dropped because the judge who issued them was under investigation for corruption in the case.[62] The definitive legal outcome of the attack investigation was the Argentine government's November 2005 identification of Berro as the suicide bomber.[63] However, in November 2006, a judge issued an international arrest warrant for Iranian ex-president Akbar Hashemi Rafsanjani and eight other top former Tehran officials in the 1994 bombing of AMIA. Judge Rodolfo Canicoba Corral told AFP he had asked the government of Iran as well as Interpol to hand over the former president on a warrant issued for "crimes against humanity" in that bombing attack.

A STRING OF TEHRAN-BACKED TERRORIST GROUPS FROM PALESTINE TO AFRICA

The Iranian regime shares a bloody history with Palestinian groups and is not shy about gloating over these groups' "achievements." After a 1996 Hamas suicide bus bombing in Israel, for example, which killed 25 people, including two Americans, Hussein Sheikholeslam of the Iranian Foreign Ministry stated, "The Islamic resistance movement is in for a glorious future. There is no peaceful solution. The Israelis must return to the countries they came from."[64] Bankrolling these terrorist groups is a high priority for the regime, which offers cash payments for successful terrorist attacks.[65] The mullahs dole out millions to those who will bomb Israelis and other enemies of the regime, which keeps Iran one step removed from the crimes. Occasionally the regime's involvement is exposed, however, such as after a terrorist attack in Gaza in 1995 in which an American was killed. A U.S. district court ruled that Iran was responsible for her death because it funded the Palestinian group that carried out the attack. The Iranian regime was ordered to pay $247 million in damages to the woman's family.[66]

Iran also has terrorist proxies in Turkey, including one group that was responsible both for a grenade attack on a synagogue in Istanbul in March 1992 and also for the killing of an Israeli diplomat in Ankara with a car bomb that same month.[67] Another Iran-backed radical Islamic terrorist group in Turkey was believed to have committed the car bombing that killed the well-known Turkish journalist Ugur Mumcu in January 1993. Mumcu was an outspoken critic of militant Islam, and after his death thousands of Turkish citizens marched through the streets of Istanbul chanting slogans against the Iranian regime.[68]

Iran's terrorist ties also extend into Africa, where it has been accused of supporting extremists in Algeria. The Algerian government severed diplomatic relations with Iran in 1993 as a result of this activity.[69] Algeria's primary Islamic terrorist group committed atrocities against the civilian population of Algeria during the civil war of the 1990s, using extreme forms of violence that overshadowed all the other terrorist acts against the populace. Iran's other sphere of influence in Africa has been Sudan, which the United States designated as a state sponsor of terrorism in 1993. The fundamentalist party called the National Islamic Front has led Sudan for decades, and the U.S. Department of State labeled Iran as "the main supporter and ally of the fundamentalist regime in Sudan."[70] In the two decades following the institution of Islamic law in Sudan in 1983, two million Sudanese were killed in battles between the government's military forces and non-Muslim rebels in the south.

Iran's support of Sudan includes military training for Sudanese troops provided by the Islamic Revolutionary Guards Corps. Iran's choice for ambassador to Sudan also reveals the type of experience that the regime wanted to install there: Kamal Magid, ambassador to Sudan until 1994, was a terrorist leader who had previously "served as Iranian Charge in Beirut, where he played a leading role in developing the Hezbollah terrorist infrastructure in the 1980s," according to the U.S. Department of State.[71]

THE MULLAHS AND AL-QAEDA

Theories abound about Iran's involvement in al-Qaeda, but the *9/11 Commission Report* published in 2004 offered strong evidence about the relationship—evidence based on U.S. intelligence reports, interviews with FBI and CIA operatives, and other sources. According to the commission, al-Qaeda operatives met with Iranian officials in Sudan when Osama bin Laden lived there between 1991 and 1996. These meetings evolved into "an informal agreement to cooperate in providing support—even if only training—for actions carried out primarily against Israel and the United States." Following this agreement, senior al-Qaeda operatives traveled to Iran and the Bekaa Valley in Lebanon for training in explosives, intelligence, and security.[72]

The commission also reported that Iran helped al-Qaeda operatives travel among Saudi Arabia, Pakistan, and Afghanistan by not stamping their passports if they passed through Iran. Travel from Afghanistan to Saudi Arabia was a problem for al-Qaeda members because Saudi authorities seized all passports containing Pakistani stamps. The Iranian regime removed this obstacle: "Iranian border inspectors would be told not to place telltale stamps in the passports of these travelers," the commission explained. "Such arrangements were particularly beneficial to Saudi members of al-Qaeda."[73] The report also highlighted that a number of al-Qaeda's top "muscle" operatives involved in the 9/11 attacks took advantage of this arrangement. "There is strong evidence that Iran facilitated the transit of al Qaeda members into and out of Afghanistan before 9/11, and that some of these were future 9/11 hijackers," the report concluded.

The U.S. Department of State concluded in 2002 that after 9/11, Iran's record with al-Qaeda was mixed:

> While it has detained and turned over to foreign governments a number of al-Qaida members, other al-Qaida members have found virtual safe haven there and may even be receiving protection from elements of the Iranian Government. Iran's long, rugged borders are difficult to monitor, and the large number of Afghan refugees in Iran complicates efforts to locate and apprehend extremists. Nevertheless, it is unlikely that al-Qaida elements could escape the attention of Iran's formidable security services.[74]

CALLING ALL TERRORISTS: LET'S MEET IN TEHRAN

Based on Tehran's continuous hosting of international conferences on terrorism, Iran could be called "terrorism conference central." In the 1990s, for example, the regime hosted such affairs as the "World Conference on Palestine" (1990), attended by members of Hamas, Hezbollah, the Palestine Islamic Jihad (PIJ), and others such as "Intifadah and the Islamic World" (1991) and "Liberation Movements" (1997). Iran's 2003 "Intifadah" conference featured an Iranian official's input about the need for more suicide operations from Palestinian resistance groups in order to ensure the destruction of Israel.[75] And 2005's "The World without Zionism" conference exposed the new Iranian president's true hard-line colors when he quoted Ayatollah Khomeini's sentiment that Israel should be "wiped off the face of the earth."[76] In spite of the global furor that arose over Ahmadinejad's assertion in 2005 that the Holocaust is a "myth," the Iranian regime announced in 2006 that it would host a conference dedicated solely to the issue. When British Prime Minister Tony Blair pronounced the regime's plans as "shocking, ridiculous," and "stupid," Tehran responded by inviting Blair to participate in the conference and present evidence that Nazi Germany's slaughter of six million Jews during World War II was a historical fact.[77]

FATWA-STYLE TERRORISM: THE SALMAN RUSHDIE AFFAIR

When the Iranian regime decided that Salman Rushdie's novel *The Satanic Verses* (1988) was an act of blasphemy against Islam, it did not send out a Qods Force hit squad against Rushdie but rather put a $2 million bounty on the author's head. Ayatollah Ruhollah Khomeini issued a fatwa that condemned the author and his publishers to death. "I call on all valiant Muslims wherever they may be in the world to kill them without delay, so that no one will dare insult the sacred beliefs of Muslims henceforth," Khomeini announced on Tehran Radio on February 14, 1989.[78] The mullahs in Iran viewed Rushdie's novel as just one more calculated effort by the West to undermine Islam. A report on state radio following the fatwa demonstrated this paranoia: "The book . . . is the result of years of effort by American, European and Zionist so-called experts on Islam gathering in international seminars and conferences on the religion with the aim of finding the best way to insult and undermine Islam's highest values and traditions."[79]

Rushdie went into hiding in England and received protection from the London police, while people associated with the book in other parts of the world fell victim to the ayatollah's fatwa. Hitoshi Igarashi, the Japanese translator of the book, was stabbed to death in 1991. The Italian translator, Ettore Capriolo, was also stabbed that year but survived the attack. In 1993, an unknown assailant shot William Nygaard, the publisher of the Norwegian edition on the novel, three times in front of his home in Oslo. He also survived, but none of the assailants in any of the attacks was ever caught.[80]

Eight years after Khomeini made the religious edict, Iran increased the reward for Rushdie's death to $2.5 million under the condition that he be killed during 1997's 10-day anniversary celebration of the Islamic revolution.[81] One year later, Iranian foreign minister Kamal Kharazi told the British government

that the Iranian regime had no intention of carrying out the fatwa, and Rushdie
came out of hiding. But in January 2005, Ayatollah Ali Khamenei reignited the
controversy during a sermon, describing Rushdie as an apostate who deserved to
die.[82] The mullahs in Iran explained that the fatwa lived on because only the person who issued the fatwa could lift it; therefore, Khomeini's death prevented the
edict from being cleared.

Iran's IRGC echoed Ayatollah Khamenei's unflinching position with a statement in February 2005 announcing that the fatwa was still in effect. "The day
will come when they will punish the apostate Rushdie for his scandalous acts and
insults against the Koran and the Prophet," the statement read.[83]

After resuming his public life, Rushdie remarked about the regime's reaction
to *The Satanic Verses:* "I do think that, as somebody once said, you can judge the
importance of literature by the apparatus that tyrants set up to repress it."[84]

———•◦•———

Iran's direct terrorist operations and its role in terrorist acts committed by other
groups all coincide with the regime's policy of "servicing" terrorist organizations
throughout the world. Not only does the Qods Force assassinate Tehran's enemies beyond Iran's borders, it shares its skills in kidnapping, torture, explosives,
and murder with other terrorist groups across the globe. One source lists 216 terrorist operations conducted by Iranian forces in the Middle East, Europe, and the
United States between 1980 and 1999.[85] This list of attacks, in addition to the
operations discussed in this chapter, reveals how thoroughly the Iranian regime
has committed itself to terrorism as the primary tool for furthering its goals. In
addition, much of the regime's terrorist resources have been funneled into operations in Iraq since the fall of Baghdad in 2003—operations that have profoundly
derailed the democratic process in that country. Iran's meddling in Iraq, which
came only gradually to the world's awareness, was the result of years of high-level
planning and is one of Tehran's most crucial tactics in achieving its goal of
spreading Islamic rule.

CHAPTER 6

THE ENEMY NEXT DOOR: IRAN'S ROLE IN IRAQ

We are happy with all that has happened in Iraq, including the elections and the victory of the encompassing and Islamist alliance. . . . A stable Islamic rule is being established in this country.

—Ahmad Jannati, chairman of Iran's Guardian Council,
December 30, 2005[1]

We are handing the whole country [of Iraq] over to Iran without reason.

—Saudi Arabian foreign minister Saud al-Faisal to the
Council on Foreign Relations, September 20, 2005[2]

Since the launch of Operation Iraqi Freedom in 2003, the Iranian regime has provided massive funding, training, and weaponry to militant groups engaged in terrorist activities against coalition forces, has sponsored assassination squads, and has installed a vast espionage network in Iraq. It has bought political influence, manipulated elections, seized control of police departments, and recruited Iraqis into terrorist operations by bribing them with medical aid and other services. The regime has forced a radical Islamic ideology into Iraq's mosques and seminaries and enforced a repressive dress code on women through armed proxy militias.

The flow of Iranian infiltrators into Iraq grew to staggering proportions by the spring of 2006. Of the 1,972 foreigners arrested as insurgents between May 2005 and May 2006, 1,577, or 80 percent, were from Iran.[3] Zalmay Khalilzad, the U.S. ambassador to Iraq, stated in March 2006 that the Iranian military presence in Iraq covered a wide swath of illegal activity. "Our judgment is that training and supplying, direct or indirect, takes place," he said, "and that there is also provision of financial resources to people, to militias." Khalilzad added that Iran's presence included members of Iran's Islamic Revolutionary Guards Corps and Ministry of Intelligence.[4] The Iranian regime's operations escalated in 2006, according to the top U.S. commander in Iraq, Army General George W. Casey, Jr. In a blunt and explicit statement at a June 2006 Pentagon news conference, he reported, "Since January, we have seen an upsurge in their support, particularly to the Shia extremist groups. They are providing weapons, training and equipment to Shia insurgents, and that equipment is being used against us and Iraqis."[5]

As the number-two commander in chief of all of Iran's armed forces—behind only Ayatollah Ali Khamenei himself—Mahmoud Ahmadinejad holds carte blanche to all the resources that Iran can offer to battle democratization in Iraq, resources including a 40,000-man intelligence and terrorism force and the wealth of the entire Iranian regime. The mullahs have sent their notorious Qods Force into Iraq and built up pro-Iranian Shiite militias to form the most active and dangerous elements of the insurgency.[6] The success of the Tehran regime's military infiltration became apparent to coalition forces in Iraq when bearded, machine-gun-wielding Iranian extremists began patrolling the streets of southern Iraq, and when Iran-friendly Shiite political parties mysteriously gained power in Basra and Amara. These and many other examples of Tehran's deep meddling in Iraq filled intelligence reports following the launch of Operation Iraqi Freedom. In September 2004, the *New York Times* reported that U.S. Secretary of State Colin Powell, Secretary of Defense Donald Rumsfeld, and other administration officials were concerned about this powerful interference from Tehran; Powell stated that Iran was "providing support" for the insurgency, and Rumsfeld expressed "no doubt" that financial backing for the insurgency was coming from Iran.[7] Former president Akbar Hashemi Rafsanjani himself confirmed Iran's commitment to supporting the insurgency in November 2005, when he told a Tehran newspaper that Iran has an important and decisive role in shaping the future of Iraq. He described the United States' situation in Iraq as a quagmire and claimed that Iran can make the United States' problems in Iraq worse.[8]

MULLAHS AT THE DOORSTEP

A major factor behind the Iranian regime's ability to influence Iraq at many levels and to interfere in its political, religious, and economic structures is the physical proximity of Iran to the most populated regions of Iraq. The majority of Iraq's population lives near the 900-mile border with Iran, which generates a heavy movement of people: Shiite pilgrims visit the major shrine cities of each country, friends visit back and forth, businesspeople make trips, government agencies engage in trade. The governor of an eastern Iraqi province who needs to acquire more electricity for his cities will purchase that utility from a neighboring province in Iran long before he would consider buying it from a country on Iraq's western border, for example, because the infrastructure connecting his province to Iran is already there.

At the same time, this expansive 900-mile border makes it easy for people to smuggle arms, explosives, and all kinds of consumer goods. Iranian television and radio broadcasts (local, not satellite or cable) are picked up in neighboring Iraqi provinces, so Arabic programming from southern Iran or Kurdish broadcasts from the northwest provide the Iranian regime with ample opportunity to send propaganda into Iraq. And Iranian spies and terrorists can come and go between the countries under the cover of businesspeople and pilgrims. The Iran-Iraq border, filled with marshlands, wooded regions, mountain and valley areas, and other hiding places, is much more convenient for those who want to sneak into the country than are Iraq's borders with Jordan, Syria, or Saudi Arabia. When it comes to the most basic fact about Iran's ability to influence Iraq, it is location, location, location.

Turning to a map of Iraq, we see that the nearest Iraqi city to Jordan, for example, is Ar Rutbah, which lies about 70 miles away from the Jordanian border. I've been to Ar Rutbah, and it is no commercial center. Rather, it is a one-street town in the middle of the Iraqi desert. The entire western and southern border of Iraq that borders Syria, Jordan, and Saudi Arabia is desolate territory with barely a handful of villages dotting the region. Doing business with these countries would entail high transportation costs; dealing with Iran does not. The table on the following page shows that 11 of Iraq's top 20 most populous cities, which account for approximately 70 percent of Iraq's population, lie within 100 miles of the Iranian border. A majority of Iraq's small towns and villages also fall within the 100 miles.

Iran looms over its neighbor with a land area that is four times as large and a population that is approximately three times as large. The physical relationship between the two countries is an intimidating one for Iraq, and Iraq's geographic vulnerability to Iran can be compared to the situation between Syria and Lebanon. Trapped between Syria and the Mediterranean Sea, Lebanon has been dominated by Syria for decades, led by prime ministers and parliamentarians who were puppets of the Syrian government.

Given this scenario, let's take a closer look at Iran's big-picture goal in Iraq.

The 20 Largest Iraqi Cities, Their Provinces, Their Populations,* and Their Approximate Distances from the Iranian Border

Iraqi city	Province	Population	Distance from border (miles)
Baghdad	Baghdad	5,605,000	100
Mosul	Ninawa	1,739,000	125
Basra	Basra	1,337,000	15
Irbil	Arbil	839,000	80
Kirkuk	Ta'mim	728,000	100
Sulaimaniya	Sulaimaniya	643,000	35
Najaf	Najaf	563,000	220
Karbala	Karbala	549,000	195
Nassiriya	Dhi-Qar	535,000	90
Hilla	Babil	524,000	195
Ramadi	Anbar	423,000	175
Diwaniya	Qadisiya	421,000	175
Kut	Wasit	381,000	80
Amara	Maysan	340,000	45
Baquba	Diyala	280,000	60
Fallujah	Anbar	256,000	150
Samarra	Salah ad-Din	201,000	100
Alzubar	Basra	168,000	25
Tallafar	Nineveh	155,000	170
Samawah	Muthanná	124,000	225

*Based on census figures from 2002, Utrecht University Library (www.library.uu.nl/wesp/populstat/Asia/iraqt.htm)

IRAN'S GOALS FOR IRAQ

The Islamic Republic of Iran's number-one foreign policy agenda is, and always has been, exporting its extremist brand of Islamic rule to the rest of the Middle East and the world. Iraq, given its Shiite-majority population, important Shiite shrines, and long border with Iran, has been the most advantageous starting point for achieving this goal. Far from being simply a theory or a sensationalized viewpoint, the mullahs' global ambitions are a fact written into Iran's constitution. Article 11 spells out Iran's "duty" to create a political "unity" of Muslims throughout the world (italics mine):

> In accordance with the sacred verse of the Quran ["This your community is a single community, and I am your Lord, so worship Me" (21:92)] . . . the government of the Islamic Republic of Iran . . . *must constantly strive to bring about the political, economic, and cultural unity of the Islamic world.*

This global mission was founded on Khomeini's personal interpretation of Islam and his vision of political power based on fundamentalist extremism. The global nature of Khomeini's vision is outlined in a series of newspaper editorials written in 1988 by a senior Iranian cleric, under orders of Khomeini, who states that the *vali*'s rule extends over "all that exists." This guardianship "applies to the entire world and all that exists in it," he wrote, "whether earthbound or flying creatures, inanimate objects, plants, animals, and anything in any way related to collective or individual human life, all human affairs, belongings, or assets."[9]

With global dominance at the heart of the agenda in Tehran, it came as no surprise that Khomeini's successor, Khamenei, and his mullahs greeted the 2003 Iraqi invasion as a golden opportunity to step in and remake Iraq in their own image. "If Iran and Iraq become united," said Iranian Expediency Council chairman Ali Akbar Hashemi Rafsanjani in June 2006, "the enemies will not be able to force anything against Islam in the region."[10]

Iraq had been threatened by Iran's religious extremism in the past— Khomeini's efforts to incite the Shiite majority in Iraq to overthrow Saddam Hussein's secular government was one of the issues that triggered Saddam's invasion of Iran in September 1980. In a series of radio addresses from Tehran in early 1980, for example, Khomeini made direct appeals to the Iraqi people to oust Saddam, whom he called the "puppet of Satan," and to "topple this non-Islamic party in Iraq."[11] The chief judge of the Islamic Revolutionary Court, Sadeq Khalkhali, minced no words in explaining Iran's true intentions for Iraq: "We have taken the path of true Islam and our aim in defeating Saddam Hussein lies in the fact that we consider him the main obstacle to the advance of Islam in the region."[12]

An important lesson from Iran's history clarifies the crucial differences between Iraqi Shiism and that of Iran—differences that have been largely overlooked by the West. When the Iranian regime made a big push to incite Iraqi Shiites to overthrow Saddam Hussein in 1991, it failed completely. This failure was not because of a lack of operatives or materials or strategy, but because of the very nature of Iraqi Shiism. Unlike Iran's ruling Shiite clerics, who control everything from politics to religion to the price of oil, Iraqi Shiite clerics have never been tied to the society at large. In modern Iraq, leaders of the Shiite religious community did not connect with the business and merchant classes, did not receive any significant financial backing, and did not enjoy a major popular following. In Iran, however, the state is run by the Shiite clerics, and rich bequests and *bonyads* (foundations) give the religious establishment tremendous resources.[13]

Another crucial difference between Shiism in the two countries is the role of preaching: Shiism in Iraq never connected to the masses because preaching was not part of the clergy's academic style; Friday sermons as a major political vehicle to mobilize the population, for example, are a purely Iranian-regime twist on Islamic tradition. In addition, Saddam Hussein's secular government curtailed what influence the senior Shiite clerics had in the holy cities of Karbala and Najaf, further inhibiting religious influence in Iraqi life. As a result, "Sunni governments in Iraq . . . managed to isolate Shi'i Islam and establish clearer boundaries between religion and state," writes Brandeis University professor of Shiism Yitzhak Nakkash.[14]

With virtually no political or social influence, Iraqi Shiite religious leaders could not muster revolutionary zeal among the majority Shiite population in Iraq in 1991. The Iranian regime dropped the mission and waited for the next opportunity to topple Saddam and bring the Islamic revolution to Iraq. It found this opportunity 12 years later when the United States invaded Iraq and Saddam's forces fled. Suddenly Saddam, his government, and his army were out of Baghdad, and the doors to Iraq were wide open. With this new access, the Iranian regime could work from the ground up to build Tehran-friendly relationships with ordinary Iraqis, clerics, local government officials, political parties, businesspeople—everyone. The mullahs in Iran knew very well that Iraq's Shiite religious establishment did not have influence or power, but they also knew that they could change that. That is what an Islamic regime's special forces are for.

After the Iran-Iraq War, two events opened even greater opportunities for Iran to try to defeat secular governments in the Middle East and export its brand of Islamic radicalism. First, the collapse of Communist governments in eastern Europe and the breakup of the Soviet Union created a political and ideological vacuum in which newly autonomous nations looked for an alternative system. The Muslim states in the southern region of the former Soviet Union were particularly vulnerable to the Islamic fundamentalists' message, which claimed to be able to solve the problems of poverty, corruption, and immorality. Muslims who were opposed to western "decadence" and Arab corruption were easy prey for the Iranian regime, which told them that Islamic fundamentalism would save them, bring them back to their moral and religious values, and create a strong nationalistic identity based on their own religion and culture.

The second event of the early 1990s that broke new ground for radical Islam was Saddam Hussein's defeat in Kuwait, which took the air out of Arab nationalism. In the 1980s, Saddam had become a symbol of this movement through his confrontation with Khomeini and the mullahs in Iran; his defeat in Operation Desert Storm deflated that symbolic identity. This created another ideological vacuum and more fertile ground for Islamic extremism.

The mullahs in Tehran are committed to claiming Iraq as Tehran's first stepping stone to the expansion of Islamic rule beyond Iran's borders. The mullahs' global Islamic vision depends on it, which explains why they have invested so heavily in personnel, intelligence, training, and financial support. As British prime minister Tony Blair reflected, "Why does Iran meddle so furiously in the stability of Iraq? The answer is that the reactionary elements know the importance of victory or defeat in Iraq."[15]

KNOW YOUR ENEMY: LESSONS LEARNED FROM THE IRAN-IRAQ WAR

Iran's goal of establishing Islamic rule in Iraq *at any cost* was made clear during the Iran-Iraq War of 1980–1988. Khomeini's ironfisted policy of keeping up the fight solely to prove his commitment to this goal revealed that the regime is dedicated to its self-proclaimed duty to achieve global rule more than to its duty toward Iran and its citizens.

Stoked by Khomeini's declaration that the war was a spiritual battle against the infidel rather than a political war over territory, the Islamic Revolutionary Guards Corps (IRGC), also known as the Pasdaran, managed to recruit thousands into their ranks. Khomeini framed the war as a battleground for Islam itself. Four weeks into the war, Khomeini said, "It is not a question of a fight between one government and another; it is a question of an invasion by an Iraqi non-Muslim Baathist against an Islamic country, and this is a rebellion of blasphemy against Islam."[16]

This approach worked in the first two years of the war because Iran was an occupied country—Iranians were united in their desire to push the Iraqi army out of their homeland. From the time that Saddam attacked until June 1982, when Iran turned the war around by reclaiming the cities of Khorramshahr and Abadan, there was an element of nationalism among the Iranian people. For instance, during this period even the Iranian resistance, the Mujahedin-e Khalq (MEK), sent its members and supporters to fight against the occupying army in the southern fronts, where a number of them were killed and dozens were captured by Iraqi forces.

Iraqi forces finally retreated that summer of 1982, and Iraq declared its readiness to reach a negotiated settlement of the conflict. But instead of ending the war, Khomeini ignited a new offensive strategy and ushered in the second phase of the war. The offensive phase expanded one of the most gruesome operations of the Iranian military—recruiting boys under age 18 (many as young as 12), older men, and women into a new Islamic Revolutionary Guards Corps unit called the Vahid-e Bassij-e Mustazafin (Unit of Mobilizations of the Deprived). The Bassij fighters were identified by the imitation brass key that hung from their necks, reminding them that their martyrdom would be their entry into heaven. With clerics urging them on, the boys locked arms to form lines of up to 1,000 fighters each, creating a human wave to walk over and clear minefields so that Pasdaran and armored units could follow.

With this new offensive phase, the Iranian regime devoted all its resources to the battlefronts, draining the country's coffers and effectively throwing Iran into the huge inferno of war. The offensives succeeded in capturing some small territory in Iraq's Kurdish region and Al Faw in the south, but the Karbala campaigns of 1986 and 1987 were crucial failures that resulted in huge numbers of casualties and further weakened national support for the war. The final straw came with Karbala V, in which Iran tried once again to capture the Iraqi city of Basra. Up to 70,000 Iranian soldiers were slaughtered in that one campaign alone.[17]

The horrendous failure of the Karbala offensives that started in 1986 set off a third phase of the war that was highlighted by two major developments: (1) growing resentment about the legitimacy of continuing the war, which as a result of the direct involvement of Iran's main opposition had reached new heights, and (2) a weakened and demoralized Iranian military. The public resentment was fueled by many factors, including a controversy over the entire idea of launching the offensive phase of the war. Confronted with hundreds of thousands of deaths at the front and missile-attack devastation during the so-called War on the Cities, Iranians questioned Khomeini's insistence on pursuing an offensive strategy. Some clerics made the argument that Islam permitted only military self-defense, not offense, and that jihad, or holy war, could not be declared during the absence of the twelfth imam, who has sole authority over such decisions.[18] Resentment over the war among ordinary Iranians erupted in a demonstration on the streets of Tehran in April 1985, which was followed by demonstrations in other cities. The regime stamped these out with beatings and arrests, but opposition to the war seethed in silence. In 1987 people again marched in protest through the streets of Tehran, and a senior cleric from Mashhad, Grand Ayatollah Qomi, dared to contradict Khomeini by announcing that the regime's promise that those who died in the war would go to heaven was not true.[19] By this time, parents were refusing to offer up their children to the Bassij, despite years of messages from the regime that martyrdom was the highest cause in life for true followers of Islam.

Turning against Khomeini's central message reflected the low morale of those suffering from unemployment, food and housing shortages, missile attacks, a constant stream of dead bodies coming back from the front, and overall exhaustion from seven years of war. Iranians had also been shocked to learn in 1986 that the supreme leader had actually struck a deal with the United States, "the Great Satan," to obtain weapons in exchange for helping free American hostages in

Lebanon. Not only had Khomeini slaughtered their youth in the name of a fake religious ideal, he had betrayed the revolution by cooperating with the "infidels."

After Islamic Revolutionary Guards Corps faced a major defeat in Karbala V, the operation proved to be the last major offensive that the regime could muster during the eight-year war. In addition, the morale among the IRGC and the Bassij was extremely low, and the regime was unable to replace its aging and damaged military equipment. Beneath all this lay Iran's crumbling economic infrastructure.

It was during this third phase—filled with public dissent and a disintegrating Iranian military—that the Mujahedin-e Khalq engaged in significant military offenses against the regime. The MEK, which had moved its leadership and forces from France to Iraq in June 1986, organized its own army in Iraq called the National Liberation Army (NLA) and launched offensives into Iran.[20] By the summer of 1988, the NLA had become a determining force and captured the Iranian border town of Mehran. What was significant about this operation was that an entire division was routed and the most elite armored division of the regime, the 16th Qazvin, surrendered to the NLA, with some of its soldiers actually joining forces with the NLA. In that operation, the NLA brought back the division's arms and machinery to its camps in Iraq to add to their own. This included hundreds of tanks, armored personnel carriers, and field guns totaling hundreds of millions of dollars worth of equipment. The NLA's victory was a crippling blow to the morale of the regime's military forces and to Tehran's mobilization effort. I accompanied an NBC television crew to Mehran just after the NLA launched its attack. By the time we arrived, NLA forces had captured the city, and they kept it for three days before drawing back to their bases in Iraq.

Only three months prior to capturing Mehran, the NLA had inflicted a heavy blow on the 77th Armored Division of the regular army, the Artesh. It was not unimaginable for the Mujahedin-e Khalq to liberate beyond a border town into a provincial capital and farther. In the end, Khomeini was forced to accept the United Nations' cease-fire, Resolution 598, in large part because of the military advances of the MEK into Iran from camps based inside Iraq. The United Nations Security Council had drafted the resolution in 1987, but Khomeini rejected it, saying that the war would continue until the last house was left standing in Iran. He was forced to throw in the towel, however, after the major military losses to the MEK; nothing else could stop the tide that had already turned against the mullahs. The *New York Times* reported in August 1988 that in addition to the Iraqi Army's success, it was a series of military successes by the "Mujahedeen forces that analysts say swung the tide of the gulf war."[21] Khomeini accepted Resolution 598 in 1988 while stating that his decision to end the war

without a military victory was "more deadly than taking poison."[22] A grim record
of destruction lay at his feet: War damages totaled $1 trillion, industry was devas-
tated, every Iranian "became 50 percent poorer during the war," and one million
Iranians were killed and an equal number wounded.[23]

Some Iran observers contend that the Mujahedin-e Khalq popularity in Iran
has suffered as a result of its presence in Iraq, a country that the Iranian regime
fought for eight years.[24] According to a "U.S. official with long experience in the
region" quoted in the *Christian Science Monitor* in July 1988, the largest handicap
the Mojahedin faces "is that it has had to base its operations in Iraq since being
expelled from France in 1986." Yet, he quickly adds, "If the Mojahedin is hated
for this in Iran, 'why does it continue to attract large numbers of Iranian volun-
teers to its army?'"[25] The war was already unpopular with the Iranians in the last
stages, as the regime had major problems with mobilization and was unable to
launch any major offensives since 1986. Ali Akbar Hashemi Rafsanjani, who ran
the war operation on behalf of the supreme leader, blamed Khomeini for the decision to continue the conflict after 1982, when the Iraqis were pushed out of the
Iranian territories. Rafsanjani said, "After the Liberation of [the southern port
city of] Khorramshahr, I was no longer responsible for the war. I was Imam
Khomeini's representative in the Supreme Defense Council, but Imam did not
allow anyone to discuss with him whether to stop the war or to agree to a cease-
fire."[26] The MEK, which had fought against Iraq when it invaded Iran in September 1980, had called for peace and signed a peace agreement with Iraq in
1983, calling the continuation of the war as illegitimate. On a number of occasions, the MEK had managed to get the Iraqi government to halt its air raids on
Iranian cities.[27] As a result of this high level of frustration with the regime and its
continuation of the war, following the July 1988 incursion into the Iranian territory by the MEK, Iranian residents welcomed the group. In 1988, for example,
the *Financial Times* reported that Tehran officials arrested and executed people in
one western Iranian town for cooperating with the MEK, stating, "in particular
many people are said to have been killed in the small town of Kerend, halfway between Kermanshah and the Iraqi frontier. This is the one place where the people
are known to have welcomed the Mujahedin."[28] During the same period a
Philadelphia Inquirer article stated, "Iran said that seven people were hanged in
the western city of Bakhtaran (Kermanshah) on Monday for collaborating with
the National Liberation Army [MEK]."[29]

Khomeini exacted a very high price from the Iranian people in using the war
to consolidate his power and rally the country behind his rhetoric of defending
Islam and the revolution. The chilling fact is that the end of the war did not mean
the end of the regime's plans for Iraq. Instead, since 1988, Tehran has been work-

ing on what can be called an "Iraqi Plan B" to export the Islamic revolution to its neighbor through a complex program of infiltration at every level.

A central part of this plan is the IRGC, which came into its own during the war, growing from 10,000 troops in 1980 to 450,000 in 1987.[30] With the Artesh nearly decimated after the revolution began, the regime spent the bulk of its efforts building up the IRGC for the war. Born with the revolution, the IRGC was made up of commanders and personnel very closely aligned with the mullahs, and therefore served as the ultimate ideological war machine. After the Iran-Iraq War, Iran created the Qods Force, whose sole mission was and is both to export the Islamic revolution beyond Iran's borders through terrorist acts against Iran's opposition and also to build up the Iranian ideology in other nations. Without the war, the Qods Force would probably not exist today. And without the Qods Force, coalition forces in Iraq would enjoy much more success in stabilizing the country.

The central headquarters of the Qods Force is at the Ramezan garrison in western Iran, and Iraqi operations are conducted out of the following four headquarters in Iraq: Nasr Headquarters in the city of Naqadeh, which coordinates operations in Iraq's Kurdistan region; Raad Headquarters in Marivan, where operatives work with the radical Kurdish Islamic group Ansar al-Islam; Zafar Headquarters in Kermanshah, which directs operations in this border area; and Fajr Headquarters in Ahwaz, which because of its location in heavily Shiite-populated southern Iraq is the Qods Force's most active headquarters.

If Iran's intentions in Iraq during the Iran-Iraq War were solely to oust the invader and perhaps gain more territory, then the official U.N. cease-fire that ended the war would have left Iran open to a new relationship with Iraq. But Iran consistently refused Saddam Hussein's invitations to enter into a peace agreement after the cease-fire. During Operation Desert Storm in 1991, for example, Iraq made significant offers in order to secure an official peace with Iran, but Tehran refused to sign. The reason is simple: The Iranian regime has no desire to live in peace with Iraq. Its prime agenda is to export the Iranian revolution, and signing a peace agreement would forfeit any chance of implementing that plan in Iraq. Tehran knows that if it cannot export Islamic rule to its most vulnerable neighbor—the most fertile ground for establishing an Islamic republic—it has little chance of fulfilling its global vision.

AN OLD OBJECTIVE FINDS A NEW WAR

By prolonging the Iran-Iraq War, Khomeini sacrificed millions of Iranians, who were either killed or wounded, as well as the nation's economy. He prolonged the war solely to export his Islamic revolution to Iraq. Since then, the regime has not wavered from this goal but has moved on to a new tactic: destabilizing Iraq from within. Since the end of the Iran-Iraq War, the regime in Iran has devoted vast resources to making deep inroads in Iraq through seven spheres of influence: economic, political, religious, social, propagandistic, intelligence gathering, and terrorist. The intervention began early and was quite extensive. "We have seen a rather steady increase in Iranian activity here, which is troubling," Paul Bremer said in the interview with ABC News on May 28, 2003, less than two months after the fall of Baghdad. "What you see at the most benign end of it is Iranian efforts to sort of repeat the formula which was used by Hizbollah in Lebanon . . . [which] is to send in people who are effectively guerrillas and have them get in the country and try to set up social services and decide that these social services are their ticket to popularity,"[31] Bremer warned.

The first Iraqi interim government, led by Prime Minister Ayad Allawi, had no tolerance for Iranian meddling. A number of the top ministers in Allawi's cabinet were moderate Muslims who, like many of the nation's Shiites, were opposed to the very idea of religious political parties. About two weeks before the January 2005 elections, for example, Iraqi defense minister Hazem al-Shaalan publicly accused Iran of investing a fortune in interfering in his country, claiming that Iran had "spent more than $1 billion on meddling in the internal affairs of Iraq."[32] Allawi's group also had heavy financial backing from the United States and plenty of media coverage, with Allawi appearing frequently on national television as the levelheaded guiding force of the newly democratic nation. Why, then, did Allawi's list of candidates for the National Assembly win a mere 14 percent of the vote in the January 2005 elections, virtually wiped out by the fundamentalist Shiite parties? The answer is that neither the Americans, its coalition partners, nor the interim government, were in control of the election process. The mullahs in Iran ran that show for months as a result of their deep penetration into Iraq's political and social fabric. The mullahs' experience from the 1979 revolution in Iran came in handy. No coalition or political party could compete with the network that Iran had built in Iraq, nor with the enormous portion of the national budget that Iran had devoted to its interference. Tehran had infiltrated Iraq so completely by January 2005 that the new Iraqi government and the coalition forces that supported it were in no position to challenge the Iranians.

Iran did everything possible to empower the pro-Iran Shiite parties in Iraq throughout 2005 in order to win an absolute majority in the December 15 parliamentary elections. Tehran knew that if it succeeded it would single-handedly form its own Shiite government. The results were a close call, but the mullahs lost by a slim margin—the Shia-led United Iraqi Alliance won 128 of the 275 seats, 10 short of an outright majority. This was a major blow to Tehran's goal of dominating Iraq.

The mullahs exploited the outcome, however, by calling it a solid move toward establishing Islamic rule in Iraq, the starting point from which the regime would spread this rule throughout the Middle East and the world. Guardian Council chairman Ayatollah Ahmad Jannati celebrated the Iraqi election "victory" as proof of "the emergence of Islam and the establishment of Islamic rule all over the world."[33] An editorial in an Iranian hard-line newspaper described the outcome as "the creation of the first Islamic state in the Arab world," and Iranian interior minister Mostafa Pour-Mohammadi called the results "an echo of the revolution and the messages of Imam Khomeini."[34]

Coalition intelligence pointed to Tehran's role in building up Iraq's Shiite parties, and one day after the election, General George Casey, commander of the Multi-National Force-Iraq, predicted that Tehran would continue "to influence the formation of this government."[35] The same day, former Iranian president Ali Akbar Hashemi Rafsanjani confirmed U.S. accusations of Iran's meddling in the Iraqi elections during a Friday prayer sermon in Tehran. "We share this victory with the Iraqi nation," he said, "since we paid a heavy price to lay the groundwork for the elections."[36]

TWO SIDES OF ECONOMIC INFLUENCE IN IRAQ

Iran's domineering position vis-à-vis its neighbor to the west allows it to exploit trade and business partnerships as a means to gain political influence. In late 2005, I had a conversation in Washington, D.C., with Dr. Abdullah Rashid Al-Jabouri, who had served as the governor of Diyala Province in eastern Iraq from April 2003 to March 2005. The Diyala Province is one of Iraq's biggest, home to about 1.5 million inhabitants, and Dr. Jabouri told me that the province ran low on electricity shortly after the fall of Baghdad. To remedy this problem, he arranged a meeting to purchase electricity from officials in Iran's Kermanshah Province, just over the border.

The governor and his aides had a single purpose for their trip—making a business deal—which they soon accomplished after meeting with Iranian officials and technical personnel. But the Iranians expanded the talks to discuss a variety of other services they could provide to their neighbor. "Your province is in trouble," they told Jabouri. "We can fix your roads, your hospitals, your medical systems." They came up with all kinds of suggestions. Jabouri responded that it sounded good, but what did they want in return? Then the Iranian officials made their purpose clear: political influence—basically through buying Dr. Jabouri. Their primary demand was for the governor to turn over the Mujahedin-e Khalq, which was headquartered at Camp Ashraf in the Diyala Province. Jabouri realized what they were asking for and wanted no part of it. He countered the intimidation and bribes with a simple "no," explaining that he was interested in purchasing just electricity and nothing more. The officials kept pushing, however, and despite their threats, Jabouri worked tirelessly over the next two years to improve border control and purge Diyala's government offices of agents working for Iran. Iran reacted to this with deadly force, including 14 assassination attempts on Jabouri. Jabouri survived them all, but a number of his relatives and bodyguards were killed. In addition, his brother was kidnapped and murdered in September 2006.

Utilities such as electric power are among the most common subjects of trade agreements between Iran and Iraq in the 2000s. In July 2005, Iraq purchased 200,000 tons of flour from Iran, which confirmed for many that Iran had found new allies in Iraq. An Arab businessman familiar with the deal told Reuters that no one had anticipated such a large transaction. "The Iran flour deal came out of the blue, demonstrating the extent of Iran's postwar influence in Iraq, with Tehran not short of friends in the new government," he said.[37]

Iran's move toward closer economic ties with Iraq became official during Iraqi prime minister Ibrahim Jaafari's visit to Tehran in July 2005. At that three-day meeting, the two countries established five cooperative councils, including one on trade. Jaafari told the press that Iraq needed the help of its "Iranian brothers" in order to rebuild a free, new Iraq.[38] Coinciding with this meeting, Iran announced that it was also launching a joint oil project with Iraq that would include building an oil pipeline between the cities of Abadan in Iran and Basra in Iraq.

Jaafari also announced at that news conference that Iraq would receive approximately $1 billion from Iran for building schools, hospitals, and libraries, and that Iran and Iraq would work together to promote religious tourism to Iraq's holy cities of Najaf and Karbala.[39] Regime documents obtained by dissident sources in Iran reveal that approximately one year earlier, in June 2004, Khamenei had met with Sheik Mohamed Baqer Attar, a cleric from Qom commissioned to Najaf in Iraq after the fall of Saddam, to discuss a new strategy for spreading the regime's brand of fundamentalism in Iraq. That meeting resulted in an order from Khamenei to build Islamic libraries in all Iraqi cities and to reopen all the Islamic centers that were closed by Saddam. It would not be unreasonable to make the connection between this order and the new promises for building libraries announced in July 2005.

Evidence of increased economic cooperation at the regional level between Iran and Iraq came in September 2005, when an official agreement was reached between the chambers of commerce of Iran's Ilam and Iraq's Karbala provinces. This agreement stipulated that the organizations would work together to finalize the export of goods between the two provinces, oversee the finalization of trade agreements, and hold mutual trade, technical, and industrial exhibitions. An Iranian news agency article about this "Memorandum of Understanding" (MOU) also reported that "providing better services for tradesmen from both countries, and granting them the six-month and one-year visas are among the main issues focused upon in the MOU."[40]

As I noticed during a trip through Iraq years ago, the Iraqi marketplace is filled with Iranian products, and one Iraqi source commented on "the warm reception of Iran-made products in Iraq, particularly among the Shiite population," in a report about a bank merger that took place in late 2005. This merger brought together Iran's Bank Keshavarzi (Agriculture Bank) and Iraq's Regional Investment and Development Bank, a merger that would, according to the article, "play an effective role in expansion of economic relations between two neighboring countries."[41]

In addition to gaining influence through business deals and trade, Iran has used blatant negative tactics against Iraq's economy in order to undermine the overall stability of the country and open up more opportunities for influence. These actions have taken place at a very basic level, literally uprooting some of Iraq's infrastructure. Since the fall of Baghdad, Iranians have either encouraged or directly participated in stealing telephone and electrical poles, wires, lampposts, and other hardware from along the streets and highways of Iraq and taking them to Iran for sale. As a result, Iraq must purchase new materials and hire the labor to install these enormous communication and power systems. This calculated effort drains the infrastructure of Iraq and tends to make it more dependent on Iran.

Even more prevalent are the smuggling operations that bring Iranian goods into Iraq. Most of this activity occurs along the border between Iran and Iraq's Kurdish region in the north, far from the control of Baghdad. This part of the border is still filled with land mines left over from the Iran-Iraq War, and smuggling is a dangerous business for those who do not know the cleared pathways. Nonetheless, all kinds of products come through this route, including food, housewares, clothes, sandals, tools, counterfeit drugs, and Persian rugs. In any country, smuggling hurts local economies: Every item that is smuggled into Iraq from Iran cuts into the profits of a legitimate Iraqi business.

OIL SMUGGLING

The most damaging smuggling operations from Iraq to Iran are the petroleum and gasoline thefts conducted on the highways and waterways. These crimes are part of the rampant oil industry sabotage that is striking Iraq, a sabotage that is costing the country billions of dollars a year. As much as 30 percent of the gasoline that Iraq imports from other countries is stolen and resold by smugglers, which forces Iraqis to buy more of their gasoline from the expensive black market and impacts Iraq's overall economy.[42]

Iran is a major player in Iraq's gasoline and petroleum smuggling crisis. Operations uncovered by my sources in Iran show that gasoline smuggling into Iran occurs on a large scale. On February 25, 2006, for example, about 10 smuggled gasoline tanker trucks were traveling in the Shalamcheh border area in southeast Iraq toward Iran. They were stopped by the commander of the border guards' brigade, who called the governor of Shalamcheh (in Iran) and informed him that the trucks did not have the proper documentation. The governor instructed the commander to release them, but he refused until a fleet of cars from the governor's office pulled up to intimidate the border guards into allowing the trucks to pass through the control gate into Iran.

My sources also discovered a smuggling operation headquartered at a house in Abulkhasib in southeastern Iraq, where deals are set up for weapons to be smuggled into Iraq in return for petroleum smuggled into Iran. The person in charge is affiliated with the pro-Iranian Organization for Islamic Conduct, and the boats that carry the stolen materials back and forth sail through the passageway called the Alziady passage, between Faw and Sibeh islands. A person on the Supreme Council for Islamic Revolution in Iraq (SCIRI) payroll, who owns a small rowboat, is one of the figures involved in this smuggling operation.

Many of the smuggling operations involve the exchange of Iraqi petroleum for Iranian weapons or narcotics. The smugglers conduct their business in the fish markets and other shoreline businesses on the Shatt al-Arab, flooding Iraq with narcotics and bleeding it of its gas and oil supplies. Four main locations in the Abulkhasib region of Basra Province are used for these back-and-forth deals, and members of SCIRI and the al-Dawa party are involved in the operations. These primary locations are in the Yousefian area, located behind the former palace of Saddam Hussein; the Sabilat area, including a port where boats fill up with petroleum to cross into Iran; the Mahijran area, a kilometer-long agricultural swath where a cleric operates smuggling operations; and Abou Alfolos, where three parties—SCIRI, al-Dawa, and Muqtada Sadr's Mahdi Army—divide the passages among themselves. These agents regularly use the local uniformed police forces and their vehicles for smuggling. Two individual members of the pro-Iranian 15 Shaban Organization in Basra operate a petroleum-smuggling operation through the Sibeh passage, in which they exchange the Iraqi oil for Iranian narcotics.

The piracy on this crowded, small waterway includes shootouts between Iraqi coastal security forces and smugglers, the confiscation of large, floating water tanks carrying Iraqi petroleum into Iran, and the transfer of Iranian weapons and ammunition into Iraq to support the Iran-backed militias that are trying to derail the democratic process.

RELIGIOUS INFLUENCE

A top-secret intelligence report uncovered in July 2005 outlines some of Iran's broad strategies in Iraq, with a focus on exploiting religious sites, theological students, and clerics. According to an Iranian Foreign Ministry official who filed the report, investing money, manpower, and resources in Iraq is a priority for the regime because "Iraq is the first country with a 70 percent Shiite population where we can expand Islam." By this time, the regime had succeeded in bringing so many clerics and programs to Iraq's pilgrimage cities Karbala and Najaf that they "are regarded as Iranian provinces and there will be more influence and control in the future." This stunning report clarifies the underlying purpose of the Islamic Revolutionary Guards Corps' programs in Iraq and its concentration on exploiting the Shiite shrine cities of Karbala and Najaf. "The Islamic Republic has spent large sums of money on Iraq . . . because it knows that it will gain huge benefits and it will be through [this] expansion that the way will be opened for the Islamic Revolution," the official wrote. "Our radio and television played an important role in the Iraqi elections, electing [Prime Minister] Ibrahim Al-Jaafari and the parliamentary elections," he boasted. The memo also remarked on a surge in real estate transactions in the region: "Many Iranians are now investing in Najaf, Karbala, Kadhimieh and Samarra," it stated, through purchasing hotels, property, factories, and companies in order to create a "foothold in Iraq's economy." The strategy appeared to be safe from American interference: "The Americans cannot prevent two things; first, [visiting] the holy shrines and second, [our influence on] the economy." The report also revealed that the highest-ranking Qods Force commanders had taken up the cause of the Iraqi religious cities and were responsible for imposing their influence in the religious centers and the holy shrines. The report also noted that Iran paid the salaries and bonuses of political party officials in Baghdad and other Iraqi cities, and that these officials worked in close cooperation with Qods Force commanders.

The religious centers of Iraq provide fertile ground for Iran to spread its radical message and foment anti-Americanism, and I received more details about Iran's efforts to gain control of the spiritual heart of Iraq from my sources in the summer of 2005. For example, an Iranian cleric named Mohammad Mehdi Asefi, stationed in Najaf, provides scholarship grants and living expenses to seminary students, and plans were underway in July to expand seminaries and build new dormitories. An Iranian fundamentalist organization called the Ahl Al-Beit World Assembly (ABWA) began a reconstruction project in the area around the holy shrines in Karbala, and this group also interacts with the local populations of Najaf, Karbala, and Kadhamieh by offering medical treatment. As a result, this organization is helping expand the Iranian regime's social influence in this heavily Shiite region.

In addition, the Iranian regime distributes books, cassettes, and CDs containing material about its brand of radical Islam to mosques in Iraq. Through these free materials, the regime attempts to attract students and clerics to Iran's version of fundamentalist Islam. Some of the regime's tactics with Iraqi clerics are more overt, however. Clerics who agree to support the Iranian regime's agenda in Iraq are backed by Iranian money and armed forces that allow them to bully themselves into positions of power. A pro-Iranian Shiite cleric in Kut, for example, showed up at a mosque one day with 300 armed Iranians and a large supply of cash, declared himself mayor, and started to "make the rules" in his new corner of the city.[43]

The ultraconservative clerics' influence in southern Iraq also shows up on the streets and in the schools. For the first time, young Iraqis are forced to conform to social standards that have never been part of their society. In Basra, according to a *Time* magazine reporter, "militants frequently 'investigate' youths accused of un-Islamic behavior, such as couples holding hands or girls wearing make-up." By August 2005 it was common knowledge that the Iranians, not the local police or officials, ruled the streets and the political infrastructure. "From the beginning, the Islamic parties filled the void," an Iraqi police officer told *Time*. "They still hold the real power. The rank and file all belong to the parties. Everyone does. You can't do anything without them."[44]

Juliana Daoud Yusuf, the editor of the Basra newspaper *al-Manar*, told an American reporter in the summer of 2005 that Iran's influence was not something invented by the West to stir up trouble for Iran, but a reality. "We see Iran's interference in all kinds of affairs: the closing of nightclubs, the disappearance of liquor stores," she said. "They're taking advantage of the absence of government, and they're doing it in a very planned way." In the same article, a 24-year-old clerk in a Basra shop discussed the crackdown that Iran's religious zealots were making on "immoral" behavior: "In Baghdad, you can still drink a beer if you want," he said. "But here, you would be in big trouble if you were caught. I think they're going to start patrolling here just like the Iranian religious police."[45]

Cultivating the shrine cities in Iraq has also given Iran the colossal advantage of exploiting the porous border between the two countries. Posing as pilgrims, Iranians working for Iran's various aid agencies can come and go easily. Between the fall of Baghdad in April 2003 and September 2005, approximately three million pilgrims traveled from Iran to Iraq's holy shrines in Najaf and Karbala.

Iran's focus on the holy Shiite cities of Iraq comes as no surprise to those who remember Khomeini's description of the Iran-Iraq War as a divine blessing that gave Iran the chance to take the revolution to Iraq. His vision, still very alive within the regime today, was to "liberate Jerusalem via Karbala"—to create an Islamic Middle East with Iraq as the first stepping stone. All of the evidence about the Iranian regime's religious influence in Iraq has been a dramatic wake-up call to anyone who doubted Iran's deep-seated plans for Iraq. As Iraqi minister of state Kasim Daoud told the U.S. Department of Defense in January 2005, Islamist fundamentalists are "doing a very, very destructive role in our society."[46]

PUBLIC INFLUENCE THROUGH SOCIAL AID PROGRAMS

Detailed information has come to light about various aid associations that Iran has set up in Iraq as strategies for gaining a stronger foothold in the country and exporting the Islamic revolution. As an unnamed U.S. official told the *New York Times* in 2004, "Now that these [Iranian] folks are starting to provide services that should be provided by the Iraqi government, their purpose is to provide a political base to extend Iran's influence in Iraq."[47]

Setting up charitable organizations is one of Tehran's principal strategies for gaining influence in other nations. This strategy serves two purposes. First, it allows the regime to make itself appealing to the poorer sectors of the target society, which is followed up by using these same people to further its primary objective of installing Islamic rule. Second, the regime's terrorist and intelligence agencies use charitable organizations as covers to facilitate their presence in Iraq. Agents from these agencies appear in the guise of directors and managers of the institutions and recruit locals for their intelligence and terrorist network in Iraq.

After the fall of the former Iraqi government, the mullahs' regime immediately dispatched tens of thousands of salaried agents of the Qods Force to Iraq. As a next step, Tehran ordered all the groups and agencies affiliated with it to do their utmost to help the Qods Force establish a firm footing in Iraq. The charities, communications centers, Internet cafes, computer stores, and other businesses provided a legal cover for the work of the Qods Force. This took place in numerous cities in southern Iraq, as well as in Baghdad.

In a confidential memo of June 2004, the Iranian Ministry of Intelligence and Security (MOIS) reported that the Iranian regime spent $70 million per month funding the aid organizations coordinated by the IRGC's Qods Force in Iraq. Five million of this amount was designated specifically for the agents' use in influencing religious figures. This means that within one year of the fall of Baghdad, Iran was pouring $840 million per year into its charity schemes in Iraq.

Iran's statement of purpose for all the charity groups in Iraq declares that they must be mobilized to seek out and recruit the poor of Iraq. The well-funded, high-priority charity organizations that are fulfilling this call include the Red Crescent, the Imam Relief Committee, the Persian Green Relief Institute, the Kowthar Logistical Headquarters, and the Imam Mohammad Baqer Charitable Institute.

THE RED CRESCENT. This long-established Iranian aid organization, a rough equivalent of the Red Cross, has operated extensively in Iraq since the fall of Saddam's regime. Just one month after Baghdad fell, Iran's Supreme National Security Council issued a top-secret document that instructed the Red Crescent to act as a cover for the Qods Force in Iraq. Part of that April 19, 2003, document states: "The urgent needs of the Iraqi people will be determined by the Qods [Jerusalem] Force and through public announcement, to gather support by the Iranian nation for the people of Iraq." Red Crescent workers were responsible for collecting the people's contributions and sending them into Iraq, through coordination with the Qods Force. The Red Crescent was also enlisted to set up medical centers and hospitals in Iraq, using all the resources of Iran's Ministry of Health and Medical Education but always under the cover of the Red Crescent.

At face value it would appear that the regime was rushing to aid Iraqi victims of the war by mobilizing an agency to gather contributions and set up emergency medical units. That the operation is under the secret coordination of the Qods Force, however, shatters that humanitarian appearance. Every mission of the Qods Force is created specifically to support the regime's strategy for exporting the Islamic revolution to Iraq. Formed at the highest level and approved by Khamenei, the Red Crescent reveals how quickly the regime moved to take advantage of the chaos in the first weeks of the war. By setting up new facilities in Iraq, the regime dug in its heels more deeply and created new opportunities to infiltrate Iraq under the cover of a medical aid project. The original letter showing how the Red Crescent has been used in Iraq as a cover for the activities of the Qods Force can be found in the Appendix.

THE IMAM RELIEF COMMITTEE. This charity was founded on the order of Khomeini on March 5, 1979, in accordance with Khomeini's policy of exporting the Islamic revolution. Its programs in Iraq are created by a central council, head-quartered in Tehran, that answers directly to Ayatollah Khamenei.

The Relief Committee's declared objective is to realize the supreme goals of the Islamic Republic of Iran and the *velayat-e faqih* system by offering financial aid and services to the needy. As outlined in its constitution, however, the mission of this institution goes far beyond that merely superficial humanitarian agenda. Objectives of the Relief Committee include supporting Iranian intelligence operations in Iraq by recruiting and training personnel; conforming to Iran's supreme leader in all policies and programs; searching out, attracting, and providing support to the needy in Iran and foreign countries; and providing cultural and spiritual growth among supported individuals, especially teenagers and youth.

The underlying purpose of the Imam Relief Committee—to make inroads into Iraqi society and thereby forge Iran-friendly alliances—is also revealed by the fact that the Qods Force coordinates the organization. Any Iraqis hired to work for the Imam Relief Committee in their local area or to receive its services must be approved by officers at the Qods Force Ramezan garrison in western Iran, about 80 miles from the Iraqi border.

After the fall of Baghdad, Iran put a top man on the job to run the Imam Relief Committee in Iraq. In December 2003, the regime named Mehdi Eskandari, former director general of the Imam Relief Committee in Qom Province, as head of the Iraq program. His experience in dealing with the senior clerics in Qom made him a perfect choice for working with the Shiite clergy in Iraq. After receiving his new appointment, Eskandari immediately met with senior grand ayatollahs in Qom to formulate his agenda. He then traveled to Iraq to make his case to Iraqi clerics, religious scholars, and political authorities to win their support for launching Imam Relief Committee projects in their cities. The regime had chosen the right man: Within six months, Eskandari had opened offices in Karbala and Najaf and distributed relief packages through them. In the following 12 months the project expanded to include new offices in Kut, Basra, Nasseriya, and Sadr City, where the organization runs under the name of the Khomeini Institution. This branch tries to draw the Shiite environment of Sadr City toward the Iranian regime under the cover of giving financial aid to impoverished families and school supplies to students.

The committee's overall strategy in Iraq is to recruit local residents to work in the organization's offices, which not only provides the residents with jobs but puts an Iraqi face on the organization. By giving food, blankets, heating supplies, medicine, and other household goods to needy Iraqis, the committee wins their loyalty and support and, in many cases, convinces them to spy and collect information for the Iranian regime's intelligence-gathering networks in Iraq. Eskandari personally ingratiates himself among the people of Iraq in several ways, such as by paying for the weddings of more than 100 people in Karbala and Sadr City who have become friends of the Iranian regime.

Another key aspect of the committee is its ability to bring Iraqis to Iran and indoctrinate them into the fundamentalist ideology of the Iranian regime. Iraqis who sign up to work for the Relief Committee in Iraq are taken to Iran for one-month training courses. During these lengthy trips, the new recruits learn about the administrative policies of the committee and are exposed to Iran's brand of religious extremism through talks and visits to Shiite pilgrimage sites.

THE PERSIAN GREEN RELIEF INSTITUTE. This organization was created to develop alliances with Iraq's Ministry of Health by helping it procure medicine and medical equipment. The regime's goal was to infiltrate this ministry and establish contacts, and the Persian Green Relief Institute also studies Iraq's medical supply situation in order to be prepared to provide materials when crises occur in any region of the country.

Set up by an Islamic Revolutionary Guards Corps member named Haj Mehdi Haidari, the institute began providing medical services to needy people in Karbala on the Tassooah holy day (the ninth day of the holy month of Moharram, a day that marks the martyrdom of Hossein, the third Shiite imam) in February 2004. The agency sent 15 specialist physicians, general practitioners, and health care professionals, along with supplies and medicine, from Iran to Karbala, a city that was suffering heavy attacks in Operation Iraqi Freedom. In 2005, for example, members of the institute's personnel were kept very busy treating victims of a spate of bombings in Karbala. The institute is headquartered at the Kadhimieh Clinic, where the nonmedical staff includes Qods Force agents. While Iraqis come to the clinic for care and medicine at the modest price of 250 dinars (less than 25 U.S. cents) per visit, the Iranian regime obtains its own benefits. Members of the IRGC can reside in Iraq for months on end under the guise of working for this charity, and Iranian intelligence agents freely travel between Iran and Iraq under this pretext. The clinic serves both as a headquarters for the regime to transmit intelligence to and from Iran, primarily through a Qods Force computer kept in the clinic office, and also as an information-gathering center for the Iraqi cities of Kadhimieh, Sholeh, and Baghdad—which is very important to Tehran's overall intelligence operation in Iraq.

THE KOWTHAR LOGISTICAL HEADQUARTERS. This agency distributes food and supplies to Iraqis and, most important, serves as a command center for coordinating other Iranian charities in Iraq. As of 2005, Kowthar was led by IRGC brigadier general Mansour Haqbin, who reports directly to the commander in chief of the Qods Force, Qassem Soleimani. General Haqbin's staff also works to build relationships with Iraqi businesspeople and government authorities in order to open new businesses that operate as front companies for Qods Force agents. This allows the agents to pose as legitimate businessmen while carrying out intelligence operations in Iraq.

The volume of Iranian agents infiltrating Iraq under the guise of business owners did not go unnoticed in the press. A newspaper from Dubai, United Arab Emirates, reported in September 2005 that Iran was using an "army of merchants" to infiltrate Iraqi towns and cities in order to gather intelligence for Iran's Ministry of Intelligence and Security and to rile up political agitation.[48]

THE IMAM MOHAMMAD BAQER CHARITABLE INSTITUTE. Named after the fifth imam of Shiite Islam, this charity was founded by the Iranian regime in 1980 as a means to infiltrate both Afghanistan and Iraq. After the fall of Baghdad in 2003, the program in Iraq was stepped up specifically to provide financial and other forms of aid to Iraqi widows, orphans, and others impoverished by the war. In 2005 the charity continued to be led by the Iraqi cleric Mohammad Mehdi Asefi, a former leader of the Iran-backed al-Dawa political party in Iraq.

———•◦•——

Not all Iraqi officials fall prey to the Iranian regime's attempts to infiltrate their communities, of course. In early 2005, the governor of the Iraqi province of Wassit, which borders Iran, spoke out in the press and accused Tehran of meddling in Iraqi affairs, disrupting the peace, and creating instability and havoc in his province. "The Iranian ambassador in Baghdad came to meet me and called for friendly relations," he told a reporter from the Baghdad newspaper *Al-Shahid Al-Mostaquel.* "I told him, the people of Al-Kut [Wassit's capital] are suffering from the actions of Iranian agents who are involved in acts of theft, narcotics distribution, smuggling, and assassination of personalities." The governor also had strong words about the charity agencies sprouting up in Iraq and explained how he reacted to the regime's invitation to set them up in his province: "The Iranian ambassador in Baghdad also asked for my permission for Iranian charities and foundations to be able to operate in our towns," he said, " but I strongly rejected such an idea since we have intelligence that these centers quickly turn into places for meddling and instigating trouble, and we have not had a good experience with such centers."[49]

Led by Iran's most elite military group, the IRGC's Qods Force, all of these charity organizations have given Iran solid connections to Iraq's social infrastructure.

Their putting a face of humanitarian aid on a vast intelligence-gathering network and terrorist operation reveals much about the nature of the Iranian regime in Tehran.

MEDIA INFLUENCE

As soon as coalition forces moved into Iraq in March 2003, Iran began building an extensive network of radio and television outlets in order to have a pervasive voice throughout the country. That very month, Iran launched a new 24-hour television news network called Al-Alam (The World), broadcast in Arabic—a clear indication that its purpose was not to better inform Iranians (who speak Farsi) but to reach Iraqis. And soon afterward, radio programs that had been broadcast from Iran began airing in Iraq, and Tehran began pouring money into existing television and radio stations to gain new programming.

By 2006, Iran had set up at least seven Arabic-language television stations broadcasting into Iraq, and in one well-reported instance, Iran's propaganda programming went too far and ignited a backlash of violent protest by Iraqis. On June 14, about 500 Iraqis attacked Iran's consulate in Basra in response to an Iranian television program that condemned the Iraqi Shiite Ayatollah Mahmoud al-Hassani, a well-known critic of Iran's meddling in Iraq. The protestors set fire to the consulate building, demanded an apology from the leadership in Tehran, and chanted slogans against the state-owned Iranian television station, al-Kawthar, that ran the broadcast.[50] In spite of this violent outrage against Iran's media presence in Iraq, however, the Iranian regime managed to make an agreement with the Iraqi government later that month that opened the door to setting up additional radio and television stations in Iraq. The two countries signed a memorandum of understanding in which they agreed to exchange radio and television programs and launch new Iranian media outlets in Iraq.[51]

My sources in Iran informed me in August 2006 that television and radio stations set up by Islamic political parties in Iraq such as the Supreme Council for the Islamic Revolution in Iraq (SCIRI) and Al-Daawa are also financed directly by Iran. Funds from the military unit's budget provide the stations with technical hardware, production support, and training, which the Iraqi employees receive at the National Iranian Television and Radio headquarters in Tehran. Networks receiving this support include the Afaq and Baladi satellite TV stations, both run by the Al-Daawa political party, and Al Furat TV, a SCIRI media outlet. The Iranian regime controls the programming at these stations, and at least one station director travels frequently to Tehran. According to my sources, he often travels to Iran to meet with authorities and the Qods Force on strategies for implementing the regime's policies through programming in Iraq.

On the print-media front, the regime set out to bribe Iraqi journalists into writing pro-Iranian columns, and in one of the boldest bribery schemes that I have ever encountered, the mullahs in Tehran orchestrated a lavish real estate giveaway for these writers in June 2004. According to my sources, the Iman Relief Institute distributed parcels of land to the media in an event attended by members of the journalists' guild and a number of other journalists. In exchange for parcels of land in the Karkh and Rasafi districts of Baghdad, a number of the Iraqi journalists traveled to Iran, where various regime officials met with and briefed them. They asked the journalists to write against the occupation and against the Mujahedin-e Khalq's presence and to portray the interim government as a "lackey" government.

Dozens of Iran-funded newspapers and magazines also sprouted up across Iraq after the launch of Operation Iraqi Freedom. These new publications include a biweekly called *Al-Shahid*, funded by the Iranian embassy in Iraq, which publishes articles critical of the MEK. The daily paper called *al-Dawa* is an organ of the Islamic al-Dawa Party, the Iran-backed political party that is fully financed by the IRGC's Qods Force. A new weekly called *Al-Musharaka* is published by the Islamic Assembly Organization, a group led by the Qods Force member Abu Mahdi Muhandis, who, according to my sources, is widely believed to be a terrorist in Iraq.

GATHERING INFORMATION: IRAN'S INTELLIGENCE NETWORK IN IRAQ

When Saddam Hussein's government fell, the Iranian regime created an unprecedented espionage-intelligence system in Iraq. Detailed reports of these activities provide hard data on a complex, comprehensive, and top-secret network.

In addition to sending Iranian operatives to enter Iraq posing as religious pilgrims, the Iranian regime has recruited an enormous network of agents within Iraq itself. As of July 2005 the number of active agents and accomplices in Iraq hired by the Qods Force exceeded 40,000. Many of them have infiltrated Iraq's police, government bodies, and security agencies. The Iranian regime has secretly purchased more than 3,000 houses, apartments, hotels, and shops across Iraq, many of which are used as covers for these operatives.

After hiring Iraqi agents, Iranian officials often bring them to training sessions in Qom or Mashhad under the guise of cultural or pilgrimage trips to Iran's holiest cities. The recruits are given the opportunity to worship at the shrine of the eighth imam in Mashhad, for example, while also attending seminars that involve the real agenda of the trip—learning how to participate in spy networks in Iraq. An intercepted report from one such Iraqi recruit—written after he had returned from a trip to Iran—stated, "We were about 35 people from Misan province that had gone for this visit. We were supposed to be there for 10 days but the visit lasted for 26 days." His group went on a pilgrimage visit to Mashhad, where the weekly program consisted of four days of instructional classes and three days of sightseeing and trips to other cities. He noted that all of the instructors were Iranian intelligence officers, and that the training included religious propaganda, as well as political and military affairs.

Long before the coalition forces invaded Iraq, the Iranian regime carried out espionage operations in Iraq that targeted its main opposition force, the Mujahedin-e Khalq. These operations, directed through Iran's Ministry of Intelligence and Security (MOIS), were expanded after Operation Iraqi Freedom to undermine the coalition and to open up more opportunities for exporting Islamic rule to Iraq. Iran's MOIS had already installed agents, intelligence-gathering protocols, and supply routes during its 10-year fight with the MEK in Iraq, so it had an enormous head start when the new opportunity of Operation Iraqi Freedom began. In the chaos of the invasion, the lack of Iraqi security forces burst the field for intelligence gathering wide open, and the agents of dozens of groups affiliated with the Qods Force stepped up their operations.

Shortly after the January 2005 Iraqi elections, *Newsweek* reported that some U.S. analysts believed that Iran had infiltrated Iraq at the grassroots power level, taking jobs in local governments and police forces. These analysts also had intelligence about Iran's strategy of planting operatives in various ministries such as intelligence and security, oil, public works, and finance. According to these U.S. officials, Iran's goal was nothing less than "taking over the government of Iraq."[52] Information gathered by my sources confirms this analysis. The Iranian regime's Foreign Ministry, for example, is another route for intelligence gathering in Iraq. Under the guise of diplomacy, this ministry establishes relations with political groups and invites them to Iran, making them easy bait for influence by the Qods Force and the MOIS. Both the Foreign Ministry and the MOIS are coordinated out of the Iranian regime's embassy in Baghdad, which has many facilities for hiring, commanding, controlling, and communicating with these recruits. In 2005, Iran's charge d'affaires in Iraq was Hassan Kazemi Qomi, believed to be a veteran and high-ranking member of the Qods Force with extensive experience in Lebanon and Afghanistan. He has since been promoted to the rank of ambassador.

According to my sources in Iran, for several years the Iranian regime has run two intelligence teams out of its Baghdad embassy. These operatives work independently of the affairs of the embassy, carrying out their covert missions and reporting back to their supervisors in Iran. Both teams expanded after the fall of Baghdad, and as of 2005 new members allegedly included Ebrahim Kashani (head of Consulate Affairs), who, along with other intelligence personnel, has held many meetings with Iraqi political party leaders and journalists in order to form a widespread intelligence-gathering network. The goal of much of this intelligence appears to be to track down the Iranian regime's enemies in Iraq and formulate terrorist attacks and assassinations against them. Other new operatives included Farhad Shahin, a Baghdad resident who was recruited by the MOIS to work with Fatemeh Qomi (wife of the Ambassador) in pressuring Iraqi journalists to be sympathetic to the Iranian regime.

Tehran also integrated spy networks into the Iran-Iraq trade bureaucracy, opening up an office in Darbandikhan in northern Iraq in August 2004. This office supposedly coordinates the import of commercial goods from northern Iran, but sources in Iran report that the office is an intelligence operation that uses its connections to Iraqi trade officials.

By December 2005, the Iranian intelligence network in Iraq had set up a series of secret detention centers where Iranian officers tortured Iraqis who were not sympathetic to the Iranian regime. An Iraqi general disclosed that Tahseer Nasr Lawandi, a senior Iranian intelligence officer known as "the Engineer," was in charge of these rogue interrogation centers, located in Baghdad and in the Shiite regions of southern Iraq. The six centers in Baghdad included two centers for women, where the detainees were tortured and raped.[53]

DEADLY INFLUENCE: TERRORIST OPS

Two days before Operation Iraqi Freedom, the Badr Corps proudly made its presence known with a large military parade in a Kurdish area of northern Iraq. This military wing of the Supreme Council for Islamic Revolution in Iraq (SCIRI), an Iran-backed Iraqi political party, invited the international press to witness the march of 1,500 Badr fighters carrying rifles, mortars, and multiple-rocket launchers as they paraded past the viewing dais. Badr commander Abdulaziz al-Hakim made Iran's goal of ousting Saddam's secular regime clear when he told his troops, "You are the basic factor in changing the situation in Iraq. Your responsibility is great, and your readiness must be great, to save all the Iraqis and rid them [of Saddam Hussein]. It is either victory or martyrdom."[54]

Even though the Badr Corps has been officially integrated into Iraq's security forces, it continues to carry out its own operations on behalf of the Iranian regime. Iraq's security apparatus is allied with the United States and other coalition forces, but the Badr Corps has participated in terrorist attacks ranging from assassinating enemies of the Iranian regime to launching missiles and bombing British troops in southern Iraq.[55] This fact was made clear in May 2005 when Basra's police chief described the overwhelming takeover of his police force by the Badr Corps and another militia group, Moqtada al-Sadr's Mahdi army. The police chief, General Hassan al-Sade, explained that Iraqi police forces were not strong enough to weed out members of these two groups. "The militias are the real power in Basra and they are made up of criminals and bad people," he said. "To defeat them I would need to use 75 percent of my force, but I can rely on only a quarter." Sade also confirmed that some of these renegade police officers were involved in assassinations, and that he was trying to filter them out by putting numbers on police cars so that they could be tracked.[56]

In July 2006 my sources in Iran uncovered facts about Iran's training and support of Iraqi militias, including the Mahdi fighters. In March of that year, 50 members of the Mahdi Army were sent from Basra to Iran for training in explosives, arms, and mines. The director of the training program, an Iranian mullah, told the company, "You are the future of Iraq and you must expel the occupying forces." The group returned to Iraq in two yellow Mercedes Benz buses and organized into a company called Ghassem. My sources also uncovered information about a 30-day training course for Mahdi soldiers that began in late May. The Iranian trainers, based in Baghdad, hid the military program under the guise of a series of religious lessons, but the attendees were trained in using hand grenades, RPG–7 rocket launchers, and bombs. In May 2006, another group of 27 Mahdi Army men left Al-Amareh for Iran for training and receiving special instructions from the Qods Force.

In August 2005, U.S. military officials in Baghdad said that two members of the Mujahedin-e Khalq living under American protection in Iraq had been kidnapped. The members, Hussein Pouyan and Mohammad Ali Zahedi, were grabbed while purchasing supplies in Baghdad's Karrada shopping district. Eyewitnesses reported that the two abducted members were bundled out of the back door of the Ministry of Interior later that day and placed into two white sport-utility vehicles with tinted windows. The Badr Corps was believed to be behind the abduction.[57]

The Iranian regime's terrorist operations running throughout southern Iraq are commanded from the Fajr headquarters in Ahwaz. The IRGC established the Fajr headquarters to conduct terrorist operations and attacks against British forces in this area.

The military leaders at Fajr set up intelligence groups to gather information in area cities including Amara and Basra. Each intelligence-gathering group consists of 20 members, and the members—commonly known as *Ettela'at*, the Persian word for "intelligence"—carry out their missions while dressed in Arab clothing in order to blend in with the locals.[58] Their individual duties range from standing watch near coalition force centers and posing as street peddlers to working as sidewalk vendors.

Uncovered Iranian intelligence reports revealed that a new group of committees was formed in June 2005 to more closely organize assassination operations against Iran's enemies in Iraq. That these committees worked out of an operation room in the Interior Ministry building in central Baghdad proved that the Qods Force had forged alliances with officials at high levels in the interim government. With these alliances, the assassins acquired Iraqi police uniforms and cars that enabled them to approach their victims easily, "arrest" them, and subsequently carry out their murders. Iranian intelligence documents reveal that in the first half of 2005, an assassination occurred once every four days, on average, in the Al-Azizieh district of Baghdad alone. Assassin squads of the Badr Corps carried out these murders.

A *Washington Times* report from January 2006 profiled the Badr Corps' recruitment of a young Baghdad man who boasted about his training when he returned home with an AK–47 strapped to his chest after a one-month trip to Iran. He had been recruited with several others at the large Husseiniya mosque in Baghdad, where Iranians invited them to visit a Shiite site in Iran. The group was actually taken to a camp, where they were lectured on the pro-Iranian Shiite fight for control of Iraq and were convinced to become warriors for the cause. Their militia training over the next four weeks included drills on how to patrol Iraq's streets, how to intimidate people, how to pull Iraqis out of their homes and execute them. "He was brainwashed," the recruit's uncle said; "he was very proud when he was talking to us."[59]

In June 2006, after coalition forces killed Abu Musab al-Zarqawi, the al-Qaeda leader in Iraq, American and Iraqi forces arrested many insurgents in the area north of Baghdad in which al-Zarqawi had been found. Among these insurgents from the town of Baquba in the Diyala Province were approximately 50 Iranians. These fighters were suspected of committing the murders and kidnappings that plagued the area, and provided further evidence that Iran was directly involved in the most violent insurgent operations in Iraq.[60] Although al-Zarqawi was expected to have sought hiding in the Sunni areas, he was killed in Hibhib, a small Shiite village about 40 miles north of Baghdad. The village is known to have many residents with close ties with Iran. The Iranian regime also targeted Iraqis in Diyala Province who worked at base camp of the main Iranian opposition group, the Mujahedin-e Khalq, in Ashraf City. In the early morning of May

29, 2006, a roadside bomb ripped through a bus carrying Iraqi workers on their way to Ashraf, killing 10 and wounding 15 others.[61]

The Badr forces, flush with weapons and cash from Tehran, infiltrated Iraqi security forces and prisons in droves. By December 2005, some 17,000 Badr fighters had made their way into Iraq's Interior Ministry alone, acting as police and prison interrogators. A former Iraq special forces commander reported in December 2005 that he had witnessed Farsi-speaking interrogators inflicting brutal tortures on Iraqi prisoners. All of these torturers were either Iranians or Iraqi Shiites who had lived in Iran in exile in order to escape Saddam Hussein's regime.[62] As accusations about the Iranian militia heated up, Badr's leader, Hadi al-Amari, made an irate outburst to the press about Badr funding compared to that of a rival Shiite political group. Al-Amari lashed out at secular Shiite political leader Ayad Allawi, who, he said, "receives money from America, from the CIA, but nobody talks about that. All they talk about is our funding from Iran." He angrily admitted, "We are funded by some Gulf countries and the Islamic Republic of Iran. We don't hide it."[63]

In Basra, the Iranian military and political presence is so pervasive that in May 2006 an aide from a government office approached a reporter, whom he mistook for an Iranian, and said, "Don't be afraid to speak Farsi in Basra. We are a branch of Iran." Iraq's paramilitary National Police includes large numbers of Iranian fighters who were integrated into the force by Iraqi interior minister Bayan Jabr. After Jabr assumed his post in January 2005, his Iranian militia recruits became what some called Jabr's "Shiite shock troops." A British officer, Major Rob Yuill, reported that Jabr had very close ties to the Badr Corps and that Jabr had ordered the Basra police chief to fill the National Police ranks with Badr fighters. Yuill saw a letter from Jabr to the police chief, in which Jabr requested the hiring or promoting of 50 Badr fighters to the force. As the Iranian presence became more and more entrenched in Basra, Yuill surmised that Jabr was Iran's point man for "creating a separate, almost Iranian state in Iraq." Coalition officials also believed that the provincial governor of Basra hired Iranian heavy police forces as hit men to eliminate his enemies and enforce his power by carrying out assassinations and extortion.[64]

As Iran's intelligence networks expanded from 2003 onward, they provided the Iranian regime with the increased information and personnel necessary to continue to expand violent operations in Iraq. In October 2005, Iraq's former interior minister Falah al-Naqib warned that not only was Iran's interference a reality, but it was growing stronger. "Without any doubt, Iran has a role in attacks against the Iraqi people," he said. "This country's infiltration has increased and this is occurring through its large-scale providing of capabilities for certain insurgent groups."[65]

The dark shadow of suicide missions that were so prevalent with the Bassij fighters during the Iran-Iraq War also looms over Iran's terrorist strategy in Iraq. In May 2004, an IRGC-coordinated group called the Headquarters for Tribute to the Martyrs of the Global Islamic Movement began canvassing Iranian cities to recruit suicide bombers for missions in Iraq and Palestine. Although there was no evidence that suicide attacks had yet occurred in Iraq when Radio Free Europe reported about the issue in October 2005, the recruiting efforts were backed by the Iranian regime's rhetoric about the values of martyrdom. In a May 1, 2002, speech, for example, Khamenei said, "It is the zenith of honor for a man, a young person, boy or girl, to be prepared to sacrifice his life in order to serve the interests of his nation and his religion. This is the zenith of courage and bravery . . . [m]artyrdom-seeking operations demonstrate the pinnacle of a nation's honor."[66]

The regime's recruitment of these suicide fighters included advertisements in Iranian newspapers. Complete with mail-in application coupon, the ads were entitled "Lovers of Martyrdom Garrison: Application for Membership Request." The ad featured a logo with the words "The Blood of God" imprinted on a globe (similar to the IRGC logo), and stated that suicide divisions would be formed in each province. Applicants were to fill in name, address, and phone number, and complete a line that read, "I request to join the suicide division of the province of _____."[67] As of July 2006, more than 55,000 Iranians had signed up.

It is difficult for anyone unfamiliar with the radical fundamentalists in Iran to comprehend how thoroughly they embrace the concept of martyrdom for accomplishing their malevolent objectives. The concept is so deeply entrenched in the extremist ideology that President Ahmadinejad was moved to express his devotion to it at a talk that he gave to Iranian artists and filmmakers in July 2005. During this discussion about art, Ahmadinejad called the martyrdom of Iranians who died in suicide human-wave attacks during the Iran-Iraq War "the most beautiful, the most divine and the most eternal of all arts."[68]

In August 2006, my sources in Iran provided information about several of the Iranian organizations established in southern Iraq to conduct espionage and terrorism and spread the regime's ideological influence. Many of these networks are headquartered in Basra, including a group that gathers intelligence on the British and Danish forces in that city. Most of the group's agents are young, armed with pistols, and outfitted in black clothes and headscarves. When working undercover, they disguise themselves as street vendors with push carts. The Islamic Dialogue Institute in Basra is involved in religious activities and promotes Iran's policies in Basra. The majority of this group's 60 employees are Iranian, and all are armed with folded-butt AK–47s, Uzi machine guns, and pistols. Another institute in Basra was established to spread the Iranian regime's propaganda about the virtues of establishing an Islamic republic in Iraq and federalism in the south, and is closely affiliated with the Basra branch of the Iraqi Al-Daawa Party. A Tehran-created group in Basra carries out assassinations and other operations against Sunnis and coalition forces in the south. An Islamic extremist group in the town of Zubeir, just south of Basra, is comprised of agents with criminal backgrounds who have been trained to conduct terrorist activities in Basra. The group takes control of the roads at night in most parts of Zubeir by setting up heavily armed check points, and my sources learned that in March 2006 a group representative made a trip to Iran to collect large sums of money from the Qods Force.

The Iranian regime's complete control of Shiite sections of southern Iraq reveals how successfully it has developed a vast terrorist network in Iraq. In a summer 2005 report to the Qods headquarters in Ahwaz, Iran, an official from the southern Iraq network confirmed Iran's hold on the entire Meissan Province:

> The situation in Al-Amareh is excellent. The provincial governor, the provincial council members and others are all supporters of the Iranian regime. In other words, Al-Amareh is all Iranian. As Ayad Allawi said while visiting the city, "I traveled to Al-Amareh and I did not understand anything, all the officials in that city were Iranians. The Hizb Al-Daweh, the SCIRI, the Iraqi Hezbollah and the Hezbollah Movement led by deputy governor Abu Maryam are all Iranians."

Coalition forces in Amara have come under steady attacks by Iranian terrorist groups. I have learned that a terrorist earns 150,000 Iraqi dinars (100 U.S. dollars) for each rocket fired at the British base. Some of the mortar-rocket night attacks on the base have been made from the Al-Hussein district cemetery, and 107-millimeter rockets used against the British forces were hidden in the home of a man in Awasheh. These rockets were regularly transferred to the fruit groves in the Al-Ziout district, where they were fired on the British troops.

The Iranian-backed terrorist groups in this region are also responsible for some of the roadside bomb attacks against coalition forces. On July 16, 2005, for example, three British soldiers on patrol in Land Rovers in Amara were killed by a roadside bomb, and four months later British Royal Marines major general James Dutton announced that the deadliest types of roadside bombs being used in Iraq were believed to be coming into the country from Iran.[69] These technically advanced bombs, called improvised explosive devices, or IEDs, were the leading cause of coalition casualties in Iraq to date, and Dutton told the press, "we believe the technology is coming across that [Iranian] border. We're not, regrettably, capturing these arms as they come across the border."[70] U.S. military officials reported that this type of bomb accounted for more than half of all U.S. casualties in Iraq, and explained that IEDs are usually placed on roadsides, either buried in the gravel or hidden in debris or animal carcasses. After they hide the devices, the attackers detonate them by means of remote controls.

Dutton made his report from Basra in southern Iraq, but roadside bombs were used in other parts of Iraq as well, including farther north, in the Diyala Province. Iranian attacks in this province bordering Iran are supported by an intelligence network that operates out of government offices and private businesses. According to a 2005 report for example, two such agents are members of the electricity board in Miqdadiyah, a town in which other operatives frequently meet at a veterinary clinic owned by a member of the al-Dawa party. This network carries out roadside bomb attacks against coalition forces and police and local government officials on the Khalis highway. In early July 2005, 150-millimeter cannon shells intended for use as roadside bombs were moved between two private houses by a terrorist. Two terrorists working out of the village of Hibhib planted 150-millimeter cannon shells as roadside bombs on the Khalis-Hibhib highway on July 7, 2005, but these shells were discovered by military forces before they were detonated. That same day, another group from the Diyala network fired 10 missiles at the U.S. Anaconda base, a base that has come to be called "Mortaritaville."

As the war dragged on, Iran increased both the deadliness and the number of IEDs it sent into Iraq. By the spring of 2006, coalition forces had identified specific welding designs and materials that traced the bombs back to one factory in Iran, which confirmed the suspicions that Tehran was behind the roadside bomb attacks. By supplying IEDs, the Iranian regime gave the insurgency its most effective weapon against coalition troops and gave Iran a means to attack U.S. troops without engaging in a direct confrontation. "I think it's very hard to escape the conclusion that, in all probability, the Iranian government is knowingly killing U.S. troops," said former White House counterterrorism official Richard Clarke in March 2006.

More details about Iran's bombs in Iraq surfaced in June 2006, when London's *Daily Telegraph* published a photograph of the Iran-designed "off-route mine," revealing for the first time the look of this precision-made, armor-penetrating weapon. The mine had been seized by British troops in Iraq earlier in the year and sent to a British forensic lab for analysis. The device pierces the armor of tanks and personnel carriers with an explosively formed projectile, or EFP, which allows the explosion to hit directly inside the vehicle and inflict death or horrifying injuries on the soldiers inside. This type of mine also completely destroys the British forces' armored Land Rovers and accounts for many British troop deaths. The off-route mine appeared in Iraq for the first time in May 2005, and military experts are convinced that the bombs are built in Iran and smuggled into Iraq to supply Iran-backed militias. The devices can be easily camouflaged to make them impossible to detect, and are ignited by infrared technology, command wire or remote control.[71]

Information I received from my sources associated with the Mujahedin-e Khalq inside Iran in July 2006 not only confirmed that Iran is building these devices, but identified for the first time the munitions factory complex in north Tehran where the EFPs are produced. Within the Ordnance Factories Complex, a subdivision of Iran's Defense Industries Organization, a company named Sattari specializes in making various types of anti-tank mines, including EFPs. A satellite photo of the Ordnance Factories Complex shows that the facility is accessed through an entrance gate off the Nobonyad Circle in the Nobonyad neighborhood of the Lavizan section of north Tehran. Sattari, along with Sayad Shirazi and Shiroodi, are the three industries producing munitions at the complex. The IRGC's Qods Force secretly orders EFPs from Sattari through a high-security protocol that includes specially designated codes. The Qods Force utilizes its network of agents within Iraq to deliver the bombs to Iran-backed militias and terrorist groups. In June 2006 the Sadr Movement smuggled several consignments of missiles and explosives into Iraq through the eastern and southern borders with Iran. According to my sources, in June 2006, a large consignment of missiles, including shoulder-operated AA missiles as well as sophisticated IEDs manufactured by the Defense Industries Organization, have been smuggled into Iraq through Shalamcheh and Badra border routes. The weapons have been mostly moved to Sadr City and provided to the Mahdi Army.

Military personnel and anti-Iranian clerics are not the only targets of Iran's attacks in Iraq. Two professors at the University of Basra who frequently spoke out about Iran's growing presence in Iraq were executed in the summer of 2005: Literature professor Ala Al-Rumi was murdered on the campus, and a short time later, history professor Jamhur Karim Chammas was kidnapped. Chammas's dead body, which bore signs of torture, was found four days later under a highway overpass.[72]

———— ◆ ————

From death squads to prison torture to IED attacks, Iran-backed militias became one of the biggest challenges to coalition forces and also the primary threat to Sunni insurgents in Iraq. In May 2006, Iraqi president Jalal Talabani explained that the entire dynamic of the insurgency had changed because the Sunnis "do not think that the Americans are the main enemy. They feel threatened by what they call the 'Iranian threat.'" Talebani warned that if Iran's interference in Iraq's internal affairs continues, "we'll support the opposition."[73]

Terrorist operations in Iraq became even more crucial to the Iranian regime after Iraq's December 2005 elections, when the Shiites failed to win an absolute majority in the Iraqi parliament. The lack of the fundamentalist Shiites' total control of the parliament created problems for the Tehran-friendly prime minister who was seeking a second term. Although the Shiite-led parliament nominated Shiite prime minister Ibrahim Al-Jaafari for a second term, the Sunnis and secular Shiites railed against his nomination and eventually rejected it. Tehran knew that its ally was on his way out, and this blow, on top of not winning an absolute Shiite majority in the parliament, drove it to decisive action. Tehran launched a new phase of escalated terrorism to make up for this loss of political clout and began planning an attack that almost catapulted Iraq into civil war.

HOLY SHRINE BOMBED

On the morning of February 22, 2006, a series of bombs exploded in the Askariya shrine in Samarra, which contains the tombs of two descendents of the Prophet Muhammad and is one of the holiest shrines in the Shiite world. One bomb shattered the mosque's gold dome, which had dominated the city's skyline for more than 100 years. Several details point to Tehran as the perpetrator of the attack, the first of which is the regime's implicit confession, in an editorial published three days after the bombing, that its militias in Iraq were responsible. The state-run Iranian newspaper *Shargh* described the operation and boasted about the bombers' expertise: "A group wearing Iraqi military uniforms entered the security office of the shrine, arrested the security personnel and started planting bombs in the shrine," the editorial stated. The agents used "sophisticated engineering and planning" in the mission, and the explosives were not the type available to "rag-tag insurgency groups" or even to Abu Musab al-Zarqawi forces, but only to the "committed players" who can "disrupt the entire Iraqi society." The writer stated that these forces had turned Iraq into "a revived prototype of Lebanon in the 1970s," and that their ability to inflame "the feelings of the Shiites" and provoke the Sunnis was an asset that "could be used to gain concessions from the Americans." This type of terrorist activity, the state-run editorial concluded, would be a crucial factor for blackmailing Americans.[74]

Iraqi authorities affirmed that the attack had been carefully planned and executed. After forensic experts had investigated the site, the minister of housing announced that "at least six locations of the shrine were detonated and at least two tons of explosives were used. About 50 to 60 percent of the blast was implosion, which required planning, engineering, moving explosives with vehicles and several hours of work on the site."[75]

There are several motives for why Tehran would want to carry out this attack. First, the bombing occurred two days after U.S. ambassador Zlamay Khalilzad condemned Iran's involvement in Iraq and warned Iraq's leaders that unless they rid the government of religious factions that are tied to militias, they would lose U.S. support.

Tens of thousands of Shiites took to the streets in Iraq's cities after the bombing, and some groups bombed and set fire to dozens of Sunni mosques and killed Sunni citizens in retaliation. The Iranian regime had the most to benefit from this outrage and chaos that bordered on civil war, and President Ahmadinejad immediately fanned the fire of violence by blaming the United States for the attack. "They invade the shrine and bomb because they oppose God and justice," he said on Iranian television, adding that the United States had earned the "anger of Muslim nations." By inflaming anti-American and anti-Sunni passions throughout Iraq, Ahmadinejad aimed to widen the rifts among the factions of Iraq's fragile democracy.

Finally, a significant detail pointing to Iran as the attacker is that the Iranian regime is the only entity with a history of bombing a Shiite holy site. No group had ever considered bombing a Shiite mosque until 1994, when Iran's Ministry of Intelligence and Security orchestrated an attack on the holy shrine of the eighth Shiite imam in Mashhad in order to harm the Mujahedin-e Khalq by framing it for the bombing.[76] That unprecedented 1994 attack proved that the mullahs in Iran were capable of blowing up one of the Shiite world's most revered sites in Iraq.

INFLUENCING AND DISRUPTING
THE POLITICAL PROCESS IN IRAQ

Iran's large-scale plan for the Middle East includes a laserlike focus on transforming Iraq. Politically, this plan includes Iranian support of political parties such as the well-funded Supreme Council for Islamic Revolution in Iraq (SCIRI). Western nations recognized Iran's involvement in SCIRI even before the start of Operation Iraqi Freedom, as evidenced by a United Press International article of 2002 that quoted a SCIRI adviser discussing that Iran supplied SCIRI with offices and funding for its soldiers in southern Iraq.[77] A United Press International article in January 2003 stated that SCIRI activities are coordinated by the Nasr command of Iran's Islamic Revolutionary Guards Corps, the "same organization [that] is responsible for funding and training Hezbollah and the Palestinian Islamic Jihad."[78] Days before the coalition forces launched Operation Iraqi Freedom in March 2003, U.S. officials described SCIRI as an extension of the IRGC and stated that it "would not welcome any role for them in the looming conflict."[79] Six months later, U.S. authorities continued to observe Iran's role in Iraq's political parties; according to a report in the *Washington Post*, "U.S. officials say . . . [that] over the past year, Iran has provided tens of millions of dollars and other material support to a range of Iraqi parties, including the Supreme Council for Islamic Revolution in Iraq, the Islamic Dawa Party and rebel cleric Moqtada Sadr's Mahdi Army."[80]

Iran's Supreme Leader Ayatollah Ali Khamenei held a meeting with SCIRI leader Abdul Aziz al-Hakim in June 2006, in which they discussed their mutual goal to see the U.S. "occupiers" depart from Iraq.[81] My sources in Iran uncovered that during that meeting, Khamenei personally presented Hakim with funds for SCIRI's military operations and also for Iraqi seminaries and their students. Khamenei and other Iranian leaders also discussed the aid that Iran gives to Hakim to support his additional role as the head of the United Iraqi Alliance (UIA) in the National Assembly. Prior to his 10-day trip to Tehran, according to a confidential report prepared by the Iranian embassy in Baghdad and sent to the Iranian FM in Tehran, Abdul Aziz Al-Hakim met with Muqtada Al-Sadr in Najaf. The two agreed on the unity of action between their forces against the U.S., the Multi-National Force and their supporters in Iraq.

The military arm of the SCIRI organization, the Badr Corps (also called the Ninth Badr Corps), was formed during the Iran-Iraq War when the Iranian regime recruited Iraqi Shiites who had fled Iraq and settled in Iran. As the muscle of the SCIRI party, Badr Corps members carry out the organization's missions—including election meddling, which played out on a massive scale preceding the January 30, 2005, Iraqi elections for the National Assembly. According to information received from sources in Iran, Tehran spent $80 million to buy Iraqi votes and to help campaign for pro-Iran candidates in the January elections. During that period, Iraqi defense minister Hazem al-Shaalan warned that over a million Iranians had entered the country to pose as Iraqis in the upcoming elections. He charged that Tehran was determined to "build an Islamic dictatorship and have turbaned clerics rule in Iraq."[82]

With deep pockets and a policy with no rules left unbroken, the Iranian regime heavily influenced campaign activities leading up to the January 30, 2005, elections in Iraq. One of its most effective tricks was plastering full-color photos of Grand Ayatollah Ali al-Sistani on posters advertising SCIRI-backed candidates, implying that he endorsed them. Sistani, the most senior Shia cleric in Iraq and opposed to an Iranian-like theocracy, did not explicitly back these candidates. This ruse helped the Iranian regime succeed in getting more of its candidates into the National Assembly, the group entrusted with drafting the new Iraqi constitution.

In addition to supporting existing pro-Iranian political parties in Iraq, Iran also created new ones in the period leading up to the election. These parties, which asserted platforms for creating an Islamic republic in Iraq, included the Hezbollah in Iraq (separate from the existing Iraqi Hezbollah group), the 15th Sha'ban based in Nasiriyah, and the Seyyed ol-Shohada group based in Basra.

By 2006, Iraq's interim government was deeply influenced by Iran, including the Interior Ministry, which was dominated by pro-Iranian elements. Working out of the seventh floor of the Interior Ministry building in Baghdad, Iran-friendly officials take their orders directly from Tehran. This is an extraordinary boon for Iran because this ministry is responsible for running the police forces in Iraq, coordinating municipal governments, and conducting elections.

Another aspect of Iran's success in dominating Iraq's political system is its tactic of preventing targeted candidates from participating in the election process. Iranian agents use Iraqi judges whom they have bought off to obtain summonses or arrest warrants for the candidate, which forces the candidate to devote precious time and resources to clearing up the problem. In the meantime, news of the warrant smears the candidate's reputation and taints his campaign. By the time the authorities notify him that the warrant is dropped (with an explanation that it was simply an investigation), the deadline for declaring his candidacy has passed. Dr. Abdullah al-Jabouri of the Diyala Province fell victim to this tactic in late 2005, when he began his campaign for a local office.

Iran was also partly responsible for swaying the Iraqi Sunnis away from the election process in January 2005, having emphasized that the Sunnis' best interests would be served by boycotting the polls. The Iranian regime's strategy of supporting the Shiite parties with money, manpower, and campaign materials while discouraging the Sunnis from voting was very successful. With a majority of Iran-backed Shiites installed in the new interim government, Iran achieved more fertile ground for political influence.

During the January 2005 campaign season, Tehran's ability to direct the political process in Iraq continued to strengthen as more agents filtered through the porous Iran-Iraq border and set about their missions to bribe and intimidate officials. The election results gave the United Iraqi Alliance, a Shiite coalition party led by SCIRI leader Abdulaziz Hakim, 48.2 percent of the seats in the National Assembly, while the Democratic Patriotic Alliance of Kurdistan came in second place with 25.7 percent. Third was Allawi's Iraqi List, with 13.8 percent.[83]

After the January 2005 elections, it was easy to assume that the Shiite leadership in the new National Assembly represented the religious and political views of Iraq's Shiite majority. This assumption was wrong, however. Many Iran-friendly Shiites won votes because Iran had worked thoroughly at all levels to make those candidates attractive. Thousands of Iraqis who received medical aid, cash, and food from Iran's charities were drawn to the candidates supported by those agencies. Iraqis who responded to Iran-friendly clerics in the mosques and received aid and instruction from those mosque communities were also led to vote for specific Iran-backed parties. In addition, Iran mobilized thousands of Iraqis to go to the polls and cast their votes. How could Iran lose?

As a result, many of the Iran-backed Shiites who were elected to the National Assembly represent Iran's radical version of Islamic rule, which is not the view of the majority of Iraqi Shiites. Clerics in Iraq do not hold the same influence that those in Iran do: In Iraq, there is a wide gap between the clergy and the day-to-day lives of ordinary Iraqis. The majority of Shiites in Iraq desire a secular government. They lean toward a separation of church and state as articulated by the grand ayatollah of Iraq, Ali al-Sistani, who has often spoken out about his fear that clerics would be corrupted by political positions and their religious message distorted.

Iran's influence upon the Shiites that it helped get elected to the Iraqi National Assembly became alarmingly clear when the assembly's draft constitution was released in late 2005. The document was a dream come true for Iran, filled with directives about Islamic law.[84]

The Iranian regime's efforts to win political alliances as a means to install an Islamic state in Iraq have not been limited to dealing with Islamic parties in Iraq. The regime is determined to unify radical Islamic groups throughout the Middle East in order to drive out the United States and build up its influence, and evidence of this strategy was found at Tehran's Third International Qods Conference, held in Tehran in April 2006. Attendees included leaders of Iraq's pro-Iran parties such as SCIRI and Al-Daawa and members of other Islamic parties from Pakistan, Lebanon, Palestine, Afghanistan and many other nations. Although the official theme of the meeting was "Support for the Palestinian Nation," the Iranian hosts stressed the importance of coordinating all Islamic groups as a unified force against the West. President Ahmadinejad told the assembly that "the criminal United States" faced severe challenges due to its "interferences in internal affairs of nations around the globe," and offered a solution for the near term. "Relying on unity, resistance, and awareness of the free nations," he said, "the final defeat of the paper powers of the world would be a near future event."[85]

FIGHTING IRAN'S INFLUENCE IN IRAQ

Iran's extensive efforts to influence Iraq has been faced with considerable opposition by the Iraqis who see their country rapidly moving toward a religious theocracy. Many Sunni leaders who eventually chose to join the political process found themselves having to counter both Iraqi extremists as well as the big bully next door, Iran.

Iraqi political leaders such as former Foreign Minister Adnan Pachachi, former Prime Minister Ayad Allawi, as well as prominent Sunni leaders Adnan al-Dulaimi and Saleh Mutlak, have tried to reclaim their country from Iranian influence. During the December 2005 legislative elections, a joint statement issued by 35 political groups that competed in elections complained to the Independent Electoral Commission of Iraq about election fraud in favor of the Iranian-preferred Shiite list. Saleh Mutlak, who headed an independent Sunni slate, said: "This election is completely false. It insults democracy everywhere. Everything was based on fraud, cheating, frightening people and using religion to frighten the people. It is terrorism more than democracy." Mutlak said he had expected his slate to capture 70 parliamentary seats, but that it seemed likely to win fewer than 20, according to the preliminary results. Alluding to Sunnis who chose to abandon their earlier rejection of Iraqi politics and participate in the election, Adnan Dulaimi, a leader of the main Sunni coalition, the Tawafaq front, demanded: "What would we tell those whom we indirectly convinced to stop the attacks during the election period? What would we tell those people who wanted to boycott and we convinced them to participate?" The preliminary results, he said, were "not in the interest of stability of the country."[86]

Adnan Pachachi said: "Weapons and members of Iran's Intelligence Ministry are smuggled into Iraq." Thousands of Sunni Arabs took to the streets calling for the general election to be invalidated and for the holding of new polls. A banner demanded that "Iran stand aside so that Baghdad could be free." The subject of Iranian interference was the main theme of the demonstration in Samarah. "The electoral commission sold Iraq to Iran for free, because it is run by people in the pay of Tehran, even if they pretend to be impartial or honest," Sheikh Mahmud al-Abbas, a Front candidate told the AFP.[87]

A U.S. official in Fallujah said there was some validity to the claim but that "the total shortfall was probably closer to a few seats." Those few seats were exactly what the Iranian regime was looking for to give the pro-Iran Shiites the absolute majority in the parliament and the ability to form the government on their own. Days later, White House national security adviser Stephen Hadley said, "Everybody understands the Sunnis need to be part of this process going forward in Iraq and need to be part of this government."[88] U.S. Ambassador Zalmay Khalilzad said "final results will not be announced until those red complaints have been looked at."[89] The Sunnis' fighting paid off and the pro-Iran Shiites who had claimed victory in the beginning fell short of the majority.

Realizing that Iran is the main threat to Iraq and its independent political process, Iraqis formed de facto coalitions that included the Sunnis, Shiites, and ethnic Kurds. Some 10,000 Iraqis gathered on a solidarity congress held at the headquarters of the MEK, at Ashraf City, north of Baghdad. Organizers of the congress released a statement signed by 5.2 million Iraqis warning of the threat of Iranian meddling in Iraq and emphasized the MEK members' right to political asylum in Iraq. The statement also recognized the MEK as a balancing factor to keep Iraq clear of Iran's domination.[90]

Although many factors have contributed to the escalating chaos in Iraq, Iran is undoubtedly the main player instigating violence and instability and derailing the political process in that country. Iraq is now a battleground for the clash of two alternatives: the Islamic extremist faction, which gets its orders from Tehran and seeks to establish an Islamic republic in Iraq, and a democratic alternative seeking a pluralistic democracy. The former seeks sectarian violence and fans the flames of civil war, while the latter seeks to ease tension, provide security and stability and establish democratic institutions.

In an interview with CBS's "60 Minutes" in November 2006, General John Abizaid warned about a need to prevent World War III by fighting Islamic extremism: "At the same time that the government of Iran is talking about stabilizing Iraq, these Revolutionary Guard Qods Force people are supporting the Shia death squads of some of the various splinter [groups]," Abizaid explained. He added: "I believe that there are people within the Iranian government . . . [who] would prefer to see a southern Lebanon-like solution to Iraq, where they can control the militia and have a weak central government as opposed to having a strong central government emerge."[91]

Abizaid's observations are firmly in line with the realities of Iran's agenda for Iraq. As U.S. forces were preparing to invade Iraq and topple Saddam Hussein's regime, the rulers of Iran decided to turn Iraq into the frontline to confront the United States and make way for the spread of Islamic extremist rule in the Middle East. Although Iran's nuclear weapons program is of great consequence, Iraq is the crucial battleground that would make or break Iran's grand agenda to establish a global Islamic rule.

Unfortunately, U.S. policy since 2003 has unintentionally yet effectively helped the Iranian regime. Following the fall of the Iraqi regime in 2003, with its incorrect assessment that the main threats to Iraq would come from the Sunnis, the Baath Party, and the former Iraqi army, the U.S. threw open its doors to the Iranian regime proxies, giving the Iranian regime a golden opportunity to expand its presence in Iraq.

According to a senior U.S. official who spoke to *Newsweek* in November 2006, some in the Bush administration believed that in order to "get help on Iraq," the U.S. might be forced to accept Iran as a nuclear state.[92] This highly controversial move would only add fuel to the fire: if the U.S. reached out for help from Iran in return for a free pass to continue its nuclear program, the mullahs would be two-time winners, advancing their agenda in Iraq and proceeding with their nuclear weapons program. The strategy met stiff resistance in late November when American intelligence officials learned that up to 2,000 fighters from the Mahdi Army and other militias in Iraq had been trained in Lebanon by the Iran-backed Hezbollah. This news heaped more weight on CIA Director General Michael V. Hayden's testimony to Congress earlier that month that "the Iranian hand is stoking violence" in Iraq.[93]

There is only one viable solution to avoid civil war and bring about security and stability in Iraq: stop the Iranian regime's meddling in Iraq. There is still a chance to bring the crisis under control and establish democracy if the following steps are taken: (1) the formation of a national unity government consisting of a wide spectrum of Iraqi people and free from Iranian operatives; (2) full immediate disarmament and disbanding of militias including the Badr Corp and the Mahdi Army and a purge of Iran-backed personnel from the security forces and military; (3) open dialogue with and protection of the MEK members based in Ashraf City and reaffirmation of their refugee status as a strategic asset in the fight against Islamic fundamentalism and a balancing weight against the Iranian regime's influence in Iraq. Since 2003, the MEK has unveiled a major part of Iran's terrorist conspiracies in Iraq; (4) modification of the constitution to guarantee Iraqi unity and sovereignty; and (5) open dialogue with resistance forces that are not controlled by foreign powers in order to move them away from the insurgency and into the political process.

This strategy would cut out the gravest challenge facing Iraq at its root and pave the way for democracy and peace.

Part IV
MARCH TO THE BOMB

CHAPTER 7

NUCLEAR COMMAND: THE MILITARIZATION OF IRAN'S NUCLEAR PROGRAM

In a country like Iran, with a sophisticated and well-capitalized energy sector, it is more than curious that a nuclear program—said to be purely civilian in nature and purely for power generation purposes—seems to have much closer ties to the Iranian military than it does to the rest of the civilian energy sector.

—Kenneth C. Brill, U.S. ambassador to the IAEA[1]

Even louder than Ahmadinejad's rants that the Holocaust is a myth and that Israel should be "wiped off this map" have been his demands about Iran's "rights" to a nuclear power program. Since his election as president in 2005, Ahmadinejad has depicted western countries as bullies who want to punish Iran by preventing it from developing peaceful nuclear technology. He shouts, with his fist in the air, that Iran will never back down from pursuing this technology, and he joins other leaders in Tehran in giving repeated denials that the regime has ever pursued nuclear weapons. For all this yelling and commotion, by late 2006 these denials had grown very thin.

The Iranian regime's strategy for hiding its nuclear weapons program involves several elements, including secret operations hidden within the legitimate nuclear organization, the Atomic Energy Organization of Iran (AEOI), which interacts with international agencies and provides a legal nuclear "face" for the regime; a top-secret military command that operates the clandestine weapons program, including nuclear weapons technology purchases; and the use of research centers and companies as front organizations for nuclear weapons work. All of these elements have been high-priority missions of the mullahs' regime in its attempt to acquire a nuclear bomb.

The biggest red flag signifying an undisclosed nuclear weapons program is military involvement. A military component within a nation's nuclear program indicates an agenda for using nuclear technology for defense—in short, a nuclear bomb. In Iran, the profusion of evidence about nuclear projects run by the Islamic Revolutionary Guards Corps and the Ministry of Defense and Armed Forces Logistics (hereafter also referred to as the Ministry of Defense) constitutes one of the strongest arguments that the regime is pursuing nuclear weapons. For several years, I have reported evidence about the deeply entrenched and highly active military element of Iran's nuclear program, all of which solidly contradicts the regime's claims that its program is solely for peaceful purposes.

According to my sources who have been responsible for the groundbreaking information revealing the nuclear sites in Natanz and Arak in 2002, the project to achieve nuclear weapons and to involve the military in this goal is supervised and pursued at the highest level of the regime by Supreme Leader Khamenei. In order to keep the nuclear project secret and to expedite the acquisition of nuclear weapons, many of the regime's nuclear program sites have been put under the supervision of military organs, and many of its nuclear experts have been transferred to these organizations. The military operations devoted to the nuclear weapons program are staffed by nearly 400 experts and researchers who work beyond the framework of the Atomic Energy Organization of Iran. Extremely cautious about keeping their work secret, a number of them function under the guise of university professors.

The military dimension of the secret nuclear weapons program involves the Islamic Revolutionary Guards Corps, the Ministry of Defense, and the Joint Chiefs of Staff. The official military involvement began in 1983 with the creation of a strategic research and nuclear technology section within the IRGC. The regime has never admitted the existence of this special unit, but over the years my sources in Iran have uncovered several details about its actions and location, including the site of its headquarters in a building in north Tehran near Vanak Square. In many cases, nuclear experts and engineers who went through the two-year training program at the research division of the AEOI were subsequently hired by the IRGC to work in the special nuclear unit. The IRGC hired these and other experts and engineers at very high salaries to join the top-secret group.

The militarization of the regime's nuclear program also extends into the Ministry of Defense, the department that manages all sections of the Iranian military. The officer in charge of the covert parallel nuclear weapons program is the number-two man at the Ministry of Defense, IRGC brigadier general Dr.

Seyed Ali Hosseini-Tash. The military's role in Iran's nuclear program has grown steadily through the years, weaving more fully into the secret program that finally came to light in 2002.

My revelations in August 2002 about two hidden nuclear facilities in Natanz and Arak revealed that the regime's clandestine program had been in the works for at least 18 years. But there is hard proof that the regime's plans for building nuclear weapons go back much further. Among those who know, without a doubt, that the regime has pursued a nuclear weapon since the early eighties are a handful of former Iranian officials and scientists who were approached by the regime to work on the nuclear weapons program. Not only are they eyewitnesses to the regime's plans, but in some cases they nearly lost their lives by refusing to cooperate. Unfortunately for the regime, they lived to tell the tale and can now testify to the true history of the regime and the bomb.

LIVING PROOF: EVIDENCE THAT THE REGIME HAS SOUGHT NUCLEAR WEAPONS SINCE THE EARLY 1980S

Physicist Alireza Assar was teaching at Shahid Bahonar University in Kerman, Iran, when he was first contacted in 1985. He was western educated, having received his master of science degree in physics from the University of St. Andrews in Scotland, his Ph.D. in mathematics from the University of Vienna, and further study in physics at the International Centre for Theoretical Physics at Trieste, Italy. Commanders from the IRGC held meetings with Dr. Assar in the governor's office of Kerman Province after recruiting him to work as a nuclear program consultant for the Ministry of Defense.

In 1987, two of Assar's meetings were attended by the commander in chief of the Islamic Revolutionary Guards Corps at the time, Mohsen Rezai (currently secretary general of the State Expediency Council). Rezai and two senior commanders of the IRGC went to the Kerman meetings to discuss a specific aspect of nuclear weaponry: nuclear triggers. The meeting was first attended by the then governor of Kerman Province, Hossein Mar'ashi, but Mohsen Rezai later asked Mar'ashi to leave the room "because he said we need to discuss some very sensitive issues," Assar told the author in an interview in November 2006. Rezai started by discussing the Iran-Iraq war as the focal point of all the affairs in the country, and the need to win the war, Assar recalled. Rezai went on to say that "Iran needs to arm itself with anything needed for victory, and we need to have all the technical requirements in our possession to even build a nuclear bomb, if and when needed." When Assar told Rezai that the development of these elements would cost $100 million, Rezai informed him that he had already allocated $800 million to the project. "This and other conversations with the top commanders of the Revolutionary Guards proved to me that they were after the nuclear bomb and that this was a state policy," Assar said. "Could commanders of the Revolutionary Guards act just on their own and dole out 800-million-dollar budgets? No way."[2]

Also attending these meetings were two nuclear scientists, both of whom worked for the Ministry of Defense.

Assar, who left Iran in 1992, went public with this information in July 2005. Days later, the Iranian regime responded by blaming the United States for co-ercing lies from Iranian scientists. Iranian intelligence minister Ali Yunesi cautioned Iranian scientists living abroad to be suspicious and vigilant because "America and Israel are trying to get close to [our scientists] by establishing emotional ties, then they put them into a situation where they are forced to give information."[3]

Another scientist, Manouchehr Fakhimi, fled Iran after years of harassment, imprisonment, and torture by the regime because of his refusal to cooperate with the regime. A geophysicist who received his Ph.D. from the University of Kiel, Germany, Fakhimi began his government work in the AEOI in the 1970s, under the order of the shah. He was specifically assigned to supervise the nuclear power plant project at Bushehr on the Persian Gulf, which was part of the shah's long-range nuclear energy plan. Blueprints for the twin reactors at Bushehr were secret, and upon analyzing them Fakhimi discovered that the building was not adequately designed for the seismic activity of the area. He calculated that the facility needed to be able to withstand an earthquake of magnitude 6 on the Richter scale, but it was designed to withstand only a magnitude–4 quake. "I couldn't accept this plan," Fakhimi told me in an interview, "so I moved from this department to the exploration of uranium." The uranium exploration project, undertaken by Ur-Iran, a subsidiary company of the AEOI, included an extensive airborne survey by helicopter and plane. Fakhimi discovered uranium in the Saghand desert near the city of Yazd in central Iran, and follow-up confirmed that the natural uranium had a concentration that was suitable for mining.

After Khomeini took power, Fakhimi began working for an Iranian steel company while teaching at the university in Kerman. He was obliged to accept a new job as an exploration superintendent at the National Iranian Oil Company. The Khomeini regime wanted to benefit from his knowledge and experience, and just a few months after the revolution he got a visit from Tehran officials. In exchange for Fakhimi's acceptance of the full party line, they offered him a high position, a beautiful home, and a car. Their specific requirements were threefold: He must take part in Friday prayers, wear a beard, and become a member of the

Islamic Republic Party. Fakhimi had no interest in becoming a propagandist for the regime, and he refused the offer.

While working on uranium mining in his new position, an IRGC officer contacted Fakhimi and asked, "Now that we have the mine, how can we build an atomic bomb?" Fakhimi told him that this would not be easy because the natural uranium was concentrated to less than one percent, and it would be necessary to have an enrichment plant near the mine. The officer responded that this was not a viable option because satellite photographs would surface and "everyone would know." In spite of this problem, the officer was still interested in recruiting Fakhimi for the secret nuclear weapons program. "They promised me that I would get a house, car, and passport and be able to travel everywhere," Fakhimi recalled. "I said, 'No, I'm not working for an atomic weapons purpose.' I was sure of myself, I wanted to use my knowledge for the exploration of mines, uranium and oil, and to study earthquakes, that was my job." The officer left, but the IRGC was not finished with Fakhimi.

Eventually three more young officers from the IRGC arrived at Fakhimi's office at the oil company. Armed with rifles, they accused Fakhimi of being an enemy of God because he did not obey the statements of those who were a "delegation of God." Fakhimi refused to cooperate, and a series of interrogations began. On any given day, guards would arrive at his office and tell him that they needed to have a conversation, then take him away for sessions that lasted one or two days. "They kept me many hours," said Fakhimi.

With no passport and $120 in his wallet, he bought a map and trekked illegally into Turkey. After weeks of hardship, he finally managed to get to Austria, where he asked for political asylum, which he eventually obtained. After two years of planning, Fakhimi's wife and two children also escaped to Austria.

The regime's efforts to recruit these scientists are a chilling dose of reality about the regime's deeply entrenched, long-term mission to get the bomb.

AN ATOMIC GRAND PLAN

After the revolution, the Iranian regime inherited remnants of the shah's ambitious nuclear program. That program had been launched in the 1960s when the United States provided the shah with a five-megawatt (MW) light-water research reactor and laboratory equipment, all of which was installed at the Tehran Nuclear Research Center (TNRC) at Tehran University. These materials were provided as part of the U.S. "Atoms for Peace" program, in which nuclear energy technology was given to nations throughout the world in exchange for those countries' commitments not to develop nuclear weapons. In 1968 the shah signed the Treaty on the Non-Proliferation of Nuclear Weapons (NPT), and Iran ratified the NPT in 1970. Iran made a $1 billion loan to Commissariat a l'Energie Atomique (CEA) in 1974 to build a uranium enrichment plant at Tricastin, France, for the Eurodif consortium. In return, Iran would receive a 10 percent stake in the plant. Iran also asked for French assistance in uranium prospecting.[4] In 1974, the shah signed an agreement with the International Atomic Energy Agency (IAEA) to allow full inspections of all of Iran's nuclear material. Also in 1974, the shah founded the Atomic Energy Organization of Iran (AEOI) and announced a 20-year nuclear energy plan that included building 22 power reactors throughout the country. In 1976, the budget for the Atomic Energy Organization of Iran was increased from 30.8 million dollars to one billion dollars a year.[5] In 1977, the United Sates and Iran signed an agreement to exchange nuclear technology and cooperate in nuclear safety. A former financial advisor in charge of all contracts of the AEOI, who was with the organization since 1977, told the author in an interview in October 2006: "We had a hard time keeping up with all the various contractors; we were dealing with more than 20 foreign companies working on Iranian nuclear projects by 1978."

By January 1979, two nuclear plants were under construction in Bushehr on the Persian Gulf, under contract with the German Siemens subsidiary Kraftwerk Union AG (KWU). One of the two 1,200–1,300-megawatt nuclear power plants near Bushehr was already 85 percent completed, and preliminary work had begun on another pair of 930-megawatt reactors to be built near Ahwaz, about 75 miles north of the Persian Gulf, by the French company Framatome. The shah had also signed letters of intent to purchase 18 more reactors from Germany, France, and the United States.[6]

To coincide with the nuclear-power deal making of this period, thousands of Iranians were studying nuclear technology in Iran, Germany, France, India, the United Kingdom, and the United States.[7] A study published in 1987 concluded that after the revolution, the Khomeini regime inherited "a substantial nuclear infrastructure" from the shah's regime.[8]

An important piece of evidence that the shah was funding research that the mullahs could eventually use came from the discovery of a laser enrichment program that began in 1975. An American scientist, Jeffrey Eerkens, revealed in 1987 that during the time of the shah the TNRC commissioned him to build a set of lasers that could separate weapons-grade uranium from natural uranium. This technology can also produce plutonium. Eerkens obtained permission from the U.S. government to ship this classified laser technology to Iran, and four lasers were delivered in 1978.[9] In its entirety, the nuclear program that Khomeini inherited in 1979 was "by far the most ambitious in the Middle East."[10]

NUCLEAR DEVELOPMENTS IN THE 1980S

Khomeini viewed the shah's nuclear program as a remnant of evil western influence. As a result, the regime canceled the German and French contracts, and work on the Bushehr and Ahwaz plants came to a halt. But despite Khomeini's abhorrence of western innovations, the regime did not turn its back on nuclear weapons technology.

Tehran's drive for a nuclear program met stiff challenges in the 1980s, but despite these setbacks, research and planning for a nuclear arsenal continued. Factors that slowed some aspects of the overall nuclear program included the Iran-Iraq War and the refusal of the German company Kraftwerk to resume work on the two reactors at Bushehr because of Iraq's repeated air attacks on the site. Israel's attack on Iraq's nuclear reactor at Osirak in 1981 further deepened concerns about the vulnerability of Iran's nuclear sites, but that attack also raised the mullahs' hopes that they would win the race to the bomb and gain power over Iraq. With help from foreign nations and an underground nuclear black market, the regime made definite progress with the nuclear weapons program in this decade.

In 1984 the regime built a new nuclear research laboratory at the Isfahan Nuclear Technology Center (INTC), the facility that had originally been built by the shah in the 1970s as a training center for Bushehr personnel. With assistance from China, the regime's expansion included several new buildings, some underground, resulting in a large complex that later grew beyond the needs of peaceful research. China's impact on the development of the INTC in the 1980s included supplying a "training reactor" in 1985, the first of four small research reactors that China would install at the research center over the next ten years.[11]

Activities at the INTC reveal that the trail of the regime's deliberate and successful deception about its nuclear program goes back very far. Hidden from the IAEA, the research at this center involved experiments in uranium conversion and fuel production—flagrant violations of its NPT obligations.[12] And not only did the regime hide uranium experiments performed at the INTC and at the Tehran Nuclear Research Center, but it also hid the fact that it secretly imported uranium in 1982 for use in these activities.[13] The IAEA later reported that, contrary to what the Iranian regime had told them up to 2003, "practically all of the materials important to uranium conversion had been produced in laboratory and bench scale experiments [in kilogram quantities] between 1981 and 1993 without having been reported to the Agency."[14]

In 1985, with the country deep in the throes of the Iran-Iraq War, the Iranian regime decided to restart a full-fledged nuclear program.[15] This new decision led to a series of secret cooperative agreements with various nations to acquire training, expertise, and materials. Former Iranian president Akbar Hashemi Rafsanjani had placed high emphasis on the Chinese cooperation even before he became president, and the Chinese cooperation continued throughout his presidency. The regime's agreement with China stipulated that China would train AEOI engineers and supply the regime with nuclear equipment and data about designing nuclear facilities. Iranian nuclear experts began training in China in 1985, and in that year China provided Iran with a research reactor and a calutron, which became operational in 1987. A cooperative agreement initiated with North Korea on nuclear weapons development included assistance with uranium mining and exploration.[16] And the 1987 cooperation agreement with Argentina stipulated that Argentina would sell Iran 20 percent enriched uranium for use in the small reactor at the Tehran Nuclear Research Center.[17]

In 1987 the Iranian regime also formed a nuclear cooperation agreement with the Soviet Union, which raised even more concerns in the United States about the Soviet Union's inroads into Iran during the cold war. A declassified top-secret memo from June 1985 from National Security Adviser Robert McFarlane to Secretary of State George Shultz and Secretary of Defense Caspar Weinberger outlines the Iranian regime's wartime crises and the White House's increasing concerns that the crises made Iran more vulnerable to Soviet influence. "The most immediate U.S. interests [regarding Iran] include," McFarlane wrote, "limiting the scope and opportunity for Soviet actions. . . . Our primary short-term challenge must be to block Moscow's efforts to increase Soviet influence (now and after the death of Khomeini)."[18]

The failure of the Iranian regime to win the Iran-Iraq War with conventional weapons reinforced its determination to develop a nuclear arsenal in the 1980s. Even though Iran had fought a smaller nation—Iran is four times as large in land area and has three times the population of Iraq—and had branded conquering Iraq as the first step in creating an Islamic government throughout the Middle East, none of this was enough. For all its tremendous resources and ideological fervor, the Iranian regime could not capture Iraq through conventional weapons, so the mullahs became even more convinced that the bomb was the way. After the cease-fire in 1988, Iranian president Hashemi Rafsanjani declared in a speech to the IRGC, "We should fully equip ourselves both in the offensive and defensive use of chemical, bacteriological and radiological weapons. From now on you should make use of the opportunity and perform this task."[19] A critical element of achieving this goal would be obtaining nuclear weaponry design and materials from the world's foremost entrepreneur of weapons of mass destruction, A. Q. Khan.

IRAN AND A. Q. KHAN'S NUCLEAR BLACK MARKET

Until his arrest in 2004, Abdul Qadeer Khan operated a clandestine international nuclear weapons supply network that provided nuclear technology and materials to nuclear weapons programs in his home country of Pakistan, as well as in Iran, Libya, and North Korea. Khan, a western-educated scientist known as the father of the Pakistani bomb, began his covert career in the 1970s by stealing uranium centrifuge designs from his Dutch employer, Physics Dynamic Research Laboratory (FDO). Khan had access to Europe's most cutting-edge centrifuge technology, because FDO was a subcontractor for Urenco, Europe's sole commercial enrichment firm set up exclusively for producing low-enriched uranium (LEU).[20] With easy access to sensitive areas of FDO and Urenco facilities, Khan gathered classified technological and contact information for a vast network of European experts in nuclear technology and manufacturing, all of which information he brought to Pakistan in 1975. After four years working on Pakistan's uranium-enrichment program, President Zia ul-Haq renamed the government lab in his honor, calling it Khan Research Laboratories (KRL).

By the mid-1980s, Pakistan's nuclear program had developed enough highly enriched uranium for a nuclear weapon, thanks to Khan's smoothly running network of financiers, importers, middlemen, and front companies. (Pakistan's bombs were later tested in 1998.) In the late 1980s, Khan had an overflow of equipment to sell on the black market because of an overordering of materials and an inventory of outdated aluminum-based centrifuges that were being replaced by new steel designs. This overflow launched Khan's expansion into the international marketplace, making use of the vast network he had put in place for the Pakistani program.[21] Khan's network went beneath the radar of international intelligence agencies for decades, and only after his criminal investigation is complete will a picture of his extensive involvement in various nuclear programs come to light. "Khan and his network had been unique in being able to offer one-stop shopping for enrichment technology and weapons design information," said CIA director George Tenet in 2004. "With such assistance, a potentially wide range of countries could leapfrog the slow, incremental stages of other nuclear weapons development programs."[22]

Iran was among the first buyers in Khan's venture into the international marketplace. The Iranian regime admitted to the IAEA in 2003 that it had begun uranium enrichment in 1985 and had received blueprints for centrifuge design "through a foreign intermediary in around 1987."[23] After his arrest, Khan confessed that he was this foreign supplier who had provided Iran with designs, drawings, and components related to nuclear weapons. (Khan also accepted full responsibility for his proliferation activities and insisted that the Pakistani government was in no way involved; after his public apology, Pakistan's president Pervez Musharraf granted him a pardon but put him under house arrest in Islamabad.) The deal that Khan began with the Iranian regime in 1987 included the training of at least six Iranians in two Pakistani facilities, the Institute of Nuclear Science and Technology in Islamabad and the Nuclear Studies Institute in Nowlore. Khan also set up training for Iranian scientists at his own facility.[24] Additionally, Khan revealed that he personally met with Iranian scientists in the city of Karachi in Pakistan and in Malaysia.[25]

As the investigation into Khan's network continued, his chief financial associate, a businessman named Buhary Syed Abu Tahir who lived in Malaysia, confessed details about one Khan hardware deal with the Iranian regime. Tahir told police that Khan sent used centrifuges to Iran aboard a ship that sailed from the port of Dubai in the United Arab Emirates. In exchange for these two containers of centrifuges, Tahir was given two briefcases filled with UAE dirhams in an amount equivalent to three million U.S. dollars. Tahir described Khan's network of middlemen from Great Britain, Germany, Turkey, and Switzerland who facilitated the secret deals and deliveries, and he described the overall operation as "a loose network without a rigid hierarchy or a head and a deputy head."[26]

In August 2005, I received from my sources inside Iran new details of Iran's association with Khan that, in addition to providing insights about Khan's activities, provided evidence about the military oversight of the Iranian regime's nuclear weapons program. The regime repeatedly insisted that its meetings and contacts with Khan had been conducted in a nonmilitary context, but my sources in Iran provided information that proved otherwise. Khan's main counterpart was Islamic Revolutionary Guards Corps commander Mohammad Eslami, the chief of the IRGC's nuclear research center. In 1986 and 1987, Eslami and two other IRGC commanders met with A. Q. Khan in Tehran for meetings that were coordinated by the head of the Atomic Energy Organization of Iran at the time, Reza Amrollahi. (Mohammad Eslami is currently a brigadier general of the IRGC and leads the Defense Ministry's Institute for Defense Education and Research.) At the time of the meeting, the main mission of the research center was nuclear weapons research. Following these meetings, relations between the IRGC and the A. Q. Khan network intensified, as the recent investigations into Khan's network have revealed.

My sources also revealed that a delegation from the Atomic Energy Organization of Iran also met with A. Q. Khan in 1986 and 1987. The participants in these meetings included Mohammad Reza Ayatollahi, then deputy director of the AEOI, and Seyyed Mohammad Haj Saeed, chief of the AEOI's directorate of research. Currently Ayatollahi is the director of the National Organization for Civil Registration, and Haj Saeed remains a member of the AEOI.[27]

The arrest of A. Q. Khan was a direct result of IAEA inspections of Iran's top-secret uranium-enrichment plant in Natanz, which had been built and developed from 2000. That revelation in August 2002 launched the IAEA's investigation of the site, which in turn uncovered technological evidence that pointed to Pakistan as the supplier of the centrifuge technology. The IAEA's findings at Natanz blew the lid off Khan's extensive network and ultimately brought its founder down.[28]

The global black-market network that Khan created still poses a threat by virtue of what Tahir described as its "loose" international design. International Atomic Energy Agency director general Mohamed ElBaradei described Khan's individual involvement as just the "tip of the iceberg" of illegal nuclear technology trafficking throughout the world.[29] In his essay on A. Q. Khan for *Atlantic Monthly*, journalist William Langewiesche pointed out "the likelihood that much of the network [Khan] established remains alive worldwide, and that by its very nature—loose, unstructured, technically specialized, determinedly amoral—it is both resilient and mutable, and can resume its activities when the opportunity arises."[30]

ACCELERATING THE NUCLEAR PROGRAM IN THE 1990S

When Khomeini finally accepted the cease-fire that ended the Iran-Iraq War in 1988, the Iranian regime initiated a more ambitious phase of its secret nuclear weapons program. That year, the IRGC created a top-secret nuclear weapons program at the AEOI under the code name the "Great Plan," to which was allocated a budget of $200 million. This secret budget increased rapidly over the years; just four years later, in 1992, for example, the Great Plan was allocated $800 million. At the same time, two nuclear experts at the Ministry of Defense began supervising a new project to obtain nuclear technology from foreign countries.[31]

After Khomeini's death in 1989, the regime's new supreme leader, Ayatollah Seyed Ali Khamenei, and its new president, Ali Akbar Hashemi Rafsanjani, expanded Iran's secret nuclear program and launched a new series of agreements with foreign suppliers. Increasing pressure from the United States for nations to stop nuclear cooperation with Iran brought on problems for Rafsanjani's plans in the 1990s, such as Germany's refusal to resume construction of the two plants at Bushehr and Argentina's cancellation of its agreement to provide nuclear technology. As a result, the Iranian regime turned to China and Russia.[32]

China was very willing to do business with the mullahs, and in September 1992 Rafsanjani traveled to Beijing to attend a signing ceremony for China's agreement to build at least four nuclear power plants and another research center. Reza Amrollahi, director of the AEOI, and Song Jian, Chinese minister for science and technology, signed the agreement.[33] The first Chinese facility to be delivered was a 300-megawatt nuclear reactor, which China insisted was for "peaceful purposes," to be built at Darkhovin, a site in southwest Iran that lies 25 miles south of the city of Ahwaz. This site had been slated for a German-built nuclear reactor as part of the shah's program in the 1970s, but the deal was never completed. The Chinese reactor would be modeled after the new Qinshan reactor in the Zhejian Province, which had been operating in a trial mode for less than a year. I revealed in a September 11, 1992, press conference that by the time of the official signing in Beijing, the Iranian regime had already sent 20 technicians and engineers to China for training, and at least 4 Chinese nuclear experts were already working at the Darkhovin site. I also revealed, based on information from my sources in Iran, that 22 Iranians were already in Pakistan for nuclear training and that Rafsanjani had stopped in Pakistan on his way to China.[34]

Another crucial deal with China in the early 1990s involved the construction of an industrial-scale uranium conversion plant and zirconium production plant at the Isfahan Nuclear Technology Center (zirconium is a corrosion-resistant metal used in nuclear reactors). As a report from the International Institute for Strategic Studies stated, this deal was a significant development for the Iranian regime:

> [These plants] could produce large quantities of materials for enrichment and fuel fabrication. As a sweetener to these deals, China shipped just over a ton of natural uranium in various compounds to Iran in 1991. This allowed Iran to carry out undeclared conversion, reduction and enrichment experiments during the 1990s.[35]

The Iranian regime's nuclear cooperation with Russia solved one of the thorniest ongoing challenges facing Iran's nuclear program: completing construction of the twin reactors at Bushehr. In 1993, Russia committed to the project, and in January 1995 the Russian minister of atomic energy, Viktor Mikhailov, and AEOI chief Reza Amrollahi signed an $800 million contract for Russia to finish construction of one of the 1,000-megawatt reactors in four years.[36] The structural frame of one of the reactors was 75 percent complete, awaiting only the core reactor components, and the second reactor was 60 percent complete. According to an Iranian exile who visited Iran in 1987, both reactor silos were being used to store grain at that time.[37]

Although the Bushehr contract was public, a secret deal was made at the same time between Moscow and Tehran that would have given the Iranian regime a complete domestic fuel cycle. Russia was ready to supply a large research reactor, plants for manufacturing nuclear fuel, and a centrifuge enrichment facility, but when U.S. intelligence uncovered the secret deal, President Clinton urged Russian president Boris Yeltsin to halt the covert program. Yeltsin agreed to scrap all nuclear assistance except construction at Bushehr.[38] In February 2006, Iranian foreign minister Manouchehr Mottaki announced that construction on the plant was completed and that it would "be soon ready to receive nuclear fuel, which Russia has pledged to supply."[39] Russia and the Iranian regime had signed contracts in 2005 formalizing an agreement that fuel for the reactor would be provided by Russia, and spent fuel would not remain in Iran— where it could be reprocessed for a nuclear weapons program—but would be returned to Russia.[40] As of 2006, the Bushehr reactor is not yet operating.

It is important to remember Iran's devastating economic condition in the early 1990s, despite which the regime secretly spent hundreds of millions of dollars on a covert nuclear weapons program. As I reported at a Morning Newsmaker presentation at the National Press Club in June 1990, Rafsanjani's biggest motto during his campaign had been his promise to reconstruct Iran's economy, but after his first year in office the state of the nation's finances had only gotten worse. By the summer of 1990, half of the nation's workforce was unemployed, according to the government's announced figures; one-third of the population of Iran lived below the poverty line; one-third was homeless; people suffered from tremendous shortages of food, medicine, and basic goods; inflation was skyrocketing at nearly 200 percent on the flourishing government-controlled black market; corruption was spreading throughout all the governmental offices; and industry was working at only 25 percent of its production levels. In addition, the budget deficit in 1990, despite all the promises from Rafsanjani, had increased 20 percent from the year before.

In October 1989, when Rafsanjani introduced his five-year economic plan, his remarks revealed that he was aware of the rock-bottom situation of the regime's economy. He admitted that things could not get any worse: "If you don't offer *any* plans into the economic market," he said during a speech about his five-year plan, "even this very dismal condition cannot continue. I swear to

God, it cannot continue." Many deputies in the parliament themselves protested the plan, asking how in the world Iran's export capabilities could grow, in five years, to 200 times the number of items exported in 1988 and 1989. Some of the Majlis (parliament) members also threw up their hands at Rafsanjani's proclamation that his plan would bring an annual growth rate of 2,000 percent. I also recall one of the Majlis members complaining loudly that the budget allocated to rebuild seven war-stricken provinces would not suffice to repair even 100 of the 2,000 fishing boats damaged during the war. Iran needed a realistic postwar economic recovery plan, but Rafsanjani and the rest of the regime's top leadership had other priorities—militarizing the nuclear program and developing a nuclear weapon.[41]

The regime's ambitious nuclear deals of the 1990s, both in the public eye and underground, bled the country of much-needed funds and further isolated the regime from the United States and other western nations.

THE TWO FACES OF THE ATOMIC ENERGY ORGANIZATION OF IRAN

Despite the Iranian regime's bullying insistence that it is only pursuing nuclear technology for energy, the reality is that there are two nuclear programs in Iran. One, the Atomic Energy Organization of Iran (AEOI), presents a legitimate nuclear face to the IAEA and the rest of the world. During most of the regime's nuclear history, the AEOI has been involved with handling all the issues surrounding the very public nuclear power program at Bushehr, which the regime has been struggling to complete for approximately two decades. The second nuclear program in Iran is secret in every aspect, from its invisible budget to its military-command hierarchy and its operative direction from the highest levels of power in the regime. Since the first months of the regime's existence, hiding this top-secret program from the IAEA and all Iranian government personnel—including the Majlis—who are not involved in the covert program has been the number one priority of the regime.

As the official organ of the Iranian regime that deals with nuclear energy and the ability to gain access to complete nuclear fuel cycles, the AEOI successfully distracted attention from the regime's covert nuclear weapons program until my revelations about the two secret nuclear facilities in Natanz and Arak in 2002. As evidence about the regime's long-held secret program surfaced in the wake of these revelations, the AEOI and, most recently, President Ahmadinejad worked strenuously to portray Iran's nuclear program as a point of national pride and independence, hoping that this spin on the regime's real intentions would rally many Iranians to join the rants against the West who would take away this "right" to nuclear technology.

The AEOI is an executive agency that reports directly to the president, and the official director is an appointed vice president, currently Gholamreza Aqazadeh. Formerly the regime's oil minister, Aqazadeh was named head of the AEOI after the election of President Mohammad Khatami in 1997. The director has a set of advisors and a team of deputies who manage the five main divisions of the agency. In the Ahmadinejad administration, these deputy directors are Dr. Vahid Ahmadi, Research Division; Assadollah Sabouri, Nuclear Power Plant Division (NPPD); Dr. Mohammad Ghannadi-Maragheh, Nuclear Fuel Production Division; Dr. Barat Ghanadian, Planning, Education and Parliament Affairs Division; and Dr. Seyed Ismail Khalili-Pour, Nuclear Regulatory Division.

Since its founding in 1973 and throughout its expansion in the mullahs' regime, the supposedly transparent AEOI has received cooperation and support from the IAEA in the form of joint projects and other programs. As Deputy Director Ghannadi claimed at a London conference in 2002, "All the sections and centers under AEOI are under regular inspection and supervision by the IAEA, through the visits of expert teams from the IAEA. The declared policy of the Islamic Republic of Iran is to utilize the peaceful applications of nuclear power for the improvement of lives of its people."[42] The operative word there is "declared." The hidden side of the AEOI is a central part of the regime's nuclear weapons program.

This official mission and structure of the AEOI is vastly misleading. Even though AEOI officers officially report to the president of the regime, the entire agency is actually controlled by the Supreme National Security Council. In closed-door meetings, most of the AEOI's planning and operations are conducted secretly. For example, the construction of the uranium-enrichment facility in Natanz and the heavy-water facility in Arak were done without informing the Majlis and without appropriating a budget from the Majlis budget committee. Instead, these massive projects were funded by a special budget that was allocated by the supreme leader.

After my revelation about the secret Natanz and Arak programs in 2002, the regime established an investigative committee to research these two sites. After 18 months the committee issued a report that described the great surprise among members of the Majlis who said that they had never heard anything about these two programs until my announcement. They stated that the budget for these programs did not come from the parliament, and that they had been kept completely out of the loop. Khatami's response to this report was simply that the secret programs benefited the government and were in the best interest of the regime.

The AEOI's official budget, as appropriated by the Majlis and stated in the annual budget of the regime, was $255 million in 2005. But the secret budget, allocated by the Supreme National Security Council, must be several times that amount, in accordance with the Great Plan figures that my sources in Iran uncovered about the budget of 1992.

———————•••———————

A remarkable string of revelations in 2005 and 2006 about secret nuclear facilities proved that the regime's nuclear weapons program has accelerated in recent years. The parallel nuclear weapons program that is controlled, operated, and run by the IRGC, with its own nuclear experts and facilities, had grown alongside the so-called civil program that was rapidly advancing through the AEOI. The military program could easily benefit from all the work that the civilian program was doing. But the sharing is a one-way street: The IRGC's program fully benefits from the AEOI program, making use of their experts and research centers, but not the other way around. In fact, most of the personnel who work in the civilian program do not even know that such a parallel program exists. And the regime goes to great lengths to ensure that they do not learn more. Some senior officials are aware of the scope of military program, but they are a small minority within the regime.

The militarization of Iran's nuclear program sped into high gear after the election of Ahmadinejad in 2005. Senior members of the IRGC were installed in the Supreme National Security Council (SNSC), including Ali Larijani, the secretary general of the SNSC, Brigadier General Ali Hosseini-Tash, Brigadier General Mohammad Bagher Zolqadr, and Brigadier General Mohammad Ali Jafari. Because the SNSC, chaired by President Ahmadinejad, is commissioned with policy making on all foreign policy, defense, and security issues, the move to add IRGC members to the SNSC essentially further brought the entire nuclear program under the direct control of the IRGC.

This new, highly visible military oversight reveals the urgency with which the regime seeks to finish work on a complete nuclear fuel cycle. The urgency is not over completing the power reactors in Bushehr, because that facility requires only fuel, which Russia can provide. What the regime is rushing toward is exactly what the West does not want it to have: a complete fuel cycle that would enable it independently to create fissile material for nuclear weapons. Tehran's determination to get its enrichment program running at any cost also explains its increasingly confrontational attitude in negotiations between it and the IAEA, the EU3, and the United States. The mission to create a complete nuclear fuel cycle takes precedence over any and all other political priorities of the regime, evidenced by

Ahmadinejad's fiery rhetoric as well as by actions such as the AEOI restarting uranium enrichment at Natanz in February 2006.

THE BIG SECRET EXPOSED:
UNCOVERING THE SECRET NUCLEAR SITES
AT NATANZ AND ARAK IN 2002

In 2002, my sources in Iran completed their investigation of two secret nuclear sites, both coordinated by the supposedly transparent and aboveboard AEOI, and subsequently blew the lid off Iran's top-secret nuclear program. Thanks to extensive research and investigation by the Committee of Defense and Strategic Studies of the National Council of Resistance of Iran and the command headquarters inside Iran of the Mujahedin-e Khalq (MEK), facts came to light about these nuclear sites that had gone undetected by the world community. My August 14, 2002, press conference announcing these findings compelled the IAEA to investigate both sites.[43]

The older of the two facilities is a heavy-water production plant (HWPP) in Arak, about 150 miles south of Tehran. The AEOI began construction in 1996 under the direction of Dr. Mohammad Ghannadi-Maragheh, chief of the Nuclear Fuel Production Division. The location was selected to provide access to the nearby Qara-Chai River, because the heavy-water production process involves steam power. Heavy water, which contains a higher proportion of heavy hydrogen (deuterium) atoms than ordinary water, is used in heavy-water nuclear reactors. The heavy water creates a sustained chain reaction in the reactor, which allows the reactor to be fueled by natural, unenriched uranium. Plutonium, which is used in nuclear weapons, is a by-product of heavy-water reactors. The spent-fuel waste produced by a light-water reactor, like the one at Bushehr, contains plutonium. Iran can quickly separate out the plutonium in relatively small facilities (as little as 65 square feet), which can easily be hidden, and use it to make a nuclear bomb.

Following my revelation in August 2002, the IAEA, in a formal letter, requested a visit to the heavy-water facility in Arak. After several delays, Iran had little choice but to agree to the IAEA visit. The IAEA visit to Iran in February 2003 confirmed that Iran was building the heavy-water production plant in Arak. In a letter written to the IAEA three months later, the regime confirmed that it planned to construct a 40-megawatt heavy-water research reactor, the IR–40, at the same site.[44] IAEA inspectors visited Arak in March 2005 to carry out their standard design information verification (DIV) and observed that construction was ongoing on both the HWPP and the reactor. The regime informed the inspectors that they planned to have the heavy-water reactor online in 2014.[45]

The other site exposed in the August 2002 press conference is the regime's centrifuge enrichment facility at Natanz, about 200 miles south of Tehran. Construction began at the site in 2000 by two companies, Jahad-Towseh and Towseh-Sakhteman, and the cover story created by the AEOI was that it was a desert eradication project. The facilities included buildings both above and below ground, and they were spread out over an area of about 25 acres. Centrifuge technology allows fast-spinning cylinders to separate enriched uranium (U–235) out of natural uranium (U–238). Unstable U–235 is the fissionable material used to fuel nuclear power plants and to create nuclear bombs. When U–235 is drawn out of one cylinder, it flows into another to enlarge the quantity, flows into yet another cylinder, and continues on in a series called a centrifuge cascade.

The Natanz site contained a pilot-scale centrifuge plant and a partially completed industrial-scale centrifuge facility. The regime first declared that an old European-designed centrifuge called P–1 was in use at Natanz, but inspectors later discovered that Iran was developing P–2 centrifuges, a newer and more sophisticated design. When IAEA inspectors first visited the site in February 2003, there were more than 100 centrifuges installed at the pilot facility, which was constructed to hold a maximum of about 1,000 centrifuges. The large plant was designed to hold approximately 60,000 machines in two large underground cascade halls.[46]

A few days before I held my press conference announcing the existence of the Natanz and Arak sites, former Iranian prime minister Hossein Moussavi secretly visited the Natanz project as the representative of Supreme National Security Council. The AEOI surrounded the Natanz site with high security, causing quite a stir among some officials in the area. Natanz is located in the Kashan region of Isfahan Province, and when the governor's office of Kashan could not obtain any information about the construction going on at the site, a major quarrel broke out between that office and the AEOI. Further, the deputy governor General of Isfahan Province was turned away when he tried to pay a visit.

After its initial inspections of Natanz in 2003, the IAEA determined that the Iranian regime had violated its IAEA Safeguards agreement by not reporting the nuclear material, as well as the subsequent processing and use of that material, and by not declaring where the material was stored and processed.[47]

That the regime hid the Natanz and Arak projects raised suspicions in the international community that Tehran was working toward creating a complete fuel cycle that would produce highly enriched uranium and plutonium, the two fissile materials needed for nuclear weapons. The great lengths to which the hidden side of the AEOI went to create separate budgets, independent bureaucratic operations, and front companies in order to sidestep IAEA supervision make these suspicions very plausible. But these two sites were just the tip of the iceberg, as my sources inside Iran uncovered in the years that followed.

The Iranian regime's network of secret nuclear weapons sites was designed not only to expand the program, but also to keep the program alive if any of the nuclear facilities came under attack. The mullahs' regime, understanding the threat that would be posed to its nuclear facilities if they were uncovered and drawing on lessons from the raid on Iraq's Tammuz nuclear facilities in 1981, has adopted a twofold method to foil such surgical military strikes. The first part of this plan is showcasing the nuclear site in Bushehr and turning it into the focal point of outside attention, thus providing legitimate cover for the development of other nuclear sites in the country. At the same time, the regime built up other nuclear laboratories and uranium-enrichment sites in different parts of Iran, so that even if one or two sites were destroyed in an attack, the project would survive and be continued at other sites.

This policy has created three types of nuclear sites in Iran. The first is open sites such as Bushehr, which the regime intentionally places under the monitoring of the International Atomic Energy Agency. The second type is secret facilities such as the uranium-enrichment plant in Natanz, the heavy-water production plant in Arak, and the Kalaye Electric facility near Abali in Tehran. These sites were critical for the regime's efforts to reach its ultimate goal of a complete nuclear fuel cycle, and it worked very hard to keep them secret. The third type of nuclear site is the smaller, more dispersed sites used for research and development and for uranium enrichment. Not only do these sites complement principal sites such as Natanz, but they also ensure that in the case of air attacks or more intrusive intervention by the IAEA—which might suspend activities in places like Natanz—these sites would still allow the mullahs to continue enriching uranium.

The entire nuclear program, both public and secret, is supervised by the supreme leader and carried out under the de facto direction of the military. The military personnel, scientists, and officials from the Islamic Revolutionary Guards Corps and Ministry of Defense who run these secret operations operate, in many cases, behind the facade of academic research centers and front companies.

LAVIZAN-SHIAN

One of the regime's most outrageous nuclear cover-ups occurred at a nuclear site in Tehran following my revelations about the site in a May 2003 press conference. In that announcement, I revealed a program for secret weapons of mass destruction based at the Lavizan-Shian Technological Research Center in the

Lavizan-Shian district of northeastern Tehran. The Ministry of Defense formed this biological and nuclear weapons center in the late 1990s during Khatami's presidency (1997–2005), when it accelerated both of these weapons programs. Based on information from my sources in Iran, I revealed on May 15 that the Ministry of Defense had created a special organization called Special Chemical, Biological, and Nuclear Industries, headed by IRGC brigadier general Seyyedi, which conducted secret research at the site now known as Lavizan 1.[48]

After this revelation, the Iranian regime realized that the IAEA would most likely inquire about the site and request a visit. Therefore, the Nuclear Committee of the Supreme National Security Council held a meeting and decided that the entire site had to be demolished. Before the bulldozers arrived, Iran's Ministry of Defense moved all of the nuclear and biological equipment to a nearby 60-acre military facility, now known as Lavizan 2, in the same Tehran district.[49]

Among the materials moved out of the Lavizan-Shian Technological Research Center before it was razed to the ground were two whole-body counters used to detect radiation contamination in the human body. Although the regime had purchased these counters from western countries in the 1990s, stating that they would be used for peaceful purposes, they had been installed at the secret nuclear research facility. As noted in a report by the Institute for Science and International Security, "the equipment itself is not direct evidence of a nuclear weapons program, but it is out of place at a site that was not declared by Iran to have any nuclear activity." This report also stated that spare parts for the radiation detection machines had been sent to the site, which "may actually have allowed modifications to the whole body counter that would make it more useful for a nuclear weapons program."[50] Before tearing down the secret site, the Ministry of Defense moved one of the body counters to a research facility at Malek Ashtar University in Isfahan and the second one to a private medical clinic in Tehran.

By the time that the IAEA arrived to inspect the Lavizan-Shian Technological Research Center in June 2004, there was nothing to see. The buildings were gone and the ground had been plowed over to remove six inches of topsoil.[51] The regime claimed that they were forced to remove the facility because the Tehran city authorities planned to build a public park on the property, but documents from the city government proved that this was a complete fabrication. The city had not had any communication with the research center about building a park, and when they visited the area to observe the demolition, they "were not allowed to enter the site [but] only reported the event to their superiors," according to the city document.[52]

The IAEA took soil samples during its visit to Lavizan-Shian in late June 2004, as well as samples from the two body counters and from one of the trailers that housed them. The regime did not give the IAEA access to the second trailer. In its November 14, 2004, report, the IAEA said that it did not find any nuclear material in the soil samples, but qualified this fact very explicitly: "It should be borne in mind, however, that detection of nuclear material in soil samples would be very difficult in light of the razing of the site." The report added that it could not verify what sort of activities had taken place at Lavizan-Shian, "given the removal of the buildings."[53]

In response to the IAEA's questions about the site, the regime stated that the first facility built there was the Physics Research Centre (PHRC), established in 1989. It described this as a military support center for "preparedness to combat and neutralization of casualties due to nuclear attacks and accidents (nuclear defense) and also support and provide scientific advice and services to the Ministry of Defense." Although the regime gave the IAEA a list of 11 "activities" carried out at the PHRC, it refused to provide a list of the equipment, claiming that such a list would compromise the nation's security. The regime also flatly denied that any nuclear work related to the fuel cycle was conducted at the center, and that "no nuclear material declarable in accordance with the Agency's safeguard[s] was present." The PHRC was closed down in 1998 and replaced with the Biological Study Centre, which focused on "biological R&D and 'radioprotection' activities," according to the regime. Tehran stated that in 2002 the Applied Physics Institute was added to the site, and most of the education and R&D needs of the Ministry of Defense was subsequently conducted at university research centers such as Malek Ashtar University in Isfahan.[54]

THE CENTER FOR READINESS AND
NEW ADVANCED DEFENSIVE TECHNOLOGY (LAVIZAN-2)

The structure of the Iranian regime's secret nuclear program underwent a major change in 1993 because of the anticipation of IAEA inspections and a need to merge a wide variety of covert programs into a more central organization. In 1993, the regime transferred to the Defense Ministry all of its secret nuclear programs run by the IRGC at nuclear research centers and other military and university centers. Following this merger, the Research Center of the IRGC changed its name to the Ministry of Defense Educational Research Center. All of the IRGC's nuclear experts were transferred to this center, putting the Defense Ministry's program completely under the command and control of the IRGC. Since then, the Defense Ministry's main research center, which coordinated the covert nuclear weapons program, has been known as the Center for Readiness and New Advanced Defensive Technology (CRNADT; *markaz amadegi va fannavari novin pishrafteh defaee*). In April 2004, the NCRI revealed the existence of the CRNADT, as well as of some of the top personnel involved in it. Located on Mojdeh Street in the Lavizan district of Tehran, the center is headed by Dr. Mohsen Fakhrizadeh. This top-secret, 60-acre site is protected by many closed-circuit cameras, and visitors are prohibited from entering, even employees who work in other sections.

The site was previously occupied by the Ordnance Factory Support Center, a subunit of the Ministry of Defense. Following my May 2003 revelation of the Lavizan-Shian site, the equipment and devices used for nuclear and biological activities at the razed site in Lavizan-Shian (known as Lavizan 1) were completely moved to this site (known as Lavizan–2).

Owing to the importance of this center, Brigadier General Dr. Seyed Ali Hosseini-Tash is based at this site and directly oversees nuclear-weapons-related activities. These projects include laser enrichment, which is directed by Dr. Fereydoon Abbassi, one of the Ministry of Defense's laser experts and one of the few with expertise on isotope separation. Dr. Abbassi is also director of the Nuclear Research Division at the Ministry of Defense and is in charge of the Physics Group of the IRGC's Imam Hossein University. In addition to laser enrichment, many nuclear tests on neutron initiators and recycling are pursued at the CRNADT. Some of the other personnel at the facility are Mansour Asgari, Mohammad Amin Bassam, and Majid Rezazadeh.

As of November 2006, the IAEA has still not inspected Lavizan 2, and the regime continues to sanitize the area. In February 2006, Tehran mayor Mohammad Baqer Ghalibaf gave the order to cut down more than 7,000 trees in the parklike area near both Lavizan 1 and Lavizan 2, intending to eliminate the possibility that inspectors could analyze them for traces of nuclear material. His order was prompted by IAEA tests that had found uranium contamination on the leaves and branches of the trees, but the mayor's official explanation for the tree clearing was that a national park was planned for the site.[55]

When I first learned about the mayor's story, I thought, "Another park story—not very original!" But the silliness of this excuse is overshadowed by the regime's ability to hide the nuclear secrets of Lavizan from the IAEA to this day.

IMAM HOSSEIN UNIVERSITY

In 1986, during the Iran-Iraq War, the IRGC created a training school in northeast Tehran that was named after Prophet Muhammad's grandson. Imam Hossein University is the main academic facility for training the personnel and commanders of the IRGC and members of the regime's intelligence security. Patterned after a military organization, the university organizes all the students into a brigade with a chain of command that runs from company commander to platoon commander and team commander.

As I revealed in March 2006, this school contains a large and sophisticated nuclear physics department that serves as a secret nuclear weapons research and production site for the IRGC. The nuclear physics program at Imam Hossein University is as extensive as that at the Sharif University of Technology, which has the oldest and largest nuclear physics major in the country. If the regime's nuclear program was solely for energy, the question was, Why did the IRGC military school have one of the biggest nuclear physics departments in Iran?

My sources identified the two company commanders of the nuclear physics program as IRGC commanders Seyyed Hassan Hosseini and Reza Haj Beiglou. At the time of my revelation, the commander of the school was IRGC brigadier general Ali Akbar Ahmadian, who was also serving as chairman of the Joint Chiefs of Staff of the IRGC—a clear indication that Imam Hossein University is a central institution in the IRGC. Ahmadian had succeeded IRGC brigadier general Ahmad Fazaeli in October 2005, who held the position of commander of the school for six years, until he was appointed as an advisor to the commander in chief of the IRGC. Ahmadian's deputy was IRGC commander Majid Soleimanpour.

A number of nuclear experts were transferred to the university when the regime reorganized its military nuclear programs in 1993. Among those high-level experts was Mohammad Tavalaei, who was transferred from the IRGC research center to Imam Hossein University's research center.

The regime's top nuclear expert at the university is Fereydoon Abbassi, director of the physics program and member of the IRGC since the beginning of the revolution in 1979. After fighting in the Iran-Iraq War, Abbassi obtained a Ph.D. in nuclear physics and in 1993 became a member of the college physics board at Imam Hossein University. In tandem with his work at the university, Abbassi conducts nuclear research at the Ministry of Defense, including work on a neutron generator, which he built for the agency. Abbassi is one of the regime's two top experts on the neutron generator, which, along with nuclear fuel and launching systems, is one of the three main components of a nuclear bomb. As I announced in March 2006, my sources in Iran discovered that Abbassi ran a neutron generator test at Imam Hussein University.[56] In this test, neutrons are produced when a high-energy beam targets a very small amount of enriched uranium or plutonium in the presence of beryllium. This neutron initiator is the element of a nuclear bomb that triggers the fission chain reaction. The second expert on

the neutron generator in the regime is Javad Rahighi of the AEOI, who, according to sources inside the regime, can make, at a cost of $100,000 (U.S.), a neutron
generator with a life span of seven to eight thousand hours.[57]

NUCLEAR ENRICHMENT SITE IN LASHKAR AB'AD

In 2000, the regime began constructing an enrichment facility in the Hashtgerd region of Tehran Province, an agricultural area about 25 miles west of Tehran. This
site, which I revealed in May 2003, was set up as a laser enrichment facility. The facility is located on Soheilieh Road just outside the village of Lashkar Ab'ad, in an
area dubbed by the local people as the "Presidential Orchard." The walled 200-acre
compound contains a four-story administrative building and a 165-foot by 100-foot
hall that contains several pieces of equipment used for laser enrichment.

The Lashkar Ab'ad site was designed to serve as a parallel program to uranium
enrichment in Natanz, giving the regime an additional means to enrich uranium
(laser enrichment), especially if the Natanz facility were hit by military strikes. This
facility was under the direct supervision of AEOI director Gholamreza Aqazadeh,
whose agency also acquired surrounding plots of agricultural land to use for nuclear
testing. The site was built by Jahad-e Tosse-eye Silou (Silo Development Jihad
Company), the same construction firm that worked on Natanz. All the workers,
even manual laborers, were brought in from Tehran, and no indigenous construction workers were employed—a highly unconventional practice for building construction in Iran. After construction was completed, all the workers and employees
of Silo Development Jihad Company were required to pledge in writing that they
would not disclose any information about the site to anyone.

My sources also uncovered details about the heavy security involved in keeping this facility strictly classified. The telephone numbers of the site were not
given to anyone, even senior officials, and on-site personnel were under strict orders not to give the address of their workplace to anyone. Only authorized per-
sons were allowed to approach or enter the site.

Despite all the security measures and the tremendous effort by the regime to
keep this site secret, my revelation in May 2003 once again threw the regime off
balance. The Iranian regime was already busy explaining away its concealment of
the nuclear sites at Natanz and Arak and had informed the IAEA that no enrichment-related laser activities had taken place in Iran.[58] Then the cat-and-mouse
game between Iran and the IAEA began a new round. Following my revelation,
the IAEA immediately asked to visit the site. Iran paused. In its visit to Iran, which
was held from July 10 to 13, 2003, the IAEA's team inquired as to whether they

could visit the Lashkar Ab'ad site near Hashtgerd. The Iranian authorities "indicated that they were not yet ready" to accede to the IAEA's request to visit the site in Lashkar Ab'ad. Iran eventually allowed the IAEA inspectors to visit the site in August 2003, after it moved away some key equipment.[59]

Interestingly, Iran tried to play down its program in Lashkar Ab'ad and told the IAEA that "the laboratory had originally been devoted to laser fusion research and laser spectroscopy, but that the focus of the laboratory had been changed and the equipment not related to current projects, such as a large imported vacuum vessel, had been moved."[60] But when was the equipment moved? In May 2003, according to the IAEA. What a coincidence that my revelation about the site took place in May 2003, the IAEA asked to visit the site in the same month, and Tehran also moved an important piece of equipment that same month. But the story was not over. During the inspectors' follow-up visit to Iran in November 2003, Iran acknowledged that a pilot plant for laser enrichment had been established at Lashkar Ab'ad in 2000. Iran also conceded that "uranium laser enrichment experiments had been conducted between October 2002 and January 2003 using previously undeclared natural uranium metal." Further, it became evident that following my August 2002 revelations about Natanz and Arak, which triggered IAEA inspections of Iranian nuclear sites, Tehran rushed to move equipment around and adjust its program to be better able to evade inspections, disperse the program, confuse the inspectors, and waste the inspectors' time chasing equipment and connecting the dots. For instance, in October 2002, "the laboratories, and the nuclear material, were moved from TNRC to Lashkar Ab'ad. None of these activities involving nuclear material were reported to the Agency." In addition, the IAEA stated that experiments "were conducted from October 2002 through January 2003 using 22 kg of the 50 kg of imported natural uranium metal." According to Iranian authorities, "the uranium metal was located at Lashkar Ab'ad from December 2002 through May 2003. The equipment was dismantled in May 2003 and transferred together with uranium metal to Karaj."[61]

The Iranian authorities told the IAEA that the equipment, dismantled following my May 2003 revelation, "had been imported in 2000, that it had never been used, and that it had now been packed for shipment back to the manufacturer." The Iranian regime's officials later admitted that they had lied and that the equipment was actually used for carrying out experiments involving about 500 grams of uranium metal. What is more important is that the equipment, a large vacuum vessel, was an advanced machine not only capable of enriching uranium to the peaceful range of 3.5 to 7 percent; as IAEA experts confirmed, "the system, as designed and reflected in the contract, would have been capable of HEU production."[62] HEU (highly enriched uranium) could be used as the fissile material for building a nuclear bomb.

Laser enrichment activities are now taking place at Lashkar Ab'ad. According to the information I received in September 2006 from my sources inside the Iranian regime, contrary to Iran's claims that it has stopped all laser enrichment activities, that it does not now have an active laser enrichment program, and that it has already dismantled the equipment at the Lashkar Ab'ad site, Iran is in fact involved in laser enrichment of uranium at that site. Laser enrichment at Lashkar Ab'ad is reportedly done under the disguise of a front company named Paya Partov that is involved in the acquisition and distribution of laboratory equipment for industrial and medical purposes. The resumption of the laser enrichment activities at Lashkar Ab'ad has produced favorable results, sources say.[63]

THE MINISTRY OF DEFENSE'S BERYLLIUM PROGRAM AT MALEK-ASHTAR INDUSTRIAL UNIVERSITY

The Ministry of Defense's laboratory at Malek-Ashtar Industrial University in Tehran provides a crucial element for the nuclear trigger program. In a top-secret project, the ministry's lab at Malek-Ashtar produces beryllium oxide, the sturdy yet lightweight metal component of a neutron initiator. In February 2003, the National Council of Resistance of Iran (NCRI) announced that its sources inside Iran had discovered this facility in the Chemical Labs Science Complex of Malek-Ashtar Industrial University. The project is directed by Dr. Nasser Ehsani, the president of the university, and supervised by IRGC brigadier general Dr. Seyyed Ali Hosseini-Tash of the Ministry of Defense's Institution for Training and Research. A scientist with the last name Teimourian, who heads the chemistry section of the university, and an engineer named Abbas Soleimani work with Dr. Ehsani on producing the beryllium material for a nuclear trigger mechanism.

Because of its lightness and very high melting point, beryllium is used in missiles, spacecraft, satellites, and other defense and aerospace products, and also in the construction of nuclear power reactors. It is also the essential metallic component of a nuclear neutron initiator, used in conjunction with the radioactive element polonium–210 to trigger the fission chain reaction for a nuclear explosion. Ehsani and his fellow scientists at Malek-Ashtar have worked for several years on the process of mixing polonium-210 with beryllium to provide a source of neutrons.

Beryllium's dual-use nature puts it on the IAEA's list of items that are banned for sale to "a non-nuclear-weapon state in a nuclear explosive activity or an unsafeguarded nuclear fuel-cycle activity, or in general, when there is an unacceptable risk of diversion to such an activity, or when the transfers are contrary to the objective of averting the proliferation of nuclear weapons."[64] In short, selling it to Iran is banned.

As a result of this difficulty in purchasing beryllium on the open market, the Ministry of Defense and the IRGC looked for domestic sources and initiated a search for copper-beryllium alloy deposits in Iran. The NCRI's sources discovered that in 2001 the regime launched a project code-named TAVA to find mines containing this alloy, and in June 2004, Mohammad Ghanadi of the AEOI announced in a private meeting that TAVA had successfully discovered beryllium mines.

In addition to mining beryllium, the regime has also smuggled the substance into the country through a top-secret military program. With the exception of a few grams of beryllium imported from Great Britain, the regime has not reported any of its clandestine imports to the IAEA. In 2004, the Foreign Purchase Directorate of the Ministry of Defense made a secret purchase of beryllium. Sources inside Iran informed the NCRI that the person directly involved in the purchase was an IRGC colonel. Reports intercepted by the NCRI's sources reveal that the regime's efforts in producing and importing beryllium have provided it with enough material to produce initiators for approximately 12 nuclear bombs.

SECRET NUCLEAR WEAPONS COMPONENTS AT THE MATERIALS AND ENERGY RESEARCH CENTER

Twenty-five miles west of Tehran, the regime conducts more secret nuclear weapons development under the cover of a legitimate research center set up by the Ministry of Science. In January 2006, the NCRI revealed that the Materials and Energy Research Center, located just outside the city of Meshkin-Dasht, contained hot isostatic press machines.[65] These presses can be used to shape the uranium spheres of a nuclear bomb and, like beryllium, are dual-use items banned for export to Iran. The NCRI's sources also revealed that because of the difficulty of obtaining hot presses, the regime was working on manufacturing its own.

When making its announcement about the machines at the Materials and Energy Research Center, the NCRI noted that Belgian authorities had conducted an investigation into the illegal attempts of some Belgian companies to export these items to Iran. A Belgian newspaper reported in April 2005 that the Belgian Finance Ministry sent a classified fax to its customs agents to alert them to "pressing equipment used for isostatic nuclear materials" that could be "exported to Iran."[66]

Until the revelations of January 2006, the regime's hot isostatic presses at the Materials and Energy Research Center were hidden from the world. According to the research center's Web site, the center operates as a lab for "organic and in-organic material analysis" using infrared spectrometers and other standard equipment. There is no mention of hot isostatic presses on the Web site's list of equipment.[67]

THE ISLAMIC REVOLUTIONARY GUARDS CORPS' SECRET CMC PROGRAM

In 1986 the Islamic Revolutionary Guards Corps' nuclear research center began experiments for producing ceramic matrix composites (CMC), a lightweight, heat-resistant, and very strong graphite material that can be used in heat shields for missiles that carry nuclear warheads and in other nuclear weapons applications. In May 2005 my sources in Iran informed me that the regime had managed to manufacture a small amount of the material at the IRGC research center and allocated $450 million in 2004 for expanding the program's ability to produce larger amounts. In addition, the same sources discovered that the regime has been smuggling CMC into the country in a covert program run by the Defense Ministry. Although CMC was not an item that Iran was obligated to report to the IAEA, an international agreement involving 30 nations bans the material from being traded for use in nuclear weapons. Gary Milhollin, director of the Wisconsin Project on Nuclear Arms Control, stated that CMC "would likely have to be smuggled into Iran because no reputable manufacturer would fulfill such an order."[68]

In May 2005, I revealed how the Ministry of Defense's smuggling scheme works: Each operation begins with the purchase of the material from China, India, or other countries and proceeds by routing the sale through a third country, usually in the Persian Gulf. These operations are coordinated by a Ministry of Defense official, and one of the companies that operates as the go-between is an Iranian firm based in Dubai named the Gulf Resources Development Corporation. This company, headed by an Iranian engineer who travels frequently between Dubai and Iran, secretly diverts Chinese sales of CMC into Iran. My sources also uncovered an operation run through an Iranian company based in Great Britain, which bought CMC from an American company and diverted the material through several countries before it ultimately arrived in Iran.

I also learned that in May 2004, Iran began constructing a large graphite electrode plant that will allow the regime to master graphite technology (only 19 countries have this capability), including the technology to produce CMC and other graphite components. Minor changes in the production line of this plant would enable the Iranian regime to produce the graphite products needed for a nuclear bomb. A $450 million budget was allocated for building this plant on a site spanning nearly 200 acres near Ardakan in central Iran. The plant will have the capacity of producing 30,000 metric tons per annum of UHP (ultra-high power) electrodes, which are normally used in the steel industry.

The regime gathered a consortium of several companies for this graphite-production program, including an Iranian company named IRITIEC, which is 40 percent owned by the state-run Iranian Mines and Mining Industries Development and Renovation Organization (IMIDRO). The second Iranian company involved is IRASCO, based in Italy, which is responsible for equipment purchasing and procurement from abroad. An Indian company named HEG was brought in to provide technical assistance, as was the German company SCS Technology.[69]

KHOMEINI CONFESSES TO THE BOMB IN HIS LETTER IN 1988

In a letter written by Ayatollah Ruhollah Khomeini to top officials in the final days of the Iran-Iraq war in 1988—made public in September 2006—Iran's top Islamic Revolutionary Guards Corp Commander is quoted as saying that Iran may need a nuclear bomb to win the war against Iraq. This statement, which the supreme leader considered significant enough to share with his inner circle, is yet another proof of the mullahs' long-held ambition of obtaining the bomb. The letter, made public by former President Hashemi Rafsanjani, is at odds with Tehran's official statements that Iran is not seeking a nuclear weapon because it is against Islam. The letter from Khomeini lists the requirements of military commanders if they are to continue fighting against Iraq. It mentions more aircraft, helicopters, men and weapons, and also quotes the top commander's remarks that Iran would within five years need laser-guided and atomic weapons in order to win the war.[70]

What other roles do any of Iran's uninspected sites play in its journey toward a "peaceful" nuclear program? It is a question that led the IAEA in early 2006 to bemoan the many gaps in its knowledge of Iran's nuclear activities. "After more than three years of Agency efforts to seek clarity about all aspects of Iran's nuclear programme," wrote IAEA director Mohamed ElBaradei in April 2006, "the existing gaps in knowledge continue to be a matter of concern. . . . Because of this, and other gaps in the Agency's knowledge, including the role of the military in Iran's nuclear programme, the Agency is unable to make progress in its efforts to provide assurance about the absence of undeclared nuclear material and activities in Iran."[71]

A HISTORY OF DECEPTION: IRAN'S NUCLEAR FUEL CYCLE AND NUCLEAR WEAPONS CAPABILITY

We are not questioning [the Iranians'] right to civil nuclear power. . . . But because of a track record of 18 years in which they were not clear and not transparent with the International Atomic Energy Agency, that civil nuclear power cannot include the ability to enrich and reprocess on Iranian territory, because when you learn to do that you've learned the key technology to making a nuclear weapon.

—U.S. Secretary of State Condoleezza Rice, April 19, 2006[1]

Iran's nuclear weapons program is extremely advanced. The military oversees programs that together provide all the ingredients necessary to build and deliver the bomb, and the regime has deceived the world at nearly every turn of its journey to a complete fuel cycle and the production of nuclear weapons. The level to which Iran's leaders have misled and outright lied to the IAEA reveals nothing less than contempt for anyone who tries to get in the way of its nuclear ambitions, which are tied to its ideological ambitions to export its "Islamic" revolution throughout the Middle East.

As critical elements of the nuclear program increasingly move underground into tunnels, the regime operates at an even greater level of secrecy than it did before the revelations about the Natanz and Arak facilities in 2002. Controlled by the Islamic Revolutionary Guards Corps, Iran's wholly militarized nuclear program poses the gravest threat to the world in the new millennium. Ahmadinejad's mission is to give the mullahs their first nuclear bomb at any cost, and his mission is well underway.

The most puzzling contradiction in the Iranian regime's nuclear program is its longtime pursuit of a complete domestic nuclear fuel cycle. Although the regime claims that it is committed to building nuclear reactors solely for electricity, its programs for creating nuclear fuel flagrantly contradict this argument. In a 2002 agreement with Russia over the Bushehr reactors, the Iranian regime agreed that Russia would fuel the reactors for as long as they operated and would reclaim the spent fuel rods so that the rods could not be used to make reprocessed fuel. If the fuel problem was resolved in 2002, why did the regime make a point of reminding the world of its ambitious uranium mining program in 2003?

Just two weeks before the IAEA inspectors were to arrive in Iran in February 2003 to visit the Natanz and Arak sites for the first time, AEOI chief Gholamreza Aqazadeh announced that uranium was being extracted from underground mines in the Yazd region. This prompted U.S. State Department spokesperson Richard Boucher to comment that "Iran's admission that it's been mining uranium when Russia has agreed to provide all the uranium fuel for the lifetime of the Bushehr reactor raises serious questions about Iran's supposedly peaceful nuclear program."[2]

In fact, the IAEA had been aware of Iran's uranium mining operations for years and inspected them for the first time in 1992, but Aqazadeh's statement provided an update on the mining operations in Yazd. Most significant was Aqazadeh's additional remark that Iran hoped "in the not so distant future" to "complete the fuel cycle."[3] The regime's heavy investment in mining uranium and in producing fuel for nuclear reactors stood in stark contrast to its claims that it was interested only in nuclear power.

Such a glaring contradiction exposes the Iranian regime's attempts to reconcile its legitimate nuclear agenda with its covert nuclear weapons program. Facts coming from my sources inside Iran continue to break through this facade, revealing a military-run nuclear program with one purpose: to manufacture nuclear bombs. Evidence of the regime's deception has been uncovered at every point, from its acquiring uranium to its building missiles capable of carrying nuclear warheads.

STEP ONE: OBTAINING NATURAL URANIUM—
MINING, MILLING, AND SECRET ACQUISITIONS

The two uranium mining projects in Iran noted in the IAEA's reports are at Saghand in the Yazd Province and at Bandar Abbas. The regime has been developing the Yazd mine in the Kavir Desert, about 125 miles from the city of Saghand, since the 1980s. The ore is mined from two deposits that lie 50 feet and 230 feet below the surface, and the mining is expected to yield about 50 tons of uranium per year.[4] The regime built a corresponding mill near the mine at Ardakan, which grinds the uranium into the ore concentrate called yellowcake (U_3O_8). The second mine, called Gchine, is an open-pit mine near the city of Bandar Abbas in southern Iran. This mine, and the nearby mill that accompanies it, is expected to produce about 21 tons of uranium per year.[5]

The cost of mining and producing yellowcake at the Ardakan site "is likely to exceed current world market prices several times over," according to an analysis by the International Institute for Strategic Studies.[6] Iran's pursuit of mining and processing its own uranium does not fall in line with the economic realities of fueling a small reactor program, as Iran has only one nuclear power reactor. Most countries with only a few operating nuclear power reactors have not found it economical to develop their own enrichment facilities.

In addition to mining, the Iranian regime has acquired uranium through secret, illegal purchases. In 1982, it purchased 531 tons of yellowcake from South Africa, an enormous stockpile that it did not report to the IAEA until 1990.[7] The London *Observer* reported in 1987 that the Iranian regime had secretly purchased uranium from a British-owned mine in Namibia between 1979 and 1987. The regime owned a stake in the mine that provided this eight-year supply line.[8] In 1991, the regime imported from China one ton of uranium hexafluoride (UF_6), a uranium compound that becomes a gas when heated and can then be fed into centrifuges for enrichment, and 800 kilograms of uranium tetrafluoride (UF_4), a compound that can be converted into UF_6.[9] The regime did not report these imports to the IAEA until February 2003.[10]

STEP TWO: CONVERSION

The second step in the nuclear fuel cycle is the conversion of yellowcake into other uranium compounds that can be used for enrichment or for making reactor fuel. The chemistry involved in these activities is no secret, but the various types of uranium compounds produced in a uranium conversion facility (UCF) such as the one at Isfahan can be used both for peaceful nuclear energy programs and for nuclear weapons. The Iranian regime hid some of its crucial work on conversion from the IAEA, first by hiding the program entirely and then by declaring only part of its conversion work.

The process at the UCF at Isfahan begins with the conversion of yellowcake (U_3O_8) to ammonium uranyl carbonate (AUC). This compound is then converted to uranium dioxide (UO_2), which is processed into uranium tetrafluoride (UF_4)

and finally into uranium hexafluoride (UF_6), or "hex." The uranium compound UO_2 can be used as a component of the fuel pellets that go into running a nuclear power reactor like the ones at Bushehr. Hex can be reconverted into UO_2 for this purpose, and it can also be processed into uranium metal in a technique called reduction. In addition to its uses for making nuclear fuel and parts for nuclear reactors and nuclear weapons, uranium metal can also be used to produce enriched uranium through the laser enrichment process.

The Iranian regime did not inform the IAEA about its conversion and reduction experiments at the Tehran Nuclear Research Center (TNRC) until February 2003, in the wake of the NCRI's August 2002 revelations about the Natanz and Arak sites. In its early 2003 declaration, the regime told the IAEA that it had conducted the experiments at the TNRC between 1995 and 2000, using uranium compounds that it had secretly purchased from China in 1991. The regime admitted that it had used some of the Chinese uranium for reduction experiments in order to design a uranium metal production line at the Isfahan facility. The regime also informed the IAEA in this declaration that its research activities at the TNRC did *not* include certain types of conversion experiments, such as converting UO_2 to UF_4 or converting UF_4 to hex.[11]

This declaration revealed that the regime tried to carry out its conversion phase in secret by setting up a hidden program at the TNRC and using uranium compounds that it had secretly purchased from China. Soon after this declaration, it became clear how the regime continued deliberately to hide aspects of this critical conversion phase. After the IAEA followed up on the regime's declaration in 2003, it discovered that the regime had lied when it stated that it had not conducted some of the more complex conversion experiments. Backed into a corner by the IAEA's findings, the regime admitted in August 2003 that it had indeed converted UO_2 to UF_4 at the TRNC between 1989 and 1993. In October 2003 the regime also admitted that it had run experiments for converting UF_4 to hex at the TRNC between 1991 and 1993—thereby admitting that it had lied to the IAEA in previous declarations.[12]

Another lie that came to light in the regime's October 2003 declaration involved some UF_4 that it had previously declared as lost. The regime originally told the IAEA that about 9 kilograms of UF_4 were lost in processing during reduction experiments that were conducted from 1995 to 2000. In the October declaration, the regime admitted that it had in fact used this "lost" uranium tetrafluoride in the 1991–1993 TRNC experiments for converting UF_4 to hex.[13]

The regime also lied to the IAEA about how some of the uranium metal produced at Isfahan would be used. Originally Iran told the IAEA that the metal would be used exclusively to make "shielding material," but it later admitted that it actually also planned to use the metal for laser enrichment.[14]

Iran also repeatedly deceived the IAEA about its conversion program ever since it first declared the Isfahan UCF site in 2000, claiming that the UF_6 produced from yellowcake at the facility would be enriched outside the country and brought back for conversion to UO_2. In February 2003, however, after the world learned about the Natanz enrichment facility, the regime changed its story and admitted that it intended to produce the UF_6 at Isfahan to be used for uranium enrichment at the Natanz site.[15]

Activities at the UCF were presumably shut down in late 2003, when Iran signed an agreement with Britain, Germany, and France— the EU3—to suspend all of its enrichment activities. The regime breached the agreement in August 2005 by resuming its conversion work at Isfahan (and again a few months later when it resumed enrichment at Natanz). Why the urgency? The mullahs were determined to continue their fast track to a nuclear weapons arsenal, regardless of how many treaties or threats of sanctions by the United Nations Security Council got in the way. This was abundantly clear in the regime's ability to make a "positive" out of the suspension agreement in terms of its conversion work at Isfahan.

According to one of Tehran's top mullahs, the suspension period was the perfect time to exploit the international crisis over its nuclear program. The cleric Hassan Rowhani, former deputy head of the Supreme National Security Council, stated in a speech at the Supreme Council for Cultural Revolution in October 2005 that work at Isfahan actually sped up after the EU3 suspension agreement was signed. Rowhani, who was the chief nuclear negotiator with the European Union from 2003 to 2005, explained that the regime "only accepted suspension in areas that we did not have technical problems." He said that work on the UCF at Isfahan was completed during the enrichment suspension period of 2003 to 2005. "At the same time when we were talking with Europeans in Tehran, we were installing the equipment in some of Isfahan's sections and a lot of work had still remained to complete the project. In fact, we managed to finish the Isfahan project by creating a calm environment."[16]

The facility at Isfahan is designed to produce enough UF_6 to meet the annual fuel requirements for the Bushehr nuclear power plant. Between September 2005 and May 2006, the site produced approximately 110 tons of UF_6.[17] Approximately 5 tons of UF_6 is required to make enough highly enriched uranium for a single atomic bomb. So 110 tons of UF_6 could potentially give the Iranian regime enough fissile material for 22 bombs. Annually, UF_6 from Isfahan will be enriched at Natanz to yield about 25 tons of low-enriched uranium for the Bushehr reactors. The Isfahan conversion facility is also designed to produce about 11 tons of UO_2 per year, enough to meet the fuel needs of the heavy-water research reactor at Arak.[18]

STEP THREE: ENRICHMENT

Because natural uranium contains only 0.7 percent of the fissile uranium isotope U–235, it must be enriched for use as either fuel for a reactor or fuel for a nuclear bomb. The fuel that runs nuclear power reactors contains 3 to 5 percent U–235, a concentration classified as low-enriched uranium (LEU). Uranium enriched to 20 percent U–235 or above is considered highly enriched uranium (HEU), and a concentration of at least 90 percent is needed for a nuclear weapon. Centrifuge technology uses the centrifugal force of spinning machines to separate the U–235 and U–238 isotopes found in natural uranium. Both isotopes are siphoned off and refed into a series of connected machines until the desired enrichment of U–235 is achieved.

The most important thing to understand about this process in terms of Iran is that it takes much more time and resources to enrich uranium to LEU levels than it does to subsequently enrich LEU to HEU levels. The vast majority of the work is done in producing the LEU, and once that is accomplished, the cascades can be rearranged in a matter of weeks to use LEU as feed material to produce HEU.[19] As analysts from the British American Security Information Council noted, "Roughly speaking, only an additional cost and effort of 20 percent is needed to produce HEU from LEU, compared to the cost and effort involved in producing LEU from natural uranium."[20] Therefore, by the time that Iran successfully produces LEU on a large scale, it will have done 80 percent of the work in producing HEU for use in nuclear weapons, putting Iran only a screwdriver's turn away from building the bomb.

The Iranian regime's centrifuge program, begun in 1985, was hidden from the IAEA until my revelations of August 2002. The program comprises various military research sites and a million-square-foot enrichment facility in Natanz, about 200 miles south of Tehran. Since my revelations, the regime has continued to use delay tactics and deception in order to conceal its long history of enrichment from the IAEA.

Centrifuge research and production began as a secret project at the Tehran Nuclear Research Center and in 1995 was moved to an undeclared AEOI site in Tehran called the Kalaye Electric (Electric Goods) Company. I revealed the existence of the nuclear workshop at Kalaye Electric in February 2003. In 1987, the regime bought centrifuge design drawings and parts from the A. Q. Khan black-market network to boost its work at this site. Iran bought another set of designs and 500 used centrifuge components from the network for about $3 million in the mid-1990s. This second sale, which was handled through a company in Dubai, was revealed by Khan's associate, Buhary Tahir, during the investigation of Khan's network in 2004.

The regime went to great lengths to hide its activities at the Kalaye Electric Company after the workshop was identified, starting with the denial that any nuclear material had been used in its experiments. In its "full disclosure" report to the IAEA of October 2003, however, the regime confessed that it had used UF_6 in centrifuge tests at the site. This tactic—deny first and delay the truth as long as possible—became the regime's prime directive in dealing with the IAEA after its covert nuclear program was exposed.

The regime did not allow the IAEA to visit Kalaye Electric until March 2003, and during that visit it prohibited inspectors from taking samples to check for traces of enriched uranium. When the regime finally agreed to let the IAEA return and take environmental samples in August 2003, it prepared for the visit by painting the entire interior, ripping up and replacing all the flooring, and moving all of the equipment to another AEOI-operated company in Tehran called Pars Terash. Despite these desperate measures, the IAEA found traces of HEU at 36 percent, 54 percent, and 70 percent in its Kalaye Electric samples, and more traces of HEU from samples taken at Natanz, Pars Terash, and a centrifuge quality-control site in Isfahan called Farayand Technique.

Forced to reveal more details based on this evidence, the regime admitted that it had run centrifuge tests at Kalaye Electric, but it insisted that these tests achieved only 1.2 percent enrichment. The regime claimed that the previously used centrifuge equipment at these sites must already have been contaminated with the HEU when it was received from its foreign supplier (A. Q. Khan), and that the IAEA's analyses "tend, on balance," to support Iran's claim about the foreign origin of some of the observed HEU contamination. However, analysis of the environmental samples collected at some other locations is still in progress.[21] The IAEA announced in May 2006 that additional tests on equipment from Lavizan 1 had again uncovered traces of HEU. In its ongoing analysis, the IAEA must compare the HEU to uranium on similar Pakistani equipment to determine if the sample material entered Iran on the imported equipment or if it had been enriched at Lavizan 1.[22]

The revelations about Iran's enrichment facilities at Natanz and Kalaye Electric shook many leaders awake to the possibility that Iran had been developing a nuclear weapons agenda for nearly two decades. "As Iranian diplomats had told their European counterparts for many years that Iran was not interested in the development of enrichment technology, the exposure of the facility aroused concerns about Iran's nuclear intentions," noted the International Institute for Strategic Studies.[23] Iran's first response about its project at Natanz was to explain that the site was not secret at all, but had been openly under development since 1997, using Iranian know-how to model centrifuge design. This story did not hold up with the experts, however, and in August 2003 the regime admitted that it had actually begun its centrifuge program in 1985 and received designs and materials from a foreign source, which was eventually revealed to be the A. Q. Khan network.

The regime's deception about uranium enrichment has been broad and deep. In its "full" disclosure of October 2003, the regime claimed that it would be fully transparent about its nuclear activities, stating that Iran was committed to "removing any ambiguities and doubts about the exclusively peaceful character of these activities and commencing a new phase of confidence and co-operation in this field at the international level."[24] But AEOI director Gholamreza Aqazadeh must have been crossing his fingers as he wrote this declaration, because in addition to the cat-and-mouse deceptions about its P–1 centrifuges, Iran failed to mention that it had been working on a P–2 centrifuge program since 1995.

The P–2 centrifuge is a Pakistani design that features steel rotors that spin much faster than the aluminum rotors of the P–1, which allows the P–2 to enrich uranium at twice the speed of the older machine. After developing this new model, Pakistan converted all of its cascades to the P–2 model and sold off its old P–1 machines. Following its investigation of the sites that I revealed in August 2002, the IAEA found evidence that the Iranian regime had been building and testing P–2 centrifuges. The regime's response was a classic example of Tehran's tactic of denial, deception, and delay.

First, Iran claimed that it had "neglected to include" the P–2 centrifuges in its October 2003 declaration because of "time pressure in preparing the declaration." The IAEA found this excuse "difficult to comprehend." In its first declaration about the P–2 program, the regime stated that it received P–2 drawings in 1995 from a foreign source and that it engaged in some testing without nuclear material. It claimed that actual testing did not begin until 2001, and that all the manufacturing was done at a private company in Tehran, with no materials imported from foreign countries.[25] This declaration was filled with falsehoods, as affirmed by the IAEA report of June 2004. The regime's P–2 program was much more extensive than the regime had declared: It had purchased raw materials and related equipment from foreign suppliers, including some magnets for the centrifuges from Asia, and it had an outstanding order for 4,000 more magnets from a European supplier. These facts flew in the face of Iran's repeated denials of importing materials for the program. "Iran even had the effrontery to circulate an official document at the IAEA board meeting last February [2004] denying any foreign P–2 procurement," stated then Under Secretary of State for Arms Control and International Security John Bolton.[26] The size of the European magnet order signified plans for building thousands of centrifuges. The regime had also lied about the location of all the P–2 manufacturing: The rotors were not built at Kalaye Electric, but at a military manufacturing workshop run by the regime's Defense Industries Organization (DIO).[27]

To denounce the regime's pattern of withholding information about the P–2 centrifuges until evidence demanded it, the IAEA issued a resolution in March 2004 stating that it "deplores that Iran . . . omitted any reference, in its letter of 21 October 2003 . . . to its possession of P–2 centrifuge design drawings and to associated research, manufacturing, and mechanical testing activities—which the Director General describes as 'a matter of serious concern, particularly in view of the importance and sensitivity of those activities.'"[28] In April 2004, the NCRI named a senior IRGC nuclear scientist at the Defense Ministry involved in the research and development of the advanced P–2 centrifuge machines and reported that most of the work was conducted at the Center for Readiness and New Advanced Defensive Technology located at the Lavizan–2 nuclear site.[29] In April 2006, President Ahmadinejad finally conceded that Tehran was "presently conducting research" on the P–2 and boasted that it would quadruple Iran's enrichment powers.[30] NCRI Foreign Affairs Committee Chair Mohammad Mohaddessin charged later in the month that work on P–2 machines was conducted at various sites, including military facilities, as well as in the workshops in Abali, northern Tehran, and at the Natanz uranium enrichment facility in central Iran. Mohaddessin announced in August 2006 that Iran has built at least 15 advanced P–2 machines at a secret site run by the "Iran Centrifuge Technology Company."[31]

The regime began construction on the enrichment facility at Natanz in 2000, after many years of centrifuge research and development at the TNRC and at Kalaye Electric. Nine aboveground buildings make up the pilot fuel enrichment plant (PFEP), where a cascade of about 1,000 centrifuge machines is designed to enrich uranium to 5 percent. The biggest work at Natanz goes on 25 feet underground, where two massive halls are designed to hold a total of 60,000 centrifuges. This fuel enrichment plant (FEP) will be capable of producing about 25 tons of low-enriched uranium per year, enough to run the Bushehr reactor but far from enough for the regime's stated plans to generate 7,000 megawatts of nuclear energy by the year 2021. This would require seven nuclear power plants and thus seven times more LEU than Natanz can provide.

Why does Iran invest in such a facility—and the extensive mining and conversion operations that accompany it—to fuel one reactor when it already possesses other vast energy reserves? Experts believe that Iran has the second largest gas reserves in the world and flares enough gas annually to generate electricity equivalent to the output of four Bushehr reactors.[32] This glaring contradiction is enough to rouse suspicions that the regime is investing in nuclear facilities for weapons, not energy.

Technicians at Natanz conducted a brief test of a 164-centrifuge cascade before the regime suspended activities at the PFEP in October 2003. The demand to suspend came from the EU3 in the wake of the 2002 revelations; by agreeing to suspend its enrichment program, Iran averted having the case sent to the United Nations Security Council. After the regime's announcement that it would suspend its activities, Hassan Rowhani, the secretary of Iran's Supreme National Security Council, attempted to save face by explaining that Iran was in full control of the situation: "We will suspend our activities for as long as we deem necessary," he said on October 21, 2003. "This could be for one day, one year or longer. The decision is ours."[33] Former president Mohammad Khatami belittled the global reaction to Iran's top-secret, 18-year nuclear program as nothing more than bullying incited by the United States. "It's been like a boxing match with a powerful, unjust rival trying to sway world opinion," he said after Iran agreed to shut down the activities at Natanz. "Now it has turned into a marathon run. The world has learned that we have been sincere."[34]

Sincerity was the last thing that the regime displayed after it signed the suspension agreement, as well as an additional protocol to the Treaty on the Non-Proliferation of Nuclear Weapons (NPT) that would allow snap inspections by IAEA inspectors. The protocol was signed on December 18, 2003, four months after the regime's covert program was exposed. In August 2005, the National Council of Resistance of Iran (NCRI) revealed that thousands of centrifuges were built after the late 2003 agreements were signed. The NCRI's sources inside Iran—who had provided the facts about the secret sites at Natanz and Arak in 2002—revealed that teams were working around the clock in secret military manufacturing companies to build centrifuges for the Natanz facility.[35] Based on these same sources, I announced in January 2006 that approximately 5,000 centrifuges were completed, all built during the so-called suspension period.[36]

The regime broke the suspension agreement in January 2006 by removing the IAEA seals on the equipment at Natanz and restarting pilot-scale enrichment. Mohammad Saeedi, deputy head of the AEOI, claimed that the regime had relaunched enrichment activities "merely in the field of research," and that the production of nuclear fuel was still suspended.[37] A statement by the president of the United Nations Security Council in March 2006 gave Iran until April 28 to suspend all enrichment-related activities. In April 2006, Ahmadinejad staged an elaborate event in Mashhad to announce that the PFEP at Natanz had successfully enriched LEU to 3.5 percent, a sufficient concentration to fuel the Bushehr reactor. "Iran has joined the nuclear countries of the world," he said.[38]

The event was staged one day before IAEA chief Mohamed ElBaradei made an official visit to Tehran to discuss the looming deadline for Iran to suspend enrichment, and Ahmadinejad took advantage of the event to show his contempt for all western authorities. Remarking on the anger aroused in the world over Iran's completion of the nuclear fuel cycle, he said, "We will tell them to keep on being angry and die from it."[39]

After Iran ignored the April 28, 2006, Security Council deadline to shut down its activities at Natanz, the IAEA issued a report confirming that the site had achieved the production of LEU at 3.6 percent and that UF_6 was still being fed into a 164-machine cascade. In addition, two more 164-machine cascades were being built. On the day of the deadline, Ahmadinejad took the stage once again to proclaim that the regime was not intimidated by the prospect of U.N. Security Council sanctions or other measures. "The Iranian nation won't give a damn about such useless resolutions," he said.[40]

The regime also hid its laser enrichment program from the IAEA until my sources in Iran uncovered the secret facility that housed it in 2003. This experimental type of enrichment can be carried out using two different methods: atomic vapor laser isotope separation (AVLIS), in which a laser ionizes U–235 atoms so that they can be collected on an electrically charged plate, and molecular laser isotope separation (MLIS), which exposes UF_6 to laser light in order to isolate U–235 molecules. Laser enrichment is faster and less expensive than the gas centrifuge method—and also easier to hide. According to the Federation of American Scientists, "because of their small size and potential for high enrichment in few stages, laser isotope enrichment techniques could prove to be difficult to detect and control if successfully developed in a clandestine program."[41]

The shah's regime had conducted laser enrichment research at the TNRC, but the program was dropped after Khomeini came to power. The program was restored in 1991 when the regime purchased laser enrichment technology from China, as well as the uranium to use in the experiments, in complete violation of its safeguards obligations under the NPT.[42] This covert activity was discovered only after the IAEA was compelled to investigate following my May 2003 revelations about the enrichment site at Lashkar Ab'ad, about 25 miles west of Tehran. This revelation provoked a round of regime denials and deception about its laser enrichment activities that have not yet been completely resolved.

The IAEA requested a visit to the undeclared facility the same month of my revelation, but the regime refused and immediately began taking apart the equipment in order to move it off the site. After the regime transferred the laser equipment to the AEOI's Nuclear Center for Agriculture and Medicine in Karaj,

100 miles northwest of Tehran, it allowed the IAEA to schedule a visit to Lashkar Ab'ad. During that visit in August 2003, the regime said that it had conducted laser activities at the site, but that none of the activities involved nuclear material or enrichment. In early October 2003, the regime admitted that it had illegally imported laser equipment in 1992 and 2000 that it had installed at the TNRC, and in the same declaration it agreed to let the IAEA take samples at Lashkar Ab'ad. The inspectors took samples at that facility as well as at the Karaj site, and realizing that the game was up, the regime made another confession to the IAEA before the month was over.

In its October 21, 2003, declaration, the regime admitted that it had "carried out laser enrichment experiments using previously undeclared imported uranium metal at TNRC between 1993 and 2000," according to the November 2003 IAEA report, "and that it had established a pilot plant for laser enrichment at Lashkar Ab'ad, where it had also carried out experiments using imported uranium metal." The regime soon followed up this statement with the admission that it had moved all the laser enrichment equipment to Karaj before allowing the IAEA to visit the facility.[43] Once again, the mullahs disregarded their treaty obligations and told the truth only when they were about to be caught red-handed, after working the system for as long as possible.

My sources in Iran uncovered an additional covert laser enrichment operation in early 2005. On March 24, I announced that the regime was conducting this work at the Parchin military complex in a program led by IRGC member and laser enrichment expert Mohammad Amin Bassam.[44] The regime had granted the IAEA a limited visit to Parchin in January 2005, and the IAEA visited once again in November 2005 but stated that it did not "observe any unusual activities" during this inspection, nor did it find any nuclear material in its samples.[45] However, according to the NCRI sources in Iran, the IAEA was allowed to inspect Plan 10, a few buildings in one of the subsections of an installation that dealt with antiaircraft defense. This was one of 11 plans in a huge military complex that covers thousands of acres near Tehran. The inspection was also delayed for a long period to allow the regime to clear all possible nuclear tracks. The IAEA was not allowed to inspect the buildings at "Plan 1" at Parchin, where I had revealed the regime's laser enrichment program in March 2005.

STEP FOUR: FUEL FABRICATION

In Iran, the procedure for processing low-enriched uranium into a form that can be fed into a nuclear reactor takes place at the fuel manufacturing plant (FMP) at Isfahan. The site produces UO_2 pellets that will be inserted into the fuel rods of both the light-water reactor at Bushehr and the heavy-water reactor at Arak. Once the pellets are stacked into the hollow rods, the rods are covered in a zirconium metal coating, and 312 are grouped together to form a fuel assembly. The Russian-designed Bushehr reactor contains a reactor core made up of 163 of these fuel assemblies.[46] The UO_2 that is shaped into the pellets is produced at the uranium conversion facility (UCF) at Isfahan.

The regime told the IAEA in 2003 that it would begin construction of the FMP that year for the purpose of making fuel assemblies for Arak and Bushehr and that it expected the plant to be operational in 2007.[47] Construction at the FMP has not gone as quickly as planned, however. In a March 2006 report, the IAEA noted that construction was ongoing but that the completion date "was likely to be postponed."[48]

The controversy surrounding this plant centers on global suspicions that Iran is building its heavy-water research reactor at Arak in order to produce plutonium for a nuclear bomb. The high-quality plutonium produced in a heavy-water reactor is the main component of a compact nuclear weapon. As FirstWatch International director Jack Boureston observed, "If Iran wishes to develop a nuclear weapon small enough to launch on top of its Shahab 3 or 4 missiles, it will most probably be an implosion device with a plutonium (Pu) core. . . . A heavy water reactor is among the most dangerous in existence from a proliferation perspective."[49]

STEP FIVE: THE NUCLEAR REACTOR

For all the effort that Iran exerts to showcase the nuclear power plant at Bushehr as the centerpiece of its long-range energy plans, the unfinished plant has been an engineering and financial nightmare for decades. Iran creaks along in constructing the site, which has been in the hands of a Russian company since the mid-1990s. Most of the problems stem from the Russian design conflicting dramatically with the original German design, such as the current requirement for six horizontal steam generators versus the four vertical steam generators inherent in the German design.[50]

Alexander Rumyantsev, head of Russia's Federal Atomic Energy Agency, explained that "it is easier to start construction from scratch than try to observe regulations fixed by a foreign country." He described the technological hurdles that have plagued the Russian construction team since the beginning: "We actually had no designs. We had to do everything on the results of our surveys. . . . In fact, it is a very hard task."[51] But the Russians had a good reason, in addition to the financial one, to take up the Bushehr project: obtaining access to the complete western design of a nuclear reactor.

Dr. Manouchehr Fakhimi, who saw the original classified blueprints for the Bushehr plant during the early years of Khomeini's regime, believes that the initial work on the plant prevents it from ever being a viable facility. In particular, the original structure did not meet the standards needed to withstand the seismic activity of the area, and now the buildings are simply getting too old. "The time for this plant is over," he said. "It is too old, and it could be the second Chernobyl situation."[52] The plant's beleaguered past includes multiple bombings during the Iran-Iraq War, years of standing idle, and usage for grain storage. Russia was aware of all these challenges when it made the $800 million deal to complete one of the two twin reactors in 1995.

The heightened suspicions about Iran's secret nuclear weapons program that followed the revelations of 2002 widened the rift between Washington and Moscow regarding Russia's investment in Iran's nuclear program. The United States has not been able to convince Russia to halt its work at Bushehr, and Russian president Vladimir Putin has staunchly defended Iran's nuclear program. In February 2005, Iran and Russia finalized the fuel agreement for Bushehr, stipulating that Russia would provide fuel for the plant and Iran would ship its spent fuel rods to Russia.

In the Iranian regime's eyes, the escalating U.S.-Russia friction and the years that Russia and Iran spent haggling over the financial details and other aspects of this agreement helped put the focus on Bushehr rather than on the covert nuclear weapons program. The regime is well aware of how long these political, commercial, and diplomatic issues can be drawn out, and it exploits the delays whenever possible. With every month and year that governments and nuclear watchdog agencies deliberate over the single power plant at Bushehr and the facilities that support it, the regime buys precious time in advancing its nuclear arsenal.

Although Bushehr has always been an aboveboard project that complies with IAEA regulations, experts looked at the site with extreme suspicion after the world learned about Iran's long-hidden nuclear weapons program. The enrichment program that was developed to feed the plant could easily be used to produce highly enriched uranium, and the power plant will eventually produce plutonium in its spent fuel that can be used for a nuclear bomb. Paul Leventhal of the Nuclear Control Institute remarked that if Iran did not follow through with its agreement to send its spent fuel to Russia, the Bushehr reactor could produce a quarter ton of plutonium a year, enough for about 30 nuclear bombs.[53]

But perhaps Iran's greatest long-term benefit from Bushehr is Iran's ability to use the entire project as a cover for its shadow nuclear weapons program. With Bushehr as the poster child of Iran's civilian nuclear energy program, the regime can justify having hundreds of nuclear scientists and nuclear research labs.

Another reactor at the center of global alarm about Iran's covert nuclear program is the heavy-water reactor at Arak, the Iran Nuclear Research Reactor (IR–40). This reactor is the latest development in what began as a top-secret AEOI heavy-water project first developed in 1999. The regime hid the heavy-water program until I revealed the heavy-water production plant (HWPP) in 2002, and the regime did not declare it until the IAEA's visit in February 2003. The regime hid the program from the IAEA—and from Iran's parliament—by implementing all the operations through a front company in Tehran called Mesbah Energy.[54]

News about Iran's secret heavy-water program raised red flags throughout the world because heavy-water reactors are tailor-made for producing weapons-grade plutonium. Despite these suspicions and the international crisis surrounding Iran's enrichment program, the regime went full steam ahead with its heavy-water program in 2004 by starting construction on IR–40. Although the reactor was from the beginning part of Iran's plans for its heavy-water project, it did not declare its reactor plans to the IAEA until May 2003.

Iran's stated purpose for the IR–40, according to IAEA reports, was research and development and the production of radioisotopes for medical and industrial use. The regime also claimed that the IR–40 at Arak would replace the 35-year-old research reactor at the TNRC, which was getting too old. But a powerful 40-megawatt heavy-water reactor is an odd replacement for a 5-megawatt light-water reactor. If the regime was intent on going into the medical isotopes industry, why did it not just say so in 1996 instead of hiding its heavy-water facility and heavy-water reactor plans? At one glance, the most compelling comparison of the TNRC reactor and its replacement, the IR–40, is the amount of plutonium each can produce: The TNRC can produce up to 600 grams (1.3 pounds) of plutonium per year, while the IR–40 can produce 8 kilograms (17 pounds), the amount the IAEA says is required for a nuclear weapon.[55]

Iran's deception about the IR–40 continued even after it finally declared its plans to the IAEA. In July 2003, the IAEA had questions about the drawings of the plant that Iran provided, particularly about the drawings that did not include any mention of hot cells. Every facility that works with radioisotopes requires these structures—thick-walled rooms in which the radioactive material is handled remotely with robotic arms or other large manipulation devices. The IAEA wanted more detailed design plans for the reactor and an explanation about public reports that Iran had attempted to buy large manipulators from a French company; such a purchase would be a violation of the NPT.

Iran responded to the IAEA's concerns with its usual evasiveness. Three months after the IAEA's request for information, the regime stated that it had "foreseen" the need for two hot cells during its development of the reactor design and that it now had plans for nine such structures. It was silent on the issue of trying to purchase manipulators from a foreign country. As of November 2006, the IAEA was still waiting for a response. Western experts say that the Arak heavy-water reactor is too big for research and too small for making electricity. Its size is roughly that of those used abroad to make plutonium bomb fuel. Gary Milhollin, director of the Wisconsin Project on Nuclear Arms Control, a Washington research group that tracks atomic materials, said, "If you look around the world at heavy water reactors of this size, virtually all of them have been used to make bombs."[56] Iran has told the IAEA that the reactor would be completed by 2014, but my sources in Iran say that that date is a deliberate deception and that Iran actually plans to complete the project five to seven years earlier.

STEP SIX: REPROCESSING

At the "back end" of the nuclear fuel cycle, reprocessing recovers spent fuel for recycling. The spent fuel of a nuclear power plant like Bushehr contains U–235 and plutonium that can be reprocessed into a mixed oxide fuel to be fed back into the plant. Reprocessing also reduces the amount of highly radioactive waste that must be disposed of. Because this process requires separating the uranium and plutonium from the spent fuel, reprocessing is a critical nuclear proliferation concern because the plutonium can be collected and used for the core of a nuclear bomb.

The Iranian regime performed top-secret reprocessing experiments at the TNRC for several years, and not until the revelations of 2002 was it compelled to declare them to the IAEA. Iran's declarations, begun in October 2003, came in the usual stages—misinformation followed by a series of corrections, and then only when pressed for more information. The first declaration stated that researchers produced about 200 micrograms of plutonium at the TNRC between 1988 and 1993. The IAEA's investigations proved that the regime lied about the amount of plutonium, as well as about the dates of the experiments. The IAEA concluded that 100 milligrams of plutonium were separated—not the 200 micrograms that Iran claimed—and the regime was forced to confirm that the IAEA's figure was correct.[57] These are very small quantities, but the difference is significant when dealing with research that will be applied to industrial-scale programs such as reprocessing the spent fuel from the Bushehr power plant. The IAEA also found that the age of materials in the experiment pointed to activity more recent than 1993. In May 2005, the regime admitted that it had conducted further experiments in 1995 and 1998.[58]

The plutonium reprocessing fiasco is one more example of how Iran keeps the nuclear sleuth teams of the IAEA very busy by providing false information and withholding data, thereby creating delays in the already sluggish inspections process.

Once the Bushehr power plant is operational, it will produce about 25 tons of spent fuel per year to yield "a few hundred kilograms of plutonium," according to the International Institute for Strategic Studies. This is enough to create "a few dozen nuclear weapons" that each require 6–8 kilograms (13–18 pounds) of plutonium.[59] Thus Iran is on track to produce weapons-usable material from both possible routes: acquiring plutonium from spent fuel (at Bushehr and Arak) and producing highly enriched uranium (at Natanz).

WEAPON CONSTRUCTION

Iran is working on critical chemical and hardware aspects of nuclear bomb design. These secret projects are operated by the same secret military infrastructure that operates the covert nuclear fuel cycle programs. Bomb construction activities include work on the bomb trigger mechanism, boosted-fission weapon design, and bomb casings.

As discussed in the previous chapter, Brigadier General Dr. Seyyed Ali Hosseini-Tash, the official in charge of the Ministry of Defense's weapons of mass destruction program, is responsible for the neutron initiator program. The neutron initiator, composed of polonium–210 and beryllium, acts as the trigger for the fission chain reaction that produces the explosion in a nuclear weapon.[60]

Iran's Ministry of Defense and the AEOI are both involved in beryllium projects. The Ministry of Defense's Malek-Ashtar Industrial University produces beryllium oxide for use in laboratory testing, and nuclear experts at this university are also working on a program to produce the material on an industrial scale. The AEOI runs a secret beryllium-oxide program at its primary nuclear laboratory, the Jaber Ibn Hayan Multipurpose Laboratories (JHL).

The process of creating polonium–210, also necessary for a neutron initiator, involves irradiating bismuth metal, and Iran's activities in this area continue to confound the IAEA. In September 2003, the IAEA found records that bismuth had been irradiated in the research reactor at the TNRC from 1989 to 1993. The IAEA's report noted that even though bismuth is not a banned material, "its irradiation is of interest to the Agency as it produces polonium–210 (Po–210) . . . that could be used . . . in conjunction with beryllium, for military purposes (specifically, as a neutron initiator in some designs of nuclear weapons)."[61]

According to IAEA reports, the Iranian regime has given inadequate explanations and has continuously evaded requests for information about its bismuth experiments. In November 2003, Iran claimed that the experiments were done to produce polonium–210 on a laboratory scale, with the ultimate goal of using the material in radioisotope batteries. The following February, the regime stated that the experiments had also been "part of a study about neutron sources," but that it could not offer evidence to support this claim because very few records remained about the project. In all subsequent communication with the IAEA, the regime merely restated its original story about producing polonium–210 for batteries. In a 2004 report, the IAEA stated that Iran had "reiterated in writing that it 'does not have [a] project for neither production of Po–210 nor production of neutron sources, using Po–210' and that 'there [had] not been in the past any studies or projects on the production of neutron sources using Po–210.'"[62] When the IAEA asked Iran for access to the glove box used to protect technicians doing the polonium–210 experiments, the regime said that the box had been discarded. In the November 2004 board report, the IAEA expressed its ongoing concern about Iran's flimsy explanations, stating that it remained "somewhat uncertain regarding the plausibility of the stated purpose of the experiments given the very limited applications of short lived Po–210 sources."[63]

Information gleaned from the NCRI's sources inside Iran revealed that the regime has also tried to obtain tritium, an NPT-banned material used in boosted-fission nuclear weapons. A bomb that contains a "booster" of tritium-deuterium gas achieves a much more powerful fission chain reaction than a standard implosion bomb does. In August 2005, the NCRI revealed that Iran had tried to smuggle this material in from various countries, including South Korea.[64] Tritium can also be produced in heavy-water reactors, which raises suspicions that the secret heavy-water (deuterium) research at Lavizan 2 may involve work on producing this element.[65] In 2004, a Reuters report about Iran's negotiations with a Russian company to buy deuterium gas deepened the concern about Iran's hidden bomb-making activities.[66]

There are additional indications that Iran is working on the weaponization of its nuclear program. NCRI sources in Iran said in April 2006 that Iran was seeking to build an "implosion-triggered" bomb in which conventional explosives are packed around highly-enriched nuclear fuel.

In November 2005, IAEA inspectors reported that they had found in Iran documents delivered around 1987 by the A. Q. Khan network, related to casting and machining uranium metal into hemispherical forms. The only known use for such forms is in nuclear weapons. As the November 2006 report by the IAEA indicates, Iran is yet to provide a copy of the 15-page document describing the procedures for the reduction of UF_6 to uranium metal and the casting and machining of enriched and depleted uranium metal into hemispheres.[67]

The existence of a laptop computer containing extensive documentary evidence indicating that the Iranian regime has been working on a re-entry vehicle consistent with many of the technical parameters for a nuclear warhead first surfaced in November 2004. *The Washington Post* quoted Secretary of State Colin L. Powell and other officials who shared information with reporters about Iran's nuclear program. "A 'walk-in' source approached U.S intelligence earlier that month with more than 1,000 pages purported to be Iranian drawings and technical documents, including a nuclear warhead design and modifications to enable Iranian ballistic missiles to deliver an atomic strike," according to a U.S. official who spoke on the condition of anonymity.[68] Also, U.S. officials told the *Wall Street Journal* that the materials document Iran's efforts between 2001 and 2003 to adapt its Shahab-3 missile for delivering a "black box" that experts at the nation's nuclear-weapons laboratories believe is almost certainly a nuclear warhead. The specifications for size, shape, weight and height of detonation do not change during more than two years of work and do not make sense for conventional explosives, according to several officials who have been briefed on the intelligence.[69] In a four-page report provided by the IAEA to the member countries in January 2006, the Agency refers to a secretive Iranian entity called the "Green Salt Project," which worked on uranium processing, high explosives and a missile warhead design.[70] The combination suggests a "military-nuclear dimension," the report said. According to the IAEA, as of November 2006, Iran "has not expressed any readiness to discuss information concerning alleged studies related to the so-called Green Salt Project."[71]

———————— ⋅•⋅•⋅ ————————

This brief overview of Iran's repeated attempts to hide, deny, mislead, and unabashedly lie about its nuclear program illustrates the regime's habitual bad behavior toward the international community. Each documented lie and delay tactic, combined with many reports that have not yet been investigated, leads to a few inevitable questions: What else is the regime hiding? How many other black-market purchases of uranium or missiles are yet to be uncovered? How many facilities are hidden in additional tunnel complexes beneath Iran's mountain ranges? How much expertise and material continue to flow into the country from foreign nations that have been collaborating with the regime for decades via Tehran's intricate smuggling network? The ascension to the presidency of Mahmoud Ahmadinejad signals a rise in Tehran's deceptive tactics as it marches headlong into the final stages of its nuclear weapons program.

CHAPTER 9

CAMOUFLAGE AND CONCEALMENT: HIDING THE NUCLEAR PROGRAM UNDERGROUND AND BEHIND FRONT COMPANIES

The construction of the . . . secret underground emergency command centre in Tehran . . . is part of the regime's plan to move more of its operations beneath ground.

—*Telegraph* (U.K.), March 12, 2006[1]

The regime was plunged into survival mode in 2002 after its secret nuclear facilities at Natanz and Arak were exposed. In an attempt to protect its covert nuclear programs from further exposure and possible attack, Iran took two critical actions: It brought the programs increasingly under IRGC control and moved more of the activities physically underground. These actions, the mullahs believed, would make the program leak proof, or at least extremely difficult to detect, and also more secure.

Prior to taking those actions, one of the key strategies that allowed the regime to build the nuclear weapons program and, later, to keep it hidden and extremely difficult to track has been its use of front companies. This strategy helps make the regime's covert nuclear operations extremely difficult to detect and difficult to tie to the regime itself. Using private firms as camouflage for purchasing equipment and material, researching, acquiring expertise, and building nuclear components has played a central role in the regime's ability to hide its program from the world.

TUNNEL VISION: IRAN'S UNDERGROUND FACILITIES

As one of the most mountainous countries in the world—more than 50 percent of the country is covered by mountain areas—Iran is well suited for tunneling. And Tehran itself is conveniently located near the massive Alborz range that runs across the entire northern boundary of the country, allowing vast tunnel complexes to be built around the country's capital. None of Iran's underground facilities have been inspected by the IAEA, with the exception of the centrifuge cascade halls at Natanz. Those two halls were constructed underground to protect the secret enrichment program from air attacks and from IAEA detection, and the IAEA first visited them in 2003. But none of the other tunnel sites have been investigated, which has given the regime years of uninterrupted work on nuclear weapons and missiles.

On March 24, 2005, I revealed in Washington, D.C., that the Iranian Ministry of Defense had secretly built tunnels at the Parchin Military Complex, a military site 19 miles southeast of Tehran. Based on facts that I received from my sources inside Iran, I also reported that this was the site of the regime's top-secret laser enrichment program.

Laser enrichment is one of several operations running at the complex and is concealed within a military chemical project. The chemical section accounts for five out of the eight operations at Parchin, and the entire site is directed by IRGC member and laser enrichment expert Mohammad Amin Bassam. This scientist reports to Mohsen Fakhrizadeh, director of the nuclear program at the Ministry of Defense's Center for Readiness and New Advanced Defensive Technology. The laser enrichment equipment is located in an underground bunker designated as Project 1 in the chemical section. In addition, several other tunnels have been built at Parchin for nuclear activities, and underground facilities are used for testing high-power explosions.

Together with secret research projects operating out of military research centers in Tehran, Malek Ashtar, and Imam Hossein universities, Parchin is an important site for joint top-secret nuclear projects in the regime. The Parchin site houses projects in cruise missiles (Projects 4 and 11), other missiles (Projects 7 and 9), ammunitions (Project 3), chemical weapons (Projects 1, 2, 5, 6, and 8), and anti-aircraft (Project 10).[2]

A few months after my revelations about Parchin, my sources in Iran provided additional information about this site and about the military's aggressive program to move the nuclear weapons program underground. In a press conference on September 16, 2005, I announced that the regime had created a new engineering section called the Enforcement Management of Air and Space

Organization Development Project within the Air and Space Organization, part of the Ministry of Defense. The mission of this new department was to build secret tunnels in Parchin and nearby mountain regions around Tehran.

The management team uses the cover name "Development Projects" when referring to this engineering operation, and the department is under strict security. Everyone involved in the project is prohibited from using the tunnels' names, and must refer to them by their code names. Access to all maps and documents in the department are granted only by an official permit from the manager, Yadegari, or his deputy, Khosh-Seresht. In the year leading up to my September 2005 announcement of this site, the unit had completed 14 large-scale tunnel projects and several smaller ones, including a tunnel below Parchin's Stone Hill. Some of these tunnels are dedicated to secret military nuclear factories, completely equipped with water, electricity, and air conditioning. Others are dedicated to storage for weapons and missiles built to the required technical standards. A fully militarized program, the Enforcement Management of Air and Space Organization Development Project received its orders for tunnel building for nuclear projects from IRGC brigadier general Seyed Ali Hosseini-Tash.[3]

Information about the tunnel complex in the mountainous region around Tehran continued to come out of Iran in late 2005, and on November 21, during a press conference, I presented my sources' findings about the extensive missile program operated in several tunnel complexes. Included in this new information was the regime's covert strategic plan to build missiles capable of carrying nuclear warheads. On the orders of Supreme Leader Ali Khamenei, the Ministry of Defense took over a 4- by 12-mile area of east and southeastern Tehran for use in building an underground military complex. This area is enclosed by the Ghazal Park to the north, by the Tehran-Parchin expressway to the east, by Parchin and Hessar Amir to the south, and by the villages of Hamsin and Towchal to the west. The series of facilities in this underground region were designed to connect the regime's missile production, nuclear warhead, and other underground weapons operations.

The many industries located in this sprawling complex, which the regime has been building and expanding since the end of the Iran-Iraq War and Khomeini's death in 1989, include a firm named Karimi Industries, code-named 2500, which builds nuclear warheads. Communication with this company requires a very high security clearance, and all communications are in code. The regime's most advanced missile manufacturer, the Hemmat Industries Group, builds the Shahab–3 and Ghadar missiles—both capable of carrying nuclear warheads—in this region.[4]

The Iranian regime's missile program is enormously dependent upon the tunnel complexes, and this cover has helped the regime develop an advanced missile program that is regarded as one of the largest in the Middle East. New versions of the Shahab–3 tested in 2004 reveal that the regime is working furiously to develop more sophisticated missiles that can carry a nuclear warhead. In October 2004, Iran released a video of its latest test of the Shahab–3, a version with a dramatically modified nose and, as with other Shahab–3 designs, capable of carrying a nuclear warhead.[5] Less than four weeks later, U.S. secretary of state Colin Powell remarked, "There is no doubt in my mind—and it's fairly straight-forward from what we've been saying for years—that they have been interested in a nuclear weapon that has utility, meaning that it is something they would be able to deliver, not just something that sits there."[6]

Since the mid-1980s, Iran has developed its missile program with substantial help from China, North Korea, Libya, and Russia, all of whom have supplied either complete missiles or equipment, technology, and expertise. Iran's exact inventory is unknown, but it is estimated that it possesses from 200 to 300 Shahab–1 (Scud-B; short range) and more than 200 Shahab–2 (Scud-C; short range) missiles.[7] Also, my sources inside Iran have confirmed that Iran now has more than 300 Shahab–3 (medium range) missiles. In the 1990s, Iran began building its own Shahab–3 missiles; in 1999 it announced that it was producing the Shahab–4, with a range of 1,200 miles, which some experts believe is an updated version of the Shahab–3. The regime's information about this missile has been erratic, and for the most part the program has been shrouded in secrecy. Iran originally described the Shahab–4 missile as a more capable version of the Shahab–3, but later denied that it had any military application and claimed that it was instead being designed only as a space-launch missile.[8] However, in November 2003 the Ministry of Defense denied that it had a Shahab–4 program at all.[9] In July 2005 Iranian Defense Minister Ali Shamkhani said the Shahab–3 contained a range of 1200 miles, a major increase from the previous version of the missile, which had a range of 800 to 880 miles.[10] He said the Shahab–3 developed and tested in 2004 significantly increased the range of the missile. In November 2006, Iran test fired the Shahab–3 near Qom, after which State Television reported that the missile had the range of 2000 km (1240 miles).[11] The extended range of the Shahab–3 will give the Iranian regime the ability to target all of Israel, Turkey, Afghanistan, Iraq and other Persian Gulf countries, most of India, and parts of Germany and China.

The regime's rush to acquire and build its own long-range missiles included black-market purchases of cruise missiles from the Ukraine that remained secret for several years. An investigation by the Ukrainian government in 2005 revealed that one of its former secret service officers sold 12 Kh–55 cruise missiles between 1999 and 2001: six each to Iran and China.[12] The Kh–55 has a range of 3,000 kilometers (1,860 miles), and can carry a 200-kiloton nuclear warhead.[13]

In August 2005, my sources in Iran uncovered details about what the regime did with these long-range, low-flying, jet-propelled cruise missiles after they entered Iran. After the Ministry of Defense received the illegal cargo, it was sent to the IRGC missile unit, which reconstructed the missiles and transferred them to the Cruise Division of the Ministry of Defense's Air and Space Organization. The Cruise Division consists of a command center, a research center, several independent industries and companies in Tehran, and military industries in Parchin and Mashhad. The individuals working in this sector are highly trained experts in the defense industry, many of whom have obtained their advanced training from countries such as Russia, France, Germany, China, and North Korea.

At least two of the Kh–55s were sent to the Parchin military complex to undergo a reverse-engineering process. Sections of other missiles were sent to other facilities for work on various aspects of the missile design. For the next four years, engineers successfully learned the technology and fabrication of the Kh–55, which gave the regime the capability to build the missile domestically. My sources inside Iran provided last names of the engineers in charge of this program, which opened a window to the regime's highly secretive missile organization. At the Parchin cruise systems operation, Karbalaii is the chief of staff, Mahdavi is the deputy head of the Shahid Fassihi Research Center, Moslimi is the deputy head of the cruise missile war division, and a mullah named Yasaghi heads Khamenei's delegation to the site. An engineer named Tolouii heads the cruise research center in Lavizan, and Fesharaki of the Air and Space Organization supervises many of the engineers throughout the cruise operation.[14]

After the nuclear site Lavizan 1 was exposed in 2003, the regime transferred some of its nuclear research work to secret tunnels. The secrecy of Iran's missile production—which has led to decades of varying reports about its research, development, inventory, and capability—is now based upon so much of the program being underground. North Korea has been Iran's primary collaborator in building and expanding this underground infrastructure, providing experts and blueprint designs. This is the latest in a long history of missile cooperation between the two countries, which began with a 1985 agreement in which Iran funded North Korea's Scud-B program in exchange for missile technology and an option to buy the Scuds.[15]

In September 2005, I shared more details about Iran's missile operations in the secret tunnels associated with the Parchin military site, and a few weeks later I was able to provide new information about the massive size and operations of the regime's tunnel complexes. Accessible only by private military roads, the largest tunnel complex is beneath the mountains of the Khojir region just east of Tehran. This is where Movahed Industries, housed in the largest tunnel in the Khojir complex, builds the main body of missiles, carries out the final assembly, and warehouses the final product. The tunnel is about 1,000 meters long and 12 meters wide, and inside are six forklike, 500-meter extensions. The tunnel extends from deep inside the central area of Khojir to the Bar Jamali Mountain. The eyewitness accounts of my sources inside Iran described this tunnel as an underground township complete with its own firefighting system, steam boilers for an independent heating system, air conditioning, water pumps, and water-resistant electrical system.[16]

Hemmat Industries Group, the primary and most advanced organization in Iran's Aerospace Industries Group, builds Shahab–1, Shahab–2, Shahab–3, and Ghadar missiles. The prototype, nuclear-capable Ghadar–101 and Ghadar–110, designed with North Korean assistance, will have a range of 2,500 to 3,000 kilometers (1,150 to 1,850 miles). The top of this range puts the Ghadar in the category of an intermediate-range missile (3,000 to 5,500 kilometers), the next step up from medium-range missiles (1,000 to 3,000 kilometers). As I remarked in an interview with George Jahn of the Associated Press in March 2006, the Ghadar at that time was 70 percent complete, and once these missiles are operable, Tehran will have a weapons delivery system that can target all the cities in the Middle East and several in eastern Europe. Iran's work on the Ghadar model coincides with mass production of the medium-range Shahab–3; in 2004, the regime significantly increased the Shahab–3 production line and began turning out 90 missiles a year.[17]

The security measures in the tunnel facilities include a code-naming system for the industries that work on various aspects of the program. For example, Karimi Industries, the section that builds the warhead and is the most secretive part of the program, is known as 2500. Movahed Industries, which builds the missile body and conducts the final assembly, is 7500. Varamini Industries, or 6000, builds the missile guidance and control systems; Cheraghi Industries, or 3000, builds the missile; Rastegar Industries, or 4500, builds missile engines; and Kolhar Industries, or 1500, builds the launcher systems.[18]

In addition to this tunnel, the Khojir complex contains dozens of other well-equipped tunnels that vary in length from 150 to 300 meters and contain more industries and warehouses in which missiles are kept. Among these is Bakeri Industries Group, whose five facilities in the Khojir complex produce surface-to-surface missiles including the Iran-designed Fateh A–110, Nazeat, and Zolqadr.[19]

One of the regime's newest underground sites, the Hormuz Tunnel, is located in the foothills of the Alborz Mountains, north of a township called Shahrak-e Bazi (Mini City) in northeast Tehran. Running beneath an unsuspecting northern section of Mini City, the tunnel reaches from a residential neighborhood to the southern edge of the mountains. The regime drew up the designs for this tunnel complex in 2004 and began construction in 2005.

Hara Company, an engineering firm associated with Khatam Al Anbia, which is the main engineering headquarters for the Islamic Revolutionary Guards Corps, built the Hormuz Tunnel. The Ministry of Defense has repeatedly used this firm for building underground nuclear facilities, because Hara is experienced in building antiradiation walls and air-ventilation systems that are specially designed to prevent radioactive traces from escaping into the surrounding soil. Hara's employees are members of the IRGC's engineering corps and other groups trusted by the regime.

The entrance to the Hormuz Tunnel consists of a 165-foot vertical shaft that leads down to the largest section of the site. At the bottom of the shaft are entrances to four parallel tunnels, 20 to 30 feet wide. The multilayered walls include a lead layer that prevents radiation leakage and fiberglass layers that render the tunnel soundproof. The design is highly fortified with a double layer of concrete, unlike the single layer found in other military tunnels built by the regime. The facilities set up inside the complex include workshops, administration offices, and warehouses for nuclear research and development.

The Hara Company group working on this tunnel was strictly forbidden to talk about the project to anyone outside the team. The workers who built metal frames in January 2006 for the tunnels at a Hara workshop called Imamzadeh Hashem were never told the purpose of the frames or where the frames would be installed. My sources also learned that the location of the tunnel in a residential area forced the workers to switch to less noisy equipment during the excavation phase.

One of the two major branches of the Hara Company is devoted solely to defense contracts, and the president of the company is IRGC brigadier general Ehtesham. With the general's oversight, this project fulfills both of the regime's goals: to bring more of the nuclear weapons program under military control and to drive the program underground.

While global alarm about Iran's nuclear program escalated in 2005, heightened by the regime's resumption of uranium conversion at Isfahan, engineers were hard at work deep beneath the streets of Tehran. I learned from my sources in Iran that by early 2006 the workers had completed a secret underground complex designed to protect senior government officials during attacks and to hide various operations from the prying eyes of satellites. Building this site suggests that Iran's leaders were preparing for a confrontation by going underground.

Located near the Abbas Abad district in the northern section of the city, and hidden beneath a key religious center called the Mossalla Prayer Grounds, this underground command headquarters is connected by means of tunnels to other government centers. A number of key government buildings including the Energy Department, State Security Forces, and the Organization of Islamic Culture and Communications are located nearby.

In an interview with the French daily *Le Monde* on February 25, 2005, nuclear negotiator Hassan Rowhani responded that reports that Iran was building tunnels to hide its nuclear technology "could be true." He added, "From the moment the Americans threaten to attack our nuclear sites, what are we to do? We have to put them somewhere." This is a clear violation of Iran's NPT commitments.

Iran's underground nuclear weapons facilities are dispersed enough to make it very difficult for military strikes to wipe out the entire operation. "Although stealth airplanes might be able to penetrate the radar systems of Iran," said Raymond Tanter, president of the Iran Policy Committee in Washington, D.C., "it is unclear whether it would be possible for the bombs to penetrate Iran's underground nuclear and missile facilities."[20]

The regime has not been able to keep the sites described here under the radar of the committed sources in Iran who risk their lives to uncover the mullahs' secrets and bring them to the world. Thanks to them, the regime's nuclear goals, which first came to light in the summer of 2002, have awakened the world to its most imminent nuclear threat—and the evidence keeps coming.

FRONT COMPANIES

The regime developed the front-company approach when its international nuclear purchasing powers were strongly curtailed in the late 1980s and early 1990s. Because of international pressure, the power reactor projects underway by the Chinese in southern Iran and by Russia in northern Iran near the Caspian Sea were canceled. Those cancellations, in addition to other difficulties in acquiring nuclear materials from abroad, compelled the leaders in Tehran to find another route for importing nuclear expertise, equipment, and material for their secret nuclear weapons program. The solution was to hide nuclear purchases and activities behind private Iranian companies.

Many of these companies—I exposed more than 50 of them between August 2002 and January 2006—were directly operated by the AEOI, with members of the organization registered among the company executives (without their AEOI titles, of course). This allowed the regime to buy nuclear-related materials from a number of foreign countries under the cover of benign civil purchases. By selling to these Iranian companies, even while knowing the illegal end use in some cases, foreign countries including China, North Korea, Pakistan, and India could justify the sale of dual-use chemicals, materials, and components because they were written up as sales to nonmilitary and nongovernmental entities. This would keep the paperwork beneath suspicion in terms of the selling nation's commerce and export officials.

A few of the Iranian regime's nuclear imports managed by front companies have been detected en route and halted, but these have been the minority. In December 2003, for example, an Iranian firm called Pars Refractories Company ordered graphite from China, guaranteeing in its end-user certificate that "we will not use the above-said FLAKED GRAPHITE in the storing, processing, producing and treating of weapons of mass destruction and their delivery systems."[21] Despite these promises, correspondence between Pars Refractories and the seller, Sunstone International Industry & Trade Company, revealed that the Chinese company had a difficult time getting authorization to export the material. It apologized for the delays and said it would "do our best to pass customs declaration," but repeated attempts did not look promising.[22] The regime then turned to another graphite supplier in China, Beijing Guoruiminfu International Trade Company, which would sell the material to a German company, who would in turn send it to Iran. However, in November 2004 the Chinese firm notified Germany that the sale was off, because "customs officials said that this goods [sic] is prohibited to export to Iran by government order."[23]

The NCRI's astounding revelations about the regime's secret beryllium program included disclosure not only of the lab at Malek-Ashtar Industrial University but also of the front company through which the illegal imports were made. The sources inside Iran discovered that the regime operated the imports out of the San'at Gostar Majd Company on Azadi Street in Tehran, located next door to the Sharif University of Technology. This company was set up specifically to import beryllium and to legitimize the secret program in the event that the IAEA learned about it and began to make inquiries. The regime formulated the company's records to reflect that the beryllium was for peaceful purposes only, used in manufacturing centrifuges for Iran's uranium-enrichment program to make fuel for nuclear power reactors. Among the San'at Gostar Majd Company's recent smuggling operations was a June 2004 order for 5,000 pieces of copper-beryllium alloy, ostensibly for the manufacture of centrifuge machines. The order was placed by AEOI deputy Mohammad Ghanadi and by an engineer named Mehdi Panahi. The sources learned that the company CEO is a scientist and beryllium expert named Ehsan Mar'ashi, who is assisted by the company's director general, an engineer named Mohammad Jamil-nia.[24]

Novin Energy is a front company that I first exposed in August 2002, elabo-
rated upon in May 2003, and gave further details about its activities and location in
August 2005.[25] Due to its clandestine nuclear activities on behalf of Iran's nuclear
program, the company was sanctioned by the U.S. government in January 2006.

Another firm with a similar name, Rah-e kar-e Sanayea Novin (New Industries
Solutions), is a front company involved in the regime's deuterium program. It is officially registered with the authorities as a company designed to "present and conduct
services necessary for industrial plans." The registration lists AEOI director Gholamreza Aqazadeh as president of the executive board, and the "services" provided
support for the import of nuclear-related equipment and materials including deuterium, or heavy water. As the NCRI revealed in September 2004, this company imported deuterium from Central Asian Republics for use at the nuclear research
facility at Isfahan.[26] The regime also uses this secretly imported pure deuterium to
produce tritium, the material that acts as the neutron initiator and booster in a
boosted-fission nuclear bomb. The regime planned ultimately to use its own deuterium, produced at the heavy-water facility in Arak, but until that facility is operational, it set up the top-secret import program through Rah-e kar-e Sanayea Novin.

That the regime has been able to purchase deuterium for an undeclared nuclear research program is topped only by the location of the front company itself—
Rah-e kar-e Sanayea Novin's offices are in the AEOI building in Tehran!

Revelations about the regime's deuterium purchases raised deeper concerns
about how much the world did not know about the Iranian regime's nuclear program. In the summer of 2004, U.S. Department of State Under Secretary John
Bolton stated, "Why should Iran be seeking deuterium, when as I have said Iran
is building a production facility for heavy water, another name for deuterium, to
supply its heavy-water reactor program? What other roles does deuterium play in
the Iranian nuclear program?"[27]

The regime has successfully smuggled another material used in nuclear
weapons, maraging steel, through its network of front companies. Banned by the
NPT, maraging steel is twice as strong as stainless steel and is used for the rotors
of P–2 centrifuges, missile components, and casings for nuclear weapons.[28] The
Iranian Ministry of Defense set up the illegal imports through Iran's National
Steel Company (NSC) and a series of front companies including an Iranian international firm called ASCOTEC. This metals company, a subsidiary of the Organization for the Development and Rebuilding of Iran's Mines and Industries, has
offices in Tehran, Japan, the United Arab Emirates, and Düsseldorf, Germany.
The NCRI's sources inside Iran uncovered information about one smuggling
route in which maraging steel is purchased from Malaysia and shipped to the
United Arab Emirates, where the manifest is altered and the shipments sent on to

Iran.[29] Iran's clandestine imports of this material had also come to light in May 1998, when a British citizen of Iranian descent, Ali Asghar Manzarpour, was convicted for attempting to export 750 kilograms, or nearly one ton, of U.S.-origin maraging steel from Britain to Iran for nuclear purposes. He served nine months in British prisons. According to the United States Department of Homeland Security, British authorities noted that the high-strength steel, which is used to build centrifuges for enriching uranium, was destined for Iran's nuclear weapons program. British authorities said Manzarpour had been working with the Iranian government for at least a decade.[30]

In an aim to produce this grade of steel domestically, Iranian scientists carry out research on both the analysis and the production of maraging steel at Malek-Ashtar Industrial University, one of the research centers affiliated with the Ministry of Defense, Tehran's Technical University, and Sahand University in Tabriz. Iranian sources also uncovered a classified maraging-steel production line at the Mobarakeh Steel Factory in Isfahan. The new assembly line was created in 2004, and the high security attached to the project includes making the site off-limits to scientists and other experts who are not affiliated with the secret program.[31]

After this information was revealed by the NCRI in July 2005, an IAEA spokesperson said that the agency was investigating, and its initial findings were revealed in the November 2005 board report. The IAEA stated that "after September 2005" Iran provided documentation about maraging steel that it had acquired through "a contractor." Iran explained that these purchases were for the P–2 research and development done between 2002 and 2003 that it had previously declared to the IAEA.[32] Once again, the regime put off declaring a critical detail of its nuclear program until backed into a corner by new information.

Based on the success of the international front-company import operations, the AEOI expanded the scheme by setting up firms that could secretly support and operate Iran's nuclear activities in several other ways. I revealed the first of these firms, a Tehran company called Kalaye Electric (Electric Goods), in my August 2002 press conference. This front company, which was officially registered as a watch-making factory, had already been operating a top-secret centrifuge development workshop since 1995, when it was enlisted to support the Natanz enrichment facility, which began construction in 2000. The head of Kalaye Electric, Dawood Agha-Jani, was also the director of the Natanz operations and reported directly to AEOI director Gholamreza Aqazadeh.

Once we revealed Kalaye Electric, the regime was very reluctant to allow access to IAEA inspectors. After describing Kalaye Electric as a watch company that also happened to make a few centrifuge components, the mullahs went into full-throttle delay tactics.[33] They put off a full inspection for months, first by flat-out denying permission on the grounds that such a visit was not obligatory without an additional protocol in force. They permitted access to certain areas of Kalaye Electric in March 2003, and finally to the full workshop in May.[34]

More information about Kalaye Electric's role in the regime's secret nuclear program has surfaced since those first revelations. In November 2004, the NCRI announced that its sources in Iran had uncovered a major center of the regime's nuclear cover-up network in a building at 33 Sayed Jamaleedin Assad Abadi Avenue, at 15th Street, in Tehran. This building houses four companies that hide either nuclear weapons programs or nuclear materials import operations, and three are owned by Kalaye Electric. The NCRI revealed that another firm in this building, Pars Terash Company, also supported the secret centrifuge program. Centrifuges were discovered in the company's first-floor office, and it was discovered that the company also has a workshop outside the city.[35]

The initial revelations of August 2002 also exposed the front company that helped operate the secret heavy-water production plant at Arak. The plant was not included in the official records of the AEOI, but instead operated through a cover business called Mesbah Energy Company. Located at 77 Armaghan Gharbi Valiasr Avenue in Tehran, Mesbah was headed by an AEOI employee named Daryoush Sheibani. The covert program was directly overseen by AEOI director Gholamreza Aqazadeh, and the bureaucratic operation was handled by the AEOI's Security and Intelligence office and Central Office of Security. The operational manager, based at the site in Arak, was identified as Behnam Asgarpour. As noted, the budget for the project was not part of the regime's official budget, but was funded through a secret budget controlled by Supreme Leader Ali Khamenei.

The AEOI conducts its clandestine activities at the two nuclear enrichment sites in Lashkar Ab'ad through a front company called the Noor-Afza-Gostar Company, one of the largest covers operated by the AEOI. The nominal CEO of Noor-Afza-Gostar Company is Dr. Jamshid Sabbaghzadeh, the adviser to AEOI director Gholamreza Aqazadeh. Curiously, Dr. Sabbaghzadeh's work address is listed as the AEOI building, even though he is the CEO of Noor-Afza-Gostar Company in Tehran. The company is officially registered as an importer-exporter of "authorized materials" and is located on Zarafshan Street off of Eivanak Street, in Qods Township.

In addition to CEO Jamshid Sabbaghzadeh, the company's board of directors includes Gholamreza Aqazadeh, director of the AEOI and listed as representing the Novin Energy Company; Mohammad Saeedi, deputy CEO whose other job is deputy director of the AEOI; two additional members named Mahmoud Ashraf Kashani and Babak Khodadoust; and an alternate member named Mohammad Hossein Bagheri Rastegar. That the AEOI director and his deputy are on the board of this company is an indication of the crucial importance of Noor-Afza-Gostar to the AEOI.

Among the many front companies located in Tehran is Pishgam Development Industrial Energy, launched in the early 1990s as an electronic company and used by the regime to cover up its nuclear fuel production site at Isfahan. Rather than working in the commercial electronics industry, the personnel on the books at Pishgam are part of the design team for the fuel manufacturing plant (FMP) and uranium conversion facility (UCF) at Isfahan. The FMP is expected to be operational in 2007. The UCF converts yellowcake (milled uranium in powder form) into uranium hexafluoride, the gas that is fed into centrifuge machines. Employees of Pishgam also work on the uranium milling project at Ardakan, in which uranium ore is ground into yellowcake.

Pishgam operates out of an unmarked building on Fatemi Square in Tehran, at the address 11 Second Street, Biston Avenue. Its main office is located on Army Avenue in Isfahan, where the president of the executive board is Mansour Habashizadeh, the head of the Esfahan Nuclear Technology Center (ENTC).

Because Iran's front-company strategy has been hugely overlooked, only two such companies have been sanctioned by the United States. These sanctions were a follow-up to the U.S. sanction of the AEOI implemented in 2005. As part of its battle against the proliferation of weapons of mass destruction, the United States acknowledged the subversive role of the AEOI and sanctioned it under Executive Order 13382 on June 28, 2005. This presidential order, implemented by the U.S. Department of the Treasury, prohibits any U.S. person or company "from engaging in any transaction or dealing with" the AEOI.[36] Seven months later, on January 4, 2006, the United States sanctioned Mesbah Energy and Novin Energy, both of which I revealed in August 2002. The U.S. Department of the Treasury designated these two companies for "their support of the proliferation of weapons of mass destruction (WMD)." Treasury described Mesbah as a state-owned company used as a front for the AEOI, in order to procure products for Iran's heavy water project. "Novin has transferred millions of dollars on behalf of the AEOI to entities associated with Iran's nuclear program. Novin operates within the AEOI, and shares the same address as the AEOI," the department's statement said.[37]

These sanctions are important, but the fact that they came four years after the companies were exposed and pertain only to two front companies (out of more than 50 companies that the Iranian opposition has exposed) highlights the frustratingly slow pace of action taken against the Iranian regime's covert nuclear program. In addition, in 2004 the regime made clear that it would continue to conduct nuclear work at its ancillary companies regardless of its promises to suspend all uranium-enrichment activities. As the IAEA reported, Tehran boldly told the agency that centrifuge work would go on in various companies after the suspension went into effect: "Iran notified the Agency that . . . due to disputes between the AEOI and some of its private contractors, three private companies would continue with centrifuge component production."[38] This demonstrates that the regime's front-company operations are so vital to its effort to speed up its path to the bomb that it will not shut them down, regardless of how many are uncovered. Every time the regime agrees to suspend enrichment, it will continue to pursue its nuclear program through its widespread network of front companies.

The vast network of front companies that support and operate Iran's secret nuclear program prevents IAEA inspectors and world leaders from getting a true sense of the size of the program, who is involved, and how many violations there are. Until all of these cover operations are investigated and shut down, the regime will continue to use them to run many aspects of its nuclear program in secrecy.

CHAPTER 10

FAST FORWARD: AHMADINEJAD ADVANCES IRAN'S RACE FOR THE BOMB

We know well that a country's backing down one iota on its undeniable rights is the same as losing everything. We will not bend to a few countries' threats.

—President Mahmoud Ahmadinejad, March 13, 2006[1]

The ultraconservative leadership of Iran, fed up with the nation's bout with "reform" of the 1990s, struck down the liberal element in the elections of 2004 by not allowing most of the candidates of the rival faction headed by President Mohammad Khatami to run. With this move, Khamenei and his inner circle initiated their move to consolidate power and adopt a new, more focused approach. With their secret nuclear program exposed, the mullahs needed to shore up their covert infrastructure with more military control. They were also committed to dominating neighboring Iraq after the fall of Baghdad in April 2003 opened up that possibility. Ahmadinejad was the mullahs' choice instrument for swaying the country toward a chest-beating attitude of Iran versus the bullying West, and after his election he hit the ground running.

In July 2005, before being sworn in as president, Ahmadinejad visited the enrichment facility at Natanz. As I revealed in a press conference in January 2006, my sources in Iran discovered that the regime planned to intensify its uranium-enrichment program at Natanz, despite being under a suspension agreement with the IAEA and with the EU3, as signed in Paris in November 2004. Shortly after Ahmadinejad's visit, Iran accelerated its two-part plan to complete the enrichment process at Natanz. The first step involved making public an-nouncements about what was called "research" developments at the site, includ-ing the building, installation, and testing of centrifuge machines. Second, the regime planned to feed uranium hexafluoride into a cascade of centrifuges and officially start the enrichment process.[2] Ahmadinejad's role in the accelerated enrichment program would include appointing hard-liners and senior IRGC commanders to key government posts and taking his brand of fiery rhetoric to the masses beyond Iran's borders in order to rally support for Iran's nuclear "rights."

Ahmadinejad's election coincided with the nuclear anxieties of the summer of 2005, as the EU3 tried to avert a crisis by drawing up a package of incentives to convince Iran to stop its nuclear conversion and enrichment programs perma-nently. In its 35-page proposal, the EU3 offered to help develop Iran's nuclear power program, but the regime insisted that it would never agree to a plan that forced it to stop enriching uranium. European leaders warned Iran that a refusal to stop nuclear fuel work would lead to a referral to the United Nations Security Council and possible sanctions, but instead of negotiating, the regime exploited these warnings by ramping up its "us versus them" propaganda. The regime com-plained that the West was bent on stripping Iran of its rights to nuclear energy, all the while failing to mention that the nuclear crisis was provoked in the first place by the Iranian regime's flagrant violation of the Nuclear Non-Proliferation Treaty (NPT).

On Ahmadinejad's inauguration day, August 6, 2005, the regime announced that it was rejecting the EU3 offer (the official rejection letter was handed over to the EU3 two days later), and the new president began the rallying cry that be-came a theme of his presidency. "I don't know why some countries do not want to understand the fact that the Iranian people do not tolerate force," he said at the swearing-in ceremony.[3] Without naming the EU3 proposal directly, he contin-ued, "We respect all international conventions, but will not surrender to any pressures which go beyond these conventions and deprive us of our legitimate rights." Ahmadinejad framed the crisis as an act of western aggression to which "the Iranian nation will not surrender," thereby setting himself up as Iran's bold new defender.[4]

Two days after Ahmadinejad's inauguration, the regime broke its November 2004 agreement with Europe and resumed uranium conversion activities at the Isfahan plant. As IAEA members looked on, Iranian engineers removed the seals that the IAEA had installed when Iran agreed to suspend all its nuclear fuel activ-ities. Workers suited up in their white overalls, face masks, and hard hats, and began feeding yellowcake into the processing system.[5] Ahmadinejad incited things further that same day, August 8, 2005, by naming a new chief nuclear negotiator. Hassan Rowhani, the head of the team that had been negotiating with Europe throughout the crisis period after August 2002, was out, and Ali Larijani, a former senior commander of the Islamic Revolutionary Guards Corps and a prominent hard-line conservative with close ties to Khamenei, was in.

Ahmadinejad's choice instantly set the tone for Iran's nuclear stance. Larijani had recently finished ten years as the chief of Iran's state broadcasting system, where his agenda included cutting down on foreign television shows and increasing "Islamic" programming. Larijani was a harsh critic of reformist figures in the government, who, he felt, were weakening Iran's Islamic value system. Larijani's idea of reform was the same as that of Khamenei and his most conservative followers, including Ahmadinejad. "If reforms are not undertaken for the sake of religion, justice and morality, they do not constitute reforms," Larijani said.[6] In 2004, after a decade at the broadcasting system, Larijani had been appointed by Khamenei to a three-year term at the Supreme National Security Council. One year into that powerful position, he was appointed as the secretary of the council and took on the role of chief nuclear negotiator.

By handing over the reigns to Larijani, Ahmadinejad declared that in the new order, Iran's nuclear negotiations would reflect the most hard-line position of the regime. If the Europeans thought dealing with Rowhani and his colleagues was bad, they were in for a whole new level of rhetoric and defiance. Within weeks, Larijani proved the point. In the wake of the August breakdown of EU3-Iran negotiations, the IAEA voiced its frustrations over Iran's "many failures and breaches of its obligations" by recommending that Iran be reported to the United Nations Security Council. When Larijani learned about this draft resolution, he threatened to retreat from the NPT altogether. The regime had never gone this far before, but Larijani declared that Tehran was prepared to withdraw from the treaty and thereby cut off the IAEA inspection process (just as North Korea did in 2003). "If they want to use the language of force against Iran, Iran will definitely review its relations with the nuclear agency and its commitments to N.P.T.," Larijani warned in a news conference on September 20, 2005. "If they want to use the language of threat, or send Iran's case to the Security Council, Iran will think twice about implementing the Additional Protocol [snap inspections] and will resume uranium enrichment," he added.[7]

Larijani left no room for question about where the regime stood. His threats drew a clear line in the sand and were accompanied during these heated weeks by Ahmadinejad's own rantings about global bullying and Iran's refusal to back down. Just three days before Larijani's ultimatum, Ahmadinejad hinted at the same thing in his address to the United Nations. "If some try to impose their will on the Iranian people through resort to a language of force and threat with Iran, we will reconsider our entire approach to the nuclear issue." In the same speech, he called the West's accusations about Iran's nuclear weapons program "nothing but a propaganda ploy."[8]

Throughout September, Ahmadinejad pumped up his rhetoric to link the nuclear program to national pride and inflame anti-U.S. sentiment: "A country, which possesses the biggest nuclear arsenal, embarks on proliferation of nuclear weapons in defiance of the safeguards and threatens to use them against others, is not competent to comment on peaceful use of nuclear know-how by other states."[9] Even though it was the Iranian regime that had been caught hiding a nuclear program for nearly two decades, Ahmadinejad went into full denial mode for a September CNN interview: "Access to nuclear fuel cycle for peaceful use is our nation's natural right and it is up to the opponents to prove otherwise by putting forth legal evidence." Contrary to Ahmadinejad's claims that the nuclear issue is a matter of national pride, an internal classified report prepared by a state-run polling center has reportedly concluded that 69 percent of Iranians do not consider the nuclear program a "nationalistic" project. In addition, the poll shows that 86 percent of Iranians believe the issue of nuclear energy is not worth the risk of entering a war. The vast majority of Iranians are opposed to Ahmadinejad's nuclear policy, which has pushed the country to the verge of a military confrontation.[10]

Confronted by all the evidence that had surfaced since August 2002 about Iran's covert nuclear program—including weapons research and development—Ahmadinejad repeatedly tried to turn the legal argument on its head. "We have concluded that the three European countries—France, Germany and Britain—do not want us to have a nuclear fuel cycle and this is against the law," he said in September 2005. "The opponents of Iran's nuclear program should revise their viewpoints and recognize our rights. They should not be under the illusion that they enjoy more rights than other nations."[11]

Ahmadinejad tried to divert his people from the facts by focusing his speeches on Iran's nuclear rights and everyone else's selfish determination to strip those rights—a complete fabrication on his part, but delivered with passion. His words may have pleased his very small group of war veterans and military followers, but—as usual—the vast majority of Iranians saw through the rhetoric and dismissed it.

In the autumn of 2005, Ahmadinejad's increasingly hostile attacks on the West and hyped defense of Iran's inalienable right to a nuclear program fed the nuclear crisis. The speech that provoked the most widespread shock was his call for Israel to be "wiped off the map," accompanied by a warning that any Islamic nation that recognized Israel's existence would "burn in the fire of the Islamic umma [nation]."[12] In the meantime, the mullahs in Tehran moved full steam ahead and planned their next breach of the EU3 suspension agreement. Ahmadinejad tried to garner more nationalistic sentiment by praising Iran's homegrown nuclear expertise: "The Islamic Republic has acquired indigenous technology for fuel production thanks to the efforts made by young, faithful and revolutionary scientists." Ignoring again the regime's long-hidden nuclear program, he said: "The West cannot deprive us of what the Iranian nation has achieved through efforts and perseverance."[13]

The official IAEA resolution of September 24, 2005, determined that Iran had not complied with its NPT obligations and that the remaining unresolved questions about Iran's nuclear program "are within the competence of the Security Council," but the resolution did not specifically call for Iran to be reported to the U.N. Security Council. Larijani's hard-line tactics obviously deepened worries that the regime might actually back out of the NPT and become a rogue nuclear state. The IAEA called for continued diplomacy, which bought the regime more time. Ahmadinejad launched a new phase of nationalistic zeal. "We are not afraid of your bogus stick known as the Security Council," Ahmadinejad sneered in December. "We will not back down from our stance. We will continue until we obtain nuclear technology."[14] He played the oil card, too, threatening to upset global supply: "If Iran's nuclear case is referred to the Security Council of the United Nations, then the response of this country will be to use different ways to stop selling oil."[15] He labeled the world's criticism of Iran's secret nuclear program as a "lack of trust"—as though the regime had never violated any of its treaty obligations—and he justified breaking more of them: "When our government reached a conclusion that they are not after building trust, the activities in Isfahan began. Now that they realized that our new government is not willing to compromise, they began to fuss and make noise about it."[16] He warned that Iran's nuclear expertise was ready for export: "Iran will never produce atomic weapons, but it is ready to transfer its atomic knowledge for energy usage to the other Islamic countries."[17] At times he tried to describe the regime's hard-line stance as basic common sense: "Any smart person must use every available source to attain its own independence. I doubt that the American and the European leaders don't realize this fact and they are smarter than that of depriving us from our rights. . . . [O]ur nation has the essential tools to defend its rights."[18] Ahmadinejad portrayed Iran's nuclear program as an unstoppable national achievement that mere words could never affect. He called Iran's nuclear program "a flood which cannot be stopped by a match stick. It's impossible to stop a nation's scientific progress with a bunch of irrelevant words. . . . It would be suicidal for a country to attack Iran . . . so we must not bend to threats."[19]

But inflammatory speeches were not the only tool that Ahmadinejad had at his disposal. The Majlis had written up a bill in preparation for actions that the regime might take if it was reported to the United Nations Security Council. On December 13, 2005, Ahmadinejad signed the bill into law, giving the government the power to "stop voluntary and non-legally binding measures and implement its scientific, research and executive programmes" if the Iranian case went to the United Nations. Armed with this law, the government was legally prepared to prevent IAEA inspectors from entering the country and to proceed with any type of nuclear research it desired. After signing off on the new legislation, Ahmadinejad ordered AEOI chief Gholamreza Aqazadeh to prepare his agency for implementing the law.[20]

In August 2006, I received striking new information that the Iranian regime was nuclear fast-tracking at the time that it was seeking to install a hard-core new president. This new information from my sources in Iran reveals the establishment of two nuclear universities in early 2005. In a classified report entitled "Initiation of Ph.D. Studies for Senior Level Expertise in Scientific Research and Development," dated February 1, 2005, AEOI deputy director Vahid Ahmadi requested the formation of an institution that would offer graduate programs in nuclear engineering, physics, and chemical engineering. The report emphasized that the university would be planned and constructed in secret because of the risk of international attention and scrutiny over such a significant expansion of Iran's nuclear training programs. To ensure the plan's secrecy, the AEOI put together a carefully selected scientific board, each member of which underwent an extensive background search by the Ministry of Intelligence and Security. The chairman of the technical committee overseeing this project is Dr. Manouchehr Rad (a professor with the nuclear engineering department at the Sharif University of Technology).

This board consists of 36 experts, including the AEOI's Ahmadi, and each member holds the rank of Ph.D. In a letter dated February 1, 2005, Ahmadi announced that the two fields of study would be senior-level expertise and a Ph.D. program in laser physics.

The second nuclear institution is a new college within Beheshti University. Although several universities in Iran offer nuclear engineering majors, an entire college dedicated to nuclear studies is a new step in the Iranian regime's nuclear program. The order to establish this college was issued in February 2005, with subjects to include nuclear reactors, nuclear engineering biomechanics, biometrical nuclear engineering, the nuclear fuel cycle, nuclear materials, and nuclear medical engineering. With such a comprehensive program, this college was designed to be one of the country's strongest nuclear engineering colleges.

The candidates for president of this college are Drs. Minouchehr, Zolfaghari, and AghaMiri, all of whom are graduates of Russian nuclear mechanics programs and share a history of working together on nuclear engineering projects. Another expert at the school is Dr. Majid Shahriari, an expert in reactors with a history of work with the AEOI.

In January 2006, the regime forged ahead in its race to complete the fuel cycle, thereby violating more of its nuclear treaty obligations. This time the violations occurred across Iran, first with breaking the seals on equipment at the uranium-enrichment plant in Natanz on January 10, and then with resuming research activities at Farayand Technique in Isfahan and Pars Terash in Tehran on the following day. Leaders throughout the world condemned these acts, which many viewed as further evidence that Iran's nuclear agenda is far from peaceful. United States ambassador to the IAEA Gregory Schulte declared that Iran's startup at Natanz proved that "the regime continues to choose confrontation over cooperation" and that the regime's choice to continue enrichment "deepens the isolation of Iran and hurts the interests of the Iranian people."[21]

Larijani reacted to the global protest with an unstatesmanlike analogy: "The West wants to frighten us with the Security Council like little children before a spider."[22] Ahmadinejad's response was equally juvenile: "Be angry with us, and from this anger die."[23] He used the crisis to pump up his rhetoric about Iran's overall lack of concern about world opinion: "The Iranian government and nation has no fear of the Western ballyhoo and will continue its nuclear programs with decisiveness and wisdom," he said. He also pointed out that the previous Iranian administration, headed by President Khatami, had acted irrationally in making an agreement with the EU3 in the first place.[24] Unlike that administration, Ahmadinejad and his hard-liners held no interest in concessions or compromise and were not afraid to say so.

The regime's blatant violations of nuclear agreements in early January 2006 exposed the growing urgency surrounding the nuclear program. There was no electricity shortage striking Iran and plunging the nation into blackouts, so why the rush? Why did the mullahs accelerate their nuclear program in the midst of a world crisis about the regime's nuclear lies and deceptions? Such moves were not about "peaceful" intentions. Iran was committed to building a nuclear bomb as soon as possible in order to change the entire political landscape of the Middle East.

The regime's resumption of enrichment activities compelled the IAEA to report Iran to the United Nations in February 2006. In response, Ahmadinejad invented a new phrase, "scientific apartheid," to describe the West's treatment of Iran.[25] He lashed out at the IAEA and the nations on the Security Council that voted for the resolution, raving that "the foes cannot do a damn thing. We do not need you at all. It is you who need the Iranian people. . . . You can issue as many resolutions as you like and dream on. But you cannot prevent the Iranian nation's progress."[26] He continued to try to frame the crisis as simply a matter of foreign powers bearing down on Iran for no reason in order to halt its amazing technological progress: "[Western nations] are even ready to say [we] do not need universities and academic research works. . . . Their demand for halting the progress of Iran toward advancement is among the funniest things we have ever heard, and it is them that need to gain our trust now, not the other way round."[27] But his declarations were not limited to denigrating the situation as a laughing matter. "The enemies want to get concessions from Islamic Iran through psychological warfare, exaggeration, and propaganda," he said in March 2006, "but the time has come for the bullies to be answerable for their crimes. . . . Our nation will give them and ill-wishers for the Islamic Republic a decisive and firm response."[28]

Throughout all the negotiations, throughout the headline-making IAEA decision finally to report Iran to the United Nations Security Council, and throughout the endless rhetoric, the regime kept its nuclear program running at top speed. The Security Council's initial response did not faze the mullahs in the least, as evidenced by events that occurred shortly afterward. On March 29, 2006, the Security Council released a Presidential Statement that noted its "serious concern" over Iran's outstanding issues with the IAEA and the "serious importance" of stopping enrichment activities in Iran. It also requested an IAEA follow-up report on Iran in 30 days.[29] Thirteen days later Ahmadinejad took the stage at an elaborate ceremony to announce that the regime had successfully enriched uranium to reactor-grade levels at Natanz. Two days later, on April 13, he incited things further by boasting that the regime was conducting research on the P–2 centrifuge. This stunned leaders throughout the world because Iran had previously declared to the IAEA that it stopped work on the P–2 in 2003.[30] Both of Ahmadinejad's announcements proved that no amount of diplomatic overtures or emergency IAEA meetings had any effect on the mullahs in Iran. On the contrary, the regime had used the opportunity to speed up the program and evade consequences by feigning cooperation.

Not only did the regime reject the IAEA's April 28 deadline to suspend its enrichment program, but Ahmadinejad took the opportunity to taunt the IAEA before a large crowd in western Iran one day before the deadline. "Did you imagine that you can impose anything on the Iranian nation or force it to retreat from its rights by frowning at us or by issuing resolutions?" he said in a speech on April 27. "You still don't know the power of the Iranian nation."[31] On the day of the deadline, when the IAEA sent its new, critical report to the United Nations Security Council, former Iranian president and current chief of the Expediency Council Ali Akbar Hashemi Rafsanjani confirmed the regime's rejection of the IAEA request. He proudly compared Iran's nuclear advancements to Galileo's greatest discovery, saying, "Back then no one believed his theory—but now we all revolve around the sun." Atomic Energy Organization of Iran chief Gholamreza Aqazadeh added his voice to the regime's air of bolstered confidence by stating that uranium enrichment was now "irreversible" in Iran.[32]

Ahmadinejad's speech on the day of the deadline was an all-out tirade against the West. "Iran does not give a damn about such resolutions," he said. "The bullies of the world should know that nuclear energy is a national demand, and thank God our nation is a nuclear nation today." But his most colorful remark of the day showed the regime's drastically inflated bravado: "The Islamic Republic of Iran has the capacity to quickly become a world superpower," he said. "The Iranian nation's achievement of peaceful nuclear energy is so important that it could change the world equation."[33] How could the development of a nuclear energy reactor turn a country into a world superpower and change the world equation? Ahmadinejad is clearly talking about the bomb.

The Iranian regime not only refused to halt uranium enrichment by August 31, 2006, as ordered by United Nations Security Council resolution 1696, but made two moves to rebuke the IAEA and the entire issue. On August 24, exactly one week before the deadline, Iran began enriching a new batch of uranium in the 164-machine cascade at Natanz.[34] As if to ensure that the message was getting through, on August 26, Ahmadinejad inaugurated the heavy-water production plant in Arak. When the adjacent nuclear reactor is complete, that facility will produce large quantities of plutonium that could be used in a nuclear weapon.

Although the leaders in Tehran had rejected yet another deadline and treaty responsibility, the global reaction was understated at best. The deadline came and went, the United States talked about possible sanctions, European leaders set up new meetings to discuss the Iran problem, and Ahmadinejad and other officials continued to rant about Iran's refusal to back down. Mohammad Reza Bahonar, Iran's deputy parliament speaker and a close ally of Ahmadinejad, pointed to the regime's designs to build the nuclear bomb in comments published by Iran's *Sharq* newspaper, "Be afraid of the day that the Iranian nation comes into the streets and stages demonstrations to ask the government to produce nuclear weapons to combat the threats," he said.[35] When United Nations Secretary General Kofi Annan visited Tehran during the first week of September 2006, Ahmadinejad snubbed his efforts to mediate by insisting that Iran would not suspend enrichment before entering negotiations.[36]

Ahmadinejad's speech before the United Nations General Assembly in September 2006 echoed the preachy, rambling, and belligerent tone that he had presented one year earlier at the same podium. He railed against those who "seek to rule the world," lectured on the perils of weapons of mass destruction, lambasted the "occupiers" in Iraq, gave a lengthy history lesson on Palestine and Lebanon, and lashed out at the Security Council as an illegitimate organization. He claimed, once again, that all of Iran's nuclear activities "are transparent, peaceful and under the watchful eyes of IAEA inspectors."[37] His appearance at the United Nations drew protests by several thousand Iranians who chanted "Ahmadinejad is a terrorist" from the plaza across from UN headquarters. Ahmadinejad continued in this vein at more hotly protested appearances in New York that week, including a meeting with members of the Council on Foreign Relations. After hearing Ahmadinejad at close range that evening, council member Robert D. Blackwill remarked, "If this man represents the prevailing government opinion in Tehran, we are heading for a massive confrontation with Iran."[38]

Ahmadinejad's strategy in the first one year of his presidency reflected the regime's goal of consolidating power among the most conservative, hard-edge elements of power in Tehran. In terms of the nuclear agenda, Ahmadinejad managed to speed up the nuclear weapons program while prolonging negotiations in order to buy more time to advance the regime's nuclear goals. In spite of international pressure, the strides in Iran's uranium enrichment program during this period included the resumption of uranium conversion at the Isfahan facility in August 2005 and of research and development at Natanz in January 2006, accelerated construction of the two large underground cascade halls at Natanz, the enrichment of uranium to nearly five percent in June 2006, stepped-up development of P-2 centrifuges, completion of construction phases at the heavy-water production plant, sped-up completion of the heavy water reactor in Arak, and restart of laser enrichment at Lashkar Ab'ad.[39] Nuclear negotiations during Ahmadinejad's tenure were drawn out by Iran providing vague responses to IAEA and other international inquiries, which instigated further questioning for clarification; repeatedly building false expectations of Iran's willingness to negotiate, only to refuse such options later; and exploiting Iran-friendly Security Council members Russia and China in order to slow negotiations and postpone sanctions. On the foreign policy side, Ahmadinejad's presidency has seen the strengthening of Iran's position in the region, especially in Iraq and Lebanon; Tehran utilized the crises in both countries as political capital to gain concessions from the west.

Analyzing the presidency of Ahmadinejad demonstrates how nothing has prevented the Iranian regime from stepping up the pace of its nuclear program. The regime's hand-picked new president gave the program the benefits of no-holds-barred rhetoric, a hard-line chief nuclear negotiator, and a cabinet dominated by the Islamic Revolutionary Guards Corps—the perfect combination for the final leg of its race to the bomb.

PART V

IF AND WHEN

CHAPTER 11

WORST-CASE SCENARIO: CONSEQUENCES OF A NUCLEAR-ARMED IRAN

The use of even one nuclear bomb inside Israel will destroy everything. . . . It is not irrational to contemplate such an eventuality.

—Akbar Hashemi Rafsanjani, chairman of Iran's Expediency Council, 2001[1]

Proof of the international consensus that Iran must not acquire nuclear weapons came in February 2006 when the nations that make up the IAEA board of governors voted 27 to 3 to report Iran to the United Nations Security Council. Even Russia and China, who both have enormous financial investments in Iran's nuclear power program and would have much to lose if the United Nations punished Iran with sanctions, voted to report the regime because of its nuclear violations.

As the IAEA board recognized, to understand the mission and mind-set of the Iranian regime is to be horrified at the prospect of Tehran armed with nuclear weapons. The United States recognizes that "the greatest immediate threat posed by the Ahmadinejad government is Iran's clear desire to acquire a nuclear weapons capability," according to R. Nicholas Burns, the U.S. Department of State under secretary for political affairs. "There is no international debate about Iran's aims—it is universally agreed that Iran is seeking nuclear weapons," Burns said in March 2006. "With the possible exception of Cuba, Syria, and Venezuela, no other country wants to see Iran succeed."[2] (Those three countries voted against reporting Iran to the Security Council.)

In the Arab world, Jordanian king Abdullah II famously envisioned a "crescent" of Shiite governments stretching from Iran to Lebanon if Iran succeeded in creating Islamic rule in Iraq and expanded its base from there. Abdullah hoped that preventing Iran from such expansion would be "just a clash of words and politics and not a clash of civilizations."[3] The Arab League expresses its concerns about Iran's nuclear threat in a wider context than the Europeans and the United States do, promoting a policy of making the entire Middle East, including the Persian Gulf, a nuclear-free zone. "What we have anxiety about is the stability and security of our region," said Saudi Arabia's foreign minister Saud Al Faisal in May 2006, "and definitely . . . the threat of the spread of atomic weapons in the region is a threat to the countries of the region."[4]

Israel knows that it would probably be the Iranian regime's first nuclear target and is adamant that the mullahs not succeed in building a bomb. "Under no circumstances, and at no point, can Israel allow anyone with these kinds of malicious designs against us [to] have control of weapons of destruction that can threaten our existence," said acting Israeli prime minister Ehud Olmert in January 2006.[5]

The consensus against a nuclear-armed Iranian regime also extends into Iran. Contrary to Ahmadinejad's mantra that the Iranian people demand their right to a nuclear program, the people themselves say otherwise. The nuclear rights demonstrations, at which supposed students make a human shield around nuclear sites to symbolize their support and protection of them, are not examples of civic activism but rather carefully staged events. Thousands of IRGC members infiltrate Iran's universities to act as the regime's eyes and ears among the youth. The mullahs created quotas at each university in order to ensure a high IRGC presence throughout Iran, and these are the "students" who load onto the buses and demonstrate at the nuclear sites. Iran's nuclear facilities are the most heavily protected areas of the country, yet somehow busload after busload of young people arrives with cameras to take pictures and carry out their rallies. Iranians realize that this is pure propaganda, and each time a nuclear rights demonstration floods the media it becomes another source of jokes and ridicule toward the mullahs in Tehran. The popular joke "nuclear energy, on sale for 200 toomans (Iranian currency) a box," made its way into the Iranian newspapers and politicians were frequently asked to comment about the joke.[13]

This critical attitude holds throughout the majority of the Iranian population, but the people's opposition to the regime does not get the media coverage that Ahmadinejad's supporters enjoy. Only a small minority, from four to five percent of the population, believes Ahmadinejad's rhetoric. These are the ultraconservative clerics, veterans of the Iran-Iraq War, and other military personnel. Every speech that Ahmadinejad gives is for this audience, which the regime tries to portray as the entire population of Iran. But the most significant evidence that the majority of the Iranian people are unified in their opposition to the regime's spending billions of dollars in its pursuit of nuclear weapons is that the nuclear program was uncovered by an organized opposition force within Iran. All the revelations about Iran's illegal nuclear work—and the global responses to them—have been thanks to the work of opposition groups. Gathering this intelligence would not be possible week after week, year after year, if the organized opposition in Iran did not have enormous support and reflect the nation's desire for democracy rather than for a religious dictatorship armed with nuclear weapons. Another undeniable reflection of the Iranian people's dissatisfaction with Tehran is the fact that thousands of anti-regime demonstrations erupt throughout the country every year, as detailed in the next chapter.

Ahmadinejad's next targets are the Muslim population in the region and Iran's proxy groups in the Islamic world, upon whom Tehran relies to pursue its agenda.

The United States' analysis of a nuclear-armed Iran in the future emphasizes six points that make this situation "intolerable." According to Robert G. Joseph, the State Department's under secretary for arms control and international security, the first reason is that nuclear weapons would "embolden" the regime to carry out its "aggressive ambitions" in the Middle East and beyond. Second, a nuclear capability in Iran would pose a direct threat to the U.S. forces in the Middle East, to its European allies, and to the continental United States. Tehran would also be more ready to use nuclear weapons as intimidation and blackmail, and it would also be more likely to use chemical and biological weapons because it would not fear retaliation from such attacks.

Joseph's third point is that a nuclear-armed Iran could open a floodgate of nuclear proliferation and undermine the world's nonproliferation program. Fourth, nuclear weapons would consolidate the mullahs' power and guarantee their survival, thus degrading the prospect of democracy in Iran. Fifth, the bomb would "represent an existential threat to the state of Israel," and sixth, Iran's role "at the nexus of weapons of mass destruction and terrorism" would make it likely that the regime would sell nuclear weapons to other countries or terrorist groups.[7]

A nuclear-armed Iran would usher in an entirely new type of nuclear terrorism. Nuclear arms in the hands of a state sponsor of terrorism are a much more dangerous prospect than any other possible scenario, such as a terrorist group obtaining a nuclear bomb.[8] As the world's leading state sponsor of terrorism, Iran already plays the central role in much of the world's terror network. If Iran gets the bomb, its old definition as a state sponsor of terrorism will sound like a tourism brochure. Suddenly a state with massive resources—resources that make it the fourth-largest oil producer in the world—would have the highest geopolitical leverage in the Middle East. Ruled by Islamic extremists whose prime directive is to export radical Islamic rule throughout the region, this new face of terrorism is beyond comparison. With the bomb, the Iranian regime would become a meta-terrorist, an annihilating combination of radical ideology and nuclear destruction.

Although North Korea is also designated by the State Department as a state sponsor of terrorism with nuclear weapons, it does not pose even remotely the same threat as Iran does because North Korea lacks the Iranian regime's extremist ideology. North Korea may use its nuclear capability as a deterrent or to gain economic concessions from the West, but it does not harbor a point-by-point plan for setting up Korean dictatorships throughout Asia, let alone the globe.

The Iranian regime's expansionist goals cannot be underestimated. Ahmadinejad's election as president in 2005 reflected Tehran's renewed investment in consolidating ultraconservative power and driving its version of Islamic rule into Iraq, and then to other states. Secretary Joseph highlighted the danger of the regime's "aggressive intentions." However, as a state sponsor of terrorism, Iran is a unique case that will redefine nuclear terrorism.

Iran's inimitable stance is made even more dangerous because the Iranian regime will not hesitate to use a nuclear bomb. Nothing in the regime's history supports the idea that Tehran would merely build up an arsenal to use for political leverage or as a deterrent from attack. The mullahs have no ethical scruples with a nuclear first-strike policy; in fact, their ideology urges them to use such a weapon to annihilate what both Khomeini and Khamenei called the "Great Satan" and what former president Rafsanjani called "global arrogance." This radical fundamentalist worldview, which does not tolerate the existence of western values, is shared throughout the power structure of Iran, from Supreme Leader Khamenei to President Ahmadinejad to the small group of clerics in the regime's inner circle.

When Ahmadinejad called for wiping Israel off the map, he meant it. When Rafsanjani, former president of Iran and chairman of the Expediency Council, preached at a Friday sermon in December 2001 about the limitations of "conventional weaponry" and condemned western support of Israel's nuclear arsenal, he meant it, too. "If one day, the Islamic world is also equipped with weapons like those that Israel possesses now," he said, "then the imperialists' strategy will reach a standstill because the use of even one nuclear bomb inside Israel will destroy everything." He added that such a strike would cause only minimal damage to nearby Islamic populations and stressed that the regime considered a nuclear attack a clear possibility, stating, "It is not irrational to contemplate such an eventuality." Rafsanjani was evidently proud of the fact that in the wake of the September 11 attacks, Iran's controversial nuclear program had the United States scrambling to deal with it: "Developments over the last few months really frightened the Americans," he said. "You can see that the Americans have kept their eyes peeled and they are carefully looking for even the slightest hint that technological advances are being made by an independent Islamic country."[9]

The former IRGC supreme commander and the current secretary for the Expediency Council, Major General Mohsen Rezai, echoed as much in April 2006 when he said, "By virtue of our influence in Iraq and Afghanistan we are changing from a national government to a regional power. If this giant, which is slowly emerging in Iran and spreading to its surroundings, would become powerful from an economic standpoint as well as in nuclear technology, we would become a small, but regional empire. The West would see this in a matter of 20 or 30 years."[10] Hossein Shariatmadari, a close confidant of Supreme Leader Khamenei, and president of *Kayhan* newspaper told *Newsweek* in August 2006, "A new Middle East is being shaped now—not one led by the Americans but by the Islamic Republic of Iran."[11]

In addition to talking about the virtues of nuclear weapons, the regime has shown that it will use any means necessary to proceed with its policy, regardless of moral, ethical, or even religious considerations. In 1994, for example, the mullahs attacked one of the Shiite world's holiest sites, on their own soil, in order to harm the opposition indirectly. The Ministry of Intelligence and Security planned and carried out a bombing at the Imam Reza shrine in Mashhad, the holiest site in Iran and one to which hundreds of thousands of Shiite pilgrims flock every year. Attacking a shrine was unheard of in the Muslim world, but the regime considered it just one more tactic in its fight against the opposition, the Mujahedin-e Khalq (MEK). After the bombing, which killed at least 24 and wounded at least 70, the regime announced that the MEK was the culprit. Later on, Abdullah Nouri, the first interior minister under President Khatami, admitted in a trial in November 1999 that the regime carried out the attack in order to confront the Mujahedin and tarnish its image.[12] If Tehran was willing to bomb a holy site on its own soil in order to frame an opposition group, it will have no reservations in launching a nuclear warhead toward Israel or toward one of the "Great Satan's" military bases in the Persian Gulf.

What makes this prospect more probable and equally more disconcerting is that a resurgent Islamic Revolutionary Guards Corps has been in full control of Iran's nuclear drive. The election of former IRGC commander Ahmadinejad as president was one more manifestation of this transformation since mid-2003 of the IRGC into an omnipresent, omnipowerful political-security force. In addition to fully supervising the regime's nuclear drive, the IRGC has been the primary organ of the regime's sponsorship of terrorism, commissioned to execute special operations and train terrorist organizations outside Iran. The Qods Force has also been the main component of Tehran's multilayered campaign in Iraq. The regime has a clear eye on using nuclear weapons to enhance the IRGC's terrorist activities.

Accepting an Iranian nuclear weapons capability would pose a monumental security risk to the countries of Iran's region and would threaten the stability and security of the democratic world. Iran's having such a capability would no doubt be seen as a failure of Washington and its allies to defuse the resurgence of an outlaw regime. Furthermore, terrorist organizations under Iran's wings would have a huge political, moral, and operational boost by the mere fact that Tehran, which has acted since 1979 as the epicenter of terrorism inspired by Islamic fundamentalism, had nuclear weapons. The junior bullies of the neighborhood would feel immensely empowered if their primary patron changed the balance of power with a nuclear weapons capability. Accepting a nuclear-armed Iran is absolute strategic madness.[13]

As Secretary Joseph remarked, nuclear weapons would allow the Iranian regime to stay in power. The clout and political leverage of a nuclear arsenal is exactly what this highly unpopular regime needs to hold itself together. Becoming a nuclear state would significantly boost the morale of the IRGC and the religious zealots who form the infrastructure of the regime. The mullahs' new power would carry through to the repressive organs that keep the population in check, including the Bassij, the IRGC, the Ministry of Intelligence and Security, and the other repressive organizations that enforce the regime's policies. Throughout its lifetime, the regime has exploited crises in order to survive, from rallying the religious zealots during the Iran-Iraq War to terrifying the population by sending out assassination squads to kill its opponents both in and outside Iran.

At the end of the day, the regime's survival depends on how much it can suppress an increasingly uneasy and critical population. The ever-growing resistance inside the country is committed to undermining these repressive policies, but a nuclear arsenal would create a more powerful and resilient repressive machine and eliminate any hope for democratic change. This is why the Iranian people, even more than the nations of the world, cannot afford a nuclear-armed Iran.

CHAPTER 12

BEYOND NEGOTIATION: TOWARD AN IRAN POLICY

> Today, the Great Satan—the embodiment of evil and cruelty against mankind—has . . . [invited] the Middle Eastern nations to democracy. . . . The bullying face of the United States and other arrogant powers has been unveiled.
>
> —Supreme Leader Ali Khamenei, January 9, 2006[1]

How do you sit at the negotiating table with the leader of a nation who, in 2006, publicly called you the "Great Satan"? Where do you start the negotiating process with a leader who tells his citizens that "the Islamic World does not need the flawed . . . prescription of the West for democracy"?[2] For twenty-seven years the Iranian regime has voiced its hatred of the United States and the West, and for the same number of years attempts have been made to change the regime's behavior through external pressures, threats, negotiations, and appeasement. All these attempts have failed, and as the Iranian regime accelerates its push for a nuclear arsenal, the world no longer has the luxury of waiting for Tehran to turn itself around and shed its medieval mind-set. The Iranian regime has not budged from its original themes of hating the West and working to export its "Islamic" revolution. Ignoring this will only further step up Tehran's rush to the bomb.

WHAT DOES TEHRAN WANT?

The goals of the Islamic Republic of Iran, ever since Khomeini wrote up its constitution, are to preserve the theocratic regime, install sister Islamic republics throughout the Muslim and Arab world, and keep an increasingly restive population in check through brute repression. Vital to achieving these goals is Tehran's commitment to building a nuclear arsenal, which will allow it to forge ahead with its expansionist policy and boost its credibility among the hard-core zealots in the regime's inner circles and among the terrorist groups that it supports throughout the world. Every act of the mullahs in Tehran supports the fulfillment of these goals, and as a result, Iran today poses a five-pronged threat with its nuclear program, its meddling in Iraq, its support for international terrorism, its opposition to Middle East peace, and its clampdown on its own citizens.

The ruling clerics have made no attempt to hide their ambitions to export their firebrand Islamic worldview to the rest of the Middle East region. "We don't shy away from declaring that Islam is ready to rule the world. . . . We must believe in the fact that Islam is not confined to geographical borders, ethnic groups and nations. It's a universal ideology that leads the world to justice. . . . We must prepare ourselves to rule the world," boasted Ahmadinejad in January 2006.[3] There is no room for compromise in such a mission, and its very existence preempts diplomatic relationships because the mission is based on a set of values and tenets that are diametrically opposed to democracy. The rulers of Iran dream of locking the Middle East into a society of rigid laws based on an extremist interpretation of Islam. Whereas the majority of Iraqis work toward a secular, democratic government, the mullahs in Tehran throw all their resources behind radical Shiite parties and militias in order to gain the upper hand in Iraq and to use that as its first stepping stone on the path to global Islamic rule. Whereas the young, well-educated men and women of Iran yearn for gender equality and liberty, the mullahs repress women, imprison and execute dissidents, close down media outlets, enforce the dress code, and rig the elections to maintain their grip on power.

Tehran wants to continue enriching uranium and wants to develop nuclear weapons and the missiles to deliver them. Ahmadinejad's pledge that Iran will never back down from nuclear enrichment demonstrates that the regime will continue to break its Nuclear Non-Proliferation Treaty (NPT) obligations and derail the IAEA inspection process. In his speech before the United Nations in 2005, Ahmadinejad explained that the Iranian regime considered the NPT an unfair, "discriminatory" instrument through which foreign nations sought to "impose a nuclear apartheid."[4] On the basis of that statement, any expectation that Iran will suddenly reverse its position and adhere to the treaty is naive at best.

With a nuclear arsenal, the Iranian regime can carry out its stated objective of wiping Israel off the map. Iran also wants nuclear weapons in order to gain the ultimate leverage in its dealings with the rest of the world. These desires were evident when Ahmadinejad warned during a September 2005 military parade—while peering over the tops of giant Shahab–3 missiles that were carrying banners reading "We will trample America under our feet" and "Death to America"—that Iran would respond with "fiery and destructive" wrath if his regime was attacked.[5]

Tehran's objectives preempt the traditional negotiation process because the West does not have anything to offer that the regime desires. The mullahs are not interested in economic and political incentives or nuclear power plants. They want to be the hegemon not only in the Middle East but throughout the Muslim world. They consider themselves to be the *Um-ol Qura* (mother of all Islamic lands). In January 2006, Supreme Leader Khamenei said, "Now, during the period of postmodern colonialism, we should . . . not once again allow the enemy to dominate our destiny for a long time." He called on all levels of Iranian society to "prevent the world-devouring U.S. from beginning a new period of colonial domination throughout the Islamic world." In short, the Iranian regime wants the U.S. to stay out of Iran and the Middle East and choke on its own "revelry, violence . . . and other fiascos."[6]

In a way strikingly similar to that of the Soviet threat that defined the Cold War, the Iranian regime wants global domination, and its pursuit of a nuclear bomb is central to that goal.

SETTING THE STAGE FOR U.S.-IRAN RELATIONS

When Iran's nationalist prime minister Dr. Mohammad Mossadeq was toppled by a CIA-backed coup d'état, many in the West praised the coup as a major success and as an indication of how the CIA could be instrumental in securing the national security interests of the United States, as well as contributing to global security. Some, however, questioned the wisdom of this policy, predicting that sacrificing liberty at the expense of assumed stability, while expedient in the short term, would have adverse ramifications in the long term. Today, more than half a century later, it is quite obvious that the overthrow of the elected, nationalist government of Dr. Mossadeq not only harmed the interests of the Iranian people, but also has significantly undercut the national security interests of the United States. To those suffering under pro-western, yet authoritarian regimes, such as the shah's, the coup projected the United States as the protector of corrupt, puppet dictatorships.

The coup against Dr. Mossadeq, the most popular leader in Iran's modern history, dramatically changed the course of developments in Iran as it paved the way for the rise of a regressive, fundamentalist current that had been kept in check until then by the force of history. In a nutshell, the coup let the genie out of the bottle. In toppling Mossadeq, the United States and the United Kingdom relied on an unholy alliance of anti-Mossadeq forces. These forces ranged from fundamentalist clerics such as influential Ayatollah Abolqassem Kashani to the pro-Moscow Communist Tudeh Party. Ruhollah Khomeini was a close associate of Kashani's. Nearly three decades later, Khomeini unveiled his antagonism toward Mossadeq when he told an audience of his zealous followers, "I told the Agha [Kashani] that [Mossadeq] would be slapped in the face. And it did not take long before he was slapped. Had he remained [in power], he would have slapped Islam."[7]

The overthrow of Dr. Mossadeq, who was already weakened by his Islamic fundamentalist opponents, did not dissuade his young followers from picking up the torch. Learning from the shortcomings of the nationalist movement, the new generation set out to form a more organized movement. To this day, the regime considers the organized opposition within Iran and outside its borders as the biggest threat to its survival.

In retrospect, by toppling the liberal government of Dr. Mossadeq and bolstering the shah in his efforts to eliminate the secular, democratic opposition, the United States unwittingly paved the way for the rise to power of Khomeini and his troglodyte disciples, who manipulated the growing anti-American sentiments among the Iranian population to consolidate their rule.

UNDERSTANDING IRAN

The mullahs are now about to arm themselves with a nuclear bomb, already enjoy significant influence in Iraq, and have close ties to Palestinian groups who do not favor peace in the Middle East.

Unfortunately, the mentality that haunted U.S. policy toward Iran more than half a century ago continues to influence some policy circles in Washington today, especially in the Department of State. The United States has either miscalculated in detecting its allies in Iran or sacrificed its own allies or potential allies in order to reach out to its enemies, whose radical and unwavering nature was never understood. Since the overthrow of the shah in February 1979, the United States has struggled to understand the nature of the regime and what makes it tick. On numerous occasions, the United States reached out to Iran's clerical rulers, provided concessions, delivered arms, engaged in economic trade, offered a "road map" for dialogue, apologized for past behavior, and gave assurances as to the "permanent feature" of the regime. But the end result is a more radical, zealous leadership in Tehran, a leadership whose behavior is far from changed.[8] In fact, many experts believe that Tehran is far more dangerous to global peace and security today than it ever was.

The U.S. State Department has failed to understand the dynamics of the Iranian political scene, the deeply ideological, hard-core nature of the regime—a nature diametrically opposed to international norms—and the regime's grand agenda to develop a global Islamic rule. Instead, the United States has invested heavily in different measures intended to change the regime's behavior. Many "Iran experts" and analysts have contributed to various administrations' perception of Iran. Gary Sick, the former White House aide for Iran during the Iranian revolution and the hostage crisis and a longtime proponent of dialogue, has made every effort to minimize the Iranian regime's regional and global ambitions and explain away its role in international terrorism. In a 1987 *Foreign Affairs* article, Sick wrote, "It is apparent that Iran has modified, at least for the time being, its millenarian goal of bringing 'Islam to the entire world' in favor of a policy that might be described as 'clericalism in one country.'"[9] On the issue of Iran's sponsorship of terror, Sick wrote, "Iran may often be falsely accused. Many of these crimes were never solved, and the degree of Iranian official responsibility may be overstated."[10]

A report published by former National Security advisor Zbigniew Brzezinski and former CIA director Robert M. Gates, who headed a task force at the Council on Foreign Relations entitled "Iran: Time for a New Approach," said that Iran "could play a potentially significant role in promoting a stable, pluralistic government in Baghdad." The report further noted that "it is in the interests of the United States to engage selectively with Iran."[11]

But engagement has already been pursued by various European countries and U.S. administrations over the years. Since the overthrow of the shah, there has been a pattern in western efforts to engage the mullahs; the outcome has ranged from failure to embarrassment to a further emboldening of Tehran, including in its incessant effort to acquire a nuclear bomb.

A HISTORY OF ENGAGEMENT

In 1985, in a secretive measure, the United States sent National Security advisor Robert McFarlane and White House national security staffer Colonel Oliver North, along with a Bible, a cake, a Colt revolver, and some 2,000 TWO antitank missiles, on a mission that came to be known as the Iran Contra affair—a major fiasco and political embarrassment that tarnished the Reagan presidency.[12] The belief was that if the United States could strengthen the hand of moderate elements within the Iranian regime, the hostages would be released and eventually the behavior of the mullahs in Tehran would change. The chief moderate whom the United States intended to empower was Iranian parliament speaker Ali Akbar Hashemi Rafsanjani. Ironically, Rafsanjani was the Iranian official who, in a humiliating speech at a Friday prayer service, revealed the details of the American overture and its secret trip to Tehran.

In 1988, the Iranian regime accepted United Nations Resolution 598, which called for a cease-fire between Iran and Iraq, ending their bloody eight-year conflict. Weeks later, high-level European delegations went to Tehran in an effort to participate in the postwar reconstruction of the country and repair the relationship between Iran and the West. Soon after taking office in 1989, President George H. W. Bush sent a signal to Tehran that was intended to settle the hostage crisis in Lebanon, where a handful of American hostages remained in the hands of Tehran's proxy groups. In his inaugural speech, he said, "goodwill begets goodwill."

In June 1989, Khomeini died, and Ali Khamenei assumed power as the new supreme leader. Soon afterward, Rafsanjani assumed the presidency. What had seemed wishful thinking in the West became reality. In summer of 1988, many analysts and Iran observers had defined three events as a turning point toward moderation that would bring Iran back to the community of nations: the end of the Iran-Iraq War, the death of Khomeini, and the election of the "moderate" and "pragmatist" Rafsanjani. In less than a year, all three desired events had actually taken place. Iran was expected to be in a rush toward moderation that nothing could stop. The Iraqi invasion of Kuwait in August 1990 and the United States' attack to push the Iraqis out of Kuwait created yet another opportunity for the Iranian regime, because the United States was preparing to focus on Iran's archenemy, Iraq, and to provide concessions to Iran. None of those events later proved to be a catalyst toward change in Iran.

When President Clinton took office in January 1993, a new round of rapprochement was initiated by his State Department. American officials used every opportunity to call for dialogue with Iran. In his famous "dual containment speech," the National Security Council's senior director for the Near East and South Asia, Martin Indyk, emphasized that it was not the policy of the United States to change the regime in Iran; at the same time, he painted Iraq under Saddam Hussein as an irredeemable regime that should be changed.[13] The new strategy was essentially a one-size-fits-all, linked policy approach to both Iraq and Iran. U.S. exports to Iran increased dramatically, and by 1995, in a sharp surge, American oil companies became Iran's biggest customers, purchasing about $4 billion of oil every year. The companies included Exxon, Bay Oil, Coastal, Texaco, Mobil, and Caltex. Other companies obtained lucrative contracts to sell high-level technology and other products to Iran. These companies included Apple Computer, Motorola, and AT&T Global Information. Rockwell International sold helicopter gear and electronics, Bell Helicopter sold helicopters, Hewlett Packard sold advanced computers, Chrysler planned a jointly operated Jeep assembly plant, and Octagon signed a contract to sell portable satellite telephones to the Iranian military.[14]

But the commercial heyday was cut short when Iranian rulers were implicated in a series of terrorist attacks. In March 1995, President Clinton issued an executive order banning U.S. investments in Iran's energy sector. Later, a May 1995 presidential order banned all U.S. investment in Iran and prohibited the export and reexport to Iran of U.S. goods and services.[15]

When Mohammad Khatami took office as the new so-called moderate president of Iran in May 1997, the United States initiated a dramatic policy change toward Iran. Clinton administration officials wasted no time in testing the new president, and they provided a series of concessions to help remove obstacles between the two countries. For his part, Khatami went on a charm offensive, including making conciliatory statements in interviews with CNN's Christiane Amanpour, who threw softballs to Khatami, providing him the opportunity to preach to Americans about their history and about the Puritans rather than dealing with Iran's human rights situation and its ambitious nuclear weapons program.[16]

Khatami's presidency led the Clinton administration to a round of successive concessions. In July 1997, the administration decided to drop its opposition to a natural-gas pipeline across Iran, "the first easing of United States' efforts to isolate Iran economically."[17] In September, Khatami's foreign minister, Kamal Kharrazi, in a speech during a session of the United Nations General Assembly in New York, pledged to "cooperate with the international community to root out terrorism," provided that western countries would "stop supporting the main armed Iranian opposition group, the People's Mujahedeen."[18] Days later, in an effort to send a conciliatory message to Tehran, the State Department designated the Mujahedin-e Khalq (MEK) as a Foreign Terrorist Organization (FTO). A senior Clinton administration official said at the time, "The inclusion of the People's Moujahedeen [sic] was intended as a goodwill gesture to Tehran and its newly elected moderate president, Mohammad Khatami."[19]

In May 1998, President Clinton waived sanctions against Russian, French, and Malaysian firms, hoping to develop Iran's South Pars natural-gas field. In June 1998, in a policy speech at the Asia Society in New York, Secretary of State Madeleine Albright announced that Washington had implemented a more streamlined procedure for issuing visas to the Iranians and offered "a road map leading to normal relations."[20] In September 1998, Khatami traveled to New York to give a speech at the United Nations General Assembly, where he spoke about a "dialogue among civilizations." Supporters of the MEK opposition organized a massive, peaceful rally, at which a bipartisan group of members of Congress addressed thousands of Iranian Americans who denounced Khatami as a terrorist. In a speech at New York's Asia Society that was considered Iran's official response to Albright's "road map," Foreign Minister Kharrazi rebuffed Albright's offer for dialogue.[21] "It did not offer a road map for the future," Thomas Pickering, U.S. under secretary of state for political affairs, said of Kharrazi's speech.[22]

Despite continuing problems, the Clinton administration embarked on a general review with the aim of relaxing sanctions on Iran. In November 1998, the Treasury Department amended its regulations to eliminate the reporting requirement for purchases or swaps of Iranian crude oil. In December 1998, Iran was removed from the list of major narcotics producers. In April 1999, the administration further amended the trade and investment ban by announcing that license applications for commercial sales of agricultural and medical products would be reviewed on a case-by-case basis, a significant easing of the trade ban.[23] In the same month, Indyk, in a speech to the Council on Foreign Relations, said that the United States had pursued several steps that could broaden U.S. engagement with Iran. In the fall of 1999, with a series of quiet approaches and inducements, the White House tried to achieve an opening to Khatami, but all of its efforts were rebuffed. In August 1999, a secret message was sent to Khatami, seeking his cooperation in solving the 1996 bombing of the Khobar Towers in Saudi Arabia, in which 19 U.S. servicemen were killed. The message also sought for the first time to reopen consular offices in Tehran. "Not interested," was the response."[24]

Former FBI director Louis Freeh wrote in his autobiography that President Clinton sidetracked the investigation into the June 1996 bombing of Khobar Towers. According to Freeh, the Clinton administration was so determined to press ahead with its campaign for a diplomatic opening with Iran that it failed to press the Saudis for access to several suspects in the case and did little to assist the FBI investigation.[25] In an October 1999 speech entitled "Iran and the United States: Prospects for a New Relationship," which was another follow-up to Secretary Albright's speech, Indyk again asked Iran to enter into a formal dialogue with the United States. He introduced a number of clear signals to Iran, including announcing that the State Department had added the National Council of Resistance of Iran (NCRI) to the list of Foreign Terrorist Organizations (FTO). Indyk explained, "the Iranian government had brought this to our attention. We looked into it and saw that there were good reasons for designating the NCRI (NCR) as an alias for the MEK."[26] Indyk probably did not want to remember that, in response to questions from reporters during a State Department briefing in June 1998, department spokesman James Rubin had insisted, "A careful review of the evidence concerning the National Council of Resistance, which is associated with the MEK, has shown that it does not meet the criteria in the law for the designation of the NCR as a foreign terrorist organization."[27] (The United States

Court of Appeals D.C. Circuit clarified at this time that the NCRI-U.S. was a separate entity and not designated as an FTO.[28])

In March 2000, Albright announced an end to the ban on imports of products such as caviar and rugs, and she apologized for the U.S. role in the 1953 coup that brought the shah to power. In response, Supreme Leader Khamenei denounced rapprochement with the United States as "treason." In the September 2000 U.N. "Millennium Summit" meetings, Albright and Clinton sent a positive signal to Iran by attending Khatami's speeches, which many described as irrelevant ramblings about philosophy and religion.[29]

THE WAR IN IRAQ

Since January 2003, when it became evident that the coalition forces would attack Iraq, the United States, through its ambassador to Afghanistan at the time, Zalmay Khalilzad, contacted the Iranian regime's representatives to ensure that Iran would not attack or meddle in Iraq if the Americans invaded. Senior American officials believed that Tehran could be persuaded to remain neutral if the United States met Tehran's demand that the Mujahedin-e Khalq be attacked and prevented from harming the Iranian regime in the future. That message was conveyed to Iran by British officials before hostilities began. U.S. officials also warned that Iran should not let fighters from the Iran-backed Supreme Council for Islamic Revolution in Iraq (SCIRI) or the Badr Corps cross into Iraq, or they would be hit as well.[30]

Five days after the start of the war, American and British planes heavily bombed almost all of the bases of the Mujahedin-e Khalq, inflicting casualties and significant damage. But Baghdad fell quickly, and on April 9, 2003, the night that the Iraqi army suddenly disappeared, Tehran violated its commitment and dispatched its own IRGC, Badr Corps, and other proxy groups into Iraq from four different positions and took up key positions in various cities, primarily in the south. The U.S. military reacted by offering a cease-fire agreement to the MEK, even though the MEK had not fired back a single shot, according to U.S. military commanders. An agreement was reached on April 15, 2003, which allowed the MEK to keep all its weapons and military equipment, including tanks and armored personnel carriers. This significantly helped secure a critical portion of Iraq's eastern border in the northeastern province of Diyala, since MEK members were familiar with the terrain, area, and population. But about one month later, Tehran intervened again.

In May 2003, in an effort both to assure the Iranian regime that the United States was not looking for supporting groups that seek to topple the Iranian regime and also to pacify the Iranian regime from meddling in Iraq, the White

House asked the Pentagon to disarm the MEK.[31] Major General Ray Odierno, commander of the 4th Infantry Division, which negotiated with the Mujahedin-e Khalq, later told the journalists, "It is not a surrender. It is an agreement to disarm and consolidate." "Speaking at a Mujahedeen base near the Iranian border, the general said they appeared to be committed to democracy in Iran and their cooperation with the United States should prompt a review of their 'terrorist' status," Agence France-Presse reported. "I would say that any organization that has given up their equipment to the coalition clearly is cooperating with us, and I believe that should lead to a review of whether they are still a terrorist organization or not," Agence France-Presse quoted Odierno as saying.[32]

The United States fully supported the nuclear dialogue that began between the EU3 and Iran in 2003 and continued itself to have direct communication with Iran. "We do have channels that we are using with the Iranians, and communicating to them that they ought to review their policies," Secretary of State Colin Powell told reporters in early May.[33] But the United States broke off the dialogue following the May 12, 2003, bombing in Riyadh.

In August 2003, when a journalist asked Powell to confirm reports that the Iranians were willing to turn over some senior al-Qaeda people in exchange for further action against Iranian opposition groups, Powell said, "This is a sensitive issue. . . . Using appropriate interlocutory, we are in touch with the Iranians on both of these issues."[34] A week later, Powell issued a special order designating the U.S. representative office of the National Council of Resistance of Iran (NCRI-U.S.) as an alias of the MEK. This was in sharp contrast with the State Department's own position and with the opinion of a United States Court of Appeals that the NCRI-U.S. was not an FTO.

Ironically, the order to close down our office came on August 14, 2003, exactly one year after the August 14, 2002 NCRI-U.S. press conference in which I revealed the nuclear sites in Natanz and Arak, and there had been dozens of other key revelations in this 12-month period. While the revelations that were brought to public attention by this small office on the tenth floor of the National Press Building stunned the world and delivered a major blow to Iran's effort to obtain a nuclear bomb, it was the Iranian regime that was rewarded for those revelations by getting the State Department to shut us down.

Six months after halting talks with Iran, the Bush administration said that it was prepared to resume discreet discussions about Iraq, Afghanistan, and other issues. "We are prepared to engage in limited discussions with the government of Iran about areas of mutual interest as appropriate," said Deputy Secretary of State Richard L. Armitage in testimony prepared for the Senate Foreign Relations Committee.[35] In December 2003, the United States briefly resumed some contact with Iran to coordinate U.S. aid to victims of the earthquake in Bam, including a reported offer to send a high-level delegation to Iran. Iran's intelligence minister, Ali Yunesi, rebuffed that offer and said that if America "were truly sincere," it would "arrest the heads of the People's Mujahedeen."[36]

Under Secretary of State R. Nicholas Burns characterized the current U.S. approach toward Iran on November 30, 2005, by stating that U.S. policy is to "isolate Iran, promote a diplomatic solution to Iran's nuclear ambitions, expose and oppose the regime's support for terrorism, and advance the cause of democracy and human rights within Iran itself."[37]

THE MILITARY OPTION

As the crisis over Iran's nuclear program escalated in the summer of 2005, President George W. Bush warned that "all options are on the table" if diplomacy failed to convince Iran to halt its nuclear program. He explained that these options included the use of military force, which the United States had used "in the recent past to secure our country."[38] The Iranian regime already felt the pressure of this recent use of force, which hemmed in Iran on the east in Afghanistan and on the west in Iraq, but the leadership in Tehran hid their anxiety behind their own threats to the United States. "I think Bush should know that our options are more numerous than the U.S. options," shot back Iran's Foreign Ministry spokesman Hamid Reza Asefi one day after Bush's remarks. "If the United States makes such a big mistake, then Iran will definitely have more choices to defend itself."[39] What is the next "choice" beyond a strike with conventional weapons? Asefi's thinly veiled threat of a nuclear attack was typical of the regime's behavior, stoking the nuclear crisis just after rejecting another European package of incentives. Bush's threat only bolstered Tehran's rhetoric and spurred on its commitment to completing its fuel cycle, as indicated by AEOI deputy director Mohammad Saidi: "The rougher and faster these countries make the game, the more decisive we become to operate the rest of our nuclear facilities," he said.[40]

The military option, which would presumably be carried out by the United States and its military allies in Europe and the Middle East, covers a range of options. At one end are limited numbers of precision air strikes targeting Iran's nuclear-related sites. The next level would involve more expanded air strikes to include the regime's military command center and other installations, as well as political command and control structures. The most advanced engagement would be a full invasion by ground forces.

A 2005 study revealed that the majority of Americans did not support a military option against Iran. Support for using force against Iran to restrain it from developing weapons of mass destruction averaged only 42 percent between 2002 and 2005, according to Richard C. Eichenberg of Tufts University. In his study of U.S. public opinion and the use of military force, Eichenberg uncovered a pattern of initial popularity followed by deflated support as conflicts become more costly. "A war fought largely with the rhetorical justification of foreign policy restraint (the famed weapons of mass destruction) was extremely popular at first," he wrote, "both because the objective has been historically popular with the public and because of the rapid success of the operation. As the objective changed from foreign policy restraint to participation in an internal political struggle, however, support waned rapidly."[41]

I do not endorse the military option for Iran because I believe that the Iranian nuclear threat should have an Iranian solution, conceived of and implemented by Iranian patriots with the support of the international community. I also believe that from both a military and a strategic point of view, a military option is not desirable on three grounds. First, the physical nature of Iran's nuclear program hinders the success of precision air strikes. Not only are the facilities broadly dispersed, which would necessitate a widespread operation that would make the bombers overly vulnerable to Iranian antiaircraft and other retaliation, but many of the facilities are buried deep underground in heavily fortified tunnels. In addition, Iran's long history of deception about its nuclear sites leads to the logical conclusion that there may be other secret facilities that have not yet been discovered. Second, a military attack on Iran would change its image from that of an antagonist—a provoker and violator of the NPT—to that of a victim of western aggression. The regime has already demonstrated how forcefully it can exploit the harshest criticisms put upon it; if it comes under military attack, those tactics will escalate into the third major issue: Tehran's option to reach out to its support base among terrorist states and Islamist terrorist groups throughout the Middle East. Tehran would consider trying to amass a coalition of armed extremists to transform the war into a terrorist Armageddon, although there is no evidence to suggest that Iran would be able to generate a significant campaign of terror.

THE DIPLOMATIC OPTION

Ever since the United States broke relations with Iran in 1980, it has maintained a policy of exerting external pressure on the regime and, at varying times, trying to initiate dialogue. United States pressures include enforcing strict sanctions, designating Iran as a state sponsor of terrorism, and objecting to Iran's pursuit of weapons of mass destruction, its support of international terrorism, and its appalling human rights record. This policy is fraught with contradictions, the most recent of which was manifested with President Bush's condemnation of Iran as part of an "Axis of Evil" in his first term, followed by Secretary Condoleezza Rice's invitation to engage in direct talks with Tehran in Bush's second term. Europe, on the other hand, has long held a policy of "critical dialogue," denouncing Iran's behavior while engaging in trade and a relatively active diplomatic relationship.

The western countries' approaches may differ, but Tehran's behavior toward the West has been unfailingly consistent. From its first months in power to its latest dealings with the IAEA, the Iranian regime has related to the West with lies, deception, denial, and outright contempt. Regardless of which president was in power in Tehran, the anti-West extremism never wavered, and ultimate control remained in the hands of the supreme leader. Instead of gradually thawing its attitude toward the West after Khomeini's death, Tehran defined its role in the world by facilitating suicide attacks in Israel, selling arms to radical Palestinian groups, and building up a covert nuclear weapons program.

The policy of containment or critical dialogue pursued by most western countries over more than two decades led to the ascension of the most radical and extremist factions in the Iranian regime. Ahmadinejad's presidency took the regime's confrontational stance with the West to new heights, from vicious rhetoric to a brazen disregard for nuclear treaty obligations.

Iran's history with the IAEA demonstrates that Tehran is not interested in honest, open relations with the international community. Since the regime's secret nuclear program was exposed in 2002, it has resorted to denials, misinformation, delays, the bulldozing of entire facilities, the continuation of illegal programs, the ignoring of requests, and outright lies. The IAEA director general's report of June 8, 2006, revealed that the regime had not changed its tune, even though it had been reported to the United Nations Security Council over its failure to comply with the Nuclear Non-Proliferation Treaty. Iran had promised, for example, to provide a timetable by May 18 that would show when it would resolve all of its outstanding issues with the IAEA; by the time of the June report, "no such timetable has as yet been received." The report also stated that Iran had not delivered any new information about its centrifuge programs, not responded to a request for clarification of its centrifuge research, not provided a copy of a requested document about procedures for working with uranium metal, declined to discuss implementing remote monitoring at one site, and ignored requests for investigators to take samples at another site.[42]

The regime's reprehensible track record with the IAEA proves that there is no historical justification for trusting it in any negotiation process. Therefore, traditional policy approaches toward Iran that center upon negotiations are doomed to failure and expose an embarrassing lack of awareness of Iran's record.

Sanctions are certainly an option, but they have their own limitations. Sanctions would hurt the regime and would slow down the nuclear program, making life difficult for the regime, but sanctions would not lead to stopping Iran from getting the bomb. Pointing a finger at Iran's human rights abuses with one hand while signing business contracts with the other has ensured the survival of the regime and allowed the mullahs to act with impunity. Defending Tehran's right to a "peaceful" nuclear program while dismissing the evidence that it is on a full-out push to become a nuclear-armed state sponsor of terror is too dangerous an option even to consider.

In some policy circles, the argument goes that we can live with a nuclear-armed Iran because the worst-case scenario is either improbable or at worst manageable.[43]

Henry Sokolski and Patrick Clawson take such an approach in their edited volume, *Getting Ready for a Nuclear-Ready Iran*.[44] To their credit, Sokolski and Clawson acknowledge that a nuclear-ready Iran would pose major threats to the international community. First, Iran's continued insistence that it acquired its nuclear capabilities legally under the Nuclear Nonproliferation Treaty (NPT) would, if unchallenged, encourage its neighbors to develop nuclear options of their own. Second, a nuclear-ready Iran could be emboldened to manipulate oil prices upward. It might attempt this either by threatening the freedom of the seas or by using terrorist proxies to threaten the destruction of Saudi and other Gulf state oil facilities and pipelines. Third, Iran would likely lend greater support to terrorists operating against Israel, Iraq, Libya, Saudi Arabia, Europe, and the United States.

While Sokolski and Clawson correctly identify some of the threats posed by a nuclear-armed Iran, they err in treating the Iranian regime as if it were a normal state, subject to containment, deterrence, and coercive diplomacy. They argue that to contain and deter Iran from posing such threats, Washington might consider discrediting the legitimacy of Iran's nuclear program as a model for other proliferators to clarify what activities qualify as being "peaceful" under the NPT: increasing the costs for Iran to leave or infringe the NPT; securing Russian cooperation in these efforts by offering Moscow a lucrative U.S. nuclear cooperation agreement; reducing Persian Gulf oil and gas production and distribution system vulnerabilities to possible terrorist disruptions; limiting Iran's freedom to threaten oil and gas shipping; isolating Iran as a regional producer of fissile materials by encouraging Israel to take the first steps to freeze and dismantle such capabilities; and backing these diplomatic-economic initiatives with increased U.S.-allied anti-terrorist, defense, naval border security, and nuclear nonproliferation cooperation.

Likewise, Geoffrey Kemp of the Nixon Center argues that "the U.S. would have to learn to live with an Iranian nuclear option and construct a deterrent policy that would be effective against the range of threats associated with an Iranian bomb."[45] Kemp concludes that the United States should be "willing to work with the current regime for the mutual interests of all parties. If this is 'appeasement' or a 'sellout,' so be it."[46] Kenneth Pollack and Ray Takeyh similarly argue that "the United States could probably deter Iran even after it crossed the nuclear threshold."[47] George Perkovich, vice president for studies at the Carnegie Endowment for International Peace, argues that in the case of Iran's acquisition of nuclear weapons, the international community could respond in two ways: it could seek to roll back this acquisition and bring Iran back into compliance with the obligations of non-nuclear weapon states, or "the world could adapt itself to Iran's new status and seek a modus vivendi through deterrence, containment and diplomacy."[48]

But because of the Islamic extremist nature of the regime in Tehran, it is not as subject to deterrent and coercive threats as are normal states. Indeed, it is because of the Islamic fundamentalist character of the regime that makes it unacceptable for Iran to possess nuclear weapons. In this respect, deterrence by threat, deterrence by denial, and deterrence by positive incentives are not as likely to be effective against a nuclear-armed Iran as against a secular state.

THE THIRD OPTION

In a reaction that has become common practice and the accepted norm in Washington, the experts, academics, and think tanks raised a commotion about the infeasibility of the military option toward Iran and then lined up to become fully entrenched in the diplomatic option—namely, more negotiations.

This traditional approach is not a realistic option in the case of Iran. Those who argue in favor of putting all their eggs in the basket of diplomacy believe that diplomacy is the best and safest path, even if it does not work, because a nuclear-armed Iran is not really a nightmare scenario. Those who do perceive the depth and urgency of the Iranian nuclear threat do not predict any greater success with other options. As a result, the policy picture toward Iran is at best worn, ineffective, and depleted.

It is difficult to argue against the proposition of a democratic government in Iran, a government that is committed to international norms and willing to build a normal relationship with the West. But the consensus has been that this is merely wishful thinking. When I appeared on Fox News Channel's *DaySide* in April 2004 and outlined a policy of supporting those Iranian people who have already called for regime change, the anchorwoman who had the last word briefly concluded the interview by saying "Oh well, easier said than done." Iran analysts and Washington talking heads consistently refuse even to consider the possibility of changing the regime in Tehran. Former CIA analyst and author Kenneth Pollack argues, "Most of the evidence indicates that Iranians are sick of revolutions and don't want another one. They may not like this regime, but they are not ready to take to the streets to depose it." He further concludes, "If Washington were to start fooling around in Iranian politics again, it would almost certainly revive all of the anti-American fervor in an instant."[49] Gary Sick, director of the Middle East Institute at Columbia University and an advocate of engaging Iran, said of those who promote regime change, "They believe that Iran is ripe for revolution, but I think this is highly questionable."[50] Others dismiss the opposition groups that are to lead the movement as "weak and disorganized."[51] They submit that even though the people might be ready for change, there is simply not a means to materialize the desire of the Iranian people. "While discontent with the clerical regime is widespread, protests are sporadic and not linked by any organized movement," an editorial writer in a major U.S. daily concluded.[52] The facts do not support these dismissals of the Iranian opposition movement as a viable option for regime change, however.

The arguments about the Iranian opposition and the means to help facilitate regime change cannot be made in a vacuum. The state of the opposition—its potentials and its true abilities to engineer change in Iran—should be viewed in light of the history of the past three decades. A serious analysis takes into consideration a long view of how the opposition has interfaced with Iran and the world. This analysis considers how much repression the opposition has absorbed, how it has responded to and adapted to that repression, how much it has been harmed or favored by the international community, and how it has handled major domestic and regional crises. Also, a serious look at the organized resistance must include an understanding of the type of democratic government platform it has proposed, promoted, and implemented in its own organization as a model for a future Iran.

The most important factor that has kept the Iranian regime in power is not that the regime is popular, not that an organized opposition does not exist, and not that the people hate the idea of another revolution. The fact is that this regime has kept itself in power by relying on three pillars: absolute repression domestically, exporting terrorism and Islamic extremism, and gaining concessions from western countries. Without any one of these, the regime could not have survived.

Any voice of dissent that could potentially threaten the existence of the regime or undermine its legitimacy was crushed by the ruthless mullahs who have relied on more than a dozen organs to clamp down on the population, including the Islamic Revolutionary Guards Corps, the paramilitary Bassij Force, and the Ministry of Intelligence and Security. From the beginning, critical voices from within have been dealt with harshly; even the most senior clerics who opposed the regime were sacked. Ayatollah Hussein-Ali Montazeri, the officially designated successor for Supreme Leader Ruhollah Khomeini, was rejected for his "weak and flexible" approach to Iran's main opposition, the Mujahedin-e Khalq. In a series of letters to Khomeini as well as judicial officials, Montazeri objected to the massacre, ordered by Khomeini, of thousands of political prisoners immediately after the 1988 cease-fire in the Iran-Iraq War. "This kind of massacre without the trial of prisoners and captives will definitely benefit [the MEK] in the long run," Montazeri wrote in one letter. "The world will condemn us and they will be further encouraged to wage armed struggle." He chastised Khomeini for trying to put down a movement through murder. "It is wrong to kill to contain thoughts and ideas," he wrote. "The People's Mujahedin are not individuals; they are an ideology and a worldview. They have logic. It takes right logic to answer wrong logic. You cannot solve the problem with killing; it will only spread."[53] Days later, Montazeri was stripped of his position and sent to Qom, where he remained under house arrest for several years. As his health deteriorated, the regime, fearing a backlash, lifted some of the restrictions placed on him. There is little doubt that Ayatollah Montazeri outranks not only all the clerics who are now in power, but all the other grand ayatollahs in theological schools in Qom.

THE CATALYST FOR CHANGE

On the path to consolidate its power, the Khomeini regime organized paramilitary thugs and IRGC members to attack the gatherings of rapidly growing secular opposition groups, beating them with clubs, stones, and chains, and making it extremely costly for anyone to join such groups. The Mujahedin-e Khalq was the only organization that stood up to the challenge and resisted the ideological, political, and military onslaught by the ruling mullahs. The group's leader, Massoud Rajavi, used the Koran and other Islamic sources to challenge the religious legitimacy of Khomeini and his ruling clique, something that no other political group dared to do or was capable of doing. In a matter of months, the MEK's publication, *Mojahed*, had a circulation of more than 500,000 copies, surpassing any other newspaper, including the government-run dailies.[54] Khomeini soon resorted to a campaign of terror to uproot the MEK in Iran.

By June 1981, Khomeini had managed to jail and torture thousands, many opposition groups were officially declared illegal, and opposition publications were shut down. As a last-ditch effort to determine if any possibility for nonviolent political opposition existed, the MEK called for a peaceful rally in Tehran and other major Iranian cities. On June 20, 1981, approximately 500,000 Tehranis showed up, despite warnings on state radio and television to not "waste their lives for the sake of 'liberalism and capitalism.'" The IRGC was ordered to shoot. Fifty were killed, 200 injured, and 1,000 arrested in the vicinity of Tehran University alone. "The warden of Evin prison announced with much fanfare that firing squads had executed twenty-three demonstrators, including a number of teenage girls," wrote one author later. "The reign of terror had begun."[55]

A book published in 2006 contains the names and particulars of 20,000 men, women, and juveniles associated with the MEK murdered by the Iranian regime since 1981 on political charges.[56] The actual number of executions is believed to be much higher, perhaps as many as 120,000, according to some estimates.

The Iranian opposition has survived a level of repression that is unparalleled in modern times. The United Nations General Assembly, the Human Rights Commission, Amnesty International, Freedom House, and many other organizations have reported on the continued human rights violations in Iran, and the situation has been deteriorating more rapidly since Ahmadinejad became president. Nevertheless, the Mujahedin-e Khalq and its associate groups in Iran have maintained an impressive level of support and structure, including a vital, experienced, and democratically inclined leadership with the ability to mobilize, plan, and lead the movement in Iran under very difficult circumstances.

The most secretive information about the Iranian regime's involvement in international terrorism, about its top-secret nuclear weapons program, and about its nefarious designs for Iraq has all come from the opposition network in Iran. I interviewed a number of U.S. military personnel who were previously stationed in Iraq or are currently there, as well as the officers who have spent time at Camp Ashraf, the MEK's main base in Iraq.[57] The officers were uniformly impressed by the members' high level of education, leadership ability, commitment, and willingness to cooperate in order to achieve democracy in Iran. The MEK's access to intelligence about all aspects of Iranian society, as well as about the most clandestine aspects of the regime, is a clear indication of its level of contact and support within Iran. Many student leaders of the July 1999 antigovernment demonstration in Tehran are now among the MEK ranks stationed in Camp Ashraf, according to these U.S. officers. The officers were also impressed with the MEK's military training, which made use of tanks, armored personnel carriers, and field guns at a level fully comparable to modern conventional armies. "I did not think highly of them," one officer told me about his first encounter with opposition leaders in Ashraf. "But by the time I left, they certainly changed my mind." Another officer who spent more than one year at Ashraf told me that each of the nearly 3,500 members of Iranian opposition in Ashraf, especially the women, was capable of managing a city in Iran.

I also interviewed a number of parliamentarians who had direct contact with various Iranian opposition groups and who traveled to the groups' headquarters to evaluate their potential. Paulo Casaca, a member of the European parliament and the president of its delegation to the NATO Parliamentary Assembly, was appalled by the extent to which Europe has conceded to Tehran and sacrificed the main opposition for petty economic gains. In an article in the *Wall Street Journal* following his visit to Ashraf, Casaca wrote, "In a region still dominated by intolerance, tyranny and blind fanaticism, this movement is advocating an Islam based on democratic governance, secularism, tolerance, and gender equality. The fact that the movement is led by a woman—Maryam Rajavi, who lives near Paris—only sharpens the contrast with a regime that bars women from high political office."[58] I also interviewed Alejo Vidal Quadras Roca, the European parliament's first vice president, who was particularly impressed with the message and the leadership of the NCRI.[59] Another member of the European parliament, Struan Stevenson, a Scottish Conservative and the cochairman of the parliament's Friends of Free Iran Inter Group, wrote a commentary arguing that the EU is best served by empowering the Iranian opposition. "By putting the People's Mujahedeen on its terror list, however, the EU has handcuffed itself," he wrote.[60]

INTERNAL OPPOSITION ON THE RISE

The Iranian opposition network within Iran registered as many as 4,000 antigovernment demonstrations in Iran between March 2005 and March 2006—an average of more than 330 protests every month. The Iranian population's visible opposition to the regime reached this remarkable number as part of a consistent trend of escalating protest against the regime since the end of the Iran-Iraq War in 1988. Some of the most significant protests from the last decade include a series of protests in several Iranian cities in the summer of 1991, as citizens lashed out about the political repression, food shortages, rampant inflation, and overall economic mismanagement that continued after the war. In Tehran, protesters threw stones at the police and set cars on fire, as reported by the *New York Times*. Others protested peacefully, such as a group of 40 men who marched in Tehran's Sabzeh Square in August with the linings of their pockets hanging out of their pants in order to protest the dire straits of the economy. Demonstrations also took place in Isfahan, Tabriz, and Rasht, 200 miles northwest of Tehran, where two bombing attacks struck the bazaar.[61]

The violent opposition to the regime grew stronger over the next year, with riots erupting in Shiraz, Mashhad, Arak, Tehran, and other cities. Approximately 300 disabled war veterans in Shiraz organized a march in June 1992 to protest the government's mishandling of funds at the veteran's agency and, as in other cities, the demonstration quickly expanded with hundreds of squatters who faced eviction. Migrants were flooding into the cities and building unlicensed homes during this period, and authorities could not keep up with providing services to the booming urban population. The regime's strategy of bulldozing the homes and covering up the areas with parks and boulevards brought a backlash of rioting, looting, and arson attacks on banks, police stations, and city buses. In Arak, massive rioting broke out in May 1992 after a 12-year-old boy was killed during a clash with government authorities over a squatter camp. Protesters burned 2,000 to 3,000 buildings in the city and fought to disarm police officers and forcibly line them up as shields against the soldiers who had been sent in to stop the riots.[62] The poor would no longer tolerate waiting for "the Islamic Government to make good on its pledges to protect their rights and improve living standards," wrote the *New York Times*.[63]

The largest of these anti-government housing policy demonstrations erupted in Mashhad on May 29, 1992, when tens of thousands of people took to the streets and burned all of the city's government buildings. Mullahs ran out of the buildings before the rioters threw computers out of the windows and set the buildings on fire. A woman journalist for *The Economist* who later reported that the riots in Mashhad were "remarkably well organized" was arrested, strip-searched, and interrogated by an army officer for ten hours. He repeatedly asked her whether she had met with any members of the MEK in Mashhad, as the regime suspected that this group organized the events. "There is little doubt that the crowd had specific targets in mind and that the rampage was planned," wrote the reporter.[64] The Islamic revolutionary courts executed at least four of the Mashhad rioters by hanging, and President Rafsanjani ordered Iran's security forces to crack down on opposition groups to prevent more such attacks on the government.[65]

To try to quell the violence in the cities and industrial towns throughout Iran that year, the regime arrested hundreds of protestors and executed some for "sabotage." The *New York Times* described the riots of 1991 and 1992 as "the worst violence in the nearly 13 years since the revolution."[66]

In August 1994, the regime was forced to give in to the demands of approximately 50,000 protesters in the northwestern city of Qazvin, who demanded that their city secede from Zanjan Province in order to retain more of its tax revenues. The government sent thousands of troops to the city to break up the demonstrations, resulting in at least four deaths and dozens of wounded during the state of undeclared martial law. The size of the uprising compelled Tehran to allow the city to secede and become part of Tehran Province, the most lucrative of the provinces, a concession which seemed "to reflect fear in Tehran that discontent in . . . Qazvin could spread throughout the economically depressed country," wrote the *New York Times*.[67]

The massive, historic anti-government uprisings of July 1999 were launched after police made a violent raid on a Tehran dormitory to put down a peaceful pro-democracy student rally. The next day, thousands of demonstrators marched in Tehran's streets to vent their rage against the regime's leadership, chanting, "Death to despotism! Death to dictators!" "Oh great leader, shame on you," and "Khamenei must quit!"[68] By later in the day, thousands of men, women, and children had joined the university students and the crowd had grown to 25,000, and the protests soon spread to Mashhad, Yazd, Shahroud, and other cities. CBS News reported that "an unmistakable sense of revolution has returned to Tehran" as the people's demand that "heads roll at the top" echoed the protests against the Shah two decades earlier.[69] Over the six-day period of national pro-democracy demonstrations, police and militias attacked protestors with clubs and tear gas, and many were arrested to be tried as "counter-revolutionaries." On the anniversary of the protests one year later, several thousand residents of Tehran demonstrated in Revolution Square, with students comprising only 10 percent of the crowd. Reuters reported that mainstream society, including unemployed youth, women, old men, and other citizens "turned on the ruling clerical elite with increasing venom."[70] The state-run daily, *Entekhab*, reported on July 9, 2000 that people were chanting, "Incompetent Khatami, this is the final warning; National Liberation Army [MEK] is ready for uprising." The wire service summed up the message of the demonstration as an event in which the people "challenged the very existence of the Islamic system, calling for an end to clergy rule in Iran and demanding a referendum on democracy."[71] The July demonstrations continued year after year, regardless of the bloody crackdowns by Iranian security forces. During the 2002 anniversary protest, the 3,000 demonstrators chanted slogans such as, "God save you the day we become armed,"[72] and in 2003 continued to demand the resignation of Khatami. During that year's July demonstrations, one member of Iran's parliament told a Reuters reporter, "our society now is like a room full of gas ready to ignite with a small spark."[73] The *New York Times* described Tehran in June 2003 as a "combat zone" with violent nightly protests "by demonstrators from across the social spectrum demanding more social, economic and political freedom."[74]

Additional large-scale protests in the mid-1990s included the April 1995 demonstrations against high utility and fuel prices in Islamshahr, a working-class suburb of Tehran, where about 100,000 Iranians marched through the streets and smashed bank windows. The protest turned deadly when the regime sent in helicopter gun ships that killed 144 of the demonstrators. In December 1996, the death of Iranian Sunni leader Mullah Mohammad Rabii, whom his supporters alleged was killed by the regime, sparked riots in the cities of Bakhtaran, Ravansar, and Javanrud. Five of the demonstrators were killed and hundreds wounded by police. In December 1999, Iranians protesting the regime's killing of the dissident Dariush Foruhar and his wife bravely shouted slogans such as "Freedom, security—that is the slogan of the nation!" at the 200 riot police poised outside the mosque in which the 2,000 people had gathered for a memorial service.

In late 2002, students launched large demonstrations in defense of Hashem Aghajari, a university professor whose critical view of the regime had landed him a death sentence. His punishment—for saying that Muslims should not follow Islamic clerics "like monkeys"—instigated a month of protests that grew to a crowd of 5,000 at Tehran University and spread to two other campuses in the city. At one point, a force of 300 Bassij fighters stormed an auditorium where a student activist was giving an address about freedom of speech, and proceeded to try to break up the assembly by throwing chairs and tables around the hall. The students responded with shouts of "Guns, tanks and the Bassijis do not frighten us!"[75] The daily outcry, which included the chanting of slogans such as, "Soon the Taliban will have to leave Iran,"[76] eventually caused the regime to rescind Aghajari's death sentence and he was released from prison in 2004.

Strong evidence of the advance of the anti-regime, pro-democracy sentiment throughout Iranian society is found in the new "tradition" of celebrating a banned annual festival as a form of rebellion. The regime tried to outlaw the festivities of Chahar Shanbeh Souri, an ancient New Year celebration held in March, but Iranians now gather in large crowds to set off fireworks during this holiday. During the March 2005 celebration/protest in Tehran, one 28-year-old student told the *Guardian* that he was participating because "we hate their brand of Islam because it spills blood; this is a sort of Islam that keeps people backward. But young people nowadays think." In the southwestern city of Ahwaz, protestors constructed an effigy of Supreme Leader Khamenei and set it on fire during the 2006 festival. Police prevented the celebrations from amassing into very large crowds by shooting teargas canisters into the gatherings and attacking with batons.

In December 2005, hundreds of Tehran University students, amid tight police security, took part in antigovernment protests to mark Iran's National Students Day. Dozens of male and female students were arrested. Many other campuses across the nation were the scenes of similar protests despite an official ban on Students Day protests. In November 2005, the inauguration ceremony for the government-appointed new chancellor of the University of Tehran turned into a fiasco as students abandoned classes and held a demonstration during which they ripped the turban from his head.

In June 2006, State Security Forces (SSF) arrested nearly 100 women in a clampdown of a peaceful demonstration in Tehran by several thousand Iranian women and men. Security forces used truncheons and tear gas to attack the women, who were chanting "Freedom, freedom!" and "We want equal rights!" The remarks of a 21-year-old demonstrator named Laila reflected the women's commitment to speaking out for rights in spite of knowing full well that the regime will use brutal force to break up even the most peaceful protests. She told the *Washington Post*, "I don't care about the police charging us with batons; I would attend any pro-human rights demonstration in the future."[77] This demonstration was held only three months after the 1,000-woman-strong International Women's Day rally in Tehran, where participants were beaten by riot police and Bassij militia.

Violent ethnic unrest in 2006 included a wave of antigovernment protests that began in dozens of towns and cities in northwest Iran after the publication of an insulting cartoon in the state-run newspaper *Iran* in May. The cartoon portrayed the Azerbaijani people as a cockroach and stated that it should be denied food until it learned how to speak Farsi. The backlash that erupted included the gathering of thousands of demonstrators outside the parliament building in Tehran, chanting demands for their rights in their native Turkish language. At least 100,000 Azerbaijanis rallied in the city of Tabriz, and tens of thousands more took part in demonstrations in the towns of Orumieh, Zanjan, Marand, Naqadeh, and Ardebil. Although the regime claims to be a champion for all Muslims, it fiercely discriminates against ethnic minorities in Iran, and the mullahs do everything in their power to marginalize them and quell their uprisings.[78] During the May and June 2006 riots, the regime's forces killed at least 13 Azerbaijanis and injured dozens more.

In January 2006, clashes erupted in Tehran between security forces and striking bus drivers. Agents of the Ministry of Intelligence and Security (MOIS), Iran's notorious secret police, raided bus drivers' homes and arrested hundreds of union activists. On May Day, the SSF and special antiriot police attacked a peaceful demonstration by 1,000 bus drivers and conductors outside the Tehran Bus Company (TBC) headquarters to protest the arrest and firing of many of their colleagues for taking part in the recent antigovernment protests. Many students joined the demonstration in unity with the transit workers, and several transit workers and a dozen students were arrested in the ensuing clashes.

In March 2006, hundreds of coal miners from the northern province of Gilan held a strike inside Sangroud Mine near Rudbar in protest of the government's failure to pay their wages for 13 months. In February 2006, hundreds of people in Ahwaz clashed with the SSF after three explosions rocked the oil-rich Khuzistan Province. Two of the blasts occurred at the local governors' offices in the cities of Dezful and Abadan, and the third occurred in Ahwaz. The city had been the scene of sporadic anti-government protests for months. A court in Khuzistan handed down 10 death sentences over the wave of unrests.[79]

In spite of the regime's powerful security forces, the Iranian people have steadily become more willing and committed to speaking out against the leaders in Tehran. What began as primarily student pro-democracy rallies in the early 1990s has grown into a full-blown environment of national unrest and activism on the part of men and women of all ages and backgrounds. The hundreds of demonstrations that erupt throughout Iran every month provide compelling evidence that the people do not tolerate the radical fundamentalist regime's domestic or foreign policies.

THE IRANIAN OPPOSITION IS THE IRANIAN REGIME'S ACHILLES' HEEL

The Iranian regime's internal opposition is its most significant domestic challenge, but the West has repeatedly used this opposition as a sacrificial lamb to reach out to the Iranian regime. The Iranian opposition has never benefited from outside help in the way that the Solidarity movement in Poland or the African National Congress in South Africa did. On the contrary, nations have complied in cracking down on the main Iranian opposition group, the Mujahedin-e Khalq, in order to fulfill the demands of the Iranian regime. For decades the regime has made the punishment of the MEK its prime negotiating point, compelling western nations to restrict the group's activities, expel or try to dismantle it, and bomb it (as was the case in Iraq).[80]

In a June 2006 letter to the editor of the *Wall Street Journal*, an official from Iran's diplomatic mission at the United Nations in New York attacked members of the U.S. Congress for their support of the Iranian opposition. "Instead of condoning acts of terrorism against Iran, U.S. lawmakers should respect Iran's sovereignty and international law and prove their goodwill toward the Iranian nation by rebuking the MEK," wrote the Iranian mission's press secretary.[81] The letter was written in response to a *Wall Street Journal* article in which members of Congress expressed their support for removing the MEK from the State Department's list of Foreign Terrorist Organizations. Representative Brad Sherman (a Democrat from California) described the MEK as "the only group on the terrorist list that's been more helpful to the U.S. and more harmful to our enemies."[82]

When in August 2003, at Tehran's request, the State Department acted to shut down the Washington, D.C., office of the National Council of Resistance, Iranian Foreign Ministry spokesman Hamid Reza Asefi asked for more: "This measure is a positive step which should apply to other countries where the United States and the Mujahedeen group are present including Iraq," he said. "The U.S. should treat the Mujahedeen very harshly in Iraq to complete its measures in this respect."[83] In February 2006, Britain's Foreign Secretary Jack Straw conceded in an interview with BBC Radio that when he was home secretary, Iran had "successfully" demanded that Britain should ban the "MEK that was working against Iran."[84] In October 2002, Spain's ambassador to Iran explained why the EU had added the MEK to their terrorist list, saying, "Spain was the EU rotating president for the first six months of 2002. There were three issues that Iran wanted to address with the EU [and] the two sides were able to resolve these differences. One of the major issues was adding the People's Mojahedin Organization [MEK] to the list of terrorist groups by the EU."[85] Tehran's official news agency confirmed this and summarized its successful efforts against the opposition in 2002: "Analysts point out that this year the EU took several major steps to improve ties with Iran: it put the MKO [MEK] grouplet on its terrorist list, decided to begin talks on a cooperation and trade accord, decided not to table a proposal in the U.N. General Assembly this year criticizing the human rights situation in Iran, and began discussions to boost cooperation in the energy sector."[86]

The 2004 Paris agreement between the EU3 and Iran that called for the suspension of Iran's enrichment-related activities included an odd item at the very end. This item read, "Irrespective of progress on the nuclear issue, the E3/EU and Iran confirm their determination to combat terrorism, including the activities of al-Qaeda and other terrorist groups such as the MEK."[87] With that, the Iranian regime was able to insert an item totally unrelated to the uranium-enrichment program and once again tie the hands of its main opposition.

In May 2005, the Canadian government designated the Mujahedin-e Khalq as a terrorist group, and opposition members of Canada's parliament said that the move undermined Canada's outrage over the killing of Canadian-Iranian photojournalist Zahra Kazemi, who died in police custody. Even though the Canadian Foreign Affairs Department denied a link between the Kazemi case and the MEK terror listing, Conservative Foreign Affairs MP Stockwell Day, who is now the

minister for Public Security, said that the MEK designation "looks like appeasement to a repressive regime."[88]

In the wake of the 1997 designation by the U.S. State Department of the
MEK as an FTO, the state-run English-language *Tehran Times* wrote, "If the
West and other European capitals are genuinely interested in combating terror-
ism, they must avail of the best opportunity of shutting down all offices of the
MKO [MEK] and extradite their key leaders to Iran to be tried for their heinous
terrorist acts."[89] In June 1998, Expediency Council chairman Ali Akbar Hashemi
Rafsanjani appealed to the United States and Europe to stop the activities of the
MEK overseas, claiming that if Washington was serious, it should close down
U.S. MEK offices.[90] In August 1998, official Jordanian sources announced that
the Iranian Foreign Ministry had called on Jordan to close the bureau of the
MEK in Amman in order "to help develop the relations between the two countries." The sources said that Jordanian foreign minister Jawad al-Anani received
the request during his visit to Iran, where he delivered a communiqué to Iranian
president Mohammed Khatami.[91]

THE THIRD OPTION:
THE IRANIAN OPPOSITION AS
THE CENTRAL ELEMENT OF IRAN POLICY

Some argue that the United States should dismiss the Iranian opposition option
for regime change because it would be difficult for it to succeed before Iran obtains a nuclear weapon. As a result, in light of the infeasible military option, the
prevailing consensus would be to negotiate further with Iran. But what does negotiation mean when one party has already announced that it "will not hold talks
about our legitimate rights with anyone"?[92] The outcome of such a negotiation
would be continued concessions to the Iranian regime.

What is evident from Tehran's interactions with its foreign interlocutors is
that it is highly threatened by its main opposition, the MEK, and has constantly
requested that these nations curb the group's activities. The bulk of Iran's domestic repression, too, is targeted at the MEK: In early 2006, for example, Radio
Farda announced that an MEK member, Hojat Zamani, was executed after
spending eight years in prison.[93] Valiollah Feyz Mahdavi, another MEK member
in his 20s, was killed in September 2006 following five years of imprisonment.

In July 2003, when the daily newspaper *Asia* published a photograph of the
Iranian opposition leader Maryam Rajavi after her release from detention, all
copies of the paper sold out in Tehran. But more important, the Iranian regime arrested and jailed the editor, publisher, and even the publisher's family members.

The editor, Iraj Jamshidi, spent 22 months in prison, most of it in solitary confinement, just for publishing a photo that Agence France-Presse had put on its wire.[94]

At issue is not whether the Iranian opposition can overthrow the mullahs before they get the bomb, but whether Tehran has the ability to convince the wider
world to ignore the crucial role the MEK has played, is playing, and will play in
shaping Iran's history. Every carrot-and-stick approach has allowed the mullahs
to eat the carrots and use the sticks against the people of Iran and its main opposition. As one European parliamentarian told me, this unproductive and damaging tango with Tehran will continue unless the international community frees
itself from Tehran's ill-intentioned designs.

The analysts who do support making the Iranian opposition a central element of foreign policy acknowledge that little progress has been made to date because the regime has successfully used the opposition as a bargaining chip. Over
the last quarter century, those in the West have not only ignored this option, but
overlooked the yearnings of the Iranian people for change. The Iranian opposition, which is organized both within and without Iran and is willing to put itself
on the line when it counts, is the answer. As Georgetown University Professor
and former U.S. National Security Council senior staff member Raymond Tanter
put it to me, "When it comes to searching for a solution for the Iranian problem,
we should stop beating around the bush. The answer is plain and simple: It's the
MEK, stupid."[95] A study conducted by the Washington-based think tank Iran
Policy Committee (IPC), released in July 2006, showed that among all opposition
groups inside Iran and abroad, Tehran is by far more afraid of the Mujahedin-e
Khalq than of any other Iranian opposition group.[96] Using English- and Farsi-
language state-run Web sites, an IPC research team performed content analyses
of Iranian leadership statements about opposition groups. "It is remarkable that
the MEK is the topic of discussion over 350% more often than all of the other
groups combined," the report stated.[97] In addition to counting the frequency, the
IPC research team conducted a content analysis to determine the intensity of
negative regime site references about opposition groups. "Across the board, the
MEK averages an antipathy score of 4.7 out of 5, whereas the next closest group,
the Freedom Movement of Iran, scored a neutral 3." The IPC concludes, "In
short, of all of the groups in Iran, the only one that receives serious attention and
provokes fear and anger among regime figures is the MEK."[98]

THE OPPOSITION'S ROLE IN DIPLOMATIC NEGOTIATION

The Iranian regime believes that it has the upper hand in negotiations between
Iran and the international community, and rightly so. It has operational cascades

of centrifuges, profound influence on the political process in Iraq, and significant leverage in Lebanon. Stretched thin in Afghanistan and Iraq, the United States is unwilling to use force. And last but not least, the United States has limited influence over Russia and China.

In addition, the Iranian regime is not at all impressed by heightened economic incentives from the United States. "They think they are facing a four-year-old child and that they can take away our gold and give us some nuts and chocolate in exchange," Ahmadinejad said in May 2006 as he ridiculed the western powers' package of incentives in exchange for stopping its enrichment program.[99] In response to the United Nations Security Council resolution, which urged Iran to freeze its uranium enrichment, a defiant Ahmadinejad said that Iran would not bow to "the language of force and threats," and insisted that Tehran would pursue its nuclear program.[100] The regime's attitude toward negotiation was summed up by Hossein Shariatmadari, editor of the *Kayhan* newspaper—mouthpiece of the supreme leader Khamenei—in August 2006, when he told *Newsweek*, "Having full relations with the Americans is not a plus point for us. It is the Americans who have been looking to reestablish relations with us for the last 27 years."[101]

The only factor that Tehran would take seriously is the West's support of, or at least neutrality toward the Iranian opposition. Removing the Iranian opposition from the FTO list would force Tehran to make concessions because it realizes how effective the opposition would be if it was fully operational rather than operating at severely reduced capacity. The leadership in Tehran recognizes that the only sword of Damocles available to the West is the Iranian opposition.

This became abundantly clear in July 2006 when the regime cancelled and later rescheduled a critical nuclear meeting with the European Union after discovering that its month-long effort to revoke the invitation extended to NCRI president-elect, Maryam Rajavi, had failed. She was scheduled to visit the European Parliament on the same day as the meeting. Iranian nuclear negotiator Ali Larijani called EU foreign policy chief Javier Solana the day of their meeting, informing him that he was postponing the talks. For her part, Rajavi held a press conference in Strasbourg but rescheduled her meeting with parliament in order to prevent the mullahs in Tehran from having an excuse to cancel the nuclear talks altogether.[102] France had just lifted travel restrictions on Maryam Rajavi and 16 other members of the National Council of Resistance of Iran in June, which had been imposed three years earlier as part of an appeasement agreement between the French government and Iran. Tehran immediately protested to the French Government for the decision of their judiciary. In addition, Iran's Permanent Ambassador to the United Nations, Mohammad-Javad Zarif, sent a letter to the UN Secretary General and the head of the UN Security Council, which could be read as threatening France. It stated, "the Government of the Islamic Republic of Iran strongly protests against the said decision and cautions the French Government about the negative consequences that it may entail."[103] It became evident that Maryam Rajavi and her NCRI act as a major leverage against Tehran.

THE CASE FOR REGIME CHANGE

The Iranian regime's ability to create chaos in Iraq, fund and train terrorists throughout the Middle East, and defiantly proceed with its nuclear enrichment program can easily be interpreted as signs of the Iranian regime's strength. That is exactly what the leaders in Tehran want the world to think. But in reality, these actions, including Ahmadinejad's bravado and grandstanding, provide a smokescreen for a regime that is struggling to survive.

In spite of Iran's oil wealth, the economy is in shambles; the most conservative estimates rank inflation in the double digits, and one out of every four Iranians living below the poverty line. One of Iran's own economic organizations estimated 52 percent unemployment among the 15–29 age group for 2006.[104] Others believe the numbers are much higher. Strikes are rampant in state-run businesses, from bus companies to soda factories, where workers go for months without pay or benefits. The ruling mullahs monopolize huge segments of the economy through ownership of massive, unregulated "philanthropic" organizations (bonyads) that form a bloated and corrupt system. The younger generation, which comprises the vast majority of the population, is fed up with all the restrictions imposed upon them and the increasing crackdown on the press and personal liberties. Civic unrest forces the government to expend enormous resources to put down the thousands of demonstrations that erupt every year before the situation gets out of hand. Iran's leaders realize that the domestic situation is a time bomb that could explode any day, and they attempt to hide that weakness and vulnerability behind "successes" abroad. The regime's defiance of the IAEA and the West regarding the nuclear program is just one attempt to try to build up Tehran's image, while repressing the population that seeks to drive them out of power.

Understanding the realities of Iran's domestic situation, any state that attempts to negotiate with Tehran while perceiving Iran as a strong, rich, and stable nation is operating under a fallacy. Tehran has never been more vulnerable. The leaders' greatest fear is that the organized opposition will continue to gain more visibility and international support. Far from leading a young, loyal nation toward prosperity and stability, Tehran is facing down an inevitable showdown with its own people.

Facilitating regime change in Tehran will require, as its central element, the efforts of organizations, not individuals. Such a group must have the infrastructure and wide support of all segments of Iran's diverse population to be able to launch a comprehensive, strong program against the regime. In order to represent the Iranian people's demand for a democratic system, this movement must hold a democratic, secular, and nationalist platform that is compatible with the history, culture, religion and national interests of the Iranians as well as the Universal Declaration of Human Rights and other international agreements. An effective anti-regime organization must be able to organize and lead the movement in Iran and abroad; contain a leadership that has passed a stringent litmus test of pro-democracy ideals; and exhibit a track record of engaging the religious dictatorship in Tehran and the IRGC, Bassij, and a score of other repressive organs. The only group that meets these criteria and that Tehran considers a formidable threat is the MEK and its larger associate secular coalition, the NCRI. If the regime is worried that the MEK has enough experience and support in Iran to tip the balance of power, the West would be wise to pay attention.

The MEK's ability to gain grassroots support, expose the regime's long-hidden nuclear program, and inspire Iranians throughout the world with a secular, pro-democracy plan for a new Iran has continued, despite being severely hampered by the terrorist designation put upon it by the State Department as well as the European Union. The designation has forced the organization to devote the majority of its resources to be used to overcome the consequences of the terrorist label rather than on its programs to expose and overturn the Iranian regime. Nevertheless, *Time* magazine reported that Maryam Rajavi, the president-elect of the NCRI, brought "the crowd of as many as 30,000 people to its feet repeatedly with the familiar message "Let my people go!" when she appeared in a rally near Paris in July 2006.[105]

"The removal of the MEK and the NCRI from the FTO list would send a signal to the Iranian people that we in the West are standing with them rather than with their oppressors," said Brian Binley, British Member of House of Commons, in his July 2006 trip to Washington to address his American counterparts.

"Delisting the MEK could unleash the great potential of the younger generation and the most feared Iranian dissident group," said former Assistant Vice Chief of Staff of the Air Force, Lt. General Thomas McInerney (ret.) in an interview with the author.[106] "Keeping the MEK on the list is limiting US options unnecessarily, while the Ayatollahs are threatening us with their nuclear bomb-making, violence and domination in Iraq, and terrorism in Lebanon," McInerney added.

Tehran knows that the opposition is committed to free and fair elections under the auspices of the United Nations for a secular republic, and that if the regime would agree to such elections, the opposition has the ability and the appeal to sweep the mullahs out of power. The opposition also has substantial military experience after nearly three decades of fighting the Iranian regime.

Removing all restrictions from the Iranian opposition would significantly empower the movement. It sends a strong signal to Tehran that the West has now shifted its policy and, contrary to the past, will not keep silent over Iran's harsh suppression of anti-government demonstrations and crackdowns on dissidents. Removal would also send a very strong message to the Iranians that their efforts to unseat the radical fundamentalist leaders would no longer be viewed by the United States as terrorism, but rather as an exercise of their legitimate right to change their future.

An unchained and empowered opposition would also have a much greater ability to organize anti-government demonstrations in a consistent way, keeping the ayatollahs in a defensive position rather than in their present offensive posture. The removal would trigger hope among the younger generation of Iranians, especially women, as the political platform of the NCRI is based, first and foremost, on the rights of women. The movement would then have the ability, for example, to enhance its television broadcasts, allowing it to have longer hours and an extended coverage area. The removal would enhance the group's ability to gather intelligence about the Iranian regime's nuclear ambitions, its terror network, and its destructive role in Iraq, which would further weaken the regime. The intelligence sources within the Iranian regime would be more encouraged to provide information to the resistance's network or to defect, should they feel the regime does not have international backing and that the opposition is on the winning side.

The third option is not only a viable opportunity for regime change due to the capabilities of the Iranian resistance, but a solid, realistic alternative that will completely reposition Iran as a non-nuclear, secular, democratic state. This option promises to rid Iran of the radical fundamentalist leadership that has transformed the country into the world's most active state sponsor of terrorism and held the Middle East and the world hostage to terrorism for decades. In its place, Iran will be led by a representational government elected in transparent elections and positioned for a peaceful, strong and prosperous future. To millions of Iranians within Iran and around the world, that is the Iran that the people, and the proud history of the nation, so deeply deserve.

APPENDIX

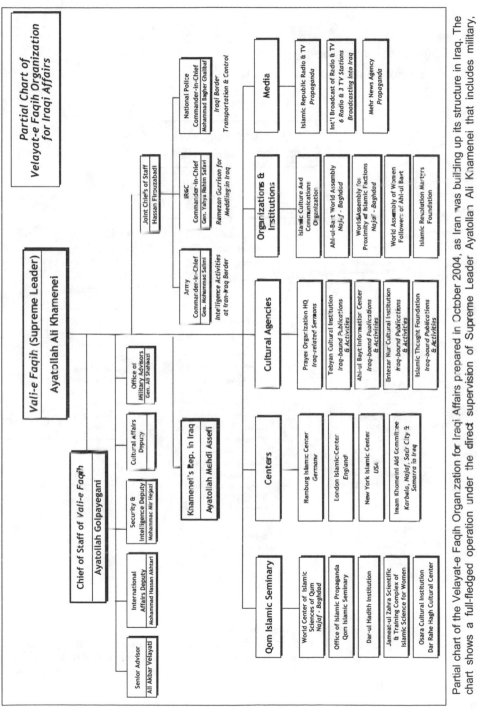

Partial Chart of Velayat-e Faqih Organization for Iraqi Affairs

Vali-e Faqih (Supreme Leader)
Ayatollah Ali Khamenei

Chief of Staff of Vali-e Faqih
Ayatollah Golpayegani

Senior Advisor — Ali Akbar Velayati

International Affairs Deputy — Mohammad Hassan Akhtari

Security & Intelligence Deputy — Mohammad Mir Hejazi

Cultural Affairs Deputy

Office of Military Advisors — Gen. Ali Shahbazi

Khamenei's Rep. in Iraq
Ayatollah Mehdi Assefi

Joint Chief's of Staff
Hassan Firouzabadi

Army Commander-in-Chief
Gen. Mohammad Salimi
Intelligence Activities at Iran-Iraq Border

IRGC Commander-in-Chief
Gen. Yahya Rahim Safavi
Ramezan Garrison for Meddling in Iraq

National Police Commander-in-Chief
Mohammad Bagher Ghalibaf
Iraqi Border Transportation & Control

Qom Islamic Seminary
- World Center of Islamic Sciences of Qum *Najaf - Baghdad*
- Office of Islamic Propaganda Qom Islamic Seminary
- Dar-ul Hadith Institution
- Jameat-ul Zahra Scientific & Training Complex of Islamic Science for Women
- Osara Cultural Institution Dar Rahe Hagh Cultural Center

Centers
- Hamburg Islamic Center *Germany*
- London Islamic Center *England*
- New York Islamic Center *USA*
- Imam Khomeini Aid Committee *Karbala, Najaf, Sadr City & Samarra in Iraq*

Cultural Agencies
- Prayer Organization HQ *Iraq-related Sermons*
- Tebyan Cultural Institution *Iraq-bound Publications & Activities*
- Ahl-ul Bayt Information Center *Iraq-bound Publications & Activities*
- Entezar Nur Cultural Institution *Iraq-bound Publications & Activities*
- Islamic Thought Foundation *Iraq-bound Publications & Activities*

Organizations & Institutions
- Islamic Culture And Communications Organization
- Ahl-ul-Bayt World Assembly *Najaf - Baghdad*
- World Assembly for Proximity of Islamic Factions *Najaf - Baghdad*
- World Assembly of Women Followers of Ahl-ul Bart
- Islamic Revolution Matters Foundation

Media
- Islamic Republic Radio & TV *Propaganda*
- Int'l Broadcast of Radio & TV *6 Radio & 3 TV Stations Broadcasting into Iraq*
- Mehr News Agency *Propaganda*

Partial chart of the Velayat-e Faqih Organization for Iraqi Affairs prepared in October 2004, as Iran was building up its structure in Iraq. The chart shows a full-fledged operation under the direct supervision of Supreme Leader Ayatollah Ali Khamenei that includes military, intelligence, security, social, financial, logistics, religious, political, cultural, public relations, and media activities.

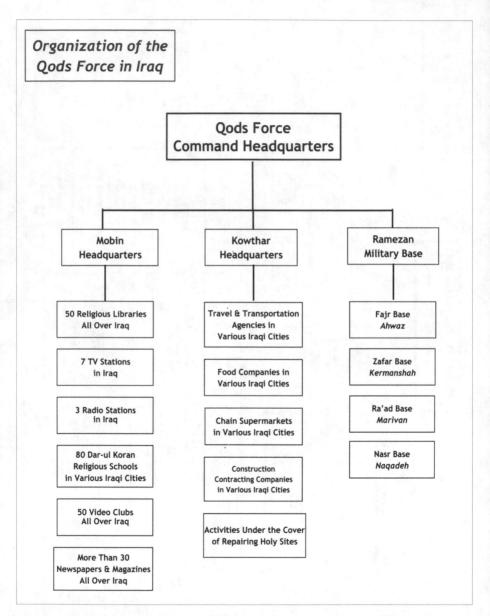

Organization of the Qods Force in Iraq

Qods Force Command Headquarters

Mobin Headquarters

- 50 Religious Libraries All Over Iraq
- 7 TV Stations in Iraq
- 3 Radio Stations in Iraq
- 80 Dar-ul Koran Religious Schools in Various Iraqi Cities
- 50 Video Clubs All Over Iraq
- More Than 30 Newspapers & Magazines All Over Iraq

Kowthar Headquarters

- Travel & Transportation Agencies in Various Iraqi Cities
- Food Companies in Various Iraqi Cities
- Chain Supermarkets in Various Iraqi Cities
- Construction Contracting Companies in Various Iraqi Cities
- Activities Under the Cover of Repairing Holy Sites

Ramezan Military Base

- Fajr Base *Ahwaz*
- Zafar Base *Kermanshah*
- Ra'ad Base *Marivan*
- Nasr Base *Naqadeh*

Organizational chart of Iran's Qods [Jerusalem] Force of the Islamic Revolutionary Guards Corps, which is responsible for intervention in Iraq. Its main garrison, Ramezan, as well as four other military bases and various support structures conduct or coordinate a wide range of military, intelligence, security, financial, logistics, religious, political, cultural, social, public relations, and media activities.

Immediate

The Islamic Republic of Iran
Supreme National Security Council

No: 6131/D/3661
Date: April 19, 2003
Attachments:

Mr. Nourbala,
Honorable Director of the Red Crescent
Of the Islamic Republic of Iran

SECRET

With greetings,

Respectfully, the items 4, and 5 of the ratifications of the 44th session of the Iraq Policy Council, in regards to providing assistance to the Iraqi people, that has been approved by the honorable president and the head of the Supreme National Security Council, is hereby being brought to your attention to be executed.

4) In order to help the people of Iraq, the urgent needs of the Iraqi people will be determined by the Qods (Jerusalem) Force and through public announcement, to gather support by the Iranian nation for the people of Iraq, the Red Crescent is responsible for collecting the people's contributions. These contributions will be sert into Iraq, through coordination with the Qods Force.

5) In order to provide emergency medical assistance to the people of Iraq, ass stance and medical centers will be set up in a number of cities in eastern Iraq by the Red Crescent of the Islamic Republic of Iran, and provide emergency assistance. If possible, a number of hospitals should be mobilized by the Red Crescent. The Ministry of Health and Medical Education, would send its resources under the cover of Red Crescent.

Ali Rabiee
Executive Director,
Secretariat, Supreme National Security Council

A document obtained from sources inside Iran showing that one month after Baghdad fell, Iran's Supreme National Security Council issued a secret document that instructed the Red Crescent to act as a cover for the IRGC's Qods Force in Iraq. Part of this April 19, 2003, document states: "The urgent needs of the Iraqi people will be determined by the Qods [Jerusalem] Force and through public announcement, to gather support by the Iranian nation for the people of Iraq." Red Crescent workers were responsible for collecting the people's contributions and sending them into Iraq, through coordination with the Qods Force.

Honorable Executive Director of Foreign Nationals Affairs of
The Military Forces of the Islamic Republic
Second Revolutionary Guards Brigadier, Borghe'i

Immediate

No: G/600/50/3435
Date: 16 Azar, 1382 (December 7, 2003)
Attachment:
Priority:

Subject: Referring to cross the border in Shalamcheh
Date exiting the border: 17 Azar, 1382 (December 8, 2003)

Peace upon you

Respectfully, the following individuals are eligible to cross; please order
the issuance of the license to cross.

1. Name and Last name: Seyyed Abolghassem Hosseini
                         Passport number: 6440943
2. Name and Last name: Yassin Moshtagh
                         Passport number: 1588833

3. Name and Last name: -   Passport number: . . .
4. Name and Last name: -   Passport number: . . .
5. Name and Last name: -   Passport number: . -

Vehicle: Plate number:

Goods accompanied: Personal belongings

Be'ssat Mobilization Center
2nd Rev. Guards Brigadier Seyyed Ali Akbar Tabatabae'i
CC: 66 for information and due action

An original letter, obtained by sources inside Iran, showing that in the months after the fall of Baghdad Iran's military and security officials
methodically arranged for continued border crossing of IRGC Qods Force personnel into Iraq. The letter was faxed from the Be'ssat
Mobilization Center of the Qods Force to the Command HQ of the Fajr Garrison in city of Ahwaz in southwestern Iran. The two individuals, for
whom entry arrangement was requested, belonged to the cultural staff of Mobin HQ of the Qods Force. Arrangements were made for the two to
return to Iran via the border town of Mehran. The code number 66 mentioned in the letter refers to the Fajr Garrison.

Front Companies Used by Tehran for Nuclear & Biological Projects

No	DATE EXPOSED	ENTITY NAME	DESCRIPTION
1	14-Aug-02	Kalaye Electric Company	Used as cover for the construction of the Natanz uranium enrichment facility
2	14-Aug-02	Jahad-Towseh	Construction, nuclear sites
3	14-Aug-02	Towseh-Sakhteman	Construction, nuclear sites
4	14-Aug-02	Mesbah Energy	U.S. Department of the Treasury sanctioned it in January 2006, for its "support of the proliferation" of WMD
5	27-May-03	Energy Novin	U.S. Department of the Treasury sanctioned it in January 2006, for its "support of the proliferation" of WMD
6	27-May-03	Noor-Afza-Gostar	Front for AEOI
7	28-Apr-04	Tehran University, physics department	Nuclear research and development
8	28-Apr-04	Center for Readiness and New Defense Technology	Nuclear research and development
9	10-Sep-04	Pars Terash Company	Building centrifuge parts
10	10-Sep-04	Pishgam Development Industrial Energy	Electronics for uranium enrichment
11	10-Sep-04	Rah-e Kar Novin Industry	Smuggling nuclear related materials
12	17-Nov-04	Malek Ashtar University in Isfahan	Nuclear research and development
13	2-Dec-04	Shahid Hemmat Industries	Missiles projects
14	19-May-05	IRITIEC	Building Graphite Electrode Plant
15	19-May-05	IRASCO	Italy-based company building graphite electrode plant
16	19-May-05	Pars Refractories Company	Importing Flaked Graphite
17	10-Jan-06	Tose'eh Silo Company	Engineering and Construction of Military and Nuclear Sites
18	31-Jan-06	Hara Company	Engineering and Construction of Military and Nuclear Sites
19	31-Jan-06	Imamzadeh Hashem workshop	Engineering and Construction of Military and Nuclear Sites

This is a small portion of the list of front companies exposed by the National Council of Resistance of Iran, between August 2002 and January 2006: These front companies, some directly operated by the Atomic Energy Organization of Iran, have been used by Iran to buy nuclear-related materials from a number of foreign countries for what it claims are benign civil purchases. Two of these front companies were later sanctioned by the U.S. Treasury Department. No charges have been brought against any of these firms.

Lavizan-Shian Site

Lavizan-Shian Site, Iran—August 11, 2003   Image: DigitalGlobe/ISIS

Lavizan-Shian, Iran—March 22, 2004   Image: DigitalGlobe/ISIS

Lavizan-Shian, Iran—December 8, 2005   Image: IKONOS satellite image by GeoEye

Satellite images of Iran's Lavizan-Shian Technical Research Center in northern Tehran. The top image was taken three months after the National Council of Resistance of Iran (NCRI) revealed that the regime allegedly conducted secret biological weapons work at the complex. Following that revelation, the regime razed the buildings to the ground and the ground was scraped, as seen in the second image, before the IAEA was allowed to inspect the site in June 2004. The regime then began planting grass and trees over the area. This activity appears to support the theory that Iran sought to remove all traces of nuclear material that it had been utilizing in its secret nuclear program at the site.

Uranium Enrichment in Natanz

September 20, 2002   IKONOS satellite Image by GeoEye

August 12, 2006   IKONOS satellite image by GeoEye

The satellite image on top shows the Natanz uranium enrichment facility shortly after I
exposed it in August 2002. The image, dated September 20, 2002, clearly shows construction
on the site, particularly the two large underground halls designed to install as many as 60,000
centrifuges. The imagery below was taken on August 12, 2006, showing the completion of the
construction of the cascade halls, now covered by dirt, as well as many new buildings above
ground.

Arak Heavy Water Production Plant and Nuclear Reactor

IKONOS satellite image by GeoEye

This satellite image taken on July 13, 2006 shows the Heavy Water Production Plant, made operational in August 2006, and the progress of a heavy water nuclear reactor on the top left. The facility in Arak could provide a parallel means for Iran to produce fissile material for a nuclear bomb, as it would be capable of producing enough plutonium for at least two bombs a year.

NOTES

INTRODUCTION

1. "Transcript: Exclusive Bush Interview; President Bush Sits Down With Bob Schieffer," CBS Television, January 27, 2006 (www.cbsnews.com/stories/2006/01/27/eveningnews/main1248952.shtml).
2. "Iran with nuclear weapons unacceptable—France," Reuters, April 19, 2006 (http://feeds.parisnews.net/?rid=7974519100ded82a&cat=fab36d240e1883d4&f=1).
3. "Putin: Iran not developing nukes," CNN, February 18, 2005 (www.cnn.com/2005/WORLD/meast/02/18/iran.russia/).
4. The official name as used by the group is The People's Mojahedin Organization of Iran (PMOI). The group is referred to by the State Department as the Mujahedin-e Khalq (which means the People's Mojahedin) or the MEK; the Iranian regime refers to it in its English-language publications as the Mojahedin-e Khalq Organization or the MKO, and in its Farsi-language publications as the Monafeqin (hypocrites). Other sources have used other spellings for the group. Based on what most of the American media, official references, and the aforementioned publications have used, I have chosen to use the term *Mujahedin-e Khalq*, or the *MEK*, for the sake of better communication, not to show preference.
5. "President's Press Conference," March 16, 2005 (www.whitehouse.gov/news/releases/2005/03/20050316-3.html).
6. "Lawmakers Defend Iranian Rebel Group," *Baltimore Sun*, November 22, 2002.
7. For details see "Front Companies," in Chapter 9.
8. Nikki R. Keddi, *Modern Iran* (New Haven, Conn.: Yale University Press, 2003), p. 218.
9. United Nations General Assembly, Resolution: "Situation of Human Rights in the Islamic Republic of Iran," December 13, 1985 (www.un.org/documents/ga/res/40/a40r141.htm/).
10. "U.N. Report on Rights and Iran Is Criticized," *New York Times*, November 24, 1985.
11. "International Arrest Warrant," Dossier No. A/289/90, Canton de Vaud, Switzerland, March 20, 2006.
12. Mohammad Mehdi Akhondzadeh Basti was appointed by Ahmadinejad as ambassador to Germany in April 2006. He was formerly ambassador in Pakistan and Bangladesh, Chargé d'Affaires in United Kingdom, and Permanent Representative of Iran to the United Nations (Vienna).
13. "Human Rights Questions: Human Rights Situations and Reports of Special Rapporteurs and Representatives," United Nations General Assembly, A/51/479, 11

October 1996, http://www.unhchr.ch/huridocda/huridoca.nsf/0/61f4b0d4b323829
58025670c00538894?OpenDocument.

14. "Khomeini fatwa 'led to killing of 30,000 in Iran,'" *The Sunday Telegraph*, February 4,
2001 (www.telegraph.co.uk/news/main.jhtml?xml=/news/2001/02/04/wiran04.xml).

15. "150 Bipartisan House Members Call for an End to Iran's Terrorist Regime and
Support for the Iranian Opposition," Press Release issued by Congresswoman
Ileana Ros-Lehtinen, November 21, 2002.

CHAPTER 1

1. "Humble Beginning That Shaped Iran's New Hard Man," *Guardian* (London), July
2, 2005, p. 15.

2. "Criticizing the executive structures in their lack of confrontation with corruption
and decay, Ahmadinejad said: 'Our executive management blows the horn into its
large end—women have no place in my Cabinet,'" *Entekhab*, June 20, 2005
(www.entekhab.ir/display/?ID=2654).

3. "Humble Beginning."

4. "Humble Beginning."

5. "Humble Beginning."

6. "Devoted and Defiant," *Newsweek*, February 13, 2006, p. 30.

7. "Mahmoud Ahmadinejad's Biography," *GlobalSecurity.org* (www.globalsecurity.org/
military/world/iran/ahmadinejad.htm).

8. Hamid Algar, translator and annotator, *Islam and Revolution: Writings and Declarations of Imam Khomeini* (Berkeley, Calif.: Mizan Press, 1981), p. 132.

9. *Islam and Revolution*, p. 43.

10. *Islam and Revolution*, pp. 52–53.

11. "With Khamenei since 1979," Rooz Online, July 5, 2005 (www.roozonline.com/
08interview/008362.shtml).

12. Iran Policy Committee, *Appeasing the Ayatollahs and Suppressing Democracy: U.S.
Policy and the Iranian Opposition* (Washington, D.C.: Iran Policy Committee, 2006),
p. 26–29.

13. Mehrzad Boroujerdi, *Iranian Intellectuals and the West* (Syracuse: Syracuse University Press, 1996), p. 117.

14. "Iran's New President Has a Past Mired in Controversy," *Iran Focus*, June 25, 2005
(www.iranfocus.com/article.php?storyid=2605).

15. Ervand Abrahamian, *The Iranian Mojahedin* (London: Yale University Press, 1989),
pp. 61.

CHAPTER 2

1. "Tehran's Mayor: Some wrong policies have limited people's participation," *Kayhannews*, January 22, 2005 (www.kayhannews.ir/831103/15.htm/).

2. History of the Ministry of Intelligence," *Sharq Newspaper*, October 6, 2004 (www.
sharghnewspaper.com/830715/iran.htm).

3. "History: Ministry of Intelligence and Security [MOIS]," Federation of American
Scientists (www.fas.org/irp/world/iran/vevak/history.htm).

4. "Ex-Hostages: Iran's President Was Captor," FoxNews.com, July 01, 2005.

5. Ilan Berman, "Understanding Ahmadinejad," American Foreign Policy Council, June 2006 (www.afpc.org/IFI/UnderstandingAhmadinejad.pdf).

6. "Ex-Hostages Demand CIA Release Its Report on Iranian President," *New York Sun*, September 14, 2005 (www.nysun.com/article/19982).

7. "Ex-Hostages Demand CIA Release Its Report on Iranian President," *New York Sun*, September 14, 2005 (www.nysun.com/article/19982).

8. "Sources: CIA finds Iranian President Likely Not Hostage-Taker," CNN.com, August 12, 2005 (www.cnn.com/2005/US/08/12/cia.iranpresident/).

9. "Leftists Clash With Moslems at Iran's University Campuses," *Washington Post*, April 20, 1980.

10. "Iran's Growing Turmoil," *Newsweek*, May 5, 1980.

11. Ervand Abrahamian, *The Iranian Mojahedin* (London: Yale University Press, 1989).

12. "Mahmoud Ahmedinejad: Justice Versus Freedom," *Al-Ahram Weekly*, June 30-July 6, 2005 (weekly.ahram.org.eg/2005/749/profile.htm).

13. The former prisoner, Gholamreza Jalal, a student at the time, was arrested on charges of supporting the MEK. He is a quality control supervisor of an industrial workshop in Ashraf City, Iraq.

14. In an interview, former female political prisoners, S.N., who was arrested at the age of 16 and spent one and a half years in Evin prison, and M.S., who was arrested at the age of 18 and spent 4 years in Evin, said that they had heard the name "Golpa" referred to as an interrogator and torturer in Evin, but did not know his real identity.

15. Author interview with R.S. who was arrested at the age of 15, charged with distributing literature and publicity activity in support of the MEK. After three years of incarceration in Shiraz prisons, she was released in 1985.

16. Author interviews in August 2006, with five eyewitnesses all incarcerated for supporting the MEK, among them M.S., 18 years old at the time of her arrest, who spent 4 years in Evin prison; J.K., arrested when he was 21 years old, who was incarcerated for 8 years, including 4 years in Evin; A.M., arrested when she was 16, incarcerated for 5 years, including 3 years in Evin; P.M., arrested when he was 19, incarcerated for 5 years, including 3 years in Evin, M.A., arrested when he was 26 years old, incarcerated for 8 years, including 5 years in Evin.

17. The interview was conducted in Washington, D.C. with the former prisoner, P.M., who was arrested by the IRGC and charged with supporting the MEK. He spent 5 years in Evin, Ghezel Hessar and Gohardasht prisons.

18. Author interview with eyewitness S.A.H. in August 2006.

19. Author interviews in June-August 2006, with several eyewitnesses.

20. *The Iranian Mojahedin*, pp. 218.

21. "Ahmadinejad's Biography," GlobalSecurity.Org, July 2005 (www.globalsecurity.org/military/world/iran/ahmadinejad.htm).

22. "History Ministry of Intelligence."

23. "Heart of the Axis," by Matthew Levitt, *National Review Online*, May 29, 2003 (www.washingtoninstitute.org/templateC06.php?CID=475).

24. "Iran's Ministry of Intelligence and Security," *Iran Focus*, May 6, 2005 (www.iranfocus.com/modules/news/article.php?storyid=2020/).

25. MOIS, Operation, Federation of American Scientists (www.fas.org/irp/world/iran/vevak/org.htm).

26. "Ahmadinejad's Biography," GlobalSecurity.org, 2005 (www.globalsecurity.org/military/world/iran/ahmadinejad.htm).

27. "US Agents Probe Past of Iran's Leader," *Sunday Times* (London), July 3, 2005 (www.timesonline.co.uk/printFriendly/0,1–524–1678496–524,00.html).

28. Kenneth Katzman, Statement at Joint Economic Committee Hearing on Iran, July 25, 2006, Congressional Research Service (www.house.gov/jec/hearings/testimony/109/07–25–06_iran_Katzman.pdf).

29. Sean O'Neill, "Terror Training 'Run by Hardline Mullahs,'" *Daily Telegraph* (London), August 12, 2002 (www.telegraph.co.uk/news/main.jhtml?xml=/news/2002/08/12/wirans212.xml).

30. "Iranian Force Has Long Ties to Al Qaeda," *Washington Post*, October 14, 2003.

31. Presidency of the Islamic Republic of Iran, "Biography of H.E. Dr. Ahmadi Nejad, Honourable President of Islamic Republic of Iran" (www.president.ir/eng/ahmadinejad/bio/).

32. "Iran Unveiled," Editorial, *The Wall Street Journal*, June 28, 2005.

33. "Interior Ministry Announced the Results of the Second Round of Presidential Elections," ISNA, June 25, 2005.

34. "Iran's New Revolutionary Guards Regime: Anti-Americanism, Oil, and Rising International Tension," (www.jcpa.org/brief/brief005–10.htm).

35. "Biography of H.E. Dr. Ahmadi Nejad."

36. "Mahmoud Ahmadinejad," *GlobalSecurity.org*, June 24, 2005 (www.globalsecurity.org/military/world/iran/ahmadinejad.htm).

37. "Kurd Murder Claim against Iran Leader," *Guardian* (London), July 4, 2005, p. 17.

38. "Controversies Surrounding Mahmoud Ahmadinejad," *Wikipedia* (en.wikipedia.org/wiki/Controversies_surrounding_Mahmoud_Ahmadinejad).

39. Author interview in August 2006.

40. Mohammad Mohaddessin, *Islamic Fundamentalism: The New Global Threat* (Washington, D.C.: Seven Locks Press, 2001), p. 223.

41. "Biography of H.E. Dr. Ahmadi Nejad."

42. "We and Mahmoud Ahmadinejad / Political Prisoner, Engineer Heshmatollah Tabarzadi," *Cyrusnews.com*, July 26, 2005 (www.cyrusnews.com/news/fa/?mi=9&ni=6042).

43. Presidency of the Islamic Republic of Iran.

44. "A Child of the Revolution Takes Over: Ahmadinejad's Demons," Matthias Küntzel, *The New Republic*, April 14, 2006 (www.tnr.com/doc.mhtml?i=20060424&s=kuntzel042406).

45. Author interview in August 2006.

46. "Senior Advisor of the President is Appointed," Sharif News, August 15, 2005 (http://sharifnews.ir/?8708).

47. "The Rash Revolutionary," *The Guardian*, November 9, 2005 (www.guardian.co.uk/elsewhere/journalist/story/0,1638503,00.html).

48. "The Man Behind Whom the President Prays," Rooz Online, November 2, 2005 (www.roozonline.com/01newsstory/011390.shtml).

49. "With Khamenei since 1979," Rooz Online, July 5, 2005 (www.roozonline.com/08interview/008362.shtml).

50. David S. Cloud, "U.S. Bombs Iranian Fighters on Iraqi Side of the Border: Pledge to Target the Group Was Made Early to Assure Tehran of War's Benefits," *Wall Street Journal*, April 17, 2003.

51. "U.S. Seeks Surrender Of Iranian Group," *Washington Post*, May 9, 2003; Page A01 (www.washingtonpost.com/ac2/wp-dyn?pagename=article&node=&contentId=A32469–2003May8&notFound=true).

52. Jehl, Douglas, " Neighbors; Iran Said to Send Agents into Iraq," *New York Times*, April 23, 2003, Page A1 (http://select.nytimes.com/gst/abstract.html?res=F3081FFD355E0C708EDDAD0894DB404482).

53. "Ayatollah Hakim Returns from Exile to Put Islam Back into Iraq," Agence France Presse, May 10, 2003.

54. "Iran's Threat to Coalition Forces in Iraq," Professor Raymond Tanter, January 15, 2004 (www.washingtoninstitute.org/templateC05.php?CID=1705).

55. "Ahmadinejad: The Country's Main Problem is that it is not Run by a Revolutionary Vision," *Kayhannews*, September 27, 2004 (www.kayhannews.ir/830806/2.htm).

56. "Main Problem with Some Managers is their Departure from Objectives for the Revolution," *Kayhannews*, March 7, 2005 (www.kayhannews.ir/831217/14.htm).

57. "In the Ceremony to Honor the City Workers, Ahmadinejad: We Can Build Tehran," *Kayhannews*, August 29, 2004 (www.kayhannews.ir/830608.115.htm).

58. "Dr. Ahmadinejad's Speech among the Bassiji's Scientific Olympiad Electives," *Kayhannews*, September 6, 2004 (www.kayhannews.ir/830616 15.htm).

59. "Tehran Mayor Praised the Athens Olympic Champions," *Kayhannews*, August 8, 2004 (www.kayhannews.ir/830618/13.htm).

60. "Segregation of Elevators for Women and Men is a Beneficial Policy / Segregation Will Cause the Advancement of Women and Men," *Entekhab*, June 19, 2005 (www.entekhab.ir/display/?ID=2648).

61. "Construction of four women-only parks in Tehran," BBC Radio, Farsi Service, November 17, 2003 (www.bbc.co.uk/persian/iran/story/2003/11/031117_a_iran_parks.shtml).

62. "The Mullahs Win Again," *Newsweek*, July 4, 2005, p. 26.

63. "Mosques and Religious Centers Are Exempt from Paying City Fees and Dues," *Kayhannews*, September 5, 2004 (www.kayhannews.ir/830715/15 htm).

64. "The Mullahs Win Again," *Newsweek*, July 4, 2005, p. 26.

65. "Ahmadinejad: Impotent Managers Blame Their Weaknesses on the System," *Kayhannews*, March 12, 2005 (www.kayhannews.ir/831222/2.htm).

CHAPTER 3

1. "President: We will experience a world without the United State and Zionism," Sharif News, October 26, 2005 (http://sharifnews.com/?10484) "Annan: 'Dismay' over Iranian comments on Israel" CNN, October 27, 2005 (http://www.cnn.com/2005/WORLD/meast/10/27/ahmadinejad.reaction/).

2. "Iran Can be a Powerful and Idol Country in the World," *Kayhannews*, January 23, 2005 (http://www.kayhannews.ir/831104/15.htm).

3. "Ahmadinejad Said: Our Executive Management Blows the Horn into its Large End—Women Have No Place in My Cabinet," *Entekhab*, June 20, 2005 (www.entekhab.ir/display/?ID=2654).

4. "Ahmadinejad: There is still time to become a (Presidential) candidate," *Kayhannews*, May 12, 2005 (www.kayhannews.ir/840222/2.htm).

5. "Ahmadinejad: No Need to Rush, a Lot Will Happen in the Next 20 Days," *Kayhannews*, May 31, 2005 (www.kayhannews.ir/840310/14.htm).

6. "Mahmoud Ahmadinejad Candidate for the Ninth Presidential Election Said: In the Country's Development Plans, Justice Has not been the Main Axis and This Has Caused Increase in Poverty, Corruption and Discrimination," *Kayhannews*, June 11, 2005 (www.kayhannews.ir/840321/14.htm).

7. "Ahmadinejad: An Islamic Country Must Be Powerful and Advanced," *Kayhannews*, April 10, 2005 (www.kayhannews.ir/840121/14.htm).
8. "Rights Violated in Iran's Last Majlis Poll: Karoubi," *IranMania*, May 12, 2005 (www.iranmania.com/news/ArticleView/Default.asp?ArchiveNews=Yes&News-Code=31782&NewsKind=CurrentAffairs).
9. Agence France Presse, "Iranian Reformer Says Election Was Rigged," *Iran Focus*, June 18, 2005 (www.iranfocus.com/modules/news/article.php?storyid=2512).
10. "Iranian Reformer Says Election Was Rigged."
11. "Iran Loser Blasts 'Illegal' Poll," *BBC News*, June 25, 2005 (news.bbc.co.uk/1/hi/world/middle_east/4622955.stm).
12. "Fraud Claims Mar Iranian Poll Run-Off," *Guardian* (London), June 25, 2005 (www.iranfocus.com/modules/news/article.php?storyid=2602).
13. "Style: The Look of a Leader," *Newsweek*, January 30, 2006, p. 9.
14. "Strong Words from Iran," *PBS NewsHour with Jim Lehrer*, transcript, December 9, 2005 (www.pbs.org/newshour/bb/middle_east/july-dec05/iran_12–9.html).
15. "Transcript: Iran President's Speech Threatening Israel," *Iran Focus*, October 28, 2005 (www.iranfocus.com/modules/news/print.php?storyid=4164).
16. "Iran's Ahmadinejad Links Cartoons to His Denial of Holocaust," *Iran Focus*, February 11, 2006 (www.iranfocus.com/modules/news/article.php?storyid=5733).
17. "IJ Leader: Teheran Won't Stand Alone," *Jerusalem Post*, April 14, 2006 (www.jpost.com/servlet/Satellite?cid=1143498855221&pagename=JPost percent2FJPArticle percent2FShowFull).
18. IRNA, "Ahmadinejad Says Enemies Will Fail to Prevent Iran Progress," February 5, 2006 (www.irna.ir/en/news/view/line–17/0602059335151351.htm).
19. "Iran Demands Patience from West on Nuclear Incentive Offer," *New York Times*, July 14, 2006, p. A3.
20. "U.N. Resolution Sets Iran Deadline," *Washington Post*, July 31, 2006 (www.washingtonpost.com/wpdyn/content/article/2006/07/31/AR2006073100353.html).
21. "Iran Set to Award Lucrative Gas Deal to Elite Militia," *Wall Street Journal*, June 29, 2006, p. A7.
22. "Iran Set to Award Lucrative Gas Deal to Elite Militia," *Wall Street Journal*, June 29, 2006, p. A7.
23. "Iran Leader Bans Western Music," *Washington Times*, December 20, 2005.
24. Amnesty International, "Iran: Worrying Trends in Use of Death Penalty," February 27, 2006 (www.amnestyusa.org/countries/iran/document.do?id=ENGMDE130202006).
25. "EU lambastes human rights abuses in Iran," *Iran Focus*, May 6, 2006 (www.iranfocus.com/modules/news/article.php?storyid=7080).
26. "Iran: Worrying Trends in Use of Death Penalty."
27. "Iran: Worrying Trends in Use of Death Penalty."
28. Amnesty International, "Iran: New Government Fails to Address Dire Human Rights Situation" (www.amnestyusa.org/countries/iran/document.do?id=ENGMDE130102006).
29. Amnesty International, "Iran: Amnesty International Condemns Violence against Women Demonstrators in Iran," March 10, 2006 (www.amnestyusa.org/countries/iran/document.do?id=ENGMDE130242006).
30. "Iran: 74 Lashes for Women Who Fail to Wear the Hijab," *ADN Kronos International*, February 3, 2006 (www.adnki.com).

31. "Iran's fashion police put on a show of chadors to stem west's cultural invasion," *The Guardian*, July 14, 2006 (www.guardian.co.uk/iran/story/0,1820248,00.html).
32. "Mahmoud Ahmadinejad," *GlobalSecurity.org* (globalsecurity.org/military/world/iran/ahma.dinejad.htm).

CHAPTER 4

1. Hamid Algar, translator and annotator, *Islam and Revolution: Writings and Declarations of Imam Khomeini* (Berkeley, Calif.: Mizan Press, 1981), pp. 330–331 and 337–338.
2. Bard E. O'Neill, *Insurgency & Terrorism* (Washington, DC; Potomac Books, 2005), pp. 9.
3. "'I Cry for Them,'" *Newsweek*, November 6, 1978, p. 80.
4. *Islam and Revolution*, p. 62.
5. Ayatollah Sayyed Ruhollah Mousavi Khomeini, *A Clarification of Questions*, translated by J. Borujerdi (Boulder, Colo.: Westview Press, 1984), p. 429.
6. *A Clarification of Questions*, pp. 429 and 432.
7. *Islam and Revolution*, pp. 185–186.
8. *Islam and Revolution*, p. 185.
9. Shaul Bakhash, *The Reign of the Ayatollahs: Iran and the Islamic Revolution* (New York: Basic Books, 1984), p. 38.
10. *Islam and Revolution*, p. 47.
11. *Islam and Revolution*, pp. 75–76.
12. *The Reign of the Ayatollahs*, p. 49.
13. "Military Cracks Down on Rebels in Iran; Moslem Leader Assails U.S. Role; Holy Man Calls for Army to Oust Shah," *New York Times*, November 7, 1978, p A1.
14. *The Reign of the Ayatollahs*, p. 72.
15. "Military Cracks Down on Rebels in Iran."
16. "Moslem Faction Opposes Monarchy; Iranian Shiites Consider Monarchy Offensive to Religion," *Washington Post*, November 12, 1978, p. A1.
17. "Ayatullah Khomeini," *Time*, January 7, 1980 (www.library.cornell.edu/colldev/mideast/1979.htm).
18. Ali Akbar Hashemi Rafsanjani, interview with *Ettela'at*, June 7, 1986, quoted in "Islam and Women's Equality: Excerpts from the Speech by Maryam Rajavi, Autumn 1995" (www.iran-e-azad.org/english/maryam/march8.pdf).
19. Nikki R. Keddie, *Roots of Revolution: An Interpretive History of Modern Iran* (New Haven, Conn.: Yale University Press, 1981), p. 250.
20. Personal interview with Ayatollah Jalal Ganjei, February 28, 2006. This applies to all the Ganjei quotations in this chapter.
21. "The Khomeini Era Begins," *Time*, February 12, 1979.
22. Said Amir Arjomand, *The Turban for the Crown: The Islamic Revolution in Iran* (New York: Oxford University Press, 1988), p. 135.
23. *The Reign of the Ayatollahs*, p. 72–73.
24. Sepehr Zabih, *The Iranian Military in Revolution and War* (New York: Routledge, 1988), p. 210.
25. *The Iranian Military in Revolution and War*, p. 211.
26. All excerpts from the Iranian regime's constitution are from the International Constitutional Law Web site of the University of Bern (www.oefre.unibe.ch/law/icl/ir__indx.html).

27. *The Iranian Military in Revolution and War,* p. 122.
28. *The Iranian Military in Revolution and War,* p. 146.
29. Mohammad Mohaddessin, *Islamic Fundamentalism: The New Global Threat* (Washington, D.C.: Seven Locks Press, 2001), p. 20.
30. *Islam and Revolution,* p. 63.
31. "Constitution of the Islamic Republic of Iran," October 1979 (http://mellat.majlis.ir/archive/1383/10/15/0001.htm).
32. *Islamic Fundamentalism,* p. 20.
33. *Islam and Revolution,* p. 357.
34. *A Clarification of Questions,* p. 428.
35. "Iran Is Back in That Old Familiar Chaos," *New York Times,* July 5, 1981, p. D2.
36. *Islamic Fundamentalism,* p. 20.
37. *The Reign of the Ayatollahs,* p.111.
38. *Islamic Fundamentalism,* p. 21.
39. Ervand Abrahamian, *The Iranian Mojahedin* (London: Yale University Press, 1989), pp. 219.
40. "Iranian Leftists Not Intimidated by Ruling Mullahs," *Christian Science Monitor,* July 13, 1981.
41. "Amid Hardship, Islamic Zeal Still Grips Iran," *New York Times,* April 21, 1982, p. A1.
42. *Islamic Fundamentalism,* p. 29.
43. *Islamic Fundamentalism,* pp. 30–31.
44. "Fascism without Swastikas," *Harpers,* July 1980, pp. 65–71.
45. "Bush Says Iran Bombs Used in Iraq," *Washington Times,* March 24, 2006 (www.washingtontimes.com/national/20060314-010558-5660r.htm).

CHAPTER 5

1. Originally, 72 hostages were seized; 6 escaped and 13 were released on November 19 and 20, 1979; another was released in July 1980, and the remaining 52 were released on January 20, 1981. See "The Hostages and the Casualties," Jimmy Carter Library & Museum (www.jimmycarterlibrary.org/documents/list_of_hostages.phtml).
2. "Mandat d'Arret International," No. A/289/90, issued by Jacques Antenen, *Juge d'instruction du Canton de Vaud,* March 20, 2006.
3. "Swiss Orders Arrest of Iranian Ex-Minister," *Swissinfo.com,* April 9, 2006 (www.swissinfo.org/eng/swissinfo.html?siteSect=106&sid=6617021&cKey=1144592966000).
4. "Court Indicts Iran Leaders for Kurd Assassinations," Agence France Presse, April 10, 1997.
5. "Berlin Court Says Top Iran Leaders Ordered Killings," *New York Times,* April 11, 1997, p. A1.
6. "Germany Opts Not to Pursue Iranian Leaders," *New York Times,* May 16, 1997, p. A12.
7. "12 terrorists hunt Danish cartoonists," Joseph Farah, G2 Bulletin, May 3, 2006 (http://g2.wnd.com/index.php?fa=PAGE.view&pageId=1049).
8. UPI, untitled report, December 3, 1987.
9. "Lebanon's Hezbollah Symbolizes Pure Islamic Thoughts," *Iran Daily,* August 2, 2005, p. 2 (www.iran-daily.com/1384/2339/pdf/i2.pdf).
10. U.S. Department of State, "State Sponsors of Terrorism" (www.state.gov/s/ct/c14151.htm).

11. Kenneth Katzman, "CRS Report: Terrorism: Middle Eastern Groups and State Sponsors, 2000," August 17, 2000 (www.ict.org.il/documents/documentdet.cfm?docid=40).

12. Beverley Milton-Edwards, *Islamic Fundamentalism since 1945* (London: Routledge, 2005), p. 83.

13. "U.S. Beirut Embassy Bombed," *New York Times*, April 19, 1983, p. A1.

14. Magnus Ranstorp, "Hizbollah's Command Leadership: Its Structure, Decision-Making, and Relationship with Iranian Clergy and Institutions," *Terrorism and Political Violence* 6, no. 3 (Autumn 1994): 305.

15. U.S. Department of State, "Country Reports on Terrorism, 2004," April 27, 2005 (www.state.gov/s/ct/rls/45394.htm).

16. FBI Most Wanted Terrorists (www.fbi.gov/mostwant/terrorists/fugitives.htm).

17. "Iran Responsible for 1983 Marine Barracks Bombing, Judge Rules," *CNN.com*, May 30, 2003 (www.cnn.com/2003/LAW/05/30/iran.barracks.bombing).

18. "Choices: Will Reagan Understand That He Finally Did the Right Thing?" *Washington Post*, February 9, 1984, p. A2.

19. "U.S. Marines to Leave Lebanese Soil," *Washington Post*, February 8, 1984, p. A1.

20. "Choices: Will Reagan Understand That He Finally Did the Right Thing?"

21. "Reagan's Surprise Retreat from Beirut," *Newsweek*, February 20, 1984, p. 36.

22. Mohammad Mohaddessin, *Islamic Fundamentalism: The New Global Threat* (Washington, D.C.: Seven Locks Press, 2001), p. 205. Additional translation by Alireza Jafarzadeh.

23. "A Flash of Gunpowder Politics," *Newsweek*, December 26, 1983, p. 24.

24. "23 Die, Including 2 Americans, in Terrorist Car Bomb Attack on the U.S. Embassy at Beirut," *New York Times*, September 21, 1984, p. A1.

25. "House Committee Says U.S. Embassy Ignored Warnings," *New York Times*, October 4, 1984, p. A1.

26. "Frontline Interview with Robert McFarlane," *PBS Frontline*, 2001 (www.pbs.org/wgbh/pages/frontline/shows/target/interviews/mcfarlane.html).

27. "Group in Beirut Says It Hanged U.S. Colonel," *New York Times*, August 1, 1989, p. A1.

28. "With Release of Terry Anderson, U.S. Hostage Ordeal Ended in Lebanon," *Washington Report on Middle East Affairs*, December 1995, pp. 79–80 (www.washingtonreport.org/backissues/1295/9512079.html).

29. Terry Anderson, *Den of Lions* (New York: Crown, 1993), p. 314.

30. A. M. Rosenthal, "Thank Them Not," *New York Times*, December 6, 1991.

31. "Hostages' Fate Linked to 4 Missing Iranians," *New York Times*, November 23, 1990.

32. "Teheran Denies Direct Discussions With U.S. on Hostages in Beirut, *New York Times*, March 8, 1990.

33. "Iran Offers Assistance on Lebanon Hostages," *New York Times*, April 21, 1991, p. 13.

34. "Iran Paid for Release of Hostages," *Washington Post*, January 19, 1992, p. A1.

35. "Kidnappings in Lebanon—President's Statement, Jan. 26, 1987" (www.findarticles.com/p/articles/mi_m1079/is_v87/ai_4991208).

36. "Iran's Hostage Hardball," *Christian Science Monitor*, July 24, 1987, p. 3.

37. "Terrorist Attacks on Americans, 1979–1988," *PBS Frontline*, 2001 (www.pbs.org/wgbh/pages/frontline/shows/target/etc/cron.html#10.23.1983).

38. Edgar O'Ballance, *Islamic Fundamentalist Terrorism, 1979–95: The Iranian Connection* (Basingstoke, U.K.: Macmillan, 1997), pp. 111–112.

39. George Bush, Inaugural Address, January 20, 1989 (www.bartleby.com/124/pres63.html), and Kenneth Katzman, *CRS Report for Congress: Iran: U.S. Policy and Options*, January 14, 2000.
40. "Iran Depicts Bush Plea as 'Arrogant,'" *Washington Post*, January 28, 1989, p. A15.
41. "Iran Urges Cooperation on Hostages," *New York Times*, April 22, 1991, p. A11.
42. "Iran Paid for Release of Hostages."
43. "Iran Paid for Release of Hostages."
44. Associated Press, "A List of Incidents Marring Iran's Ties with the West," December 30, 1991.
45. "U.S. Links Iranian-Backed Group to Hijacking of Kuwaiti Airliner," *New York Times*, December 7, 1984, p. A1.
46. "Iran Ambivalent on Hijack, despite Its Support of Lebanese Shiites," *Christian Science Monitor*, July 1, 1985, p. 14.
47. "Iran Ambivalent on Hijack."
48. "U.S. Names 3 as TWA Hijackers," *Washington Post*, October 18, 1985, p. A1.
49. "Iran May Be Behind Escalating Lebanon Tensions: US Envoy to Iraq," Agence France Presse, July 13, 2006.
50. "Iran Urges West to End Support for Israel Before It Is Too Late," Iran Focus, July 11, 2006 (www.iranfocus.com/modules/news/print.php?storyid=7871).
51. "Ahmadinejad: World Will Soon Witness the Demise of Israel," Iran Focus, July 12, 2006 (www.iranfocus.com/modules/news/print.php?storyid=7885).
52. "Lebanon Crisis Delays UN Focus on Iran Nuclear Issues—Diplomats," Agence France Presse, July 17, 2006.
53. "Iran Supreme Leader Praises Hezbollah," Agence France Presse, July 16, 2006.
54. "Islamic World Proud of Hezbollah, Says Iranian Leader," Deutche Presse-Agentur, July 16, 2006.
55. "Resistance Group Attributes Dhahran Bombing to Iranian Government," Washington Report on Middle East Affairs, June-July 1997 (http://www.washington-report.org/backissues/0697/9706063.htm)
56. Louis J. Freeh, *My FBI: Bringing Down the Mafia, Investigating Bill Clinton, and Fighting the War on Terror* (New York: St. Martin's Press, 2005), p. 29.
57. *My FBI*, p. 31.
58. *The 9/11 Commission Report* (Washington, D.C.: The National Commission on Terrorist Attacks upon the United States, 2004), p. 60.
59. "Slow-Motion Justice in Argentina," *New York Times*, March 11, 2003, editorial/op-ed.
60. Agence France Presse article from November 14, 1997.
61. "AMIA Case, People Wanted," Embassy of Argentina in Canada (http://www.argentina-canada.net/amiaen.html).
62. "Warrants in '94 Bombing Are Delisted," *Los Angeles Times*, September 22, 2005, p. 4.
63. "Hezbollah ID'd in 1994 Argentina Attack," *CNN.com*, November 10, 2005 (edition.cnn.com/2005/WORLD/americas/11/09/argentina.bombing.ap/).
64. "Roots of Terror," *New York Times*, March 15, 1996, p. A1.
65. Roger Howard, *Iran in Crisis? Nuclear Ambitions and the American Response* (London: Zed Books, 2004), pp. 55–56.
66. U.S. Department of State, "Report on Global Terrorism 1998" (www.state.gov/www/global/terrorism/1998Report/sponsor.html#iran).
67. U.S. Department of State, "Patterns of Global Terrorism 1992" (fas.org/irp/threat/terror_92/).

68. "Turks Mourn," *The Independent* (U.K.), January 26, 1993, p. 8.
69. U.S. Department of State, "Patterns of Global Terrorism 1999: Background Information on Terrorist Groups" (www.state.gov/www/global/terrorism/1999report/appb.html).
70. "Patterns of Global Terrorism 1992."
71. "Patterns of Global Terrorism 1992."
72. *The 9/11 Commission Report*, p. 61.
73. *The 9/11 Commission Report*, pp. 169 and 240.
74. U.S. Department of State, "Patterns of Global Terrorism 2002" (www.state.gov/s/ct/rls/pgtrpt/2002/html/19988.htm).
75. U.S. Department of State, "Patterns of Global Terrorism 2003" (www.state.gov/s/ct/rls/pgtrpt/2003/31644.htm).
76. "Transcript: Iran President's Speech Threatening Israel," *Iran Focus*, October 28, 2005 (www.iranfocus.com/modules/news/article.php?storyid=4164).
77. "Iran to Host Holocaust Conference Later This Year," Agence France Presse, June 25, 2006.
78. *The Iranian* (www.iranian.com/Pictory/2003/February/fatwa.html).
79. Quoted in "Khomeini Sentence Reflects Political Needs of Minority," *The Independent* (U.K.), February 15, 1989, p.10.
80. Amnesty International, "Iran: Eight Years of Death Threats Salman Rushdie," May 1, 1997 (web.amnesty.org/library/Index/engMDE130171997?OpenDocument&of= COUNTRIES percent5CIRAN).
81. "Author Salman Rushdie Talks about 'Living Day to Day,'" *CNN.com*, February 14, 1997 (www.cnn.com/WORLD/9702/14/rushdie/).
82. "Iran Adamant over Rushdie Fatwa," *BBC News*, February 12, 2005 (news.bbc.co.uk/go/pr/fr/-/2/hi/middle_east/4260599.stm).
83. "Iran Adamant over Rushdie Fatwa."
84. "Salman Speaks," *Boston Phoenix*, May 6–13, 1999.
85. *Islamic Fundamentalism*, pp. 207–226.

CHAPTER 6

1. "Top Iran Cleric Says Islamic Rule will Spread to Iraq," *Iran Focus*, December 30, 2005 (www.iranfocus.com/modules/news/article.php?storyid=5081).
2. "Two Years On, Iran Is the Only Clear Winner of War on Saddam," *Times* (London), September 23, 2005.
3. "Most Foreign Insurgents in Iraq Come from Iran—Report," *Iran Focus*, May 9, 2006 (www.iranfocus.com/modules/news/article.php?storyid=7132).
4. "Envoy Accuses Iran Of Duplicity on Iraq," *Washington Post*, March 24, 2006, p. A12. (www.washingtonpost.com/wp-dyn/content/article/2006/03/23/AR2006032301658_pf.html).
5. "General Reports Spike in Iranian Activity in Iraq," *Washington Post*, June 23, 2006, p. A19.
6. "General: Iran Planting Bombs In Iraq," CBS News, June 22, 2006 (www.cbsnews.com/stories/2006/06/23/iraq/main1745308.shtml).
7. "Iran Is Helping Insurgents in Iraq, U.S. Officials Say," *New York Times*, September 20, 2004, p. A15.
8. "Ruling Clerics Ready to Negotiate with the United States," Radio Farda, February 26, 2004.

9. Quoted in Mohammad Mohaddessin, *Islamic Fundamentalism: The New Global Threat* (Washington, D.C.: Seven Locks Press, 2001), pp. 24–25.

10. "Iran's Rafsanjani: U.S. made mistake in launching war on Iraq," *Iran Focus*, June 1, 2006 (www.iranfocus.com/modules/news/article.php?storyid=7429).

11. Quoted in Gary E. McCuen, *Iran-Iraq War* (Hudson, Wis.: GEM Publications, 1987), p. 72.

12. Quoted in Efraim Karsh, *The Iran-Iraq War: 1980–1988* (Oxford: Osprey, 2002), p. 13.

13. Yitzhak Nakkash, "The Nature of Shi'ism in Iraq," in *Ayatollahs, Sufis, and Ideologues*, edited by Faleh Abdul-Jabar (London: Saqi Books, 2002), pp. 24–29.

14. "The Nature of Shi'ism in Iraq."

15. Tony Blair, "Clash about Civilisations Speech," March 21, 2006 (www.number10. gov.uk/output/Page9224.asp).

16. Sandra Mackey, *The Iranians* (New York: Plume/Penguin Putnam, 1998), p. 319.

17. Stephen C. Pelletiere and Douglas V. Johnson II, *Lessons Learned: The Iran-Iraq War* (Carlisle Barracks, Pa.: U.S. Army War College, 1991), p. 23.

18. According to Shia Islam, the twelfth, or hidden, imam, who disappeared in 941 C.E., was the last direct descendant of Muhammad. He promised to reappear and lead his followers during the period preceding Judgment Day.

19. *The Iranians*, p. 330.

20. The MEK moved from France to Iraq in 1986 after the French government expelled it in the midst of its negotiations with Iran to release the French hostages in Lebanon.

21. "U.N. Says Human Rights Abuses Are Continuing Throughout Iran," New York Times, November 3, 1988.

22. "A Peace Worse than Poison," *The Economist*, July 23, 1988, p. 35.

23. *Islamic Fundamentalism*, p. 63.

24. "Transition 2005: U.S. Policy Toward Iran," *Council on Foreign Relations*, January 12, 2005 (www.cfr.org/publication.html?id=7605).

25. "Iranian opposition bids for power; Mojahedin tries for breakthrough before ceasefire," *Christian Science Monitor*, July 28, 1988.

26. Mohammad Mohaddessin, *The Enemies of the Ayatollahs* (London: Zed Books, 2004).

27. "Iraq Declares Two Week Suspension of Air Raids on Iranian Cities," *Washington Post*, February 19, 1987.

28. Edward Mortimer, "Iran And Iraq Turn On Domestic Opponents," *Financial Times*, August 17, 1988.

29. "Iran executing rebels without trial, chief judge hints," *Philadelphia Inquirer*, August 6, 1988.

30. Daniel L. Byman, Shahram Chubin, Anoushiravan Ehteshami, and Jerrold Green, *Iran's Security Policy in the Post-Revolutionary Era* (Santa Monica, Calif.: Rand, 2001), p. 34.

31. Reuters, "Bremer Worried about 'Iranian Activity' in Iraq," May, 28, 2003.

32. "Iran Spent over $1 Billion on Meddling in Iraq: Defence Minister," *Iran Focus*, January 17, 2005 (www.iranfocus.com/modules/news/article.php?storyid=1258).

33. "Top Iran Cleric Says Islamic Rule Will Spread to Iraq," *Iran Focus*, December 30, 2005 (www.iranfocus.com/modules/news/article.php?storyid=5080).

34. "Iran Says Khomeini's 'Message' Conquering Iraq," *Iran Focus*, December 22, 2005 (www.iranfocus.com/modules/news/article.php?storyid=5001).

35. "U.S. Commander Accuses Iran of Meddling in Iraqi Vote," *Iran Focus*, December 16, 2005 (www.iranfocus.com/modules/news/print.php?storyid=4919).

36. "Rafsanjani: Iran Expects Results It Invested For in Iraqi Polls," *Iran Focus*, December 16, 2005 (www.iranfocus.com/modules/news/article.php?storyid=4909).

37. "Iraq Buys Flour from Iran in Big Policy Shift," *Daily Times* (Pakistan), July 5, 2005 (www.dailytimes.com.pk/default.asp?page=story_5-7-2005_pg5_14).

38. "Iran/Iraq: As Senior Visit Concludes, Deals Signal Increased Cooperation," *Radio-FreeEurope*, July 18, 2005 (www.rferl.org/featuresarticle/2005/07/80a33bfc-b09b-4a5d-b0ba-1b3d1c47d626.html).

39. "Iraq Dances with Iran, While America Seethes," *New York Times*, July 31, 2005.

40. "Iranian, Iraqi chambers of commerce sign MOU," *Iraqieconomy.org*, September 28, 2005 (www.iraqieconomy.org/home/bilecon/iran/20050928).

41. "Iran, Iraq to Establish Joint Regional Bank," *Iraqi Economy.org*, October 11, 2005 (www.iraqieconomy.org/home/bank/press/20051011).

42. "Attacks on Iraq Oil Industry Aid Vast Smuggling Scheme," *International Herald Tribune*, June 7, 2006.

43. "Winning Peace in Iran and Iraq," *NewsMax.com*, April 25, 2003 (www.newsmax.com/archives/articles/2003/4/25/162507.shtml).

44. "Inside Iran's Secret War for Iraq," *Time*, August 22, 2005, p. 28.

45. "Iranian Influence Raises Anxiety in Southern Iraq," *Dallas Morning News*, August 3, 2005.

46. U.S. Department of Defense, "DoD Video-teleconference with Iraqi Minister of State Kasim Daoud," transcript, January 27, 2005 (www.defenselink.mil/transcripts/2005/tr20050127-2042.html).

47. "Iran Is Helping Insurgents in Iraq, U.S. Officials Say," *New York Times*, September 20, 2004, p. 15.

48. "Iran Uses 'An Army of Merchants' to Infiltrate Iraq," September 5, 2005, *Iran Focus*, (www.iranfocus.com/modules/news/article.php?storyid=3605).

49. "Governor Accuses Iran of Meddling in Iraq," *Iran Focus*, February 21, 2005 (www.iranfocus.com/modules/news/article.php?storyid=1527).

50. "Iranian Consulate Attacked by Followers of Shiite Cleric in Basra," Associated Press Worldstream, June 14, 2006.

51. "Iran Tries to Influence Iraq's Airwaves," *Iran Focus*, June 23, 2006 (www.iranfocus.com/modules/news/article.php?storyid=7701).

52. "Tehran: Guess Who's Trying to Infiltrate Iraq?" *Newsweek*, February 28, 2005.

53. "Ex-general Says Iranian Led Torture of Detainees," *Washington Times*, December 13, 2005.

54. "Iran-Backed Rebels Eye New Iraq Role," *BBC News*, March 18, 2003 (news.bbc.co.uk/1/hi/world/middle_east/2859173.stm).

55. "Coalition Nations Look Ahead to Exit," *Chicago Tribune*, February 1, 2005.

56. "Basra Out of Control, Says Chief of Police," *Guardian* (London), May 31, 2005 (www.guardian.co.uk/print/0,3858,5204814-103681,00.html).

57. "2 Iranian Dissidents Abducted in Capital," *Washington Times*, August 16, 2005 (http://www.washtimes.com/functions/print.php?StoryID=20050815-105438-3741r).

58. "Ex-enemy Iran May Be Biggest Winner in Iraqi Poll," *Telegraph* (U.K.), December 21, 2004.

59. "Iraqis Receive Training in Iran," *Washington Times*, January 9, 2006.

60. "Iran's Agents Arrested in Key Iraqi Province," *Iran Focus*, June 13, 2006 (www.iranfocus.com/modules/news/article.php?storyid=7585).

61. "Roadside Bomb Kills 10 People North Baghdad," Associated Press Worldstream, May 29, 2006.

62. Agence France Presse, "Iraqi Torturers on Iran's Payroll: General," December 11, 2005 (www.iranfocus.com/modules/news/article.php?storyid=4845).

63. Knight Ridder Newspapers, "Iran Gaining Influence, Power in Iraq through Militia," December 12, 2005 (www.iranfocus.com/modules/news/article.php?storyid=4852).

64. Knight Ridder Newspapers, "Iranian-Backed Militia Groups Take Control of Much of Southern Iraq," May 26, 2006 (www.iranfocus.com/modules/news/article.php?storyid=7370).

65. "Ex-Iraqi Interior Minister Rips Iran for Meddling in Iraq," *Iran Focus*, October 12, 2005 (www.iranfocus.com/modules/news/article.php?storyid=3977).

66. "Iran: Qods Day Brings Out Anti-Israeli Sentiments," *RadioFreeEurope*, October 27, 2005 (www.rferl.org/features/features_Article.aspx?m=10&y=2005&id=6BFD D196–435E–4A0E–9355–1622D610B610).

67. "Martyrdom-seeking operations embody the pinnacle of a nation's greatness and the apex of its epics," Parto Sokhan Newspaper, August 3, 2005 (http://www.partosokhan.ir/289/page03.pdf).

68. Islamic Republic News Agency (IRNA), July 25, 2005 (news.gooya.com/politics/archives/033838.php).

69. "British Victims of Roadside Bomb Named as Minister Confirms Plans for Gradual Pullout," *Guardian*, July 18, 2005.

70. Reuters, "Bomb Technology Enters Iraq from Iran," November 4, 2005 (today.reuters.com/news/newsArticle.aspx?type=topNews&storyID=2005–11–04T18590 3Z_01_SIB466548_RTRUKOC_0_US-IRAQ-BOMBS-GENERAL.xml& archived=False).

71. "The Precision-Made Mine That Has 'Killed 17 British Troops,'" *Daily Telegraph* (London), June 25, 2006.

72. "Is Iran the True Victor of the Iraq War?" *Der Spiegel*, August 22, 2005 (service.spiegel.de/cache/international/spiegel/0,1518,370990,00.html).

73. "Iraqi President Says Sunni Insurgents See Iran as Threat," *Washington Post*, May 3, 2006, p. A1.

74. Editorial, *Shargh*, February 25, 2006 (www.sharghnewspaper.com/841206/html/index.htm).

75. Alhurrah television interview, February 27, 2006.

76. "People's Mojahedin of Iran," Mission report, Friends of a Free Iran—European Parliament, September 21, 2005.

77. "Iraqi Opposition: Iran Will Not Interfere," United Press International, August 13, 2002 (located on LexisNexis).

78. "Analysis: Iraq's Divided Shiia Opposition," United Press International, January 3, 2003 (located on LexisNexis).

79. "Iran-Backed Rebels Eye New Iraq Role," *BBC News*, March 18, 2003 (news.bbc.co.uk/1/hi/world/middle_east/2859173.stm).

80. "U.S. Targets Iran's Influence in Iraq," *Washington Post*, September 25, 2004.

81. "Iran's Supreme Leader Meets with Top Iraqi Protégé," *Iran Focus*, June 20, 2006 (www.iranfocus.com/modules/news/article.php?storyid=7675).

82. "With Free Elections in Iraq, Comes Mudslinging," *Newsday*, December 16, 2004.

83. ElectionWorld.org (www.electionworld.org/iraq.htm).

84. "How Iran Won the U.S. War in Iraq," *Daily Star*, October 2005.

85. "Iran-President-Ahmad: Campaign Against Hegemony, A Global Move Today: President," Iran News Agency, distributed by United Press International, April 15, 2006.

86. "Sunni, Secular Groups Demand New Vote," *Washington Post*, December 22, 2005.

87. " Sunnis in Iraq Demonstrate Against Election Results, Agence France Presse, December 23, 2005 (www.khaleejtimes.com/DisplayArticle.asp?xfile=data/focuson iraq/2005/December/focusoniraq_December164.xml&section=focusoniraq).

88. "Bush Adviser Says Iraq Voting No Surprise," Associated Press, December 20, 2005.

89. "Sunni, Secular Groups Demand New Vote."

90. "DECLARATION BY 5.2 MILLION IRAQIS IN SUPPORT OF THE IRANIAN MOJAHEDIN KHALQ (MEK)," Congressional Record, Extension of Remarks, July 26, 2006, Page: E1541.

91. "Gen. Abizaid On Stabilizing Iraq," CBS "60 Minutes," 26 November 2006 (http.// www.cbsnews.com/stories/2006/11/26/60minutes/printable2208941.shtml).

92. "Talking with the Enemy," *Newsweek*, November 27, 2006 (www.msnbc.msn.com/ id/15788877/site/newsweek/).

93. "Hezbollah Said to Help Shiite Army in Iraq," *New York Times*, November 28, 2006.

CHAPTER 7

1. Kenneth C. Brill, "Statement on the Implementation of Safeguards in the Islamic Republic of Iran," March 13, 2004 (www.iaea.org/NewsCenter/Statements/Misc/ 2004/brill13032004.html).

2. "'Iran Is Close to a Nuclear Bomb': Iranian Scientist," *Iran Focus*, July 13, 2005 (www.iranfocus.com/modules/news/article.php?storyid=2840).

3. "Iran Says U.S. and Israel Snaring Its Atomic Experts," *Iran Focus*, July 17, 2005 (www.iranfocus.com/modules/news/article.php?storyid=2876).

4. "Nuclear Chronology," Nuclear Threat Initiative (http://www.nti.org/e_re-search/profiles/Iran/1825.html).

5. "Iran: Atomic Energy Program," United States Energy Research and Development Administration, October 1976, p. 3.

6. International Institute for Strategic Studies (IISS), *Iran's Strategic Weapons Programmes: A Net Assessment* (London: Routledge, 2005), pp. 10–11.

7. Anthony Cordesman, "Iran and Nuclear Weapons: Background Paper for the Senate Foreign Relations Committee," Center for Strategic and International Studies (CSIS), March 24, 2000, p. 4.

8. "Atomic Ayatollahs: Just What the Mideast Needs—An Iranian Bomb," *Washington Post*, April 12, 1987, p. D1.

9. "Atomic Ayatollahs."

10. Leonard S. Spector, *Going Nuclear: The Spread of Nuclear Weapons 1986–1987* (Cambridge, Mass.: Ballinger, 1987), p. 45.

11. Andrew Kich and Jeanette Wolf, "Iran's Nuclear Facilities: A Profile," Center for Nonproliferation Studies, 1998.

12. *Iran's Strategic Weapons Programmes: A Net Assessment*, p. 12.

13. IAEA Director General's Report, "Implementation of the NPT Safeguards Agreement in the Islamic Republic of Iran," November 10, 2003 (www.iaea.org/Publications/Documents/Board/2003/gov2003–75.pdf).

14. "Implementation of the NPT Safeguards Agreement in the Islamic Republic of Iran," November 10, 2003.
15. Nuclear Threat Initiative (NTI), "Iran Profile: Nuclear Chronology, 1957–1985" (www.nti.org/e_research/profiles/Iran/1825_1826.html).
16. "Iran Profile: Nuclear Chronology, 1957–1985."
17. Mohammad Mohaddessin, *Islamic Fundamentalism: The New Global Threat* (Washington, D.C.: Seven Locks Press, 2001), p. 134.
18. "'U.S. Policy toward Iran,' The White House, Draft National Security Decision Directive (NSDD), *secret*, June 17, 1985," National Security Archive (www.gwu.edu/~nsarchiv/NSAEBB/NSAEBB21/05–01.htm).
19. "Report Says Iran Seeks Atomic Arms," *New York Times*, October 31, 1991, p. A7.
20. "Tracking the Technology," *Nuclear Engineering International*, August 31, 2004 (www.neimagazine.com/story.asp?sectioncode=76&storyCode=2024442).
21. Christopher Clary, "Dr. Khan's Nuclear WalMart," *Disarmament Diplomacy*, no. 76, March/April 2004 (www.acronym.org.uk/dd/dd76/76cc.htm).
22. George J. Tenet, "The Worldwide Threat 2004: Challenges in a Changing Global Context," Testimony before the Senate Select Committee on Intelligence, February 24, 2004 (www.odci.gov/cia/public_affairs/speeches/2004/dci_speech_02142004.html).
23. "Implementation of the NPT Safeguards Agreement in the Islamic Republic of Iran," November 10, 2003.
24. "Schooling Iran's Atom Squad," *Bulletin of the Atomic Scientists*, May/June 2004, pp. 31–35 (www.thebulletin.org/article.php?art_ofn=mj04boureston).
25. "Key Pakistani Is Said to Admit Atom Transfers," *New York Times*, February 2, 2004, p. A1.
26. "Insider Tells of Nuclear Deals, Cash," *Washington Post*, February 21, 2004, p. A1.
27. "Acquiring a Nuclear-Capable Missile with the Range of 3,000 km," press conference by Alireza Jafarzadeh, President, Strategic Policy Consulting, Inc., National Press Building, Washington, D.C., August 26, 2005 (www.spcwashington.com/index.php?option=com_content&task=view&id=125&Itemid=34).
28. Sharon Squassoni, "Closing Pandora's Box: Pakistan's Role in Nuclear Proliferation," *Arms Control Today*, April 2004 (http://www.armscontrol.org/act/2004_04/Squassoni.asp).
29. "Pakistan Rejects U.N. Nuclear Role," *BBC News*, February 6, 2004 (212.58.240.35/1/hi/world/south_asia/3462907.stm).
30. "The Wrath of Khan," *Atlantic Monthly*, November 2005 (www.theatlantic.com/doc/200511/aq-khan).
31. *Islamic Fundamentalism*, p. 134.
32. *Iran's Strategic Weapons Programmes: A Net Assessment*, p. 13.
33. Nuclear Threat Initiative (NTI), "Iran Profile: Nuclear Chronology, 1992" (www.nti.org/e_research/profiles/Iran/1825_1869.html).
34. Associated Press, "Iran to Get Nuclear Technology from China, Russia," September 11, 1992.
35. *Iran's Strategic Weapons Programmes: A Net Assessment*, p. 13.
36. Nuclear Threat Initiative (NTI), "Iran Profile: Nuclear Chronology, 1995" (www.nti.org/e_research/profiles/Iran/1825_1872.html).
37. "Atomic Ayatollahs."
38. *Iran's Strategic Weapons Programmes: A Net Assessment*, p. 13.
39. "Bushehr NPP to Be Ready to Take Nuclear Fuel Soon," *RIA Novosti*, February 14, 2006 (en.rian.ru/russia/20060214/43532161.html).

40. Joseph Cirincione, Jon B. Wolfsthal, and Miriam Rajkumar, *Deadly Arsenals: Nuclear, Biological, and Chemical Threats*, 2nd edition (Washington, D.C.: Carnegie Endowment for International Peace, 2005), p. 302.
41. Alireza Jafarzadch, "Iranian Politics and Economy," National Press Club Morning Newsmaker presentation, C-Span, June 5, 1990.
42. Mohammad Ghannadi-Maragheh, "Atomic Energy Organization of Iran," World Nuclear Association Annual Symposium, September 4–6, 2002 (www.world-nuclear.org/sym/2002/pdf/ghannadi.pdf).
43. Alireza Jafarzadeh, "New Information on Top Secret Projects of the Iranian Regime's Nuclear Program," August 14, 2002 (www.iranwatch.org/privateviews/NCRI/perspex-ncri-topsecretprojects–081402.htm).
44. IAEA Director General's Report, "Implementation of the NPT Safeguards Agreement in the Islamic Republic of Iran," June 6, 2003.
45. IAEA Director General's Report, "Implementation of the NPT Safeguards Agreement in the Islamic Republic of Iran," September 2, 2005.
46. *Iran's Strategic Weapons Programmes: A Net Assessment*, p. 16.
47. "Implementation of the NPT Safeguards Agreement in the Islamic Republic of Iran," June 6, 2003.
48. Alireza Jafarzadeh, "Iranian Regime's Programs for Biological and Microbial Weapons," May 15, 2003 (www.iranwatch.org/privateviews/NCRI/perspex-ncri-cbw–051503.htm).
49. National Council of Resistance of Iran, "Disclosing a Major Secret Nuclear Site under the Ministry of Defense," November 17, 2004 (www.globalsecurity.org/wmd/library/report/2004/new-nuke-info.htm).
50. Institute for Science and International Security, "Destruction at Iranian Site Raises New Questions about Iran's Nuclear Activities," June 17, 2004 (www.isis-online.org/publications/iran/lavizanshian.html).
51. "Teheran Park 'Cleansed' of Traces from Nuclear Site," *Telegraph* (U.K.), March 6, 2006 (www.telegraph.co.uk/news/main.jhtml?xml=/news/2006/03/06/wiran06.xml).
52. "Disclosing a Major Secret Nuclear Site under the Ministry of Defense."
53. IAEA Director General's Report, "Implementation of the NPT Safeguards Agreement in the Islamic Republic of Iran," November 15, 2004 (www.iaea.org/Publications/Documents/Board/2004/gov2004–83.pdf).
54. "Implementation of the NPT Safeguards Agreement in the Islamic Republic of Iran," November 15, 2004.
55. "Teheran Park 'Cleansed' of Traces from Nuclear Site."
56. Alireza Jafarzadeh, "IRGC Imam Hossein University Involved in Clandestine Nuclear Weapons Program," National Press Club, Washington, D.C., March 20, 2006 (www.nci.org/06nci/03/Jafarzadeh_PC_Statement.htm).
57. Mohammad Mohaddessin, National Council of Resistance of Iran, "Project to Build Neutron Initiator, the Trigger to Fission Chain Reaction for Nuclear Bomb," press conference, February 3, 2005 (www.iranwatch.org/privateviews/NCRI/perspex-ncri-neutroninitiator–020305.htm).
58. "Implementation of the NPT Safeguards Agreement in the Islamic Republic of Iran," June 6, 2003.
59. IAEA Director General's Report, "Implementation of the NPT Safeguards Agreement in the Islamic Republic of Iran," August 26, 2003.
60. "Implementation of the NPT Safeguards Agreement in the Islamic Republic of Iran," August 26, 2003.

61. "Implementation of the NPT Safeguards Agreement in the Islamic Republic of Iran," November 10, 2003.
62. "Implementation of the NPT Safeguards Agreement in the Islamic Republic of Iran," November 15, 2004.
63. Alireza Jafarzadeh, "Iran Running a Clandestine Laser Enrichment," Press Conference at the United Nations Plaza Hotel, September 14, 2006 (http://www.spcwashington.com/index.php?option=com_content&task=view&id=232&Itemid=34).
64. International Atomic Energy Agency, "Communications Received from Certain Member States Regarding Guidelines for Transfers of Nuclear-related Dual-use Equipment, Materials, Software and Related Technology," May 16, 2003.
65. Associated Press, "Resistance Group Claims Iran Possesses Banned Nuclear Machinery," January 20, 2006.
66. National Council of Resistance of Iran, "Iran: Mullahs Obtained 2 Banned Machines Used for Making Atom Bomb," January 22, 2006 (www.ncr-iran.org/content/view/913/76/).
67. Materials and Energy Research Center Web site, ngdir.ir/geolab/GeoLabDetail.asp?PID=426.
68. "Iran Said to Smuggle Material for Warheads," *Los Angeles Times*, May 1, 2005.
69. Alireza Jafarzadeh, "Iran Smuggles Ceramic Matrix Composite, a Key Material for Building a Nuclear Bomb," press release, May 19, 2005 (www.spcwashington.com/index.php?option=com_content&task=view&id=141&Itemid=33).
70. "Iran Mulled Nuclear Bomb in 1988," BBC Radio, 29 September 2006 (http://news.bbc.co.uk/2/5392584.stm).
71. IAEA Director General's Report, "Implementation of the NPT Safeguards Agreement in the Islamic Republic of Iran," April 28, 2006 (www.isis-online.org/publications/iran/IAEAreport28Apr06.pdf.).

CHAPTER 8

1. Condoleezza Rice, "Opening Remarks and Q&A Session at Chicago Council on Foreign Relations," April 19, 2006 (www.state.gov/secretary/rm/2006/64797.htm).
2. Associated Press, "Iran Begins Uranium Extraction, Plans Processing Ore to Fuel," February 10, 2003.
3. "Iran Begins Uranium Extraction, Plans Processing Ore to Fuel."
4. Nuclear Threat Initiative, "Iran Profile: Nuclear Facilities" (www.nti.org/e_research/profiles/Iran/3119_3182.html).
5. IAEA Director General's Report, "Implementation of the NPT Safeguards Agreement in the Islamic Republic of Iran," November 15, 2004 (www.iaea.org/Publications/Documents/Board/2004/gov2004-83.pdf).
6. International Institute for Strategic Studies, *Iran's Strategic Weapons Programmes: A Net Assessment* (London: Routledge, 2005), p. 35.
7. *Iran's Strategic Weapons Programmes: A Net Assessment*, p. 38.
8. Nuclear Threat Initiative, "Iran Profile: Nuclear Chronology, 1957–1985" (www.nti.org/e_research/profiles/1825_1826.html).
9. Nuclear Threat Initiative, "Iran Profile: Nuclear Imports" (www.nti.org/e_research/profiles/Iran/2867_2868.html).
10. IAEA Director General's Report, "Implementation of the NPT Safeguards Agreement in the Islamic Republic of Iran," November 26, 2003 (www.iaea.or.at/Publications/Documents/Board/2003/gov2003-75.pdf).

11. "Implementation of the NPT Safeguards Agreement in the Islamic Republic of Iran," November 26, 2003.
12. "Implementation of the NPT Safeguards Agreement in the Islamic Republic of Iran," November 26, 2003.
13. "Implementation of the NPT Safeguards Agreement in the Islamic Republic of Iran," November 26, 2003.
14. "Implementation of the NPT Safeguards Agreement in the Islamic Republic of Iran," November 26, 2003.
15. "Implementation of the NPT Safeguards Agreement in the Islamic Republic of Iran," November 26, 2003.
16. Alireza Jafarzadeh, "The Islamic Revolutionary Guards Corps Use Universities for Research to Build the Bomb," press conference, March 20, 2006 (www.nci.org/06nci/03/Jafarzadeh_PC_Statement.htm).
17. IAEA Director General's Report, "Implementation of the NPT Safeguards Agreement in the Islamic Republic of Iran," April 28, 2006 (www.iranwatch.org/international/IAEA/iaea-iranreport–042806.pdf).
18. *Iran's Strategic Weapons Programmes: A Net Assessment*, p. 41.
19. R. Shock, "Proliferation-Resistant Nuclear Power Systems: A Workshop on New Ideas," March 1, 2000 (www.llnl.gov/tid/lof/documents/pdf/238172.pdf).
20. Dave Andrews and Nigel Chamberlain, "The IAEA and Iran: Crisis Averted—For the Time Being," November 23, 2004 (www.basicint.org/pubs/Notes/BN041123.htm#fn07).
21. IAEA Director General's Report, "Implementation of the NPT Safeguards Agreement in the Islamic Republic of Iran," September 2, 2005 (http://www.iaea.org/Publications/Documents/Board/2005/gov2005-67.pdf).
22. "U.N. Finds New Uranium Traces in Iran," *New York Times*, May 13, 2006.
23. *Iran's Strategic Weapons Programmes: A Net Assessment*, p. 46.
24. "Implementation of the NPT Safeguards Agreement in the Islamic Republic of Iran," November 26, 2003.
25. IAEA Director General's Report, "Implementation of the NPT Safeguards Agreement in the Islamic Republic of Iran," March 13, 2004 (www.iaea.org/Publications/Documents/Board/2004/gov2004-11.pdf).
26. John R. Bolton, "Iran's Continuing Pursuit of Weapons of Mass Destruction: Testimony to the House International Relations Committee Subcommittee on the Middle East and Central Asia," June 24, 2004 (www.state.gov/t/us/rm/33909.htm).
27. IAEA Director General's Report, "Implementation of the NPT Safeguards Agreement in the Islamic Republic of Iran," June 18, 2004 (www.iaea.org/Publications/Documents/Board/2004/gov2004-34.pdf).
28. IAEA, "Implementation of the NPT Safeguards Agreement in the Islamic Republic of Iran: Resolution Adopted by the Board on 13 March 2004," (www.iaea.org/Publications/Documents/Board/2004/gov2004-21.pdf).
29. "Supervision of Military Organs on Mullahs' Nuclear Weapons Program," Iran Watch, Wisconsin Project on Nuclear Arms Control, April 28, 2004 (http://www.iranwatch.org/privateviews/NCRI/perspex-ncri-militarynuclear–042804.htm).
30. "Iran Advances Could Speed Nuclear Process, Associated Press, April 17, 2006 (http://www.iiss.org/whats-new/iiss-in-the-press/april–2006/iran-advances-could-speed-nuclear-process-).
31. "Iran building fast centrifuges, foes say," *International Herald Tribune*, August 25, 2006 (http://www.iht.com/bin/print_ipub.php?file=/articles/2006/08/25/news/nuke.php).

32. "Iran's Continuing Pursuit of Weapons of Mass Destruction."

33. Agence France Presse, "Iran Reserves Right to Resume Uranium Enrichment," October 21, 2003.

34. Associated Press, "Iran Claims Victory over Washington in Nuclear 'Boxing Match,'" October 22, 2003.

35. "Iran Made Thousands of Centrifuges, Breaking Pledge, Exiles Say," *Bloomberg. com*, August 18, 2005 (www.bloomberg.com/apps/news?pid=10000100&sid=auKF GAFccDHM).

36. Agence France Presse, "Iran Has Built 5,000 Centrifuges, Says Opposition," January 10, 2006 (spcwashington.com/index2.php?option=com_content&task=view& id=175&Itemid=26&pop=1&page=0).

37. "Iran Breaks Seals at Nuclear Site," *BBC News*, January 10, 2006 (news.bbc.co.uk/ 2/hi/middle_east/4597738.stm).

38. "Iran Reports Big Advance in Enrichment of Uranium," *New York Times*, April 12, 2006, p. A1.

39. IRNA, "Ahmadinejad: Iran Can Now Talk to World from Vantage Point of a Nuclear State," April 13, 2006 (www.irna.ir/en/news/view/menu–234/0604131632111 023.htm).

40. Associated Press, "Iran 'Won't Give a Damn' about Resolution," April 28, 2006 (abcnews.go.com/International/wireStory?id=1901108&page=1).

41. Federation of American Scientists, *Technologies Underlying Weapons of Mass Destruction*, December 1993 (www.fas.org/spp/starwars/ota/934406.pdf).

42. *Iran's Strategic Weapons Programmes: A Net Assessment*, p. 58.

43. "Implementation of the NPT Safeguards Agreement in the Islamic Republic of Iran," November 15, 2004.

44. Alireza Jafarzadeh, "Iran Hiding a Laser Enrichment Facility Underground in Parchin Military Complex," press release, March 24, 2005 (www.spcwashington. com/index.php?option=com_content&task=view&id=144&Itemid=26).

45. IAEA Director General's Report, "Implementation of the NPT Safeguards Agreement in the Islamic Republic of Iran," March 8, 2006 (www.iaea.org/Publications/ Documents/Board/2006/gov2006–15.pdf).

46. *Iran's Strategic Weapons Programmes: A Net Assessment*, p. 59.

47. IAEA Director General's Report, "Implementation of the NPT Safeguards Agreement in the Islamic Republic of Iran," June 19, 2003 (www.iaea.org/Publications/ Documents/Board/2003/gov2003–40.pdf).

48. "Implementation of the NPT Safeguards Agreement in the Islamic Republic of Iran," March 8, 2006.

49. Jack Boureston and Charles Mahaffey, "Iran's IR–40 Reactor: A Preliminary Assessment," FirstWatch International, November 2003 (www.firstwatchint.org/ IR40.htm).

50. Nuclear Threat Initiative, "Iran Profile: Nuclear Facilities" (www.nti.org/e_research/profiles/Iran/3119_3186.html).

51. Official Kremlin International News Broadcast, "Press Conference with Federal Agency for Atomic Agency Head Alexander Rumyantsev," September 22, 2005 (transcript via LexisNexis).

52. Personal interview with Manouchehr Fakhimi, February 27, 2006.

53. "Iran's Continuing Pursuit of Weapons of Mass Destruction," testimony by then Under Secretary of State for Arms Control and International Security, John R. Bolton before the House Subcommittee on the Middle East and Central Asia, June 24, 2004 (http://www.nci.org/04nci/07/Committee.htm).

54. Alireza Jafarzadeh, "New Information on Top Secret Projects of the Iranian Regime's Nuclear Program," August 14, 2002 (www.iranwatch.org/privateviews/NCRI/perspex-ncri-topsecretprojects–081402.htm).

55. "Iran Profile: Nuclear Facilities," and Oxford Research Group, "Iran's Nuclear Activities," March 2006 (www.oxfordresearchgroup.org.uk/publications/briefings/IranNuclearMar06.pdf).

56. "Iranians Retain Plutonium Plan in Nuclear Deal," *New York Times*, November 25, 2004 (http://www.nytimes.com/2004/11/25/international/middleeast/25NUKE.html?ex=1259125200&%2338;en=e76fac2bbe2af1ab&%2338;ei=5088&).

57. "Implementation of the NPT Safeguards Agreement in the Islamic Republic of Iran," November 15, 2004.

58. "Implementation of the NPT Safeguards Agreement in the Islamic Republic of Iran," September 24, 2005.

59. *Iran's Strategic Weapons Programmes: A Net Assessment*, p. 62.

60. Mohammad Mohaddessin, National Council of Resistance of Iran, "Project to Build Neutron Initiator, the Trigger to Fission Chain Reaction for Nuclear Bomb," press conference, February 3, 2005 (www.iranwatch.org/privateviews/NCRI/perspex-ncri-neutroninitiator–020305.htm).

61. "Implementation of the NPT Safeguards Agreement in the Islamic Republic of Iran," March 13, 2004.

62. IAEA Director General's Report, "Implementation of the NPT Safeguards Agreement in the Islamic Republic of Iran," September 18, 2004 (www.iaea.org/Publications/Documents/Board/2004/gov2004–60.pdf).

63. "Implementation of the NPT Safeguards Agreement in the Islamic Republic of Iran," November 15, 2004.

64. National Council of Resistance of Iran, "Project to Acquire Deuterium and Tritium: Mullahs' Drive to Finish Heavy Water Nuclear Reactor in Arak," August 25, 2005 (www.ncr-iran.org/content/view/563/76/).

65. "Project to Acquire Deuterium and Tritium."

66. Reuters, "Iran Allegedly Seeking Nuclear Explosion 'Booster,'" posted on Nuclear Threat Initiative, July 27, 2004 (www.nti.org/d_newswire/issues/2004_7_28.html).

67. IAEA Director General's Report, "Implementation of the NPT Safeguards Agreement in the Islamic Republic of Iran," November 14, 2006 (http://www.iaea.org/Publications/Documents/Board/2006/gov2006–64.pdf).

68. "Nuclear Disclosures on Iran Unverified," *Washington Post*, November 19, 2004, p. A1. (http://www.washingtonpost.com/wp-dyn/articles/A61079–2004Nov18.html).

69. "Atomic Test: As Evidence Grows Of Iran's Program, U.S. Hits Quandary," *Wall Street Journal*, March 18, 2005, p. A1.

70. "Iran's Civilian Nuclear Program May Link to Military, U.N. Says," *New York Times*, February 1, 2006 (http://www.nytimes.com/2006/02/01/international/middleeast/31cndiran.html?ex=1164776400&en=32d4980aa83c6f6a&ei=5070).

71. "Implementation of the NPT Safeguards Agreement in the Islamic Republic of Iran," November 14, 2006, par. 19.

CHAPTER 9

1. "Iran Builds a Secret Underground Complex as Nuclear Tensions Rise," *Telegraph* (U.K.), March 12, 2006 (www.telegraph.co.uk/news/main.jhtml?xml=/news/2006/03/12/wiran12.xml&sSheet=/news/2006/03/12/ixworld.html).

2. Alireza Jafarzadeh, "Iran Hiding a Laser Enrichment Facility Underground in Parchin Military Complex," press release, March 24, 2005 (www.spcwashington. com/index.php?option=com_content&task=view&id=144&Itemid=26).
3. Alireza Jafarzadeh, "Iran Expanding Its Nuclear Weapons Program Underground and into Military Sites," September 16, 2005 (www.iranwatch.org/privateviews/ spc/perspex-spc-jafarzadeh-underground-091605.pdf).
4. Alireza Jafarzadeh, "Iran Building Nuclear-Capable Missiles in Underground Secret Tunnels," November 21, 2005 (www.spcwashington.com/index.php?option= com_content&task=view&id=149&Itemid=33).
5. International Institute for Strategic Studies, *Iran's Strategic Weapons Programmes: A Net Assessment* (London: Routledge, 2005), p. 101.
6. "Powell Says Iran Is Pursuing Bomb," *Washington Post*, November 18, 2004, p. A1.
7. "Iran: Missiles," *GlobalSecurity.org* (www.globalsecurity.org/wmd/world/iran/missile.htm). See also Iran Profile, Missile Capabilities, Nuclear Threat Initiative (NTI) http://www.nti.org/e_research/profiles/Iran/Missile/3367_3368.html).
8. "Iran Missile Milestones," *Iran Watch*, January 2004 (www.iranwatch.org/wmd/ wponac-missilemilestones.htm).
9. Central Intelligence Agency, "Attachment A: Unclassified Report to Congress on the Acquisition of Technology Relating to Weapons of Mass Destruction and Advanced Conventional Munitions, 1 July through 31 December 2003" (www.cia.gov/ cia/reports/721_reports/pdfs/721report_july_dec2003.pdf).
10. "Shahab-3," Globalsecurity.org (http://www.globalsecurity.org/wmd/world/iran/ shahab-3.htm).
11. "Iran fires missiles in war games: TV," Reuters News Agency, November 2, 2006 (http://news.yahoo.com/s/nm/20061102/ts_nm/iran_manoeuvres_dc_8).
12. "Black Market Anxieties Revived on Ukraine Arms," *Financial Times* (London), February 4, 2005, p. 7.
13. "Ukraine Reportedly Sold Nuclear Missiles to China, Iran," *Missilethreat.com*, February 2, 2005 (www.missilethreat.com/news/200502020231.html).
14. Alireza Jafarzadeh, "Acquiring a Nuclear-Capable Missile with the Range of 3,000 km," August 26, 2005 (www.spcwashington.com/index.php?option=com_content& task=view&id=125&Itemid=34).
15. "Iran Missile Milestones."
16. "Iran Building Nuclear-Capable Missiles in Underground Secret Tunnels."
17. Associated Press, "Iranian Opposition Figure Says Iran Ramping Up Missile Production, As Key European Foreign Ministers Prepare to Meet with Iranian Negotiators," March 2, 2006 (spcwashington.com/index2.php?option=com_content& task=view&id=188&Itemid=26&pop=1&page=0).
18. "Iran Building Nuclear-Capable Missiles in Underground Secret Tunnels."
19. "Iran Building Nuclear-Capable Missiles in Underground Secret Tunnels."
20. Raymond Tanter, "Iran Is Building a Secret Tunnel in Tehran for Nuclear Weapons Research and Development: Options for the International Community," January 31, 2006 (www.nci.org/06nci/01-31/Options.htm).
21. Pars Refractories Co., "End-User and End-Use Certificate," December 27, 2003, signed by S.R. Fallah, managing director.
22. Sunstone International Industry & Trade Company, Ltd., memo dated December 24, 2003, signed by Zhong Ping.
23. Memo from Beijing Guoruiminfu International Trade Co., Ltd., November 25, 2004, signed by Wang Xiangdong.

24. Mohammad Mohaddessin, National Council of Resistance of Iran, "Project to Build Neutron Initiator, the Trigger to Fission Chain Reaction for Nuclear Bomb," press conference, February 3, 2005 (www.iranwatch.org/privateviews/NCRI/per-spex-ncri-neutroninitiator–020305.htm).
25. "Sixty-nine Percent Do Not Consider the Nuclear File as Nationalistic," Roozon-line, March 8, 2006 (http://www.roozonline.com/01newsstory/014520.shtml).
26. Mohammad Mohaddessin, National Council of Resistance of Iran, "New Nuclear Revelations," press conference, September 10, 2004 (www.iranwatch.org/private-views/ncri/perspex-ncri-nuclearprogram–091004.htm).
27. John R. Bolton, "Preventing Iran from Acquiring Nuclear Weapons," Remarks to the Hudson Institute, August 17, 2004 (www.state.gov/t/us/rm/35281.htm).
28. "Iran Secretly Acquiring Super-Strong Steel for Nuclear Bomb—Exile," Iran Focus, July 28, 2005 (www.iranfocus.com/modules/news/article.php?storyid=3009).
29. Mohammad Mohaddessin, "Iran after Obtaining Maraging Steel to Build Nuclear Bomb Casing," July 28, 2005 (www.iranwatch.org/privateviews/NCRI/perspex-ncri-maraging-steel–072805.htm).
30. "Fact Sheet: Select ICE Arms & Strategic Technology Investigations," U.S. Immigration and Customs Enforcement, March 2006 (http://www.ice.gov/pi/news/fact-sheets/ICEarmsstrategic.htm).
31. "Iran after Obtaining Maraging Steel to Build Nuclear Bomb Casing."
32. IAEA Director General's Report, "Implementation of the NPT Safeguards Agreement in the Islamic Republic of Iran," November 24, 2005 (www.iaea.org/Publications/Documents/Board/2005/gov2005-87.pdf).
33. Institute for Science and International Security, "ISIS Imagery Brief: Kalaye Electric," March 31, 2005 (www.isis-online.org/publications/iran/kalayeelectric.html).
34. IAEA Director General's Report, "Implementation of the NPT Safeguards Agreement in the Islamic Republic of Iran," June 6, 2003.
35. "New Nuclear Revelations."
36. U.S. Department of the Treasury, "Executive Order 13382" (www.treasury.gov/of-fices/enforcement/ofac/programs/wmd/wmd.pdf).
37. "Treasury Employs Financial Sanctions Against WMD Proliferation Supporters in Iran," January 4, 2006 (http://www.treasury.gov/press/releases/js3069.htm).
38. IAEA Director General's Report, "Implementation of the NPT Safeguards Agreement in the Islamic Republic of Iran," November 15, 2004 (www.iaea.org/Publications/Documents/Board/2004/gov2004-83.pdf).

CHAPTER 10

1. "Showdown at U.N.? Iran Seems Calm," New York Times, March 14, 2006, p. A8.
2. Alireza Jafarzadeh, "Iranian Regime's Plan and Attempts to Start Uranium Enrichment at Natanz Site," January 10, 2006 (www.spcwashington.com/index.php?option=com_content&task=view&id=174&Itemid=34).
3. Associated Press, "Iran Rejects European Nuclear Proposal," August 6, 2005.
4. Indo-Asian News Service, "Iran Will Not Surrender to Foreign Pressure: New President," August 6, 2005.
5. "Iran Defies West by Resuming Nuclear Activity," Irish Times, August 9, 2005.
6. "Profile: Ali Larijani," BBC News, May 4, 2004 (news.bbc.co.uk/2/hi/middle_east/3625019.stm).

7. "Iran Warns against Referral of Nuclear Issue to the U.N.," *New York Times*, September 21, 2005, p. A12.

8. Mahmoud Ahmadinejad, speech before the United Nations General Assembly, September 17, 2005 (www.un.org/webcast/ga/60/statements/iran050917eng.pdf).

9. IRNA, "Iran's Ahmadinezhad Rejects Comments by Countries 'Violating Nuclear Safeguards,'" September 16, 2005.

10. IAEA Director General's Report, "Implementation of the NPT Safeguards Agreement in the Islamic Republic of Iran," August 31, 2006.

11. "Ahmadinejad Tells CNN Iran Has Right to Peaceful Nuclear Technology."

12. "Transcript: Iran President's Speech Threatening Israel," *Iran Focus*, October 28, 2005 (www.iranfocus.com/modules/news/print.php?storyid=4164).

13. IRNA, "Iranian President Says Nuclear Activities to Continue at Esfahan Facility," October 30, 2005.

14. "Ahmadinejad: U.N. Threat Won't Deter Iran from Nuclear Track," *Iran Focus*, December 1, 2005 (www.iranfocus.com/modules/news/article.php?storyid=4674).

15. FARS News Agency, "In Interview with Emirates Newspaper; Ahmadinejad: In Case of Iran's Nuclear Referral to the Security Council, We Will Use Oil Weapon," December 27, 2005 (www.farsnews.com/newstext.php?nn=8407090417 percent20).

16. "In Interview with Emirates Newspaper; Ahmadinejad: In Case of Iran's Nuclear Referral to the Security Council, We Will Use Oil Weapon."

17. "In Interview with Emirates Newspaper; Ahmadinejad: In Case of Iran's Nuclear Referral to the Security Council, We Will Use Oil Weapon."

18. "In Interview with Emirates Newspaper; Ahmadinejad: In Case of Iran's Nuclear Referral to the Security Council, We Will Use Oil Weapon."

19. "Mahmoud Ahmadinejad" (www.globalsecurity.org/military/world/iran/ahmadinejad.htm).

20. "Iran Threatens Nuke Checks," *News24.com*, December 17, 2005 (linked to www.nci.org).

21. Deutsche Presse-Agentur, "Roundup: U.S. and Europe Voice Alarm at Iran's Nuclear Moves," January 10, 2006.

22. Deutsche Presse-Agentur, "Iran Defiant on Restarting Its Nuclear Programme," January 10, 2006.

23. "Iran Defiant on Restarting Its Nuclear Programme."

24. Deutsche Presse-Agentur, "Roundup: Iran Not Afraid of Uproar over Nuclear Moves: Ahmadinejad," January 11, 2006.

25. IRNA, "Ahmadinejad: Few Strongly Armed Countries after Imposing Scientific Apartheid," February 4, 2006 (www.irna.ir/index2.php?option=com_news&task=print&code=0602046648082440&Itemid=&lang=en).

26. IRNA, "Ahmadinejad Says Enemies Will Fail to Prevent Iran Progress," February 5, 2006 (www.irna.ir/en/news/view/line-17/0602059335151351.htm).

27. "Ahmadinejad: Few Strongly Armed Countries after Imposing Scientific Apartheid."

28. "Ahmadinejad: Iran Won't Budge an Iota on Nukes," *Iran Focus*, March 27, 2006 (www.iranfocus.com/modules/news/print.php?storyid=6430).

29. United Nations Security Council, "Security Council, in Presidential Statement, Underlines Importance of Iran's Re-Establishing Full, Sustained Suspension of Uranium-Enrichment Activities," March 29, 2006 (www.un.org/News/Press/docs/2006/sc8679.doc.htm).

30. IAEA Director General's Report, "Implementation of the NPT Safeguards Agreement in the Islamic Republic of Iran," November 24, 2005 (www.iaea.org/Publications/Documents/Board/2005/gov2005-87.pdf).

31. "You Still Don't Know Iran's Power: Ahmadinejad," *The Hindu*, April 28, 2006 (www.hindu.com/2006/04/28/stories/2006042822430100.htm).

32. "Iran Is Not Cooperating, Agency Says," *New York Times*, April 28, 2006 (select.nytimes.com/mem/tnt.html?emc=tnt&tntget=2006/04/28/world/middleeast/28cnd-iran.html&tntemail0=y).

33. Agence France Presse, "Iran Can Be a 'Superpower,' Ahmadinejad Says," April 28, 2006.

34. "Ahmadinejad Inaugurates New Atomic Project," Reuters, August 26, 2006 (www.abcnews.go.com/International/wireStory?id=2359118&page=2).

35. "Iran Snubs Annan and Rejects Nuclear Plea," Telegraph, September 4, 2006 (www.telegraph.co.uk/news/main.jhtml?xml=/news/2006/09/04/wiran04.xml).

36. "Bush, Ahmadinejad Air Competing Views at U.N.," NPR, September 19, 2006 (www.npr.org/templates/story/story.php?storyId=6105334).

37. "Iran's Leader Relishes 2nd Chance to Make Waves," *New York Times*, September 21, 2006.

38. Alireza Jafarzadeh, "Iran Running a Clandestine Laser Enrichment," Press Conference at the United Nations Plaza Hotel, September 14, 2006 (www.spcwashington.com/index.php?option=com_content&task=view&id=232&Itemid=26)

CHAPTER 11

1. Akbar Hashemi Rafsanjani, "Qods Day Speech," December 14, 2001, posted on *GlobalSecurity.org* (www.globalsecurity.org/wmd/library/news/iran/2001/011214text.html).

2. R. Nicholas Burns, "United States Policy toward Iran," March 8, 2006 (www.state.gov/p/us/rm/2006/62779.htm).

3. "Iraq, Jordan See Threat to Election from Iran," *Washington Post*, December 8, 2004 (www.washingtonpost.com/wp-dyn/articles/A43980-2004Dec7.html).

4. "Remarks with Saudi Arabia Foreign Minister Saud Al Faisal," transcript of talk with U.S. secretary of state Condoleezza Rice, May 18, 2006 (www.state.gov/secretary/rm/2006/66473.htm).

5. "Israel: Iran Must Not Acquire Nuclear Weapons," *CNN*, January 17, 2006 (http://edition.cnn.com/2006/WORLD/meast/01/17/olmert.iran/).

6. "Nuclear Energy is the Desire of the Nation, not the Government," Roozonline, April 30, 2006 (http://roozonline.com/08interview/015309.shtml).

7. Robert G. Joseph, "Iran's Nuclear Program," March 8, 2006 (www.state.gov/t/us/rm/63121.htm).

8. Graham Allison, *Nuclear Terrorism: The Ultimate Preventable Catastrophe* (New York: Times Books, 2004).

9. "Qods Day Speech."

10. Quoted on Iranian state television's all news channel, April 25, 2006.

11. "Sanctions Don't Mean Anything," Newsweek, August 1, 2006 (www.msnbc.msn.com/id/14139380/).

12. "People's Mojahedin of Iran," Mission report, Friends of a Free Iran—European Parliament, September 21, 2005.

13. David E. Sanger, "Imagine: Suppose We Just Let Iran Have the Bomb," *New York Times*, March 19, 2006.

CHAPTER 12

1. United Press International/IRNA, "Islam-Mulsim-Hajj," January 9, 2006.

2. "Islam-Mulsim-Hajj."
3. "Iran's Ahmadinejad: Sharon Dead and 'Others to Follow Suit,'" *Iran Focus*, January 5, 2006 (www.iranfocus.com/modules/news/article.php?storyid=5166).
4. "Full Text of Ahmadinejad's Speech at General Assembly," September 17, 2005 (www.globalsecurity.org/wmd/library/news/iran/2005/iran-050918-irna02.htm).
5. Agence France Presse, "Iran Warns Aggressors of 'Fire and Destruction,'" September 22, 2005.
6. "Islam-Mulsim-Hajj."
7. *Kayhan* newspaper, June 16, 1981 (www.sibestaan.malakut.org/archives/2004/03/post_112.shtml).
8. Statement by Assistant Secretary of State Robert Pelletreau, quoted in Arnold Beichman, "Iranian Policy on Too Soft a Course?" *Washington Times*, September 21, 1994, p. A17.
9. Gary Sick, "Iran's Quest for Superpower Status," *Foreign Affairs*, Spring 1987.
10. Gary Sick, "Iran: Confronting Terrorism," *Washington Quarterly*, Autumn 2003.
11. Council on Foreign Relations, *Iran: Time for a New Approach*, July 2004.
12. John Tower, *The Tower Commission Report* (New York: Bantam, 1987).
13. Kenneth Katzman, *U.S.-Iranian Relations: An Analytic Compendium of U.S. Policies, Laws, and Regulations* (Washington, D.C.: Atlantic Council of the United States, 1999).
14. Stephen Green, "Double Standard in Dealing with Iran?" *Washington Times*, February 26, 1995.
15. *U.S.-Iranian Relations*.
16. CNN, transcript of interview with Iranian president Mohammad Khatami, January 7, 1998 (http://edition.cnn.com/WORLD/9801/07/iran/interview.html).
17. Irvin Molotsky, "U.S. Ends Its Opposition to Iran Gas Pipeline," *New York Times*, July 27, 1997.
18. Agence France Presse, September 23, 1997.
19. Norman Kempster, "U.S. Designated 30 Groups as Terrorists," *Los Angeles Times*, October 9, 1997.
20. Madeleine K. Albright, speech at the 1998 Asia Society Dinner, New York, June 17, 1998 (http://www.asiasociety.org/speeches/albright.html).
21. Kamal Kharrazi, speech at the Asia Society, New York, September 28, 1998 (http://www.asiasociety.org/speeches/kharrazi.html).
22. Elaine Sciolino, "A Top Iranian Aide Rejects U.S. Overture on New Ties," *New York Times*, September 29, 1998, p. A11 (http://select.nytimes.com/gst/abstract.html?res=F00D1FFC3A5D0C7A8EDDA00894D0494D81).
23. *U.S.-Iranian Relations*.
24. Jane Perlez and James Risen, "Clinton Seeks an Opening to Iran, But Efforts Have Been Rebuffed," *New York Times*, December 3, 1999, p. A1.
25. Louis J. Freeh, *My FBI: Bringing Down the Mafia, Investigating Bill Clinton, and Fighting the War on Terror* (New York: St. Martin's Press, 2005).
26. Reuters, "U.S. Extends Restrictions on Iranian Opposition," October 14, 1999.
27. James Rubin, U.S. Department of State, transcript of daily press briefing, June 22, 1998 (http://secretary.state.gov/www/briefings/9806/980622db.html).
28. United States Court of Appeals for the District of Columbia Circuit, No. 99-1438, decided June 8, 2001.
29. Kenneth Katzman, "Iran: U.S. Concerns and Policy Responses," *CRS Report for Congress*, April 6, 2006 (http://fpc.state.gov/documents/organization/64413.pdf).

30. David S. Cloud, "U.S. Bombs Iranian Fighters on Iraqi Side of the Border: Pledge to Target the Group Was Made Early to Assure Tehran of War's Benefits," *Wall Street Journal*, April 17, 2003.

31. David S. Cloud, "U.S., Iran Stall on Road to Rapprochement," *Wall Street Journal*, May 12, 2003.

32. Agence France Presse, "U.S. Says Iran Opposition in Iraq Agrees to Disarm," May 10, 2003.

33. "U.S., Iran Stall on Road to Rapprochement."

34. Colin Powell, secretary of state, interview by regional syndicates, August 1, 2003.

35. Glenn Kessler, "U.S. Ready to Resume Talks with Iran, Armitage Says," *Washington Post*, October 29, 2003, p. A21.

36. Agence France Presse, "Tehran Rules Out U.S. 'Political Mission' to Iran," January 3, 2004

37. R. Nicholas Burns, under secretary for political affairs, "U.S. Policy toward Iran," November 30, 2005 (http://www.state.gov/p/us/rm/2005/57473.htm).

38. "Bush: 'All Options Are on the Table' Regarding Iran's Nuclear Aspirations," *USA Today*, August 13, 2005 (www.usatoday.com/news/washington/2005–08–13-bush-iran-nuclear_x.htm).

39. Associated Press, "Iran Says It Won't Stop Uranium Conversion," August 14, 2005.

40. Agence France Presse, "Iran Warns EU over Nuclear Pressure," August 17, 2005.

41. Center for Strategic and International Studies and the Massachusetts Institute of Technology, "Victory Has Many Friends: U.S. Public Opinion and the Use of Military Force, 1981–2005," *International Security*, Summer 2005, p. 140.

42. IAEA Director General's Report, "Implementation of the NPT Safeguards Agreement in the Islamic Republic of Iran," June 8, 2006 (www.isis-online.org).

43. Barry R. Posen, "We Can Live with a Nuclear Iran," *New York Times*, February 27, 2006.

44. Henry D. Sokolski, Patrick Clawson, *Getting Ready for a Nuclear-Ready Iran*, (Carlisle; Strategic Studies Institute, 2005), pp 1–2 (www.strategicstudiesinstitute.army.mil/pubs/display.cfm?PubID=629).

45. Geoffrey Kemp, *U.S. and Iran, The Nuclear Dilemmas: Next Step*, The Nixon Center, April 2004, pp. 37 (www.nixoncenter.org/publications/monographs/USandIran.pdf).

46. *U.S. and Iran, The Nuclear Dilemmas: Next Step*, p. 40.

47. "Taking on Tehran," Kenneth Pollack and Ray Takeyh, *Foreign Affairs*, March/April 2005 (www.foreignaffairs.org/20050301faessay84204-p10/kenneth-pollack-ray-takeyh/taking-on-tehran.html).

48. Henry D. Sokolski, Patrick Clawson, *Getting Ready for a Nuclear-Ready Iran*, (Carlisle; Strategic Studies Institute, 2005), Chapter 8, pp. 178.

49. Kenneth M. Pollack, *The Persian Puzzle* (New York: Random House, 2004), p. 387.

50. "New Front Sets Sights on Toppling Iran Regime," *FORWARD*, May 16, 2003.

51. "Democracy Expert Says Newly Elected Iraqi National Assembly Faces Huge Challenges," *Voice of America*, February 9, 2005; Professor Larry Diamond, senior fellow at the Hoover Institution at Stanford University in California said "the opposition is weak and disorganized" (http://www.voanews.com/english/archive/2005–02/2005–02–09-voa30.cfm).

52. Trudy Rubin, "Iranian Opposition Too Weak for Regime Change," *Philadelphia Inquirer*, June 2, 2006 (http://www.baltimoresun.com/news/opinion/oped/bal-op.rubin02jun02,0,5420179.story?coll=bal-oped-headlines).

53. Mohammad Mohaddessin, *Islamic Fundamentalism: The New Global Threat* (Washington, D.C.: Seven Locks Press, 2001), pp. 194–195.

54. Ervand Abrahamian, *The Iranian Mojahedin* (London: Yale University Press, 1989), pp. 207.

55. *The Iranian Mojahedin*, pp. 218–219.

56. "Fallen for Freedom: 20,000 martyrs, Partial List of 120,000 Victims of Political Executions in Iran under the Mullahs' Regime, Volume One (Paris: People's Mojahedin Organization of Iran, 2006).

57. Interviews were conducted between June 2004 and March 2006.

58. Paulo Casaca, "People Power, Iranian-Style," *Wall Street Journal*, October 18, 2004.

59. The meeting took place on February 9, 2005, in Washington, D.C.

60. Struan Stevenson, "Risks of Appeasing Iran's Mullahs," *Washington Times*, commentary, January 5, 2005.

61. "Discontent Grows In Iranian Cities," *New York Times*, August 14, 1991.

62. "Killing of a 12-Year-Old Sets Off Clashes in Iran," *New York Times*, May 28, 1992.

63. "Iran Executes 4 More in Anti-Government Rioting," *New York Times*, June 12, 1992.

64. "Fire and Flood, Plans and Blood," *The Economist*, June 13, 1992.

65. "Iran's President Orders Crackdown on Riots," Washington Post, June 13, 1992.

66. "Iran Executes 4 More in Anti-Government Rioting," *New York Times*, June 12, 1992.

67. "Iran Yields to Demands After Riots in Northern City," *New York Times*, August 5, 1994.

68. "Iranians Want Dictators Out," Associated Press, July 10, 1999.

69. "Sense of Revolution Has Returned to Iran," CBS News online, July 14, 1999.

70. "Youth, Women, Elderly Join Students in Anti-Government Protest in Tehran," Reuters, July 9, 2000.

71. "Khatami's Faction Distance Itself from Pro-Democracy Movement," Reuters, July 9, 2000.

72. "Demonstrators, Ignoring a Ban, Clash with Riot Police in Tehran," *New York Times*, July 10, 2002.

73. "Tehran Rocked by Second Night of Protests," Reuters, June 11, 2003.

74. "Student Protests in Tehran Become Nightly Fights for Freedom," *New York Times*, June 14, 2003.

75. "Protests Grow in Iran Over Death Sentence for Professor," *New York Times*, November 13, 2002.

76. "Regime's Militia and Students Stage Rival Rallies in Iran," Agence France Presse, November 19, 2002.

77. "Women's Rights Activists Beaten in Tehran," *Washington Post*, June 12, 2006 (www.washingtonpost.com/wp-dyn/content/article/2006/06/12/AR2006061201034.html).

78. "Iran's Volatile Ethnic Mix," *International Herald Tribune*, June 2, 2006.

79. "Iran hands down 10 death sentences over ethnic unrest," Agence France Presse, July 25, 2006 (www.worldpress.org/link.cfm?http://www.iranfocus.com).

80. Douglas Jehl, "US Bombed Bases of Iranian Rebels in Iraq," *International Herald Tribune*, April 17, 2003.

81. "Why Should U.S. Support Exiles Who Are Terrorists?" *Wall Street Journal*, letters to editor, June 12, 2006, p. A13.

82. "Iranian Exile Group Aims to Build Bridges: Some in Congress See a Role for an Organization Formally Listed as a Terrorist Group," *Wall Street Journal*, May 22, 2006, p. A6.

83. IRNA, "U.S. Should Treat Mujahedeen Very Harshly in Iraq," August 18, 2003.
84. Foreign Secretary Jack Straw, interview with BBC Radio 4's *Today* program, February 1, 2006.
85. Interview with the state-run *Entekhab* newspaper, October 28, 2002.
86. IRNA, November 16, 2002.
87. International Institute for Strategic Studies, *Iran's Strategic Weapons Programmes: A Net Assessment* (London: Routledge, 2005), p. 23.
88. John C. K. Daly, UPI Terrorism Watch, May 27, 2005.
89. IRNA, October 13, 1997.
90. "Iran U.S. MKO," BBC Radio, June 5, 1998.
91. "Iran Calls on Jordan to Close Mojahidin Khalq Bureau," *Arabic News.com*, August 15, 1998.
92. Ahmadinejad speech before a gathering in Qazvin, printed in *Iran Focus*, June 8, 2006.
93. "Execution of Iranian Opposition Figure Reported," Radio Free Europe/Radio Liberty, February 17, 2006.
94. "Newspaper Editor Freed on Bail," Statement by Reporters Without Borders, 3 August 2004 (www.rsf.org/article.php3?id_article=10852).
95. Author interview with Professor Raymond Taner, August 2006.
96. Established in February 2005, the Iran Policy Committee is comprised of former officials from the White House, State Department, Pentagon, intelligence agencies, and experts from think tanks and universities (www.iranpolicy.org).
97. Iran Policy Committee, *Appeasing the Ayatollahs and Suppressing Democracy: U.S. Policy and the Iranian Opposition* (Washington, D.C.: Iran Policy Committee, 2006), pp. 40.
98. *Appeasing the Ayatollahs and Suppressing Democracy: U.S. Policy and the Iranian Opposition*, pp. 42–43.
99. "Iran Rejects EU Nuclear Proposal," CBC News, May 17, 2006 (www.cbc.ca/story/world/national/2006/05/17/iran nuclear html).
100. "Iran's President Rejects U.N. Resolution, Associated Press, August 1, 2006.
101. "'Sanctions Don't Mean Anything,'" *Newsweek*, August 1, 2006 (www.msnbc.msn.com/id/14139380/).
102. "Iran Postpones Nuclear Talks," Reuters, July 5, 2006 (news.yahoo.com/s/nm/20060705/wl_nm/nuclear_iran_dc_6).
103. "Iran's Permanent UN Ambassador Writes to Annan on MKO," IRNA, August 2, 2006 (www.irna.ir/en/news/view/menu-236/0608020691233702.htm).
104. "Iran's Unemployment Crisis," *Middle East Economic Survey*, Vol. XLVII, No. 41, October 11, 2004 (www.mees.com/postedarticles/oped/a47n41d01.htm).
105. "Are The PMOI Iran's last Hope For A Peaceful Solution?," *Time Magazine*, July 31, 2006 (www.time.com/time/europe/eu/article/0,13716,1211079,00.html).
106. Author interview was conducted in Washington, DC, on August 7, 2006. General McInerney is the co-author of a book entitled *The Endgame, Winning the War on Terror*, along with Major General Paul Vallely, U.S.A. (ret.).

INDEX